Women's Suffrage and
Social Politics in the
French Third Republic

Women's Suffrage and Social Politics in the French Third Republic

Steven C. Hause with

Anne R. Kenney

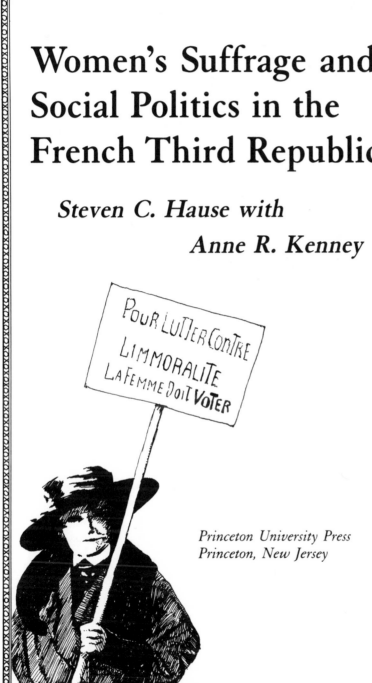

Princeton University Press
Princeton, New Jersey

Copyright © 1984 by Princeton University Press

Published by Princeton University Press, 41 William Street,
Princeton, New Jersey 08540

In the United Kingdom: Princeton University Press, Guildford, Surrey

All Rights Reserved

Library of Congress Cataloging in Publication Data will be found on the last
printed page of this book

ISBN Cloth 0-691-05427-4   Pbk. 0-691-10167-1

This book has been composed in Linotron Granjon

Clothbound editions of Princeton University Press books are printed on acid-
free paper, and binding materials are chosen for strength and durability.
Paperbacks, although satisfactory for personal collections, are not usually
suitable for library rebinding

Printed in the United States of America by Princeton University Press
Princeton, New Jersey

FOR OUR PARENTS

Charles R. Hause

Almina K. Hause

Col. William R. Kenney

Rev. Marguerite S. Kenney

Contents

Illustrations

Maps

Tables

XOXOXOXOXOXOXOXOXOXOXOXOXOXOXOXOXOXOXOXOXOXOXOXOXOXOXOXOXOXOXOXOXOXO

Preface

This is a history of the women's suffrage question in France. It surveys the political rights of French women from the twelfth century to the national elections of 1981, but it studies in detail only the period between the 1890s (when a mass suffrage movement began to develop) and the 1920s (when the French Senate soundly rejected women's suffrage). The first objective of the book is simply to bring this important subject back to the history of the Third Republic. One need only glance at the standard histories of that regime—such as those by Brogan, Bury, Cobban, Thomson, and Wolf—to see that the subject (*inter alia*) has been omitted even in traditional political history.

The unusual term in the title—"social politics"—expresses another objective of the work: to bind political and social history together. The title announces a subject in political history, but meaningful analysis in that field must incorporate lessons from social history. The fields have been too often separated. Examination of collective *mentalités* and parliamentary maneuvers should fit together, to the enrichment of both fields. Political rights are examined here in the contexts of French feminism and of French politics, but with the woman question integrated with other national concerns, in a larger social politics. Thus, French birth rates or alcohol consumption are important elements of political history. The entries under social politics and *mentalités* in the index provide access to this theme.

The publication of one's first book brings the discovery that it is more fun to write acknowledgments than to read them. It means a lot to me to be able to tell Neal Primm and Ed Fedder, of the University of Missouri-St. Louis, how much their support and confidence in me a decade ago still means; and to thank Mark Burkholder of UMSL for keeping the faith and saying so.

There is also a mischievous joy in saying that financial support for this research was hard to find in the mid-1970s, and many granting agencies declined the opportunity to be thanked here. Some repeatedly.

Perhaps they reckoned that aspiring writers actually need the formative experience of impoverished wintering in a chilly one-room Parisian flat. In the later stages of this work, however, UMSL gave me considerable help, and I am happy to give thanks for it here. The Department of History, the Center for International Studies, the College of Arts and Sciences, and the Office of Research Administration financed travel and photocopying. And this aid came at a time when UMSL was laughably underfunded by the state of Missouri.

UMSL also provided much technical assistance in the preparation of this book. The computer-generated maps which I designed and digitized would have remained designs rather than maps without the expertise of John Blodgett and the Computer Center. Similarly, Don Greer and the staff of the Instructional Technologies Center converted my Tri-X negatives into the photographs seen here. Finally, a platoon of secretaries and typists helped to prepare the manuscript, especially Sylvia Stephens, who produced the final copy. June Burton, Lanette Talley-Williams, and Richalyn Martin also earned my thanks.

The son of a librarian and the husband of an archivist is unlikely to forget the help he received in research institutions scattered around twenty cities in five countries. Among them, our greatest debt is to Madame Léautey, the librarian at the Bibliothèque Marguerite Durand in Paris. During 1976-1977, Anne and I were daily guests in her corner of the *mairie* of the Fifth Arrondissement; she gave us encouragement and tireless assistance. Special thanks are also due to Anne Perotin for her help at the Archives nationales in 1979 and for her hospitality.

Colleagues in the investigation of French history and women's history have helped to shape this book through their questions, suggestions, criticism, and sharing of materials; Patrick K. Bidelman, Karen Offen, Joan W. Scott, and Charles Sowerwine deserve special thanks. Several other scholars have generously permitted us to consult their unpublished works; our thanks to Susan D. Bachrach, Laura Frader, Sabine Jessner, Yvette Kirby, Thomas Moodie, Wayne Northcutt, Odille Sarti, Marie-France Toinet, and Elisabeth Weston for sharing such materials.

Thanks are also due to the scholarly journals in which some of these ideas first appeared in different forms. Portions of the argument in Chapters One, Four, and Nine first appeared in an essay in the *American Historical Review* in 1981; we thank the editors for permis-

sion to use copyrighted material. Other ideas were developed in the
Catholic Historical Review, the *Proceedings of the Western Society for
French History, Third Republic/Troisième République*, and *Laurels*.

The years of travel for this work also led to many debts to friends
who found themselves in the path of our peregrinations. The Order
of Heroic Friendship goes especially to Douglas and Brenda Gardner,
who must wonder at times about the hidden disadvantages of living
in London but who always have something interesting simmering on
the back burner. To Jack and Marcia Schnedler, who have a wonderful
knack of reviving tired researchers with a car trip in Crete or a
bungalow in Tuscany, and who can outwait Yugoslavian airlines. To
John Works, of Schark-Jaws and Les Trois Silos, whose hospitality
has stretched across a continent. To Tony and Sonia O'Donnell, who
reminded me to stop wearing a purse when I left Paris. To Lorna
Lennon, Michel Rieutord, and Bob Walshe, who have made me feel
at home in Paris. And to Lance LeLoup, who has been a dear friend
when I most needed one.

Finally, we come to the tradition of thanking one's spouse and
children in the acknowledgments. In this case, we produced a book
together and can thank each other. Anne and I conceived the project
together. She took off a year from the development of her own career
so that we could work on it together in Paris. The growth of her
career made it impossible to complete the book together, and I finished
the research and wrote the manuscript. Anne, however, continued to
bring her editorial skills to project. She criticized, shaped ideas, argued
with me about obtuse notions and overwriting. And she heard people
suggest that she had earned hearty thanks in the acknowledgments,
rather than her name on the title page. So I do thank her here. For
not punching them in the nose. As for the cats, all they did was
occasionally mess things up.

My last *i* being dotted, I return the proofs to Princeton with my
thanks to those who worked on this book—especially Gail Ullman,
a supportive editor who discussed it with me over several years;
Marilyn Campbell, who shepherded it through production and saved
me from many errors; and Laury Egan who designed it so nicely.

St. Louis, May 1984

Abbreviations

XOXOXOXOXOXOXOXOXOXOXOXOXOXOXOXOXOXOXOXOXOXOXOXOXOXOXOXOXOXOXO

Used in both the text and the notes:

CESC	Commission d'éducation sociale civique de la femme
CGT	Confédération générale du travail
CNFF	Conseil national des femmes françaises
FFU	Fédération féministe universitaire
GdFS	Groupe des femmes socialistes
GFS	Groupe féministe sociale
ILP	Independent Labour Party (Britain)
IWSA	International Woman Suffrage Alliance
LFDF	Ligue française pour le droit des femmes
LFF	Ligue des femmes françaises
LNVF	Ligue nationale pour le vote des femmes
LPF	Ligue patriotique des françaises
NUWSS	National Union of Women's Suffrage Societies (Britain)
POF	Parti ouvrier français
RP	représentation proportionelle
SFIO	Section française de l'internationale ouvrière
UFF	Union fraternelle des femmes
UFSF	Union française pour le suffrage des femmes
UNVF	Union nationale pour le vote des femmes
WCTU	Women's Christian Temperance Union
WSPU	Women's Social and Political Union (Britain)

Used only in the notes:

AD	Archives départementales
AHR	*American Historical Review*
AN	Archives nationales

APP	Archives du Préfecture de Police
AS	*Annuaire statistique*
BHVP	Bibliothèque historique de la ville de Paris
BMD	Bibliothèque Marguerite Durand
BN	Bibliothèque nationale
DdPF	*Dictionnaire des parlementaires français* (1789-1889)
DPF	*Dictionnaire des parlementaires français* (1889-1940)
FHS	*French Historical Studies*
HR/RH	*Historical Reflections/Réflexions historiques*
JMH	*Journal of Modern History*
JO	*Journal officiel*
PWSFH	*Proceedings of the Western Society for French History*
TR/TR	*Third Republic/Troisième République*

Women's Suffrage and
Social Politics in the
French Third Republic

Chapter One

France and the Question of Women's Political Rights

French women voted in national elections before the completion of Notre Dame cathedral. When Philip the Fair solemnly convened the first Estates General at the unfinished cathedral in 1302, he received an assembly chosen by both men and women. For over five centuries, privileged women of all estates retained the vote, both local and national. Then, in the 1790s, the revolution that proclaimed the rights of man abolished the political rights of woman. Under a succession of modern regimes that built statues of her, Jeanne d'Arc could not have voted—neither for the municipal coucil of Domrémy-la-Pucelle, her birthplace, nor of Orléans, which she liberated from the English. Until the Fourth Republic permitted women to vote again in 1945, French democracy steadfastly opposed a right that church and throne had acknowledged.

The right of medieval women to participate in local assemblies varied from region to region. The north and east of France followed the *loy et coutume de Beaumont* (1182) which granted the suffrage to widows, unmarried women who maintained their own households, and married women during the absence of their husbands. Such rights were rarely codified, so they also varied over time and social class. Yet it remains clear that from the twelfth century some women— most often *propriétaires* and heads of families—participated in town and village assemblies. By the sixteenth century, this right had disappeared in some regions and was certainly an exception rather than the rule, but legal texts of the eighteenth century, especially in eastern France, explicitly reiterated the right.[1]

The earliest record of national political rights for French women dates from the papacy of Sinibaldo de' Fieschi, a canon lawyer. As Pope Innocent IV (1243-1254), he recognized the electoral rights of all persons above the age of fourteen, male or female, without distinction by marital status or social class. French practice fell short of that remarkable standard; few women actually voted. Elections to the Estates General lacked consistent regulations, so surviving examples of the participation of women appear to have been local decisions—such as a ruling at Ferrières in the Touraine permitting some women to vote in 1308. National rights also varied with a woman's estate. Women in religious orders, notably powerful abbesses, normally voted for the clerical representatives of the First Estate; many did so in 1789. Women of the nobility, particularly possessors of fiefs, often voted in the Second Estate. Widows, the wives of absent warriors, and inheriting daughters sometimes joined them. Likewise, urban women occasionally voted for representatives of the Third Estate. In one instance, at Garchy in Champagne, records show that an electorate of 193 included 32 widows—17 percent of the votes cast. The sporadic voting of women endured into early modern times, with well-documented instances in the Estates General of 1560 and 1576. This tradition fell into desuetude with the Estates of 1614. However, the ruling of January 24, 1789 preparing for the last Estates General specifically stated that "all the inhabitants" of a town could participate.[2]

A third form of the political rights of women under the monarchy applied only to women of the nobility—the seignorial right of dispensing justice. As early as the reign of Philip V (1318) and as late as Louis XIV (1661) women attained the peerage in their own right and exercised such rights as sitting in *parlements*. For example, Mohant, Comtesse d'Artois, voted in the tribunal that judged the Comte de Flandre in 1315. A search of departmental archives has found dozens of women, such as the Duchess d'Elboeuf in Champagne, still exercising such power at the end of the eighteenth century.[3]

French women certainly did not possess political equality under the old regime. They had traditional rights and a corpus of legal precedents upon which to claim equality. The French revolution rejected both the tradition and the claim. Despite the role of women in drafting the cahiers and electing the representatives of 1789, despite the preoccupation of intellectuals with natural rights, and despite the proclamation of liberty and equality, each successive revolutionary government denied political rights to women.[4] Some revolutionaries, notably the Marquis de Condorcet, argued that women's political rights were natural rights, the denial of which would be "an act of tyranny." This earned Condorcet a reputation as "the father of feminism," but it won no victories in the assemblies.[5]

Hostility to women's rights during the French revolution appeared as early as the summer of 1789. From Mirabeau on the right to Robespierre on the left, revolutionary leaders opposed women's suffrage and legislated accordingly. Women were held to lack the physical and moral strength for politics; to be insufficiently educated; to be more suited to other spheres in life; to be unduly influenced by the enemies of the revolution, such as the church. Hence, the constitutions of 1791 and 1793 explicitly excluded them from the rights of citizenship. Other decisions cost women the right to take the civic oath, denied them freedoms of speech and assembly, closed women's political clubs, and even excluded women from attending sessions of the Convention.[6]

While women lost political rights during the revolution, they gained a tradition of feminist assertion of equality. A feminist cahier called for political rights for women because they paid taxes. A women's political club founded by Pauline Léon and Claire Lecombe also demanded political rights and denounced the Constitution of 1793 for omitting them. The most famous voice belonged to Olympe de Gouges, whose Declaration of the Rights of Women appeared in 1791. "Oh, women, women!" she cried. "When will you cease to be blind? What advantages have you received from the revolution? A more pronounced scorn, a more marked disdain." She proclaimed equality: "Woman is born free and lives equal to man in her rights." She specified political rights: "Woman has the right to mount the scaffold; she must equally have the right to mount the rostrum." Another feminist, Etta Palm, went directly to the Legislative Assembly in 1792, claiming the "natural rights, of which [women] have been deprived by a protracted oppression."[7]

Feminists suffered badly at the hands of the revolution. De Gouges did not get to mount the rostrum, but during the Reign of Terror she climbed the steps of the guillotine. A semi-official newspaper even linked her execution and her feminism: "It seems the law has punished this conspirator for having forgotten the virtues that suit her sex."[8] Etta Palm fled into exile. Léon and Lacombe were arrested in 1794. Another revolutionary feminist, Théroigne de Méricourt, ended her life in an asylum, following a thrashing by a group of Jacobin women. The beating of de Méricourt foreshadowed an important development in the women's movement: the division of activists into irreconcilable groups. On one side, advocates of women's rights often accepted the established regime. De Gouges, Palm, and de Méricourt were all political moderates. More militant women preferred to work within radical groups rather than to stress feminist reforms. The women who attacked de Méricourt, for example, preferred to collaborate with Robespierre in constructing a Jacobin France. Such splits, frequently along class lines, recurred throughout the Third Republic.

Neither the political rights of women nor advocacy of them flourished during the reign of Napoleon Bonaparte, a period typified by the misogyny of his legal code. Recent research has shown how utopian socialists reinvigorated the movement during the constitutional monarchies of the early nineteenth century. Their feminism differed from the doctrines of the revolutionary years. It stressed economic independence, incorporated ideals of sexual emancipation, and attacked the patriarchal society, but rarely claimed political rights. Although Saint-Simon asserted that a society dishonored itself by not attending to the rights of half of its number, he did not pursue the subject. Enfantin considered the perpetual minority of women incompatible with the socialist state of the future. By the 1830s, Saint-Simonian meetings in Paris were attracting perhaps two hundred women, although the hierarchy remained essentially masculine. Perhaps more important in the development of a doctrine of female autonomy, Saint-Simonian women edited their own newspaper, *La Femme libre*. Fourier, who is sometimes credited with coining the word feminism, stressed the emancipation of women, but his disciples, except for Victor Considerant, deemphasized women's rights.[9]

The breach between moderate feminists and radical women reappeared with utopian socialism. Utopians such as Flora Tristan first aspired to the reconstruction of society; within that context, they periodically addressed the woman question. Simultaneously, others created a bourgeois feminism that concentrated almost exclusively on ameliorating the condition of women without threatening the monarchy. Fanny Richomme, for example, founded *Le Journal des femmes* both to claim the rights of women and to reject socialism. Madame de Mauchamps and the women of her *Gazette des femmes* showed the same class consciousness even in their feminist activism. De Mauchamps made a career of exploiting the chief political right permitted women under the constitutional charter of 1830, the right to petition the government. Her objective was neither the reorganization of society nor even universal suffrage. She accepted the bourgeois monarchy, calling only for women taxpayers to vote on the same basis as the male electorate.[10]

The mid-century women's movement witnessed another development with profound implications for the debate about political rights. A third variety of French feminism, the most conservative but potentially the largest, emerged under the rubric of "Christian feminism." Christian (i.e., Catholic) feminists faced a generally hostile ecclesiastical tradition but found their chief foes to be bourgeois feminists and socialist feminists who shared few of the attitudes of Catholic women. Utopians propounded notions of sexual emancipation that Catholics found utterly shocking. Bourgeois feminists advocated intolerable reforms such as divorce. Both appeared to be enemies of the family and the church. Richomme stimulated the growth of Catholic feminism by defending Christian virtues against socialist theories. A Catholic women's movement slowly developed, more Catholic than feminist, but supporting reforms such as a normal school for women.[11]

The revolution of 1848 recapitulated the developments of the previous half-century. Feminists welcomed a new republic with great expectations, only to find these revolutionaries no more sympathetic than their predecessors. The Provisional Government received a feminist petition calling for women's suffrage a fortnight after proclaiming "universal" suffrage. The suffragists of 1848, led by Eugénie Niboyet and Jeanne Deroin, deluged the Provisional Government with letters, petitions, and deputations. The startling ruling of the revolutionary government was that they could not decree women's suffrage because women had never possessed this right; a new assembly might debate it. Shortly thereafter the Prefecture of Police closed feminist clubs just as the Convention had done in 1793. Suffragists pled their cause at the Constituent Assembly, but even Considerant deserted them. They urged George Sand to stand as a feminist candidate for the Legislative Assembly; she derided their "ridiculous pretension." Deroin stood herself in 1849, only to wind up in the Saint-Lazare prison for plotting against the state. One left-wing deputy called for women's suffrage in 1849, and a Saint-Simonian deputy proposed municipal enfranchisement to the assembly in 1851. They were laughed down. The only debate on the political rights of women concerned a proposal to abolish their right of petition.[12]

After Louis Napoleon's coup, French feminism lay dormant under Bonapartist autocracy for a second time. Indeed, the French patriarchal tradition even regained ground among the intelligentsia as a new generation of leftist writers, including both Jules Michelet and Pierre-Joseph Proudhon, opposed the political emancipation of women. A feminist revival began in the late 1860s, when the "liberal empire" eased repressive legislation on the press and public meetings. The new feminism of the 1860s and 1870s marked a major turning point for the women's movement: organizations appeared that would outlive their founders. The architects of the new feminism, Léon Richer and Maria Deraismes, expressly committed themselves to bourgeois standards of respectability and moderation. Both were republicans who learned caution from the events of 1793 and 1848—a lesson reinforced in December 1875 when the government of the republic suppressed their organization as a threat to public order. Their success in establishing an evolutionary strategy of making small breaches in the antifeminist wall was, in part, due to the fact that the most revolutionary women were in exile as Communards of 1871.

The organizations that emerged from the formative period, Richer's Ligue française pour le droit des femmes (hereafter, LFDF) and Deraismes's Société pour l'amélioration du sort de la femme et la revindication de ses droits (hereafter, Amélioration) endured long after the retirement of Richer in 1891 and the death of Deraismes in 1894. They attracted approximately two hundred members each, drew the backing of such luminaries as Victor Hugo, recruited young politicians including René Viviani and Ferdinand Buisson, established an adequate financial base, briefly maintained a provincial branch (the LFDF at Nantes), published monthly journals, and regularly organized national congresses from 1878 (when they attracted an audience of six hundred). They refused, however, to work for women's political rights. Women who did so, Richer asserted, "are putting their personal interests above the sacred interests of the *patrie*."[13]

The moderation of Richer and Deraismes had an important effect on the development of French suffragism. The women's movement was already divided into three forms—socialist feminism, bourgeois-republican feminism, and Christian feminism. The question of the ballot split the bourgeois movement into moderate and militant wings. The early associates of Richer and Deraismes included militant women who insisted upon working for political rights. One of them, Hubertine Auclert, created the first enduring women's suffrage league. She left Richer in 1876 to establish her own society, a group that ultimately adopted the name Suffrage des femmes. She demanded that feminists face the issue of enfranchisement and sought to debate it at Richer's congress of 1878. Moderates blocked this attempt, as they did again at the congress of 1889. As the schism deepened, small, militant suffrage societies proliferated and a militant press—led by Auclert's *La Citoyenne* (1881-1891) and its successor, *Le Journal des femmes* (1891-1910)—made it clear that they would not compromise with moderates at the price of abandoning political rights.[14]

Another result of the preeminence of bourgeois moderates was an attempted alliance between miltant feminists and socialist women. Auclert, a radical republican, first suggested collaboration. She attended the workers' congress at Marseille in 1879 to ask socialists to endorse political rights for women in return for a "pact of alliance ... against our common oppressors."[15] The Parti ouvrier français (hereafter, POF) voted Auclert's motion, a historic decision that no other party in France duplicated before the First World War. The Marseille resolution produced a suffragist-socialist entente during the 1880s, but the understanding was short-lived. Bourgeois suffragists little felt the economic plight of working women; socialists little desired to devote themselves to women's rights. Although the POF reiterated its theoretical support of women, party practice was often the opposite. As Jules Guesde said in an unguarded moment, the woman question was "an encumbrance."[16]

Auclert made the 1880s an epoch of suffragist activism. She petitioned the government relentlessly. The Chamber of Deputies told her that "opinion is not yet sufficiently prepared" for women to vote. The *conseil général* of the Seine voted 37-11 against endorsing women's suffrage. Undaunted, Auclert both ran for office and tried to register to vote. The results included feminist dissension, public ridicule, and a tightening of electoral regulations. Once she even refused to pay her taxes, because she had no voice in levying them. She fought the Treasury through the courts, capitulating only after her appeals were exhausted and her furniture confiscated.[17]

By the 1890s, suffragism was well-established in France, but it still commanded the energies of relatively few women. They were concentrated in the Parisian middle class, divided into competing organizations, and isolated from other feminists. If one evaluates the political rights campaign of the early Third Republic as collective action, it becomes clear that the movement was underdeveloped. Suffragists had articulated the interest of women in a democratic society. Permanent organizations existed, but one could not claim that significant numbers of women were mobilized for action. Suffragists remained a minority of the women's movement which itself could claim the support of only a small minority of French women. French politics would provide innumerable opportunities for collective action, yet there was little indication that a large suffrage movement would follow the militancy of Hubertine Auclert.

Political Rights and the Constitutional Law of the Third Republic

How could French suffragists succeed? The answer first depended on political grand strategy, conditioned by French history: could they work within the established regime and reasonably hope to reform its laws? Or must they aspire to create an entirely new regime dedicated to equality? Advocates of political rights for women disagreed. A minority held, as Jacobin women or the utopians had, that only a new, egalitarian France would succeed. The vast majority of French feminists, however, believed that the Third Republic could be made to accept their version of it. Two of the recurring themes of subsequent chapters derive from this division over strategy: the steadfast commitment of French suffragists to the republic and a major schism between socialist women and suffragists.

Given their faith in the republic, French suffragists had two avenues toward enfranchisement: through judicial reinterpretation of constitutional law or through legislation to amend it. By the 1890s, the first route had proven to be a dead end. Consequently, the suffrage campaign increasingly concentrated on parliament. French constitutional law was complicated on the subject of the political rights of women. This resulted partly from the number of constitutions and electoral laws elucidating them, partly from the ambiguity of the language employed in those acts. The constitutions of the French revolution explicitly excluded women from political rights. The Decree on Municipalities of December 1789 and the Constitution of 1791 both associated electoral privileges with the term "citizen" (*citoyen*, the masculine form of the noun), but the Constitution of the Year I (1793) explicitly used "man" (*homme*) in defining citizenship. Article Four of the latter constitution did discuss women and citizenship: French women conferred citizenship (and the ballot) on foreign men by marrying them, although they could not confer it on themselves. Revolutionary constitutions of the Year III (1795) and the Year VIII (1799) repeated *homme*; Napoleon's Constitution of the Year XII (1804) went to even greater lengths to exclude women from political participation. The monarchial constitutional charters of 1814 and 1830 omitted most electoral details; they were "to be determined by law." The usage of "man" ended, however, in favor of "the French" (*français*, the masculine form of the noun). Women reappeared in the electoral law of April 1831 which stated the amount of taxes that must be paid in order to vote: women were permitted to assign their tax receipts to their husbands to enable them to qualify. The Constitution of 1848 did not expressly exclude women from political rights. It proclaimed "universal" suffrage and stated that "all of the French people" (*tous les français*) enjoyed the rights of citizenship. Other articles used *français* to define electors.[18]

The constitutional and electoral law of the Third Republic employed the mid-nineteenth-century vocabulary and retained some laws in toto. The constitutional laws of 1875 derived universal suffrage from the formula *tous les français*. The Communal Law of 1871, the Departmental Law of 1871, and the Municipal Law of 1884 used *citoyen*. The typical formula in these acts provided the franchise to "all French citizens fully twenty-one years of age, in enjoyment of their civil and political rights, not being in any position of incapacity as provided in the law."[19]

The route to women's suffrage via judicial interpretation was straightforward: did universal suffrage, did the legal terms *citoyen* and *français* include women? Precedents were unambiguous in other interpretations of these terms. *Français* and *citoyen* indisputably implied women in tax law or criminal law—women paid on an equal basis with men. Auclert pressed this argument energetically in the 1880s, seeking rulings from the Ministry of the Interior, the Conseil de préfecture, the Conseil d'état, and the Cour de cassation. Eliska Vincent took the same argument to court in 1893. They lost every appeal. Three rulings of the 1880s put it bluntly: "Women cannot exercise political rights." The explanation was simple: women did not meet the stipulation that electors be "in enjoyment of their civil and political rights." Did not feminists themselves discuss the provisions of the Civil Code, such as Article Thirty-Seven which deprived them of the civil right to serve on juries? Lacking such civil rights, women "do not fulfill all the legal conditions which make the French citizen." However, the terms *citoyen* and *français* could contain a second meaning, including women, in legislation such as tax law when those acts omitted the qualification of enjoying full civil rights.[20]

French suffragists occasionally took their case to court after 1893, but they devoted their energy to seeking legislative revision of the law. The laughter that greeted women's suffrage proposals in 1851 and 1882 demonstrated how difficult this strategy would be. There were only a few auspicious signs. Some politicians belonged to feminist organizations; they constituted more than 10 percent of the membership of the LFDF in the 1880s.[21] Clovis Hugues (socialist, Bouches-du-Rhône), was a member of Suffrage des femmes and introduced Auclert's petitions. Sympathetic deputies formed a Groupe des droits de la femme in the chamber in 1895. And socialists, the most rapidly growing party in France, frequently reiterated the endorsement of 1879.

The prospects of a parliamentary victory for women's suffrage were also complicated. No party held a majority in the Chamber of Deputies, where shifting multiparty coalitions characterized politics. Socialist support amounted to only 40 to 45 votes, from a body of nearly 600, in the late 1890s. That bloc surpassed 100 deputies before World War I, but even if they voted unanimously for women's suffrage, the measure thereby won only 18 percent of the chamber. Throughout the late nineteenth century, moderate and conservative republicans of the right-center held a plurality of the seats, surpassing 40 percent in the 1890s. And they were very cautious reformers. The first elections after the Dreyfus affair, in 1902, passed that preeminent position to his principle defenders, the radicals of the left center. The Radical and Radical-Socialist Party, formally founded in 1901, held between 225 and 270 seats in the Chamber of Deputies throughout the next generation. Small factions on the right (Catholics, nationalists, monarchists) accounted for a steadily declining bloc of votes—20 percent of the chamber during the Dreyfus crisis to a smaller group than the socialists on the eve of the war.

Assuming that the socialists honored their commitment, where could suffragists find an additional 200 votes? Individual supporters were to be found in all political factions, and feminists disagreed on where cooperation should be sought. There were many reasons to concentrate on the radicals. Their numbers, added to the socialist bloc with whom they often cooperated, would mean victory; without considerable radical backing, it was unlikely. Radicals dominated the cabinets of the era; they held the committee chairmanships and administrative positions to advance a suffrage bill or bury it. Perhaps most important, there was a powerful ideological relationship between radicalism and suffragism. Radicals stood as the party of universal suffrage. Léon Bourgeois (Marne), their leading theoretician, proudly proclaimed that they were not "a party in the narrow sense of the word ... [but] French democracy itself."[22] Furthermore, most suffragists were comfortable with the radical vision of a reformist republic and considered collaboration with them natural.

Political success was not to be so simple. The radicals came to power at the turn of the century dedicated to the separation of church and state as their foremost objective. During precisely the same years that a significant suffrage movement developed in France, the government devoted tremendous time and energy to combating the church. And radicals were convinced that French women were the staunchest defenders in the land of the church. Indeed, they considered women so priest-ridden that they would reflexively vote the clergy's wishes—against separation, against the republic itself. Thus, the first congress of the Radical and Radical-Socialist Party, at Paris in 1901, voted against women's suffrage. And feminists had reasons to worry about the historical implications of Paul Painlevé's exclamation, "We are the sons of the Jacobins!"[23] When suffragists looked to the right wing for support, however, they found that conservatives did not believe they were docile daughters of the church. Indeed, on the right, political rights for women seemed to betoken revolution. As Auclert lamented in a dispirited moment, "Revolutionaries and reactionaries, believers and atheists, have shown that they are absolutely in agreement to despoil French women of their rights."[24]

If the advancement of women's rights somehow found a majority in the Chamber of Deputies, parliamentary victory was still exceedingly difficult, for they still had to persuade the Senate. The upper house was a Fabian body of such provincial conservatism that it still suggested its constitutional origins as a bastion of monarchism. For example, when the chamber finally voted a bill in 1895 to give married women control of their own wages, it took twelve more years to persuade the Senate to agree. Women's suffrage had not even been introduced at the Luxembourg Palace. Socialists there never accounted for more than 2 percent of the prewar Senate. Radicals were even more predominant there, with a plurality of 42 to 47 percent. But the senatorial radical party was deeply imbued with the social conservatism of that house, as well as the traditional anti-clericalism of the party. The political avenue to constitutional revision was not a very broad thoroughfare.

Suffragism and Anti-Suffragism in Late Nineteenth-Century French Thought

Although particularly French problems (such as the question of separation of church and state) shaped the debate, the discussion of women's political rights in France was typical of that repeated around the Western world. The primary feminist claim rested on political theory. It fell easily from French lips: Natural Right. Justice. Equality. Democracy. Political realities led suffragists to add pragmatic justifications for the vote: society would profit in innumerable ways from the contributions of women. There were likewise two principal varieties of anti-suffragist thought in France. Republicans frequently employed political arguments which acknowledged the justice of equal rights but postponed them indefinitely, until women were adequately prepared to vote without threatening the established order. Conservatives, whether republican or from the parties of the right, used social arguments about the nature of women and the family.

The conviction that nature endowed women with rights indistinguishable from those of men established a moral philosophy of suffragism. If impartial nature provided the rights of women and political man wrongfully denied them, justice demanded nothing less than their complete restoration. Without such justice, militant feminists contended, men reduced them to a state of slavery. Many suffragists treated the appeal to justice as self-evident to any thoughtful person. "*Need I even say*," wrote Georges Renard of the Collège de France in 1897, "that women, being people like men, have the same rights . . . ?"[25]

The democratic orthodoxy of the Third Republic strengthened the argument for justice. Republican sovereignty sprang from the will of the people governed—a body that undeniably included women. "Sovereignty," proclaimed the constitution, "resides in the totality of French citizens. It is inalienable and imprescriptible. No individual nor any part of the people can arrogate to themselves the exercise thereof." The exclusion of women was thus a violation of republican sovereignty. The instrument for the delegation of republican sovereignty was universal suffrage; to suffragists, what existed was a deceitful "unisexual suffrage" which could only convey a demi-sovereignty. So suffragists employed the democratic argument frequently. How, Auclert wrote, "in this country where the word equality is written on so many walls . . . can one hesitate to give women the political rights that men enjoy?"[26] How, Ferdinand Buisson (Radical-Socialist, Seine) asked his colleagues, could they not realize that "the right to vote is the first right of the citizen in all free countries?"[27]

Suffragists especially criticized the republic for selectively treating women as citizens under some laws but not others. Neither the penal code nor tax law exempted women. Yet constitutional law gave women no role in drafting the codes that punished, no voice in the levying or disbursing of revenues. "Can there exist in our democracy," feminists asked, "two categories of taxpayers? The taxpayer elector, who has all the corresponding rights and duties, and the taxpayer non-elector, who has the duties but not the corresponding rights?" This argument, well suited to terse slogans, became the most visible expression of suffragist anger. One saw it repeatedly in prewar Paris, on posters plastered to the walls, on banners carried by marching women, on handbills distributed in the streets. "Women pay taxes. Women must vote."[28]

If men could not see the justice of granting equal rights, feminists argued, surely they must recognize the expediency of doing so. The nation could draw upon twice as much talent and intelligence to solve its problems. "From the emancipation of women," Auclert wrote in the manifesto that launched *La Citoyenne*, "will flow a source of good for all humanity."[29]

Social feminists who favored this pragmatic argument for enfranchisement often held that women possessed moral force in contrast to masculine brute force. Women, according to this stereotype (perilously close to some anti-suffragist generalizations) would create a better society. This claim contained no small dose of the Protestant austerity of many leading suffragists. Women would conquer the peril of alcoholism which threatened the nation. Feminine standards of cleanliness would be applied to public health. A chamber that included women would reinforce family life and combat depopulation. Women would demonstrate their natural interest in the protection of the young, their sensitivity to the weak and disadvantaged. Such arguments served a double purpose: not only to sway political opinion, but also to recruit the less militant (men and women alike) to the suffragist cause.

Republican anti-suffragists responded that they agreed but could not act yet. One supported women's rights "in principle" but found them to be "premature." The most common version of this procrastination was the radicals' assertion that women's suffrage could destroy French democracy by giving tremendous influence to the Catholic church. Attendance at Mass was a secondary sexual characteristic of French women. As agents of a "black peril," they would elect a clerical government. Their ballots would transmogrify the republic, dismantling laic education and rewriting the concordat with the Vatican. Michelet had stated the classical formulation of this theory: "Our wives and our daughters are raised, are governed *by our enemies . . .* by the enemies of the Revolution and of the future."[30] The great leaders of French radicalism, such as Georges Clemenceau and Emile Combes, agreed and inflexibly opposed women's suffrage. Clemenceau delivered perhaps the most explicit restatement of the theory in a pamphlet of 1907. Convinced that women were "completely impregnated with the sacristy," he could only envision a distant enfranchisement, "one day, when they are rid of their atavistic prejudices." Until then, women were simply too Catholic:

> Almost all of their influence is exerted to the benefit of the reactionary parties. The number of those who escape the domination of the clergy is ridiculously low. If the right to vote were given to women tomorrow, France would all of a sudden jump backwards into the middle ages. . . . Our task is heavy enough at the moment without aggravating it in new ways.[31]

The majority of French republicans apparently reasoned this way. Even those who supported feminist aspirations balked at the vote for fear of its political consequences. Léon Richer wrote that "out of nine million women who have reached their majority, only several thousand would vote freely; the remainder would take their orders from the confessional."³² The leader of the feminist group in the chamber, Charles Beauquier (Radical-Socialist, Doubs), also told suffragists that they must wait: "The laic republic is the target of furious attacks from the clergy and in this situation it is not possible that, *solely for the satisfaction of a sentiment of justice*, one introduce a new army of enemies."³³ The best that such republicans could offer was to educate women; perhaps their daughters might then be trusted with the ballot.

Conservative opponents of women's suffrage rarely dissembled with talk of merely delaying the vote. They embraced the social theories of Frédéric LePlay and his followers who held that the family was "the fundamental cellule" of France, an institution rooted in the nature of the species and in millennia of Roman, Catholic, and French traditions. There could be no opportune moment for a reform that altered familial relations because this challenged the "natural basis of social order." How could anyone in the possession of their faculties, one baroness asked, advocate "a new breach in the constitution of the family . . . such as it has been understood by Christian civilization?"³⁴

The rhetoric of conservative anti-suffragism in France was little different from that employed elsewhere. Women belonged at home, in the family—"*la femme au foyer.*" They had their own "domain" or "sphere." Nature gave them a high and noble mission, more important than any public service: "to be the Vesta of the home and to raise children according to Latin traditions."³⁵ Change would bring discord into the household. It would imperil the authority of the husband, established in law and religion. Altered sex roles would lead to emasculation, alcoholism, licentiousness, suicide, and divorce. Virilized women would neglect their families, confuse human sexuality, exacerbate depopulation. Children would suffer.

Some held political equality to be impossible because men and women were biologically different. Small brains, frail constitutions, hypersensitive nervous systems, emotional weakness, and pregnancy excluded women from leaving the natural vocation of their organism: "What was decided among the prehistoric protozoa cannot be annuled by Act of Parliament."³⁶ Furthermore, an attempt to do so contravened the divine will, defying roles ordained by God.

Conservatives also effectively argued that women did not want political rights. They were satisfied with the traditional relationships and their power within the family. Those who sought enfranchisement were a small minority—a radical, Parisian, feminist subculture disjoined from the people.

One of the foremost tactics of the women's suffrage campaign was the vigorous rebuttal of such generalizations. The republican argument was presented as anti-democratic. It disenfranchised women for reasons not applied to men. It was a prior restraint based on how the ballot might be used. That rested on an unproven hypothesis about feminine clericalism. It also ignored the rapid increase in the laic education of women from the 1880s—from 50 percent of primary schooling in 1881 to 92.5 percent in 1906. "It is not education that makes an elector," wrote Auclert, "it is pants."[37] Suffragists also vehemently denied that political rights and family life were incompatible, often sounding like the family's most ardent defenders. Moreover, the argument did not apply to the seven million women who already worked outside the home. And it ignored unmarried women, divorcees, widows and abandoned wives.

This debate naturally led to compromise proposals—to give limited political rights to women or full rights to some women. The usual answer was the extension of women's rights by stages, beginning with municipal suffrage. "Society, like nature, proceeds by evolution," as one moderately feminist politician put it.[38] This was the pattern in most countries permitting women to vote. It circumvented the republican anti-suffrage argument and provided time for the civic education of women. It appealed to moderates, politicians, and feminists alike. Conservatives, however, often preferred the enfranchisement of widows and spinsters or a multiple balloting system of familial suffrage in which fathers voted for their children. All such plans for partial rights were to lead to serious disagreements within the women's movement.

Perspectives on the Suffrage Campaign in France

In preparing to examine the women's suffrage campaign, it is helpful to recall the context in which it developed. One of the most informative perspectives is the comparative history of international suffragism: distinct differences can be seen between France and those states in which women won the vote earlier. Such comparisons suggest several aspects of French society that need to be considered in studying the women's movement. That movement itself must also be seen as a context for the suffrage struggle, because feminist aspiration was far larger than obtaining the vote. Finally, one must return to the general nature of French politics and consider the large ways in which that nature shaped the call for enfranchisement.

France may reasonably be considered the birthplace of modern feminism. The half-century that encompassed Condorcet, the revolutionary feminists, and the utopian socialists certainly witnessed pioneering contributions elsewhere, but nowhere was the doctrine more developed than in France. France gave the world many ideas but few accomplishments. By the end of the century, she hardly seemed the homeland of feminism. Foreigners found her "woefully backward," and French feminists saw their societies as "far from having the force of those elsewhere."[39]

This international contrast was especially vivid in political rights. Bohemians permitted women to vote for the *Landtag* in 1861. From then until the beginning of the World War in 1914, thirty different states and territories in the Western world enfranchised women in local elections (see Table 1). Women were voting in ten of those states before France had her first lasting suffrage organization (1876); in

Table 1 • **States Granting Women's Suffrage in Local Elections, 1861-1914**

State	Year	State	Year
Bohemia	1861	Colorado	1893
Sweden	1862	Idaho	1896
Russia	1864	Utah	1896
Finland	1865	Norway	1907
New South Wales	1867	Denmark	1908
England	1869	Iceland	1908
Wales	1869	Washington	1910
Victoria	1869	California	1911
Utah Territory	1870	Oregon	1912
West Australia	1871	Kansas	1912
New Zealand	1878	Arizona	1912
South Australia	1880	Illinois	1913
Scotland	1881	Alaska Territory	1913
Tasmania	1884	Montana	1914
Wyoming	1890	Nevada	1914

twenty-one before she had a national suffrage league (1909). The campaign for women's suffrage in France seemed so underdeveloped at the turn of the century that Carrie Chapman Catt, the leader of international suffragism, ranked it somewhere behind the movements in Chili, Turkey, Persia, Cuba, and the Philippines.[40] The size, activity, and militancy of suffrage movements in England and the United States dwarfed French efforts, persuading both contemporary and historical opinion of the relative unimportance of French suffragism.[41] English suffragists could assemble between 250,000 and 500,000 women in Hyde Park in 1908; the French could manage 5,000 to 6,000 in the Tuileries gardens by 1914. English suffragettes were internationally renowned for window-breaking, arson, and hunger strikes; with rare exceptions, French women utterly eschewed extreme tactics.

International comparison suggests several distinguishing features of French society which clarify the contrasts between the rights movement there and those in Britain and America (or in New Zealand and Sweden). One of the most obvious, and most provocative, is religious. Suffragism apparently thrived in Protestant states rather than Catholic societies like France. The correlation is clear in Table 1: only one state of the thirty that permitted women to vote before 1914 was Catholic. And that one, Bohemia, had a powerful Protestant-dissenting tradition dating back to the Hussites. Is it reasonable to conclude that religion conditioned responses to women's suffrage? That a doctrine seeking the autonomy of women and a role for them in public life was more tolerable in Protestant societies, more revolutionary to Catholics? That Protestantism accelerated or Catholicism impeded the growth and acceptance of a women's rights movement? Clearly, the examination of the political rights issue in France must consider the role of the Catholic church and the activity of Catholic women; conversely, it must explore the small minority of Protestants in France for their response to women's suffrage.

Another striking contrast between France and those states first accepting the enfranchisement of women is in their legal systems. Not a single state among the thirty of Table 1, including Bohemia, developed within the traditions and attitudes of Roman law. Virtually all were common law societies. France, in contrast, had a very strong Roman law tradition permeating institutions and mores. Furthermore, that basis of French culture was vigorously reinforced in the Napoleonic codification of the laws at the beginning of the nineteenth century. And none of the suffrage states of 1914 came from the Napoleonic legal system. Can one conclude that the common law was in some way more conducive to women's rights, the Roman law/ Napoleonic law tradition more hostile? If that is so, would one find any difference of attitudes and behavior between northern (particularly northeastern) France, with the greater penetration of customary law, and the south with its stronger Roman tradition? International comparison thus suggests that a history of women's suffrage in France consider how differing legal systems shaped differing politics, and it requires attention to possible regional variation in France.

Comparisons based upon economic development produce a more complicated problem for analysis. It is tempting, at first thought, to consider an association between the campaign for women's rights and the stage of developing urban-industrial society. This notion is chiefly conditioned by the fact that the most famous of the successful suffrage movements were in Britain and the United States, both advanced industrial societies at the turn of the century. France, on the other hand, was a country of considerable, but distinctly different, industrialization. Her pace of development was slower, and she remained a predominantly rural society. The census of 1901 found that the majority of the nation (59.1 percent) lived in rural communes of fewer than 2,000 persons, that less than one-third of the nation (29.1 percent) lived in towns as large as 10,000.[42] Did the greater development of urban-industrial society encourage or facilitate women's rights campaigns? Did the persistence of traditional rural society retard such activity? One must move cautiously around such hypotheses, as a reconsideration of Table 1 shows. The states within the United States that granted women political rights were not the densely populated, highly industrialized states of the northeast, but the rural states and territories of the west. Highly industrialized Germany and Belgium are not on the list; Russia and Finland are. This complicated problem produces another reason for the study of French suffragism to consider regional variations, with special attention to the urban/rural problem.

The question of economic development leads to another stimulating contrast, demography. Industrialization, indeed the whole concept of modern "progress," was closely associated with population growth. While virtually all Western societies experienced rapid increases in population during the nineteenth century, France faced stagnation. A steadily falling birth rate barely exceeded the death rate. French births per thousand of population fell 29.7 percent between the revolution and the founding of the Third Republic, then another 27.4 percent before World War I; the decline between 1901 and 1911 alone was 13 percent. "Depopulation" became a national concern; eighty-two books on the subject were published in Paris between 1890 and 1914. Germany, upon whom many French still dreamt of revenge for the war of 1870, was rapidly growing. Whereas France counted a larger population than the German states in 1861, by 1911 one could foresee the day when there would be twice as many Germans as Frenchmen from whom to recruit an army. British and German birth rates also fell at the turn of the century and talk of depopulation appeared, but this was a faint echo of a deep, long-standing French concern. The intensity of the depopulation debate in France suggests that any study of the woman question must consider it as a factor, both in understanding resistance to altering the roles of women and the behavior of feminists themselves.[43]

The issue of depopulation sets the context of a larger social problem which contemporaries considered nothing less than "the degeneration of the race." The so-called *belle époque* was not a beautiful era for much of the French nation. When one started by asking what was wrong with France that caused her population to decline in the face of universal growth, one ended with an appalling inventory of perceived problems. Alcoholism, suicide, divorce, criminality, mental illness, juvenile delinquency, abortion, collective violence, and prostitution were seen to be widespread and increasing. For example: the ratio of marriages to divorces and legal separations in France fell from 93:1 in 1880 to 23:1 in 1905. Suicides in the same period were up by 33 percent, 59 percent among minors. By the end of the century, there was an establishment selling alcohol for every eighty-two inhabitants of France—versus 1:246 in Germany, 1:380 in the United States, and 1:430 in Britain.[44] Critics on the right considered this proof of degeneration and blamed it on the loss of tradition—the weakening of the family, dechristianization, the uprooting of people from the land, the decline of patriotism. On the left, these were seen as the evils of an oppressive class structure, decadent on the top and demoralized on the bottom. Just as any response to the question of depopulation affected attitudes toward the role of women, the larger question of degeneration was inextricable from the woman question. The results were complicated. Anti-feminists might exploit such social problems to argue that women must stay at home, for example, to help reduce juvenile crime. On the other hand, feminists might profit from an alliance with groups seeking to control alcoholism, the two groups collaborating to reshape France. Thus, many of the associations that proliferated during the early Third Republic, which seem at first glance to be distant from the issue of women's suffrage (such as the Alliance nationale pour l'accroissement de la population française or the Ligue nationale contre l'alcoolisme) figured prominently in the suffrage campaign.

As such varied social problems remind us, the feminist call for reform was much larger than the question of political rights for women. "One would be singularly mistaken," wrote one suffragist, "if one considered the electoral claims of women by themselves, isolated from all the rest of their rights."[45] The vote was neither the exclusive nor even the foremost ambition of French feminists. As the 1901 statutes of the Union fraternelle des femmes (hereafter, UFF) stated, "Far from concentrating on one subject, the UFF preoccupies itself with a variety of feminist concerns."[46]

The paramount restraint on women was the civil law, embodied in the *Code Napoléon* promulgated in 1804. From Article 213, which stated that women must obey their husbands, to Article 1124, which defined the condition of women before the law as perpetual minors, French women possessed few legal rights either within the family or within society. Once perceived as minors, for example, it followed that they could not witness civil acts or serve on juries. So thorough was their restriction that schoolgirls could neither own a copy of, nor even read, the code that shackled them.[47] Little wonder that feminists denounced the Civil Code as "a heap of odious, stupid, and ridiculous articles," or that its reform seemed to many women more important than the winning of the vote.

Other feminists concentrated upon economic emancipation. This issue especially attracted socialist women who considered it more urgent than political rights. Many bourgeois feminists agreed. "Where does one start?" Jeanne Schmahl asked in 1895—"with the economic interests of the married women."[48] Others recognized that a call for economic rights attracted male support more readily than a call to political rights. The simple right of women to work or to join trade unions did not exist without their husband's consent. A married woman could not even spend her own income without the approval of her husband. The rudimentary aspiration of "equal pay for equal work" required doubling or tripling of women's wages in most cases. Male laborers in private industry in the department of the Seine in 1893, for example, averaged 6.15 francs per diem whereas women received 3.00.[49] This affected no small number of women. A Ministry of Labor survey of 1900 found that 45 percent of French women worked outside the home, including nearly two million in industry. Furthermore, the niggardly salaries that the state itself paid teachers and postal workers (circa 40,000 women in 1900) meant that the disproportion in wages was not exclusively the experience of blue-collar workers.

Feminists also sought equality in education. The republican reorganization of French education in the 1880s produced the first network of free secondary schools for women (Camille Sée Law, 1880) and the first *lycée* for women (Lycée Fénélon, Paris) opened in 1883. French women, however, still did not receive the *baccalauréat*, or a curriculum as rigorous as that for men. The Third Republic trained a few women as physicians, starting with *doctoresse* Madeleine Bres in 1875, but most branches of higher education were less receptive than medicine. Women could attend the faculty of law at Paris from 1884, but Jeanne Chauvin, the first woman to complete legal training there (1892), faced a riot that halted the defense of her thesis and forced the process to be completed *in camera*. Even with her degree completed, Chauvin could not be admitted to the bar. Student riots also greeted a woman enrolling in letters at the Sorbonne in 1893; demonstrations ended only after the cancellation of her course. The *grandes écoles* were the last to accept women: the Ecole nationale des chartes was exclusively masculine; the Ecole normale supérieure had yet to train its first *normalienne*; the *doctorat* and the *agrégation*, the route to university teaching, remained closed to women. Furthermore, French women needed to be persuaded to seize the few opportunities available: the majority of women studying medicine and law in France were foreigners—52 percent of the medical students and 68 percent of the law students according to a study of 1906.[50]

The most controversial feminist programs dealt with sexual, maternal, and marital rights. The potential conflicts were immense: with bourgeois values, with masculine sensitivity, with Catholic teaching, with national interests. Most feminists responded cautiously, seeking women's autonomy and equality consonant with fundamental French attitudes. This chiefly meant stating their program in ways that did not threaten the family. They praised motherhood and marriage, deplored depopulation and immorality. Clotilde Dissard, the editor of *La Revue féministe*, presented a typical formulation of this thinking in an essay of 1895: "Feminism is in no way directed against marriage; it asks quite simply that women in the home be conscious and free, sharing with men all the rights, all the responsibilities, all the obligations."[51] This caution on subjects touching the family did not diminish feminist demands for reform. Everyone called for improvements in the legal position of the married woman. The notorious double standard of the penal code that made adultery a crime for women but not their husbands was widely denounced; the right to file paternity suits, widely claimed. But many questions split the women's movement. Militants generally called for liberalized divorce laws and two prominent leaders (Marguerite Durand and Maria Vérone) were themselves divorced. Moderates, however, were uncertain about easy divorce; Catholics, of course, were unalterably opposed. "Neo-Malthusians," such as Marie Huot, Nelly Roussel, and Madeleine Pelletier, advocated population control through sex education, the availability of birth control devices, and the liberalization of abortion laws—shocking some feminists and horrifying others. Neo-Malthusian feminism was most common among socialist women who argued, as Pelletier did, that the working class must restrict population increases in order to improve living conditions; for them, the natalist propaganda about depopulation was merely a variant of bourgeois exploitation. French feminism produced no Alexandra Kollontai, but a few left-wing feminists endorsed free love or Léon Blum's theory of trial marriage—appalling ideas to the majority of feminists.

At the opposite end of the feminist spectrum stood a reform movement that may be termed "social feminism." This did not encompass work for women's rights per se as much as it did the general reform of French society. Its leaders, such as Sarah Monod, Avril de Sainte-Croix, Julie Siegfried, and Marguerite de Witt-Schlumberger, came to feminism through years of work in philanthropy. They brought with them campaigns addressing national degeneration—for pacifism and against alcoholism, tobacco, and pornography. They brought concerns about the treatment of young women in prison, especially prostitutes, and the *police des moeurs* who harassed them. They devoted their energies to correcting juvenile deliquency and to improving public hygiene. Their crusades seldom appealed to militants, but they provided a basis for cooperation with the Catholic women's movement, established links with nonfeminist organizations, and recruited moderate women to feminism.

Given the range of feminist *revindications*, what was the relative importance attached to winning political rights? Was the ballot the cornerstone to be built upon or the capstone which only fit when other rights were in place? Could all feminists be persuaded to inscribe political rights on their program? To work for them? To collaborate with each other in a unified campaign? Auclert had fought since the 1870s to convince feminists that "the political right is the key which will give us all our other rights."[52] The prospects for a feminist consensus were not good. Not only did historic fissures separate socialist from bourgeois, republican from Catholic, even the moderate majority of the women's movement held quite diverse ideas. Could cautious social feminists be led to a political campaign? Could moderates collaborate with women who believed in the ideas associated with neo-Malthusianism?

A final context—national politics—poses other questions for understanding the women's suffrage movement in France. Some political problems, such as the ambivalence of the dominant Radical and Radical-Socialist Party, have already been seen; it is equally important to recall the broad lines of French political history. In the century between the 1790s and the 1890s, the French adopted eleven different constitutions, from the egalitarian to the authoritarian. The post-Napoleonic regimes of the nineteenth century had lasted for sixteen, eighteen, four, and eighteen years. So the twentieth anniversary of the constitution of the Third Republic, in 1895, made the regime seem near the end of its actuarial life expectancy. Very serious political crises such as the Boulanger crisis, the Panama scandal, the Dreyfus affair, and the battle over separation of church and state reinforced this impression of a government whose very survival was open to question. Virtually all suffragists were republicans who wanted that government to endure. But suffragists in other countries had a fundamentally different relationship with their government. They could agitate in public without considering that their actions might threaten the existence of the regime to which they were bound. The chance that the American republic might collapse or the English monarchy fall due to suffragists' demonstrations was so small that it did not shape women's behavior. In contrast, the republicanism of French suffragists sensitized them to the apparent instability of the Third Republic, whose two predecessors survived for a total of ten years.

Thus, very serious tactical problems were posed to French women. What political behavior, what means of demonstration was acceptable? Would demonstrations in the streets seem a threat to the regime? How would the government and the police respond to militancy? The answer to the latter question was especially important because feminists elsewhere did not confront the French tradition of state violence in response to radicalism. The French government was certainly not alone in its willingness to repress militancy, as the women confined to Holloway Prison for demonstrating in London or to Occoquan Workhouse for protesting in Washington, D.C., could testify. French governments, however, had a record of more extreme repression. British and American women might face the terrible prospect of force-feeding, but French feminists knew that greater force could be used. So what demonstrations would they dare to choose?

Chapter Two

XOXOXOXOXOXOXOXOXOXOXOXOXOXOXOXOXOXOXOXOXOXOXOXOXOXOXOXOXOXOXOXOXOXOX

The Women's Rights Movement at the Turn of the Century, 1896-1901

Why did the women's rights movement gain momentum at the turn of the century? The causes were both long range and immediate. The long-range developments have already been seen: serious grievances were present, a substantial ideological response to them presented, the pioneering experience of feminist organization acquired, and the comparatively tolerant environment of a liberal-democratic regime created. In the early 1890s, the founders of the feminist movement, Léon Richer and Maria Deraismes, passed from the scene. During the years 1896-1901, however, several stimuli led French women to take up their cause. First, the tradition of holding periodic women's congresses at Paris produced an unusually militant assembly in 1896 and three separate congresses in conjunction with the Paris world's fair of 1900. Second, in 1897 Marguerite Durand, a Parisian journalist, founded *La Fronde*, a feminist daily newspaper of high quality and large circulation. Third, under the prodding of more organized American feminists, moderate French women of the philanthropic movement founded a broad coalition of women's organizations, the Conseil national des femmes françaises (hereafter, CNFF) and affiliated with the International Council of Women.

French feminists believed that the events of 1896-1901 marked a turning point for them. As one activist put it, the late nineteenth century had been a "primitive, and a little chaotic period of feminism, a period of discoveries and not yet of organization." The events of 1900, "a year memorable among all years," she said, marked a beginning. Another wrote that they had reached "a decisive stage in the history of feminism."[1] Dramatic evidence supports their view. On the eve of the congress of 1896, there were six important feminist leagues in Paris with a combined membership of 500 to 1,000. After the establishment of the CNFF in 1901, there were fifteen feminist groups in the capital claiming 20,000 to 25,000 adherents.

The women's rights congress of 1896 was noteworthy as the first thorough airing of many militant feminist positions. It was small (c. 200 participants), it revealed some of the continuing disagreements within the women's movement, and it did not produce a comprehensive feminist program that all could work for. But it was the first congress to discuss women's suffrage, it adopted several advanced resolutions previously considered too controversial, and it produced some hope for cooperation between socialist women and militant feminists.

The congress was the joint effort of the LFDF and La Solidarité des femmes (hereafter, Solidarité), a small group of socialist-feminists founded in 1893. Maria Pognon, who succeeded Richer as president of the LFDF in 1892 and turned the league sharply to the left, and Eugénie Potonié-Pierre, the founding secretary-general of Solidarité, collaborated to present an agenda far more radical than the simple nine-point program of the last feminist congress (1892). The delegates unanimously voted their belief in the complete equality of men and women and vowed to work for a long list of legal reforms. Among the advanced beliefs discussed, but not endorsed, were abortion rights, the sexual independence of "free union," and the vote. The Parisian press, led by *Le Temps* and *Le Figaro*, was unmistakably hostile but gave the meeting heavy coverage. Some socialists stalked out due to the apparent abandonment of the class struggle, but most stayed to cooperate with bourgeois feminists. Spectators as different as the conservative Marie Maugeret and the radical Marguerite Durand were inspired to launch new feminist efforts. And Pognon's passionate plea for the right to vote won new supporters, notably Henri Rochefort, who endorsed it in an editorial in *L'Intransigeant* in April 1896.[2]

The three women's congresses of 1900 were even more important. Each assembled a separate portion of the women's movement—Catholic, moderate, militant. Preparations so excited feminists that they believed in advance that 1900 would be the year of the movement's awakening. The results did not disappoint them. They introduced feminist ideas to more people than had previously been possible, articulating so many grievances that one author called the year "our 1789—our Declaration of Rights."[3] And a large faction resolved to press ahead with a new suffrage bill.

A congress of Catholic women, the Congrès catholique des oeuvres de femmes, met first and took several advanced positions on the woman question. The origins of this assembly were scarcely feminist. A congress of French Catholics had already been planned when a group of aristocratic women asked to participate, in order to submit a motion calling for the restoration of school prayers. The organizers suggested that they meet alone instead, as a "second section" of the congress. Christian feminists, let by Marie Maugeret, constituted a minority of the participants in this endeavor but their industriousness produced a disproportionate influence on the meetings. They exposed Catholic women to a range of feminist and liberal Catholic issues, including the economic grievances of teachers, the importance of educational equality, the right of women to work, the need for paternity suits, and the revision of marriage contracts. Maugeret denounced the Napoleonic Code: "French law does not protect woman: it disarms her in economic life, it ignores her in civil life, it enslaves her in conjugal life." She even raised the question of women's suffrage, the first public discussion of the vote by Catholic women. The congress, however, refused to adopt any radical motions, and Catholic feminists took care to distance themselves from republican feminism. As Christians, Maugeret said, they must be "the resolute enemy of freethinker feminism." This was a mixture of sincere belief and adroit tactics: she knew that most of her audience was hostile to feminism in any form.[4] Republican feminists criticized Catholic women for such timidity, for being "directed by their confessors," but they acknowledged that the discussions at the Catholic congress had shown that Catholics were not "uniquely and fatally devoted to purely household questions."[5]

The second women's congress of 1900, the Congrès des oeuvres et institutions féminines, was only slightly more feminist. Most of its organizers were women active in Protestant philanthropy through the Conférence de Versailles. They were drawn to feminism, as a friend remarked, "by discovering little by little the insufficiency of charity against the problems of women."[6] Their stated goal for the congress was to adopt a feminist, but not suffragist, program—to go "beyond the questions of philanthropy ... to obtain civil rights for women, voluntarily leaving aside political questions which seem premature."[7] The honorary president of the congress, Léon Bourgeois, could comfortably subscribe to such feminism. Jeanne Chauvin provided the most aggressive reports of the meeting, calling for the abrogation or modification of dozens of articles of the Civil Code ... but no report calling for the vote. Some militants participated but did not trouble the conscience of the majority in the way that Maugeret had unsettled the Catholic congress; they were too pleased with the growing feminism of women who had previously spurned the word.[8]

The LFDF sponsored the third congress, the Congrès international de la condition et des droits des femmes. Five hundred delegates, including the militants of all Parisian leagues, debated a program larger and more systematic than that of 1896. Resolutions started with a unanimous call for "equal salary for equal work" and ended with a demand for women's suffrage. Seventy-one other motions passed. Militants wanted an eight-hour workday, payment for a wife's housework, abolition of laws maintaining the double standard of morality, coeducation of men and women in the same subjects, equal civil rights for women, divorce by mutual consent, the opening of all positions in the bureaucracy to women, and the elimination of all expressions of religious dogma from the schools.[9] The militant program of 1900 encountered criticism from both the right and the left. Catholics, troubled by the liberalism of the congress on feminine institutions, were aghast at the "socialist and anti-religious" tone of the militant congress. One abbé, who called himself a feminist, branded the congress "a crusade of hysterics."[10] Socialist women, on the other hand, thought that same assembly represented the interests of the bourgeoisie at the expense of working-class women. Their criticism crystallized during debates on the condition of domestic servants. Feminists rejected a proposal to give their maids a day off; some suggested it would lead to prostitution. Thereupon, Elisabeth Renaud (a former servant) and Louise Saumoneau denounced the middle-class stereotyping of workers. Maria Pognon, the presiding officer, answered, to widespread applause: "I know that there is a certain party that preaches class struggle; well then, I censure that party, I do not accept class struggle. ... "[11]

Ironically, the greatest progress which suffragism made during the congresses of 1900 came from a socialist deputy at the congress of women's rights. The stirrings of a Catholic suffragism at the first congress and the growth of French feminism emerging from the second contained distant promise. The vow of René Viviani to the third congress was for immediate action. Viviani had been active in the women's movement since his arrival in Paris as a law student in the 1880s. His first publication had been in Richer's *Droit des femmes*; his first parliamentary contacts had come as an officer of the LFDF.[12] Viviani endorsed legal reforms but argued that this was insufficient. "What is it worth to rewrite the Civil Code to the benefit of women," he asked, "if they are not armed for the protection of these rights with the ballot?" In an eloquent speech which suffragists of the next twenty years were to cite as a turning point in their growth, Viviani exhorted feminists to devote themselves to enfranchisement:

> I know that in speaking this way I am perhaps going to offend the sensitivities of the timid. ... Permit me to say that all the laws that we can propose will be in vain if women are not armed with the ballot to expand and to defend them. (Bravos) You will obtain—from the generosity of men, from their spirit of justice, or sometimes from their love of the paradox—some partial reforms, some slight modifications in the Civil Code or in the Code of Commerce, but you will never receive the total kindness of emancipation. In the name of a quite long political and parliamentary experience, let me tell you that legislators make the laws for those who make the legislators.

The delegates enthusiastically adopted the Viviani report, and he promised the introduction of a suffrage bill in the next session of the Chamber of Deputies. It was a climacteric moment, marking the beginning of the first sustained campaign for women's suffrage in France.[13]

The second major factor in the expansion of French feminism at the turn of the century was the development of the feminist press. Before the appearance of *La Fronde*, most feminist periodicals were affiliated with the various small groups (see Table 2). Their circulation was extremely limited, generally informing members of activities rather than reaching wider audiences. The principal exception, Maria Martin's monthly *Le Journal des femmes* (1891), obtained only a limited circulation due to its advanced opinions. *La Fronde*, with its large format, daily publication, and high circulation gave a new publicity to the movement and speeded the conversion of women to feminism. Its combination of feminist activism and radical national politics confined the regular readership to the intelligentsia and the small population of educated, independent women of the middle class. That

Table 2 • Principal Feminist Periodicals in 1902

	Founded	Editor	Frequency
REPUBLICAN			
(Militant Suffragist)			
Journal des femmes	1891	Maria Martin	monthly
(Pro-Suffrage, but not Suffragist)			
Amélioration, *Bulletin*	1894	Feresse-Deraismes	quarterly
La Fronde	1897	Durand	daily
Etudes, *Bulletin*	1898	Oddo-Deflou	quarterly
(Feminine)			
La Femme	1879	Monod	fortnightly
CATHOLIC			
Le Féminisme chrétien	1896	Maugeret	monthly
Le Pain	1900		monthly
Action sociale de la femme	1902	Chenu	monthly
Devoir des femmes françaises	1902	Dorive	monthly
SYNDICALIST-SOCIALIST			
La Femme de l'avenir	1897	Astié de Valsayre	monthly
L'Abeille	1901	Savari	monthly
La Femme socialiste	1901	Renaud, Saumoneau	monthly

base sufficed to make *La Fronde* the unquestioned center of French feminism.

La Fronde was the creation of one of the most controversial and important women of the movement. Marguerite Durand (1864-1936) was the illegitimate daughter of a general and a writer. Raised by her maternal grandparents and dispatched to a convent for a proper up-bringing, Durand rebelled against bourgeois propriety and at age seventeen left home for the disreputable career of an actress. She was an immediate success. High intelligence, a superb memory, and ar-resting beauty quickly won her the conservatory's prize and mem-bership in the company of the Comédie française. Roles as the beautiful ingenue and the coy soubrette led to the rave notices of critics, a certain celebrity about Paris, and a legion of admiring men—among them Georges Laguerre, a young radical deputy (Vaucluse) and protegé of Clemenceau. In 1886 Durand left the stage to marry Laguerre and launch a political *salon* in their Paris townhouse. When Laguerre became an ardent Boulangist, their home became a center of his machinations; Mme. Laguerre thrived on the intrigue, earning the sobriquet "the Madame Roland of Boulangism." She learned journalism when Laguerre published the Boulangist *La Presse*, and by some accounts she contributed more to the newspaper than he did. The collapse of Boulangism coincided with the collapse of the Laguerre's marriage. In 1891 Durand divorced her husband and commenced a career in journalism to support herself. She immediately obtained a position at *Le Figaro*, where she composed a column ("Le Courrier du Figaro") generally featuring a chatty view of Parisian life.[14]

Le Figaro in the 1890s was a sonorously anti-feminist newspaper which considered the equality of the sexes "contrary to natural law," but Durand was not yet a feminist. In the spring of 1896 she was assigned to attend the feminist congress organized by the LFDF and write "a humorous piece on the amazons who wanted to take the place of men and wear pants."[15] She never wrote that article. Instead, the debates of the congress converted Durand to feminism. This did not stop *Le Figaro* from lambasting "this so-called feminist movement," but it led Durand to the conviction that French feminism needed its own daily newspaper to compete with the masculine press, provide opportunities in journalism to women, and present feminist ideas to the public. Durand launched *La Fronde*—a name referring to the sling (*fronde*) with which David challenged Goliath—in December 1897 with a publicity campaign that coated Paris with her poster: a beautiful, elegantly dressed woman pointing out the horizon to a group of troubled and hopeful women of all classes. The paper was to be entirely edited, composed, and printed by women. It was a prodigious effort, involving disputes with trade unions, legal battles with the government over printing in a private residence, a difficult search for qualified women, the skepticism of the established press, and very large financial needs. To the astonishment of many, the first issue appeared with a staggering press run of 200,000. This was a gesture, to match the monthly circulation of the most successful women's publication in France, the *Petit Echo de la mode*, which was anti-feminist and survived by printing such pap as "Louise loves Gendarmes."

La Fronde immediately became the nexus of republican feminism; indeed, it employed a large portion of the feminist elite. The best-known woman in Parisian jounalism at the turn of the century, Séverine (Caroline Rémy), wrote a daily column. Clémence Royer, the French translator of Darwin, wrote on scholarly and academic subjects. Pauline Kergomard reported on education. Maria Pognon treated political questions, including a long series explaining how the communes of France were financed and administered. Hélène Sée, a member of one of France's most distinguished academic families, also wrote on politics. Avril de Sainte-Croix contributed on social problems, especially regulated prostitution. Jane Misme reviewed theater and literature. A wide range of established and beginning writers, such as Daniel Lesueur (Jeanne Loiseau Lapauze) and Mary Léopold Lacour, published poems, short stories, and serialized novels. Aline Valette and Marie Bonnevial wrote on working women and syndicalism. Camille Bélilon produced a column pointing out and rebutting anti-feminist attitudes in the Parisian press. Two of *La Fronde*'s young reporters, Maria Vérone (legal and judicial issues) and Martha Meliot (financial affairs), forced exclusively masculine institutions such as the stock exchange to accredit women as journalists for the first time.

This formidable array of talent was far greater than the staff of the average Parisian newspaper, and the world of journalism quickly realized it. Partly as a boulevard witticism and partly in respect, *La Fronde* was dubbed "*Le Temps* in skirts." A large share of the respect derived from Durand's determination to make her newspaper a competitive organ of information, covering a full range of news. Although produced by women and resolutely feminist in outlook, it did not solely record feminist activities. This had two important results. Detailed coverage of other subjects, from the political to the cultural, meant that *La Fronde* studied fewer feminist issues than might be expected from its "*grand format*" seven-day-a-week character. More importantly, it followed the model of the Parisian press and adopted a clear ideological tone—radical republicanism. This meant both ardent support of ex-Captain Dreyfus and strident anti-clericalism. Its coverage of the Dreyfus case (Séverine's longtime assignment and a strong personal interest of Durand) particularly identified the young newspaper. A large portion of *La Fronde*'s space was devoted to proclaiming Dreyfus's innocence; Durand opened two Dreyfusard fund drives, one for Emile Zola and one for Mme. Dreyfus. Such radicalism placed limits on *La Fronde*'s feminism. The newspaper was unlikely to be read by, much less to convert, conservative women. For all of her impressive accomplishments, Durand could not make *La Fronde* the instrument for creating a mass feminism; the political climate of the age did not permit it.[16]

As *La Fronde*'s affinity for the radical republic suggests, Durand initially held an ambivalent attitude about women's suffrage. The first issue stated explicitly that the newspaper expected "equal rights, equal opportunities, and equal responsibilities," but Durand believed that equal political rights could be postponed. She permitted suffragists to state their claims in *La Fronde*, but she would not endorse them. The first issue, for example, contained Pognon's survey of militant aspirations, including full political rights; within the first week Auclert also published an article on suffragism. Durand, however, angered the members of Solidarité a few weeks later by refusing to support or publicize their plans for a woman candidate during the parliamentary elections of 1898; she also infuriated Auclert by not printing or supporting her suffrage petitions.[17] Durand thus charted an exceedingly delicate course for *La Fronde*. The paper would take many advanced positions and would discuss all issues, but it would not risk losing moderates by standing on the far left. Consequently, Durand received criticism from all sides of the women's movement. Catholics occasionally contributed to the paper, but attacked her for "narrow and violent sectarianism."[18] Militants often published there, but many of them fought lifelong feuds with Durand—including Auclert and Madeleine Pelletier, who wrote that "she [Durand] is as little feminist as possible."[19] At its worst, this led to malicious gossip about Durand's well-known sexual relations with prominent men (her "regiment of lovers," said Auclert).[20] Durand paid a high price, but she created a remarkable newspaper that significantly expanded the feminist movement.

The third great stimulus to the growth of the women's movement was the foundation of the CNFF in 1900-1901, the most auspicious sign that French feminism might develop into a mass movement. The council was a federation of many different types of women's organizations. Its predominant character was more feminine than feminist, but its initial membership of 21,000 provided feminists with great hopes. Like many other groups, the CNFF did not initially call for political rights for women but soon converted.

The origins of the CNFF lay in the Conférence de Versailles, an annual meeting of feminine philanthropic organizations established in 1892. The assembly included a few Catholic and freethinking members, but it was organized and led by women of the French Protestant elite. Approximately four hundred women met each year in a social gala, under a huge tent on an estate at Versailles, to hear reports of the activities of each other's charitable works during the previous year. Gradually the format expanded to include other women's issues. When militant feminists attended to stir up the staid members, as Eliska Vincent did in 1897, they were told that the group was feminine, not feminist. Nonetheless, the Conférence de Versailles led to moderate feminism through the consideration of such issues as the legal situation of women. Simultaneously, some prominent members concluded that they could accomplish more good works if they had more rights.

As the ladies of Protestant philanthropy moved toward feminism, they received encouragement from abroad, notably a visit to France by May Wright Sewall, the American founder and president of the International Council of Women. Sewall and Frances Willard had organized a National Council of Women in the United States in 1888 as a coalition of all types of women's organizations, although its tone remained Protestant. Sewall attended the French feminist congress of 1889, attempting without success to stimulate the creation of a national council in France that would affiliate with her international council. She returned to Paris for the congresses of 1900, as an official representative of the United States at the exhibition, with the same feminist purpose. This time, she could count on the friendship of Isabelle Bogelot who had worked with the National Council of Women while living in America and served as an unofficial French delegate at several meetings of the international council. Sewall's proposal to include a broad spectrum of women's organizations—professional, educational, and charitable as well as feminist—attracted the women of the Conférence de Versailles, as did the strongly Protestant tone of the International Council. At the Congrès des oeuvres et institutions féminines, the leadership of the Conférence de Versailles (particularly Sarah Monod, Julie Siegfried, Avril de Sainte-Croix, and Isabelle

Bogelot) decided to establish a French council and called upon the militants and the Catholics of the two other congresses to join with them.[21]

The initial response to this plan was mixed. The women of the Catholic congress, including the Christian feminists, flatly refused. As Maugeret observed in an open letter to Sewall, the politics of religion in France made such cooperation impossible: "To hope that French Catholic women would rally to an organization initiated by foreigners, by Protestants, and which up to the present has still only been adopted in Europe by the Protestant nations, and in France only in the Protestant or freethinking milieux, this would be mad ... "[22] Maugeret believed that feminism could not succeed in France without attracting Catholic women. Sainte-Croix answered that the national council would "play an important, and perhaps primordial, role" in changing France, even without Catholic women's groups which acted on an "obscure and deplorable instinct ... to live in cloisters, ignoring all that passes around them."[23] Militant feminists were divided. Some, notably Auclert, remained aloof from the national council, viewing it as insufficiently feminist; others, such as Caroline Kauffmann of Solidarité, joined only at the price of precipitating a crisis in their organization. Maria Martin, however, added the prestige of the *Journal des femmes* to the council, which she considered a milestone in the history of French feminism. Led by Amélioration and the LFDF, the delegates to the congress of women's rights voted their support. This resulted in the naming of an organizing committee chaired by Bogelot with four members from the Conférence de Versailles (Bogelot, Monod, Siegfried, and Sainte-Croix), two members from the LFDF (Pognon and Bonnevial), one from Amélioration (Mme. Wiggishoff), and none from the militant suffragist or Catholic groups.[24]

The organizing committee for the CNFF initially had difficulties persuading women's groups to join the council. They sent invitations to 1,500 organizations; they received acceptances from thirteen, ten of which had been founded by members of the committee. A year of cajolery enlisted another twenty-two groups. Thus, thirty-five women's organizations founded the Conseil national des femmes françaises with 21,000 charter members. Invitations had gone to all associations "that concerned themselves with the lot of women or of children," without regard to their political or religious character. Acceptance came only from groups "of a secular spirit" and liberal politics. Consistent with the aim of the international council, the French council included women's unions and professional organizations, pacifist and temperance organizations, philanthropic groups and educational societies, as well as the moderate republican feminist leagues. The membership was immense, but most of them were not feminists. Nonetheless, the council gave the women's movement an affiliation with bourgeois respectability and an enormous potential for expansion.

The feminist conquest of the CNFF began immediately. The first formal meeting, to draft statutes and to elect officers, took place in April 1901. It surprised no one that the women of the Conférence de Versailles held a majority of the seventy delegates (two from each of the member societies). Bogelot was named honorary president and women of the Protestant elite were elected to the presidency, the secretary-generalship (the administrative head), to one of the two vice-presidencies, and a majority of the executive committee. The statutes, however, identified the council as a "federation of feminist and feminine action [oeuvres féminines] societies." Special provisions were made to facilitate the membership of small organizations, mixed groups with a large women's membership, and the women's sections of trade unions. The stated purpose of the federation was to facilitate the discussion of women's questions by diverse groups and then obtain greater influence by concerted action. Adhesion to the council, the statutes promised, "does not imply the renunciation of any particular ideas; each society keeps its autonomy." The executive committee and officers would meet five times per year, maintain the links among the member societies, and follow the program adopted at an annual congress of the full council. To establish and pursue mutual policies, the CNFF would create "sections" devoted to various areas of women's interest, such as education. These sections would conduct meetings throughout the year and seek reforms in the name of the CNFF. Sections were immediately founded for charity, education, legislation, and labor; a hygiene section was added in 1902, but initial efforts to found a suffrage section failed. The first formal program of the CNFF, however, revealed a surprising feminist strength in the council. It stated fourteen goals, many in the realm of social feminism—crusades against prostitution, alcoholism, pornography, and tuberculosis. But the majority of the vows adopted came from feminist members. The CNFF thus went on record as favoring "equal justice, liberty, morality, and rights of the two sexes." Several special measures of equality complemented this general vow: the opening of medical and administrative careers still closed to women, coeducation, the right to file paternity suits, and the improvement of women's wages. With this statement, French feminists captured the CNFF and began to use its resources.[25]

The Size and Composition of the Women's Movement

Despite the reasons for feminist optimism that a turning point had been reached, the scholarly judgment that "there was no *mass* feminist movement" is still correct.[26] Such descriptions, however, can obscure more than they clarify: it is more important to recognize the size and diversity of the movement that did exist.

The general character of the women's movement during the *fin de siècle* was a striking duplication of French national politics. Strong-willed individuals led a variety of small, competing organizations which grouped together into loose ideological coalitions. The movement was, as a prominent feminist lamented, "full of generals without soldiers"[27]—a situation little different from the multiparty politics of the men in the Chamber of Deputies. Feminist fragmentation extended beyond the historic separation of republican, socialist, and Catholic women. The bourgeois-republican majority was split into moderate and militant wings, just as the republican men at the Palais Bourbon divided into a cautious right-center and a more reformist left-center of radicals. Like republican politicians, these feminist factions were subdivided into more than a dozen groupings, each with its well-known leader. The analogy also applied to policy. Republican feminist groups usually cooperated with each other, but a cautious right-center resisted the advanced ideas of militants and disapproved of their tendency to draw close to socialist women and ideas. Just as republican men did, republican feminists found cooperation with the Catholic right-wing rarely possible. The principle difference in the parallel between male and female politics was that the radical left-center was predominant among men but the moderate right-center among women.

It is difficult to establish the precise size of the various women's rights organizations. Estimated membership in individual groups (see Table 3) can be based on feminist reports of their meetings, the

Table 3 • Principal Women's Rights Organizations, 1900-1901

Name	Founded	Leader(s)	Associated Publications	Estimated Membership
REPUBLICAN				
(Militant Suffragist)				
Suffrage des femmes	1876	Auclert	"Le Féminisme" (*Le Radical*)	under 100
Egalité	1888	Vincent	pamphlet series	under 100
Solidarité	1891	Kauffmann	(none in 1900)	under 100
(Moderate Suffragist)				
Amélioration	1876	Feresse-Deraismes	*Bulletin*	100-150
LFDF	1882	Pognon (pres.) Bonnevial (s.-g.)	(none in 1900)	under 200
(Moderate and Conservative)				
Conférence de Versailles	1892	Monod	*La Femme*	350-400
Avant-Courrière	1893	Schmahl	pamphlet series	c. 200
Etudes	1898	Oddo-Deflou	*Bulletin*	c. 100
CNFF	1901	Monod (pres.) Sainte-Croix (s.-g.)	*La Femme*	21,000
UFF	1901	Marbel	(none in 1901)	under 100
Union de pensée féminine	1901	Martial	(none in 1901)	under 100
(Provincial)				
Comité féministe républicain d'Ariège (Foix)	1889	Darnaud	"Courrière féministe"	c. 25
Société d'éducation et d'action féministe (Lyons)	1897	Laguerre	pamphlet series	under 100

Table 3 • Continued

Name	Founded	Leader(s)	Associated Publications	Estimated Membership
CATHOLIC				
Féminisme chrétien	1897	Maugeret	*Le Féminisme chrétien*	under 100
Action sociale de la femme	1900	Chenu	*Action sociale*	under 200
Devoir des femmes françaises	1901	Dorive	*Devoir des femmes*	under 100
SOCIALIST				
Groupe féministe socialiste	1899	Renaud Saumoneau	*La Femme socialiste*	under 100

accounts of the daily press, and the secret notes of police infiltrators. Such evidence suggests that the average membership of a feminist organization in 1900-1901 (excluding the CNFF) was under one hundred. As Table 3 shows, that figure is certainly true for the socialists and the three organizations of militant suffragists. Except for the National Council, no organization could claim 500 members. While the CNFF proudly announced 21,000 participants, very few of these women were active feminists—probably no more than 500. A rough overview of the feminist political spectrum therefore suggests the following proportions: 50-100 women active on the socialist-feminist left, 200-250 militant suffragists of the left-center, 1,000-1,200 moderate republican feminists, and 300-350 conservative feminists of the Catholic right. Thus, there were perhaps 2,000 active in women's rights meeting. Feminists, of course, could claim the entire membership of the CNFF, or even women who were regularly exposed to moderate feminist ideas through philanthropic societies, trade unions, or social reform lobbies. On this basis, one might calculate the outermost limits of French feminism as somewhere in the range of 20,000-25,000 women whose recruitment to activity could be expected. Whether one considers the 2,000 active feminists or the 25,000 potential feminists, a large majority belonged to moderate organizations and a very small proportion were active suffragists.[28]

Numbers provide only a partial understanding of the women's

rights movement. They help to explain some feminist actions and public responses. But the knowledge that the movement was small and just beginning rapid growth is less informative than an examination of the composition of the organizations. Who were the feminists who would conduct the campaign for political rights? How does their collective biography aid the analysis of suffragism? If one examines those organizations that worked for the vote in the period 1896-1914, the membership appears to have been strikingly homogeneous; their common characteristics, very informative.

Feminism was first of all an urban—essentially Parisian—phenomenon. More than 95 percent of the national membership lived in Paris, most of the remainder in Lyons. Although there existed a few noteworthy signs of provincial feminism, it was almost exclusively a matter of one or two energetic women in a large town trying to organize activities. There was no evidence of any rural feminism. "In the provinces," Parisian leaders realized, "the feminist idea only seems able to penetrate slowly."[29]

Feminist membership was overwhelmingly drawn from the middle classes, especially the liberal professions—"from an active and intellectual group within the bourgeoisie," as a contemporary analyst put it.[30] Even groups with links to the socialist party, such as Solidarité, were essentially bourgeois, if somewhat alienated from French society. Virtually no nobles, with the noteworthy exception of the Duchesse d'Uzès, joined republican feminist groups. The aristocratic particule occasionally appears in attendance records, but women with the background of Avril de Sainte-Croix account for a tiny share of the movement. Women of that class were more likely to join non-feminist, Catholic women's groups, such as the Ligue des femmes françaises (hereafter, LFF), which were created to defend the church against republican assaults. Some prominent feminists, such as Pelletier, came from working-class backgrounds. Unlike other cases of women's collective action in France, they were a small minority.[31] Their feminism often accompanied and encouraged their embourgeoisement, and they did not disturb the fundamentally bourgeois character or collective attitudes of the movement. The largest number of the suffragist rank and file were teachers; postal clerks and students were also numerous. Women who worked as unskilled laborers were rare. Usually workers felt ill at ease in a group of women who had maids. It will be seen that the bourgeois homogeneity of French suffragism, particularly as expressed in colllective *mentalités*, is one of the essential factors in understanding the history of the movement.[32]

In a nation that was nominally more than 90 percent Catholic, the religious composition of the women's rights movement was striking. Until the conversion of the Catholic women's movement to suffragism after World War I, the majority of suffragists were non-Catholic: Protestants, Jews, freethinkers, and atheists. Some prominent suffragists, such as Auclert, had grown up as Catholics and received conventual educations but left the church when its teachings conflicted with their own developing ideas. Many others, such as Maria Vérone, grew up in the middle-class tradition of Voltairean skepticism and republican Freemasonry. A disproportionately large number of French feminists, however, came from the Protestant and Jewish elite which defended republican liberalism. The "Judeo-Protestant coterie," as an atheist feminist labeled them, were especially influential in directing the moderate organizations such as the CNFF and the UFSF.

In addition to being urban, middle-class, and non-Catholic, French suffragism was predominantly female in membership and leadership. This may seem obvious, but it must be stressed because it has been argued that it was *"men* who started the feminist movement and ultimately it was they who brought it to success."[33] Men like Condorcet, Fourier, and Richer certainly deserve credit for their contributions to the origins of the women's movement. And it is clear that men accounted for a very large share (perhaps 50 percent) of the early membership of feminist groups. Indeed, it was possible for feminists to wonder at times if men were not in some ways more feminist than women were. Auclert's last great petition (1909), for example, bore three times as many men's signatures as women's.[34]

By the turn of the century, however, the masculine role in the women's movement was changing. By the early twentieth century, the movement was overwhelmingly comprised of women, led by women. Supportive men coalesced with them and gave essential aid where women could not go (e.g., in parliament), but it was women who brought feminism success, not men. Men probably comprised about 10-15 percent of the membership of feminist societies in 1900-1901, and that share was declining. Amélioration reported a membership of 124 in 1901, including only 35 men (28 percent). Of the 49 persons known to have attended the meetings of Solidarité in 1902, 8 were men (16 percent); of the 65 people attending Suffrage des femmes in 1904, 4 were men (6 percent).[35] The number of men in leadership positions was even lower. Indeed, some leagues explicitly excluded men from office and others extended only honorific titles. Suffragists could genuinely doubt the sincerity of some male supporters, as Pelletier did, or stress the ideological importance of women assuming the lead in their own emancipation. This angered some male supporters like Joseph Reinach, who complained that even John Stuart Mill would be rejected, but it was an important stage in feminist development.[36]

There is also an anti-feminist stereotype about the membership of women's rights organizations that must be rejected. French feminists were not spinsters who hated men, marriage, and family life. Married women (including widows) accounted for 76.7 percent of the French women in the LFDF in 1882-1883, 71.2 percent in 1892. Thirty-seven of the forty-one women active in Solidarité in 1902 (90.2 percent) were married; over 70 percent of the French women participating in the congress of 1889; 94 of the 121 participants (77.7 percent) in the feminist circle around *La Française* in 1906. Of the thirty officers of feminist societies in 1898-1902 for whom biographical data are available, twenty-three were married (76.7 percent); for the period to 1914, the rate increases to 80.7 percent. Furthermore, French suffragists repeatedly stressed their commitment to family life. "We are wives and mothers," one put it, "and we wish to remain wives and mothers."[37]

The Feminist Left: Militant Suffragism

When French feminism entered its period of sustained growth during the late 1890s, only a small portion of the movement publicly called for the vote—perhaps 10 percent of the active feminists or 1 percent of all members in women's organizations. This militant minority thus faced a double task: not only must they seek to win public opinion and political support, they also had to convert most feminists to collaboration in the suffrage campaign. Like the left wing in republican politics, suffragists shared an essential ideological unity but not unification. There were five important centers of the suffrage movement, all of them directly connected to Auclert's suffrage campaign of the 1880s.

Marie-Anne-Hubertine Auclert (1848-1914) personified French suffragism. She was born one of seven children in the family of a well-to-do *propriétaire* in Allier. Her father died when she was nine. By that age, Auclert later claimed, she had already had her revelation on "the road to Damascus." "Almost from birth," she recorded, "I have been a rebel against the oppression [l'écrasement] of women."[38] Her convent education did little to modulate Auclert's youthful outrage at the situation of women. After a few frustrating years in Allier, Auclert claimed a share of her father's estate and took her feminist anger and her *rentes* to Paris, where she immediately joined Richer and Deraismes in working for women's rights. The refusal of these prominent feminists to work for suffrage led Auclert, an extremely independent woman, to found her own society in 1876, at the age of twenty-eight. For more than a decade, Auclert created the women's suffrage movement in France. Auclert faced a personal crisis in 1887 when Antonin Lévrier, her close associate in both Suffrage des femmes and *La Citoyenne* and her intimate friend, received a judicial posting to Algeria. With great remorse she sacrificed their relationship "to my love of the idea" and declined to follow Lévrier. A year later she reconsidered, married Lévrier (keeping the name Auclert), and joined him in Algeria, where she prepared a book on the condition of women in Arab countries. Lévrier died in 1892 and Auclert returned to Paris, but she had lost her leadership of the women's movement. She lost her newspaper, *La Citoyenne*, and never forgave other militants for its death. Suffrage des femmes, which had more than 250 members at its pre-1888 peak, collapsed.

Hubertine Auclert was a person of tremendous determination. She was utterly uncompromising on "the idea"—women must vote—and relentless in its pursuit. Her passion and militancy, plus a domineering personality, separated Auclert from most feminists. As the feminist leagues grew, as moderate middle-class women joined, Auclert experienced great difficulty in reasserting her leadership. She possessed tactical flexibility and adapted in some ways, but the movement had passed her. She established a new base in Parisian journalism, as a weekly columnist ("Le Féminisme") for *Le Radical* (1896-1909); the contrast between a short article in a hostile newspaper and her previous direction of the dominant feminist newspaper typified her new position. She revived Suffrage des femmes by the turn of the century, but it was only one small society among many. A police agent who questioned Auclert's concierge in 1901 (the Prefecture kept a huge dossier on her activities) learned that she received several visitors and over thirty pieces of mail every day. Despite such activity, attendance at her meetings rarely reached fifty people; a police infiltrator claimed that the regular core of the group was "scarcely twenty members." The moderates turning to suffragism paid homage to Auclert's greatness as a pioneer, but they joined other organizations. Her "particularism," as Jane Misme delicately put it, disqualified her to lead a mass movement. The expansion of French suffragism by women embarrassed by Auclert's strindency soon left her isolated. It was the isolation of the gadfly. Auclert remained active until her death in 1914 and never ceased pushing the movement that had bypassed her. She was the suffragist who would raise the question of public demonstrations, of violent tactics, of mass rallies.[39]

Next to Hubertine Auclert, the elder stateswoman of French suffragism was Eliska Vincent (1841-1914). She learned her radicalism from a father she admired, an artisan whose republican activities led to his arrest during the "June days" of 1848 and again after Louis Napoleon's coup. She was one of the co-founders of the Société pour la revindication des droits de la femme (the predecessor of both the LFDF and Amélioration) in 1868. Three years later she participated in the Commune and narrowly escaped execution. Vincent retained her youthful radicalism as a suffragist and showed special concern for the condition of working women. She was a representative at the workers' congress of 1878 and frequenetly participated in syndicalist meetings during the 1880s and 1890s. When Auclert left Paris in 1888, Vincent left Suffrage des femmes and sought to assume the leadership of French suffragism, founding her own organization, L'Egalité. Vincent lacked Auclert's single-mindedness, however, and her society never reached one hundred members. On the other hand, Vincent found that she was better able to cooperate with bourgeois moderates than Auclert had been. She too was discouraged when moderates did not see the importance of enfranchisement, and she often had sharp disagreements about sensitivity to working-class women. But Vincent had a calmer demeanor than Auclert. Furthermore, her early widowhood with a sizable inheritance left her a wealthy landowner in the Saint-Ouen district of Paris and suburban Asnières. Her dress, deportment, and tactics became increasingly respectable. Thus Vincent was invited where Auclert was not—to address the Conférence de

Versailles or a circle of Catholic women, for example. She was also older than Auclert and after 1900, Vincent increasingly devoted her time to the feminist library she maintained in her home. She remained a delicate combination of the militant suffragist and the respectable matron of the movement but was not in a position to lead the conversion of moderates to suffragism.[40]

A third center of suffragism, Solidarité des femmes, was likewise founded during Auclert's absence by her former associates, Eugénie Potonié-Pierre and Maria Martin. Potonié-Pierre, Léonie Rouzade, and others gave the group a socialist orientation that Suffrage des femmes or Egalité lacked, but overtures to various socialist factions (to sponsor a woman candidate in the elections of 1893, for example) failed to establish any formal connection. Potonié-Pierre died in 1898 and the secretary-generalship of Solidarité passed to Caroline Kauffmann (d. 1926), who transformed the group by placing greater emphasis on the vote. Kauffman came to feminism after a troubled personal life led her to reflect on the condition of women. Despite suffering from poor health, she also devoted much time to physical fitness and founded the Ligue féminine de culture physique. Under Kauffmann's leadership, Solidarité remained republican and socialist, affiliating with the congress of independent socialists in 1899 and generally sympathizing with Jaurèsians. Nonetheless, Kauffmann alienated several of the old-line socialist members such as Rouzade and Paule Mink (the group's parliamentary candidate in 1893) and moderates alike. Thus the society was at a perigee in 1900, certainly not fulfilling the promise of its name. Membership fell to perhaps fifty, and Solidarité drifted further from the mainstream of bourgeois feminism.[41]

Solidarité was to become the center of feminist controversy and activism under the leadership of Madeleine Pelletier, whom Kauffmann recruited as her collaborator and successor. Pelletier (1874-1939) became the most advanced and outspoken feminist in France during the decade before World War I. She was an extremist whose ideas and actions alike made moderate feminism seem more acceptable, while she advanced propositions that many would later embrace. She was born in a squalid home at the back of a shop not far from the Parisian food *halles* whence her parents carted the fruits and vegetables they sold for a meager existence. Her mother, who bore the scar of a government branding iron for the crime of bastardy, was illiterate and so obsessively devout that neighbors called her "the Jesuit." Her father, who was partially paralyzed and did little work in the shop, utterly rejected his wife's beliefs and sexually abused his daughter. Pelletier was sent to a convent school where she was very unpopular as a dirty little poor girl, but where she showed considerable academic promise before running away at the age of twelve. In a remarkable feat, she completed her education on her own, and by 1899 had become one of the few women physicians in France. Consonant with her tragic youth, Pelletier became a defiant iconoclast, rejecting much of what she saw around her. The outward symbol of that rejection was her dress in masculine attire and close-cropped hair; the ideological expression of it, her attraction to revolutionary ideas. Life had already equipped her to deal with the resultant derision.[42]

Pelletier's first contacts with feminism came through *La Fronde*, which championed her when she was denied a hospital appointment because she was a woman, and the "mixed" Masonic lodges to which many republican feminists belonged. She won a medical appointment but lost her energetic battle to open Freemasonry to women.[43] Pelletier attended a few meetings of Solidarité, the group best able to tolerate her ideas, but had some reservations about its small size and actual militancy. Once Kauffmann persuaded her to accept the secretary-generalship, however, Pelletier threw herself into feminism with tremendous energy and quickly established herself as the foremost theoretician of the movement.[44]

Pelletier's demand for complete equality was stated in three unequivocal claims: the suppression of all laws that subordinated one sex to another; the admission of women to all jobs and public functions; and the acceptance of women in all political capacities. Of these, Pelletier insisted that political rights were "certainly" the most important, a belief that led her to found a monthly review in 1907 forthrightly named *La Suffragiste*.[45] Such ideas were compatible with the beliefs of many feminist militants; what set Pelletier apart from them was her additional insistence upon the total emancipation of women, including in their private lives. As a doctor, she concluded that sexual emancipation was one of the most important aspects in the general liberation of women. She was especially outraged by the plight of working-class women who came to her for treatment. Although she staunchly supported their right to sexual freedom, she was more concerned with their problems as wives and mothers. She agreed with the neo-Malthusians that excessive childbearing resulted in poverty, unhappiness, death, and prostitution. Her conclusion was to propose both birth control and abortion: "It is solely for the woman to decide if and when she wants to be a mother."[46] Pelletier wanted to make birth control information and devices readily available to all women, including young girls, and especially to the daughters of the working class, to whom it was either unknown or unaffordable. If a woman became pregnant, Pelletier believed she had a right to a legal and safe abortion. She also worked to improve facilities available to mothers and children. In later years, she became convinced that the upbringing of children should be the state's responsibility. Women, in sum, must be released from their biological bondage: "I say that marriage and maternity must only be an episode in the life of a woman as it is for a man."[47]

Such ideas were utterly intolerable in *belle époque* France. Pelletier furthered her isolation by adopting extreme militancy in seeking her ends. Her male costume made her scorned as a lesbian (she was not) and her social theories made her denounced as an enemy of the family and the *patrie* (for saying that depopulation was not necessarily bad), but her militancy made her feared as a complete revolutionary. Pelletier, who was active on the extreme left of the Socialist party, did not object to anti-suffragist characterizations of feminists "itching to unfurl the red flag." She did not intially advocate violence, but called on feminism to "virilize itself" because most of its failures were due to "the pusillanmity of its adherents." She disdained most feminists because they "have more fear of demonstrations in the streets than men do." And she tried to teach the movement that "whoever is truly worthy of liberty does not wait for someone to give it. He takes it." These attitudes increasingly led Pelletier to consider violence; by 1912, she was writing, "Feminism can never go too far."[48] With such ideas, Pelletier put Solidarité in the vanguard of the feminist left, but she provided no prospect of leading a mass suffragism.

A fourth center of the suffrage campaign derived even more directly from Auclert's pioneering efforts. The monthly newspaper of the militants, Maria Martin's *Le Journal des femmes*, was actually the direct descendent of Auclert's *La Citoyenne*. Martin (d. 1910) was English-born and (as she told an interviewer in 1899) "never dreamed of the existence of a women's question" until she married a Frenchman, Jules Martin, and moved to Paris in 1872. Her observation of the condition of French women and a philanthropic concern for the welfare of schoolchildren led her to feminism, where she became a prominent militant by the 1880s. She impressed her contemporaries with an unusual ability to tolerate divergent attitudes yet retain her own advanced opinions. Martin was an early member of Suffrage des femmes, an editor of *La Citoyenne*, a co-founder of Solidarité, one of the first women to join the Freemasons, a member of the organizing committee for the congress of 1896, and a leader in the conversion of the LFDF to suffragism—giving her impeccable credentials on the feminist left. She was also a leader of the Congrès des oeuvres et institutions in 1900, a member of the organizing committee that established the CNFF, a vice-president of the Conseil national, and the honorary president of the UFF—betokening her compatibility with moderate feminists. When Auclert left Paris in 1888, Martin assumed the direction of *La Citoyenne*. For three years, she managed her friend's newspaper; in 1891, she broke with Auclert, let her paper die, and created *Le Journal des femmes*. With the aid of her three daughters, Martin produced a monthly paper for the next twenty years. She insisted that the newspaper be neutral in national politics and religious questions and that it remain open to articles expressing any shade of feminist opinion. National questions such as the Dreyfus affair rarely appeared in *Le Journal des femmes*. Instead, Martin invited all feminist societies, whatever their political coloration, to send accounts of their activities to the paper which would serve as a central source of information for the entire women's movement. She never succeeded in this aspiration. The paper's origins on the feminist left, Martin's personal militancy, and the vigorous suffragism of *Le Journal des femmes* drove off most moderates and conservatives. "There are some questions of the first magnitude that one must never be silent about for too long," Martin wrote; "We find the question of women's suffrage in the first rank of these issues."[49]

The organization with the best prospect of leading a large suffrage campaign was the LFDF, whose predecessor Auclert had quit in 1878 when Richer refused to work for the vote. The league had a membership approximately equal to Suffrage des femmes, Egalité, and Solidarité combined—nearly two hundred. It had financial stability, wider public and political acceptance, and close connections with moderate feminists. The LFDF only gradually embraced suffragism in the decade following the retirement of Richer in 1891. This was largely the work of Amélie Hammer (who actually administered the group during Richer's last years with it), and particularly the new officers, President Maria Pognon (1844-1925) and Secretary-General Marie Bonnevial (1841-1918). Pognon was a native of Calvados who accompanied her husband to Paris in 1888. She attended the feminist congress of 1889, immediately joined the LFDF and became one of its most active members. As an officer of the league, Pognon instilled a strong anti-war tone (she was simultaneously an officer of the Ligue pour l'arbitrage international) and a more militant pursuit of women's rights. She was one of the most influential representatives at the feminist congresses of 1896 and 1900, but soon left the women's movement to follow her husband abroad.[50]

Marie Bonnevial brought working-class radicalism to the league. She was born to a poor family in a village outside Lyons and was raised by her uncle, a wheelwright and laundryman. One of the first women to profit from expanded educational opportunities, Bonnevial became a teacher at Lyons and joined the republican movement there. During the commune at Lyons she organized and directed a laic school there. Her efforts to continue laic and republican education after the war produced a conflict with the "government of moral order" culminating in the revocation of her credentials. Barred from working even as an assistant or substitute teacher, Marie Bonnevial chose self-exile and only returned to France after the adoption of the secular education laws of the 1880s, when her ideas had become the national orthodoxy and a republican government agreed to reinstate her as a teacher. Her first participation in national politics was through socialism and syndicalism. As a leader of the teacher's union, she was a delegate to many of the labor congresses of the 1890s. Her socialism was moderate and republican, rather than revolutionary, drawn from her empathy for the poor and uneducated; she was among the socialists who supported Alexandre Millerand. The feminist congress of 1896 and the establishment of *La Fronde* in 1897 drew her into the feminist movement, and it was to feminism rather than socialism that she devoted most of her energies. As secretary-general of the LFDF, Bonnevial joined with Pognon to radicalize the league and lead its membership to suffragism.[51] By 1900, Pognon and Bonnevial had prepared the LFDF to accept Viviani's pro-suffrage speech. With their call for the vote at that congress, the League became the largest suffrage society in France and the best connection between suffragism and the moderate feminists.

It was a younger woman, Maria Vérone, who was to lead the LFDF to the forefront of suffragist militancy. Vérone (1874-1938) was the daughter of an accountant and a shopworker, both left-wing republicans who introduced her to radical politics at an early age; at fifteen, she was the secretary of a society of freethinkers, and at eighteen, one of their lecturers. Vérone was a star pupil at the communal school in the working-class suburb of Levallois and won a scholarship to attend an upper-level school in Paris but had to abandon a desired career in mathematics when the sudden death of her father required her to help to support her family. Vérone worked with her mother in the ill-paying occupation of *plumassière*, ornamenting women's clothing with artificial flowers and feathers, until she obtained an appointment as a travelling substitute teacher in 1894. Much like Marie Bonnevial twenty years earlier, Vérone got into trouble as a teacher due to her political activities and was summarily dismissed without her final two months of wages in 1897. After singing in the chorus line at a small theater, Vérone, a chorus girl who read Montaigne, married a young jounalist and joined him on the staff of Clemenceau's *L'Aurore*. *La Fronde* deeply impressed Vérone and she joined it in December 1897. This led to a regular column, reporting on legal and judicial matters under the pen name of "Themis," and to the realization that she was personally capable of the legal work that she wrote about. As a divorced mother with two children and a meager income she somehow found the time to learn Latin and Greek in order to pass her *baccalauréat* and enter the Ecole de droit. In 1907 Vérone became the fifth woman in French history to be admitted to the bar. Unlike her predecessors, Vérone began an active legal career—to the dismay of a profession that had reluctantly accepted women but expected them not to appear in court. Two months after becoming a probationary attorney she became the first woman to plea before the Cour d'assises, commencing a series of firsts that later led as high as the Conseil de guerre.[52]

Her experience at *La Fronde*, especially through the involvement of Durand in the congress of women's rights in 1900, introduced Vérone to feminist associations. She joined the LFDF and almost immediately became one of the league's most energetic members, supporting Pognon and Bonnevial in leading the group to suffragism.

At the same time, Vérone joined the socialist party where she had several friends from her freethinker days. She remained active in the party for many years but never left any doubt that her first political interest was the woman question. Like Marie Bonnevial, she was a feminist who wished to be able to vote for socialism, rather than a socialist who also supported women's rights. Vérone became the head of the LFDF as a thirty-year-old law student. When Pognon retired and Bonnevial succeeded her as president, Vérone became secretary-general, the officer in charge of the daily direction of the league. Despite the numerous demands on her time, Vérone gave such energetic leadership to the LFDF that contemporaries agreed that she had almost single-handedly reinvigorated the group and restored it to the importance it once held in the feminist movement. She was a dedicated suffragist and made the ballot the primary target of the league.

Maria Vérone held an extremely important position in the evolution of French suffragist tactics. She occupied a middle ground between the militants, such as Auclert and Pelletier, who considered violence, and the moderates, who opposed all demonstrations in the streets. Was there some form of suffragist militancy that stopped short of "avenging gestures" and the prospect of violence? Maria Vérone sought such a course. She did not fear confrontations with the government and was to spend several nights in jail before her career was finished. Nor did she hesitate to consider activities in the streets or energetic challenges to authority. But her personality and training induced Vérone to seek an activist's solution within the law. In conjunction with her second husband, Georges Lhermite (an attorney and a vice-president of the LFDF), Vérone committed the league to a course of legal activism. They pursued court cases on behalf of individual women and for general principles of women's rights. For the decade before World War I, Vérone sought a careful combination of legalism and militancy that could attract moderate feminists to more active suffragism.

The Feminist Center: Reluctant Suffragists

The moderate majority of French feminists still hesitated to embrace suffragism at the beginning of the twentieth century. Like republican politicians, they generally held that women's political rights were desirable in theory but inappropriate at the moment. Their reluctance to seek enfranchisement had numerous sources. Some felt that other feminist reforms were more urgently needed or could more realistically be expected from parliament. Some shared aspects of the republican anti-suffrage argument, fearing that French women or French society was not yet prepared for such an innovation. Many sought to disassociate themselves from the militants, whose advanced ideas or behavior they deemed wrong. Virtually all would claim the vote when they found the appropriate time and means. Most of these moderates were members of the CNFF and would follow its leaders to suffragism. The feminist center, however, was also divided into several competing organizations. Some of the most widely respected leaders of the women's movement directed these small groups; when they adopted women's suffrage, the National Council and the feminist center would follow.

The oldest and best established organization of the center was Amélioration, a cautious and comfortable bourgeois society. The membership included many well-to-do women, whose contributions made it the best-financed of the small feminist groups; Auclert claimed (with exaggeration) that they hoarded a treasury surplus of 20,000 francs. Maria Deraismes had defined the group as "laic, republican, and socialist," but after her death it was not as advanced as that sounded. The membership stressed, both in their name and policy, the condition of women more than their rights. Statues adopted in 1894 committed them to concentrate on reforming the Napoleonic Code and to eschew militant tactics. In a revealing gesture, they elected an expressly anti-suffrage deputy, Charles Beauquier, as their vice-president because he supported them on the code. Amélioration was a major financial sponsor of both the moderate and the militant congresses of 1900. Only after two votes did they decide not to support the Catholic congress, but they still sent an official delegation. With similar caution, they endorsed Viviani's speech of 1900 but chose not to act on it. Their president, Anna Feresse-Deraismes (1822-1911) typified this attitude. She had been her younger sister's "intellectual mother" but lacked Maria's energy, determination, and militancy. She preserved Amélioration as a living memorial but transformed it into a more sedate organization. Daily leadership fell to the vice-president, Madame de Montaut (d. 1911), but she was chiefly interested in charity

work and devoted most of her life to the Red Cross. While Amélioration might support a suffrage campaign, it would not take a central
role in it.[53]

Among the most ardent feminists who did not yet advocate wom-
en's suffrage were Jeanne Schmahl and her followers in Avant-Courrière. Schmahl (1847-1915) desired equal political rights for women
(and even helped to finance Auclert) but stongly believed that other
rights must be won first. Born in London of an English father and
a French mother, Schmahl came to Paris to study medicine. She was
already a member of Amélioration when she had the formative experience that shaped her feminist thought, that convinced her women
must win basic economic rights first. Schmahl met a patient with an
appalling case history: habitually beaten by an alcoholic husband, the
woman once refused to turn her wages over to him, whereupon he
began collecting them at her place of work; when she complained,
she was fired by her employer and severely beaten by her husband.
Beginning in 1884, Schmahl devoted herself to changing the provisions
of the Civil Code that denied married women the right to dispose of
their own income. To obtain an earnings law comparable to the
Married Women's Property Act of 1882 in Britain, Schmahl founded
the Avant-Courrière in 1893. Schmahl dominated the group with an
iron will, refusing to work for political rights because that would
detract from her efforts for an earnings law. Her objective and her
combination of uncompromising feminism with conservative standards of behavior enabled Schmahl to attract an unusual membership
to Avant-Courrière. Not only was her group large (perhaps two hundred
members), but Schmahl recruited members ranging from the oldest
names of the *Gotha* to salon celebrities of the republican left. Among
her notable converts were Anne de Mortemarte, the Duchesse d'Uzès
(1847-1933), a monarchist but an extraordinary individualist who financed Avant-Courrière and befriended Louise Michel; Juliette Adam
(1836-1936), the grande dame of French letters and hostess of one of
the most politically influential salons of the late nineteenth century;
and Jane Misme (1865-1935), a young Parisian journalist who later
founded the principal feminist newspaper after the closing of *La
Fronde*. These women still felt that women's suffrage was (in Misme's
words) "terribly subversive." But they agreed upon a married woman's
earnings bill, and under Schmahl's tenacious leadership they kept
relentless pressure on parliament. Léopold Goirand (Radical, Deux-

Sevres) deposited Schmahl's bill in the Chamber of Deputies in 1894 and secured its adoption in 1896, but hostile senators blocked the bill. Until the adoption of the bill in 1907, Avant-Courrière worked solely to persuade the Senate to act; until that success, Schmahl kept an important group of feminists away from the suffrage campaign.[54]

A third small society that kept the feminist center away from suffragism was Jeanne Oddo-Deflou's Groupe français d'études féministes. A bourgeois matriarch who came to feminism in the 1890s, Oddo-Deflou shared the perception that the vote was desirable (she too contributed to Suffrage des femmes) but the wrong target. Unlike Schmahl, she rejected concentration on a single issue, preferring to work for dozens of changes in the civil law. This made Oddo-Deflou exceptionally flexible in her range of activities. As a leading militant put it, Oddo-Deflou was "one of those people who can do ninety-nine different things."[55] She was a member of Solidarité yet simultaneously an enthusiastic supporter of the CNFF. She was one of the few republican feminists who attended meetings of Catholic feminists; somehow she combined this with membership in a mixed masonic lodge. Her principal disagreements with other bourgeois feminists generally revealed a fundamental conservatism. She opposed public demonstrations as undignified. She was shocked that some feminists believed in free love and angered that others were pacifists. Oddo-Deflou established Etudes in 1898 when Kauffmann's militancy made Solidarité unacceptable as her primary base of action. Oddo-Deflou was able to cooperate with socialists on some issues, but she was a bourgeois who could never be completely comfortable among them. She intended Etudes to be an independent, nonpartisan feminist group with members of all political and religious beliefs. The statutes of Etudes dedicated its members to increasing the civil rights of women, a commitment soon added to the society's name: Groupe français d'études féministes et des droits civils des femmes. In addition to supporting the efforts of Avant-Courrière to obtain a women's earnings law, the program of Etudes listed several other concerns: the right of women to file paternity suits (*recherche paternité*); equal parental powers over children; the abolition of all legal incapacities of women, such as in signing contracts or serving on juries; and the right of women to be legal guardians. If Oddo-Deflou took an especial interest in any single issue, it was *recherche paternité*, and her text became the basis of the law adopted several years later.[56]

Two other small feminist groups founded at the start of the twentieth century deserve brief mention among the non-suffragists: Marbel's Union fraternelle des femmes (UFF) and Lydie Martial's Union de pensée féminine. Marbel (the pseudonym of Marguerite Belmant) was a *lycée* professor whose feminism stemmed from her profession: she recognized the obstacles confronting her students and their apparent unconcern about them. She resigned her position in 1901 to found the UFF, a feminist library, and later (1906-1908) a feminist almanac; she evisioned such as extensions of her teaching career. The UFF was a very moderate society (other feminists characterized it as timid) with the stated first purpose of introducing women to the questions affecting them, then facilitating their study. The members supported the reforms espoused by Schmahl and Oddo-Deflou, and due to Marbel's interest in the young they concentrated on the right of women to be legal guardians. Like other moderates, Marbel insisted that the feminist struggle for justice be combined with respectability and dignity.

Martial (Anna Carnaud, 1861-1929) belonged to several different groups, but aspired to be a major theorist of feminism, and created the Union de pensée féminine as a forum for her ideas. She advocated "integral feminism," by which she meant the complete equality of men and women, but taught that France must first pass through the stage of "rational feminism." This latter doctrine held that feminists should not seek full equality all at once and must first find fulfillment as mothers. Rational feminism was esentially a conservative doctrine, incompatible with militant suffragism.[57]

The most important bloc in the feminist center was unquestionably the CNFF, whose size and resources dwarfed all other organizations. The national council set the tone of moderation and caution that often characterized French feminism in the early twentieth century—particularly in response to delicate questions opened by militants, such as political rights, sexual matters, or public demonstrations. The restrained feminism of the CNFF was an extension of the personality and attitudes of its leaders who were almost exclusively models of bourgeois rectitude and propriety. They were women of considerable wealth; one feminist claimed that the council was run by an alliance of forty or fifty millionaires.[58] Their first interest was charity work and social improvement. And the common font of their reformist zeal was an austere, righteous Protestantism.

The personification of the CNFF was its first president, Sarah Monod (1836-1912), the longtime editor of *La Femme* and animating spirit of the Conférence de Versailles. She was the daughter of a celebrated Protestant pastor. Her feminism kept a powerful religious component which stressed the family, high standards of individual morality, Christian pacifism, evangelical determination, and dedication to the improvement of society. She entered charity work as a field hospital nurse during the Franco-Prussian War and continued volunteer nursing into her sixties. Monod also took especial interest in the plight of prostitutes and collaborated with Bogelot in Les Libérées de Saint-Lazare, a charity that aided women (especially prostitutes) being released from Saint-Lazare prison, the only women's prison in the department of the Seine. The first vice-president of the CNFF and Monod's eventual successor as president had a strikingly similar biography. Julie Puaux Siegfried (1848-1922) was also the daughter of a Protestant pastor. At twenty she married a wealthy cotton merchant and future deputy, Jules Siegfried, with whom she shared a lifelong collaboration championing liberal social reform. When her husband came to Paris in 1885 as a moderate republican deputy from Le Havre, Julie Siegfried became active in philanthropic causes, especially the fight against alcoholism. By the time of her death, Siegfried presided over seven different charitable organizations. Avril de Sainte-Croix (1855-1939), the secretary-general and chief administrator of the CNFF for over twenty years (1901-1922), also came to feminism through Protestant philanthropy. She founded L'Oeuvre libératrice to aid women in escaping from the life of prostitution; that work led Sainte-Croix to the Conférence de Versailles.[59] The section heads of the CNFF had similar biographies.[60]

Monod, Siegfried, and Sainte-Croix illustrate the varieties of moderate feminism within the CNFF. Monod participated in the feminist congresses of 1889 and 1900 and was an early member of Avant-Courrière. She refused to call herself a feminist, however; she preferred a description as a woman dedicated to working for the protection of women. Siegfried did not hesitate to use the label after she concluded that charity work alone produced too little social change. This same line of reasoning ultimately led her to women's suffrage as the best vehicle for the improvement of France. Sainte-Croix was the most ardent feminist in the council's triumvirate. As a writer for *La Fronde* she imbibed more militant attitudes than her friends and she gently chided them to be less timid in advancing the cause of women. The amalgam of these attitudes was to be a moderate feminism which could accept limited suffrage activities but which would always stress the importance of women being feminine and feminists being dignified.

A final important locus of moderation in French feminism was in the provincial women's rights organizations. Feminism was virtually unknown in most of France in 1900. The scant support that could be found outside Paris was essentially a phenomenon of the larger provincial cities, where a few dedicated individuals proselytized among the urban bourgeoisie. For their audiences, any doctrine of women's rights was a radical departure from tradition; merely to seek revisions in the Civil Code was a militant act. Seen in this context, it is scarcely surprising that nascent provincial feminism was not suffragist. Indeed, provincial feminists frequently shared the view of radical politicians that women's suffrage was undesirable because so many women were influenced by the church. "If you knew our villages!" one small-town feminist wrote to a Parisian suffragist newspaper, "At the present time, to give the right to vote to women in France would be to give the priest in each village the ballots of all the women."[61]

There were two active women's rights organizations outside Paris in the late 1890s, one at Lyons and the other at Foix. The Société d'éducation et d'action féministe, although not formally constituted until 1903, began with a series of feminist meetings organized at Lyons by Odette Laguerre in the 1890s. The region in which they sought to shape opinion—chiefly the southeastern departments of Ain, Rhône, Loire, and Isère—was especially difficult to penetrate. Working-class women in cities such as Lyons, Saint Etienne, or Vienne were drawn first toward syndicalism, second toward socialism, and showed little disposition for bourgeois feminism. Lyons itself was the center of the most conservative wing of the Catholic women's movement, the Ligue des femmes françaises, which offered a resolutely anti-feminist model to Catholic women. The educated women of the villages were largely practicing Catholics, little interested in the society's anti-clerical republicanism. Laguerre was married to a radical politician and proprietor who served as the mayor of Vieu and sat in the Conseil général of Ain; she learned first-hand the difficulties of reaching the women of the villages with Parisian ideas. Consequently, the Société d'éducation drew chiefly upon the traditional base of French feminism, the urban middle classes, and sought to expand by publishing educational pamphlets on feminism and omitting suffragism—which would repulse potential converts. The society had two noteworthy strengths, one a throwback to an earlier stage of feminism and the other an anticipation of future development. It relied heavily on the membership of influential men, such as Justin Godart (one of the most important feminists in the Chamber of Deputies after 1906) and the popular novelists Paul and Victor Margueritte. And, as suffragists would later do, it recruited a large share of its membership from teachers.[62]

The other outpost of provincial feminism in 1900, the Comité féministe républicain d'Ariège (the name changed frequently) was a unique phenomenon, located in a southern town of a few thousand population. It was the creation of Emile Darnaud, the least typical of all French feminists. Darnaud (1825-1914) was a lawyer and captain of Zouaves, a wounded hero of the Franco-Prussian War who retired to Foix and was repeatedly reelected mayor of the village of Roquefixade, a few kilometers outside of town. The sixty-four-year-old pensioned officer became a feminist after reading about the women's congress of 1889 and founded a feminist "committee" which received great publicity in the women's movement in Paris. Prominent feminists joined the group, represented it on the CNFF, and accepted Darnaud's invitation to lecture at Foix. Darnaud believed in "one and the same justice, one and the same morality" for women and men, but disputed many feminist opinions. He vigorously resisted feminist pacifism. As a devoted republican and lifelong southerner, he staunchly opposed suffragism (except as a distant goal), constantly writing feminists that it would not work in the provinces—an opinion with no small influence on the feminist center.[63]

The Feminist Right: Catholic Feminism

There is some truth to the assertion that the Catholic church was "the most persistent and intractable enemy of feminism" in Europe, but this must not obscure the role of Catholic feminism in French history. Separated from the republican feminist mainstream by many emotional issues, conservative feminists worked within the Catholic women's movement to win many of the same reforms that radical women proclaimed. Indeed, seen within their own context, these "Christian feminists" (as they called themselves) were as militant as republican women were in theirs. The most advanced, such as Maugeret, even took up women's suffrage before moderate feminists were willing to do so. There were several stimuli to the development of Catholic feminism at the end of the nineteenth century: the interest of the liberal Catholic movement in the situation of women, especially working women; the establishment of several Catholic women's organizations to defend the church from republican anti-clericalism; the contact of some Catholic women with republican feminism through their publications and congresses; and the Catholic congress of 1900.

The recrudescence of Christian feminism was especially facilitated by social reformers within the church who provided a favorable climate, encouraging women in their efforts and reassuring them that such endeavors could be acceptable to Catholics. A liberal Catholic record of trying to ameliorate the condition of working women was well-established. The establishment of the first Catholic union (Parisian clerical workers) in 1887, and the encouragement of Catholic associations of workers by Leo XIII's encyclical *Rerum novarum* in 1891 had led to a Catholic women's labor movement, notably the pioneering efforts of Marie-Louise Rochebillard at Lyons. Membership in Rochebillard's union was limited to professing Catholics and the group remained committed to the defense of the church; simultaneously, however, Rochebillard understood the need of some women to work outside the home and espoused a moderate feminism on their behalf. Liberal Catholic political leaders such as Count Albert de Mun and Jacques Piou worked for legislation to improve women's working conditions. Some on the Catholic left went beyond economic questions. Marc Sangnier and the Sillon, plus a group of "democratic priests" including Paul Naudet (the editor of *La Justice sociale*), Jules Lemire (a Christian socialist deputy from the Nord), and Henry Bolo, advocated reforms in the Civil Code such as the revision of marriage contracts or the right of women to be legal guardians. Their efforts stopped short of the claims stated by the republican feminists and were further distinguished from them by an emphasis on Catholic values, but they encouraged Catholic women to formulate a new Christian feminism.[64]

The organization of Catholic women also resulted from the crisis of French Catholicism. The victory of the anti-clerical Radical Party, which led to the termination of the Concordat of 1801 and the complete separation of church and state, produced passionate efforts by French Catholics to defend their church. Catholic women organized for precisely this purpose. Most of the associations created were not feminist (see Table 4). The overwhelming majority of women who joined such groups belonged to two large leagues, the Ligue patriotique des françaises (hereafter, LPF) and the Ligue des femmes françaises (hereafter, LFF). Their politics and social perspective were conservative Catholic; their ambition, the rechristianization of France, not the emancipation of women. The women of the Ligue patriotique, for example, believed that the traditional role of the woman in the home was proper; feminism was "unfeminine." The church offered women—above and beyond theological considerations—an institutional home, an identity, an ideology, and even careers, with which

Table 4 • Catholic Women's Organizations, 1897-1904

Name	Founded	Leader(s)	Associated Publications	Estimated Membership
ACTIVELY FEMINIST				
Féminisme chrétien	1897	Maugeret	*Le Féminisme chrétien*	c. 100
MODERATELY FEMINIST				
Action sociale	1900	Chenu	*L'Action sociale*	c. 5,000 (1904)
Devoir des femmes	1901	Dorive	*Le Devoir des femmes*	c. 100
Fédération Jeanne d'Arc	1904	Maugeret	(none)	c. 350,000
CONSERVATIVE				
LFF	1901	Lestra(SG)	*L'Appel à la France chrétienne*	
LPF	1902	Frossard(SG)	*L'Echo de la* LPF	320,000 (1905)

secular institutions could not compete. Furthermore, they perceived the insistence upon *rights* (such as the vote) to be a misdirection of energies, distracting women from their *duties*. Whereas Protestantism encouraged the individualism of seeking one's rights, Catholic thought led the women of the LPF to understand political questions in terms of their duty to the family, the church, and the nation.[65]

Despite their clearly non-feminist nature, such organizations of Catholic women contributed to the development of Christian feminism and ultimately to a Catholic suffragism. They did so indirectly at first. Women, according to the LPF, should use their influence, bolstered with their time and money, to obtain the rechristianization of France. This legitimized the involvement of the conservative Catholic women's organizations in national politics, particularly during the heated parliamentary elections of 1902 and 1906. Thus, non-feminist leagues wound up teaching women political organization and action. The same groups also slowly acquainted hundreds of thousands of provincial members with some of the tenets of Christian feminism simply by reporting in their journals the activities of women such as Marie Maugeret and (infrequently) by cooperating with them. This led to a gradual acceptance of some feminist ideas, such as greater legal rights for women, among women who distrusted the militant feminism of Paris. Such women represented the potential for a feminist mass movement: at a time when republican feminists were pleased to draw several hundred women at a demonstration in Paris, it was not uncommon for tens of thousands to attend an LPF rally in the provinces.[66] Their numbers became especially important for suffragism after World War I when the LPF led a membership of over 500,000 to call for the vote. The league's potential for action was also recognized by the government, leading to its infiltration by police agents.

The leaders of the LPF and the LFF insisted that such perceptions about their organizations were mistaken. The Patriotic League, which was affiliated with a Catholic political party, the Action libérale populaire of de Mun and Piou, preferred to remind women that it had been founded "to face up" to the persecution of the church. The leaders of the league did not consider their electoral activities of 1902-1906 to be either feminist or political. As the president of the LPF (and mother of two Catholic deputies), the Baroness René Reille, put it: "If it were a question of politics, I would not be here. But if it is a question of defending our faith and the souls of our children, is it not the duty of a true Christian and mother?"[67] The LFF was even more conservative. Founded at Lyons in 1901 in association with the anti-Dreyfusard Ligue de la patrie française of Paul Bourget and Maurice Barrès, the LFF vigorously denounced separation, attacked Freemasonry, defended private property, and worried about "the success of Satanism in France." During the elections of 1902, *La Fronde* interviewed the honorary president of the LFF, who summarized the league's position: "Do not assume that we are politicians or women of politics. We are only, and only wish to be, Christian wives and mothers."[68] Despite such rhetoric, the effect of the organizing of Catholic women was political, and this gradually prepared Catholics to accept suffragism.

The greatest effort to direct this conservative women's movement toward Christian feminism came from the founder of Catholic suffragism, Marie Maugeret (1844-1928). She was the daughter of a well-to-do physician in the Sarthe who left her the independent means to found and edit a literary review at Le Mans in the 1880s. This career brought Maugeret into contact with much of the Catholic intelligentsia and with Parisian ideas. As a middle-aged, devout liberal Catholic, Maugeret found republican feminism both appealing and alarming. She knew and admired Maria Deraismes; she attended the feminist congress of 1896, where she was disturbed by the preponderance of socialists and freethinkers. Although drawn to feminism, Maugeret concluded that she could only accept it in a Catholic context. Catholic feminism, she argued, "alone is French feminism, the only form that can acclimate itself to our national temperament."[69]

After the feminist congress of 1896 Maugeret founded a monthly review which bore traces of her literary career, her Catholicism, and her militancy for women's rights: *Le Féminisme chrétien et l'écho littéraire de France*. Along with it, she began a small discussion group of like-minded women, a *cercle* through which she sought to persuade Catholic women that their religion was compatible with feminism: "One can be a feminist without demanding the upsetting of society, without adding the war of the sexes to the war of the classes. . . . One can be a very good Christian while being a feminist."[70] The program that Maugeret offered included conservative and nationalist politics, attacks on the radical government over the Dreyfus affair and the Fashoda crisis; ardent Catholicism, defense of the church against radical policies and Masonic conspiracies; and a remarkably assertive feminism. She advocated the freedom of women to work, equal pay for women, the property rights of married women, and numerous other reforms in the Civil Code. Few republican militants were more eloquent in denouncing the "obstacles invented by prejudice and maintained by routine" that keep *la femme au foyer*.[71] It was only her defense of the family and the church plus her criticism of revolutionary-socialist feminism that prevented other feminists from recognizing that Marie Maugeret was one of the most militant of their number.

Maugeret also contributed to the formation of two other Catholic women's organizations that, unlike the LPF and the LFF, shared some of her Christian feminism. She was one of the co-founders and most active members of Françoise Dorive's Association patriotique du devoir des femmes françaises (hereafter, Devoir), established in 1901. Devoir shared the right-wing politics of other Catholic women's organizations born in the wake of the Dreyfus affair; indeed, its principal political advisor was Paul Copin-Albancelli, a minor author of extreme anti-semitic and anti-masonic opinions. The members of the group found Maugeret too advanced in her opinions, yet fundamentally agreed that French women had a special role to play in national regeneration and that for this they needed greater rights. Devoir's monthly bulletin ultimately became the forum for a public discussion of Catholic suffragism.[72]

Another Catholic women's group of some feminism, Jeanne Chenu's Action sociale de la femme, owed a debt to Maugeret's energetic role at the Catholic women's congress of 1900. The group began as a small discussion circle founded by Chenu (1861-1939) in 1899. Their initial interests were not feminist. They shared the same anxiety about the effects of the Dreyfus affair and a national drift toward paganism that stimulated other Catholic women; their strongest interest was the discussion of French literature. Chenu, however, was motivated by the congress of 1900 to add discussions on social topics such as the role of women outside the home. Her interests led her to work with prominent liberal Catholics such as René Bazire (the president of Jeunesse catholique) to acquire the active support of Catholic intellectuals. Action sociale was the result. By 1902 Action sociale had grown enough to establish a permanent secretariat under the direction of Chenu and to found a monthly bulletin. Two years later, it had provincial branches and was serving as the nexus for similar groups in 100 towns. Their meetings retained the nationalist, patriotic, and anti-collectivist tone of other Catholic women's groups but stressed the additional interests of literary criticism and social Catholicism. At least once a year they discussed and published articles on some feminist issue, including minimum salaries for women, the legal incapacity of women, and women's suffrage. Most republican feminists were unimpressed, but it was Jeanne Chenu who ultimately led Catholic women to suffragism, in 1918-1920.[73]

At the beginning of the century, however, only Maugeret and a few followers were Catholic feminists. They recognized the importance of other leagues of Catholic women, shared many of their concerns, applauded their occasional feminism, and nudged them to a fuller consideration of the vote. Maugeret realized that most Catholic women did not accept her ideas and that their conversion would not be easy. French feminism was unmistakably republican and anti-clerical. Catholics need only have heard (as Maugeret did) a speaker at the 1896 congress proclaim that "God is evil personified" to recognize the immensity of the gulf dividing French women.[74] The implication of Maugeret's efforts, however, was also immense: there could be no mass, national movement comparable to those in Britain and America without Catholic women.

The Feminist Left: Socialist Women and Suffragism

At the opposite end of the political spectrum, socialist women were also estranged from bourgeois, republican feminism, although not so completely as Catholic women. Many militant feminists considered themselves socialists—Bonnevial, Kauffmann, Vincent, even Auclert at one time—although most were moderate, republican socialists. Thus they had some affinity for the socialist women's movement. Socialists, however were more preoccupied with the condition of workers (as Catholics were more interested in the condition of the church) than of women. Socialist women, like Catholics, were also alienated from (often opposed to) the republic that bourgeois feminists stoutly defended. Although socialist women represented a smaller group for conversion to suffragism than did Catholic women, they were better prepared for political action. Many perceived the situation of French women in feminist terms and called clearly for the amelioration of this condition, but, no less than Catholic women, they subscribed to a transcendental doctrine which took precedence over cooperation with republican suffragists.

The center of the socialist women's movement at the turn of the century was the Groupe féministe socialiste (hereafter, GFS), founded in 1899. The two founders of the GFS, Elisabeth Renaud (1846-1932) and Louise Saumoneau (1875-1949), disagreed on the possibility of collaboration with bourgeois women. Renaud was the daughter of a carpenter and the widow of a printer who had supported herself as a domestic servant, a governess, and a teacher. She was an independent, Jaurèsian socialist who believed that the republic could be saved through a new devotion to social justice; thus, cooperation was possible with advanced republicans. Saumoneau lived the precarious existence of a piecework seamstress and burnt with a passionate anger over the working-class poverty she knew firsthand. Renaud could see working-class women as "the slave[s] of slave[s]" and middle-class women as having "the privilege of being the slaves of masters"; she did not doubt that there was a shared bondage among women of the two social classes. Saumoneau rejected the comparison. Middle-class women were "the natural adversaries" of working-class women; the shared slavery was between men and women of the proletariat.[75]

It was Saumoneau who, at age twenty-four, took the lead in founding the GFS and giving it a tone hostile to bourgeois feminism. Saumoneau had initially thought to join Solidarité and had made the considerable personal sacrifice of missing work to attend one of their afternoon meetings. She found the socialism of Solidarité to be middle-class socialism, its members to be drawn from the class of employers rather than workers. How could she be comfortable in a group of women who seriously debated dowries? With Renaud and two other working women, she created the Groupe féministe socialiste to be an "authentically working class" organization. The GFS grew to have several Parisian chapters, a few small provincial branches, and a monthly newspaper (*La Femme socialiste*), but it never numbered one hundred women. From its inception the GFS was troubled by the conflicting views of Renaud and Saumoneau. As Saumoneau was the more ardent in advocating her opinion, it became the dominant feature of the group. The GFS statutes denounced "the double oppression" of women through their exploitation by capitalism and their subjection to men.

Saumoneau made it clear in *La Femme socialiste*, however, that she saw no antagonism between men and women of the proletariat. The oppression of working women was entirely the fault of capitalists, not of their fathers, husbands, and comrades. The goals of proletarian women and men, she contended, were identical: the destruction of the bourgeois regime that enslaved them together. Therefore, there could be no question of the unity of women across the gulf of the class struggle. Bourgeois women wished to preserve the preeminence of their class which would merely be modified by the women's movement. The emancipation of women by bourgeois feminism was a "lying phrase" that distracted working-class women from the revolution that could truly set them free. "The women of the people ... must not abandon the terrain of class struggle ... to run after a chimerical ... emancipation on the bourgeois terrain." Saumoneau, thus, was anticipating the distinction that Lenin would make, in his writings on the woman question, between formal equality and real equality.[76]

Saumoneau's position had solid roots in French socialist history and theory. Paule Mink and Aline Valette had made the same argument to women in the 1880s and 1890s. The men at the head of French socialism (notably Jules Guesde) and Marxist theory itself sustained Saumoneau's view. Thus, after Auclert's success at the congress of Marseille in 1879, French socialists had a good record of verbal support for women's rights, a poor record of actually working for the vote, and a hidden record of opposing such reforms. Behind the vow of 1879 and its occasional repetition there was no significant effort to obtain equality of political rights under the republic. Instead, socialist doctrine directly discouraged women in the party from placing a high priority on questions such as the vote because they detracted from work toward the revolution that would produce full equality. Most socialists thus favored the ideas of Saumoneau to those of Renaud. The rejection of Renaud's policy became especially acute after the "Millerand case" of 1899, when a socialist deputy, Alexandre Milllerand (Seine), agreed to join the cabinet of René Waldeck-Rousseau as minister of commerce. Socialist debates over his collaboration with bourgeois reformers resulted in the condemnation of Millerand's "socialist defection." Guesde and Edouard Vaillant produced a manifesto proclaiming that "there cannot be any accord between those who have compromised the honor and interests of socialism and those in charge of defending them." Even Millerand acknowledged "Conception and method are interdependent [*solidaires*]. One cannot be revolutionary in theory and reformist in action." Thus, French socialists chose to remain revolutionary in theory and reject collaboration with bourgeois reformers; Saumoneau was in the mainstream, not Renaud.[77]

Women who aspired to be both socialists and feminists faced a personal dilemma similar to that confronting Maugeret and Catholic feminists: did they put their feminism or their socialism first? For republican socialists in the feminist movement, such as Bonnevial, the answer was easy. They were feminists who would vote socialist on the day that the republic gave them the ballot. For Renaud, who did not wish to choose, the situation was painful. She occasionally spoke in favor of cooperation with militant feminists or inserted pro-suffrage articles in *La Femme socialiste*, but she did not challenge Saumoneau's ideological domination of the GFS or openly denounce the implications of Guesde's anti-Millerand manifesto. In the delicate question of first allegiance to her class or to her sex, Renaud usually stood with the proletariat, apparently never forgetting nor forgiving the way bourgeois feminists had virtually excommunicated her at the 1900 congress of the rights of women when she outspokenly championed the rights of maids. Maria Pognon had criticized Renaud for her devotion to the theory of class struggle, just as Saumoneau blamed her for insufficient attachment to it. Viewed from Renaud's position, bourgeois feminists made collaboration as difficult as socialist opposition did. A few militants pled for cooperation, but most feminists, such as the moderates of the CNFF, did not care to work to this end. Even Auclert criticized socialists who did not put women's rights first. "There cannot be a bourgeois feminism and a socialist feminism," she wrote, "because there are not two female sexes."[78] Any program that divided the women's movement, including socialism, was intolerable. Such arguments only confirmed Saumoneau's determination to prevent collaboration; bourgeois feminists who stood in the way were "intriguing, naive, deranged, and hysterical women."[79] There was little prospect of socialist women rallying to suffragism in 1900.

Chapter Three

ΧΟΧΟΧΟΧΟΧΟΧΟΧΟΧ ΟΧΟΧΟΧΟΧΟΧΟΧ ΟΧΟΧΟΧΟΧΟΧΟΧΟΧΟΧΟΧΟΧΟΧΟΧΟΧΟ

The Growth of a Suffrage Campaign, 1901-1907

René Viviani had left ambiguous the delicate question of which women he proposed to admit to what franchise when he promised the congress of 1900 a suffrage bill. Despite a commitment to the full and equal suffrage for women, Viviani's political realism suggested their enfranchisement by gradual stages: a bill for immediate equality would probably produce immediate rejection. Viviani chose to limit his bill to municipal suffrage and to restrict the female electorate. In articles after the congress he proposed to let married women vote—to the surprise of suffragists who had anticipated the initial enfranchisement of unmarried women (*femmes célibataires*). Viviani argued that unmarried women already had more civil rights than married women and did not suffer from the husband's legal powers under French law. He also suggested that beginning with *célibataires* might close the question for many years because deputies might consider it a fair and complete solution, a compromise that did not challenge the family. Conversely, calling for the vote for married women would imply the need for further reforms. Finally, Viviani addressed the problem of republican anti-suffragism: unmarried women were "the category the least sensitive to our [republican] propoganda"; hence they were most likely to vote the confessional, so republicans would be least sympathetic to any bill proposing to let them vote.[1]

Viviani's proposal angered Hubertine Auclert. Having accepted the pragmatism of seeking the vote in stages, Auclert had for years concentrated on winning it for unmarried women. She believed that they most needed political rights because they lacked even the theoretical representation a husband provided. Her petition of 1900, calling for the vote for all unmarried women, had been deposited in the Chamber of Deputies by her old ally, Clovis Hugues, and would be in conflict with a Viviani bill when both reached the Commission of Universal Suffrage. Auclert herself would not vote under his scheme, whereas her formulation, giving the right to all unmarried women of full age (*femmes majeures*) would include widows and divorcees. Viviani's proposal would enfranchise nearly 55 percent of adult women—7.9 million married women, compared to 4.1 million *célibataires* plus 2.4 million widows and divorcees.[2] Auclert nonetheless criticized Viviani in her column in *Le Radical*, comparing his attitude to the anti-suffragism of his close friend, Léon Richer. Auclert soon made a conciliatory gesture, modulating her case in an article published by the organ of Viviani's parliamentary faction, but the quarrel was not ended.[3]

A quarter century of fractious political disputes had taught Auclert how to maneuver. With the aid of a first-term deputy, she outflanked the future premier. Jean Gautret, an independent republican elected from the Vendée in 1898, had provided one of the 3,000 signatures on Auclert's petition and had been moved to send her a letter of support. Auclert called upon the young deputy to show his sincerity by depositing a bill based upon the petition he lauded. Gautret hesitated but agreed. On July 1, 1901, he introduced a *projet de loi* in the Chamber of Deputies which was a modestly revised version of Auclert's petition. Viviani, who had apparently been in no rush to act during the ten months between his speech to the congress and the deposit of the Gautret Bill, accepted the *fait accompli* and did not introduce a competing bill.[4]

The Gautret Bill was the second formal introduction of the women's suffrage question in the Chamber of Deputies during the Third Republic. Joseph de Gasté, a republican from Finistère, had introduced the first in 1890 but had died without obtaining a committee report on his bill, which expired for want of a defender. The Gautret Bill fared little better. The one-article bill conferred the vote on all unmarried women for elections at all levels. The only exclusions from full equality were the continued disenfranchisement of married women and the ineligibility of women for election to office. Gautret thought that this form circumvented conservative anti-suffragism: women would not be taken from their marriage to vote or from their domestic roles to serve. He added a short statement calling universal suffrage a "pleasant expression" that covered the "brutal and triumphant egotism" of men, and laid his text before the chamber.[5] It went to the

Commission of Universal Suffrage without discussion and was never heard of again, never debated for a moment.

The utter rejection of the Gautret Bill has several simple political explanations beyond the powerful anti-suffragism of the epoch. The bill went to a hostile committee whose minutes show that women's suffrage never even obtained a token discussion in the entire legislative session. Gautret had designed his bill to combat conservative anti-suffragism, but it went to a committee with a majority of radicals whose anti-suffragism was different. Premier Emile Combes, a notorious anti-suffragist, took an especial interest in the work of the Commission of Universal Suffrage and regularly attended its meetings. Radicals, with their conviction that women would vote as priests directed, held the Gautret Bill precisely during the years (1901-1906) when the party's whole raison d'être seemed to be the separation of church and state. It that were not enough, the bill lacked anyone to champion it. Auclert's treatment of Viviani did not win friends for the bill or Viviani's energetic support. Gautret was a parliamentary neophyte. Furthermore, he left the Chamber of Deputies a few months after introducing the bill to accept an appointment in colonial administration, leaving the bill without a sponsor.[6] Women's suffrage had little chance of serious consideration in those circumstances.

The Gautret Bill also underscored the fragmentation of the women's movement. Saumoneau excoriated the project as a bourgeois ploy for ameliorative reform to the benefit of the few, especially women of independent means; it would not solve the true problems of the people. The bill, she concluded, was "unacceptable as much from the point of view of principle as from the practical view ... it must be repulsed by the socialist deputies." Moderates hesitated to champion any version of political rights. Militants criticized the bill for its omissions. Even if the political hour had been more propitious, suffragists were unable to apply effective pressure on parliament.[7]

Auclert, Pelletier, and the Tactics of the Feminist Left, 1902-1907

While the Gautret Bill lay buried, French suffragists began to revive the militancy that had characterized the movement during the 1880s. The principal author was once again Hubertine Auclert. Her determination to take forceful action had won few converts during the

1890s. Two events at the beginning of the new century, however, galvanized French militants to follow her in protesting vigorously: contact with foreign feminists through the Berlin Congress of 1904 and the French celebration of the centennial of the Napoleonic Code.

The Berlin Congress of 1904 was the regular quinquennial meeting of the International Council of Women. The French affiliate of the council, the CNFF, sent an official delegation (Bogelot, Monod, and Sainte-Croix) of moderate feminists which was unlikely to import militancy into France. However, a second meeting occured in Berlin that did stimulate French suffragism: an organizational meeting to create an International Woman Suffrage Alliance (IWSA). The idea of an international alliance had been proposed by the pioneering American suffragist, Susan B. Anthony, in the early 1880s. Auclert had exchanged a few letters with her and served as a "foreign corresponding secretary" with American suffrage groups, but Anthony's visit to Europe in 1883 had found insufficient backing for an alliance. Carrie Chapman Catt, Anthony's successor as president of the National American Woman Suffrage Association, revived the idea in 1899 and held a preparatory meeting at Washington, D.C., in 1902. The meeting of 1902 suggested the comparative weakness of French suffragism when no representatives attended, although delegates came from Russia, Chili, and Turkey. The resolution adopted at Washington for suffragists to meet in Berlin in 1904 and there to found an International Women's Suffrage Association, however, prompted Auclert to organize French participation.[8]

Shortly after the Washington meeting, Auclert invited all French women's organizations—including Catholics and socialists—to a joint meeting to prepare for membership in an international alliance. Only the suffrage leagues and a few small groups from the feminist center agreed to participate. Elections held in 1902 chose a delegation of Auclert, Vincent, and Schmahl to represent French interests at Catt's conference; other feminists, including Kauffmann and Oddo-Deflou, decided to attend on their own. Auclert eagerly prepared for Berlin and discussions with foreign suffragists on how to obtain the vote. Her enthusiasm produced such assiduous effort that even the Municipal Council of Paris was persuaded to provide a subvention for the travel costs of the three representatives.[9]

After its revitalizing origins, the organizational meeting of the IWSA became a fiasco for French suffragism. Auclert and Catt soon fought over several issues such as dues and meeting times. The great American suffragist was unimpressed with an "auxilliary" delegation and with the size of the French movement. She furthermore appears to have suffered from a prejudice against the Catholic countries of "Latin" Europe. Auclert, for her part, was uncompromising and did not care to organize a national women's suffrage society in France along different lines to suit the tastes of foreign suffragists. The result was that Catt created the IWSA at a rescheduled meeting before Auclert arrived in Berlin, with no French representatives present; women from the United States, Great Britain, Canada, the Netherlands, Norway, and Sweden—all northern, Protestant countries—established the alliance. Meanwhile, the International Council of Women, without CNFF support, voted a resolution calling for "strenuous efforts" to obtain the vote. France was outside the international suffrage movement.[10]

The Berlin Congress taught several lessons to French suffragists and angered them enough to do something about it. The meeting highlighted their comparative underdevelopment and lesser support from moderate feminists. This alone might have stimulated French suffragists to greater efforts on their return. In addition, Auclert, Vincent, and Kauffmann met privately with foreign militants; they concluded that French women were too slow to undertake forceful public demonstrations. Within five months of their return to France, they acted on this conclusion and took their cause into the streets of Paris.[11]

The feminist demonstrations of 1904 resulted from the decision of the Combes government to celebrate the 100th anniversary of the promulgation of Napoleon's Civil Code with festivities costing thousands of francs. Two days of ceremonies in late October were to culminate in a rally in the grand amphitheatre of the Sorbonne, with speeches by President Loubet, the minister of justice, the president of the Cour de Cassation, and the dean of the Faculty of Law—followed by a lavish state banquet. Even moderate feminists were outraged at the glorification of what they considered the principal instrument of their oppression. The feminist press bristled with angry articles. Maria Martin excoriated the code as accepting women only "to produce cannon fodder." Celebrants, wrote Gabrielle Petit in *La Femme affranchie*, should not forget flowers because "champagne will be insufficient to drive away the cadaverous odors." Durand organized a broad women's coalition for a countercelebration to brand the code "a shame to the republic." Between 800 and 1,000 women—a huge crowd for the feminist movement in 1904—paid to hear Nelly Roussel (widely considered by feminists to be their most effective orator) excoriate "the humiliations imposed on women by the Napoleonic Code."[12]

The militants returned from Germany less satisfied with polite protests held in lecture halls. Auclert, Vincent, and Kauffmann, with the hesitant support of Jeanne Oddo-Deflou, decided upon a series of public demonstrations to "express in a vehement fashion their indignation." Their societies surreptitiously posted announcements and distributed handbills on the streets, proclaiming "The Code Crushes Women" and calling for a rally outside the Palais Bourbon. Privately, the groups discussed dramatic "avenging gestures" they might make, such as burning a copy of the Code in public. Kauffman proposed that they then take an urn containing the ashes of the Code and deposit them on the head table during the celebratory banquet. Most militants, led by Oddo-Deflou, bluntly opposed such "grotesque" violations of the standards of respectable behavior and refused "to brave the ridicule." A lack of support notwithstanding, Auclert organized a march to the Napoleonic memorial column at the Place Vendôme for the burning of the Civil Code on October 29th. A parade would then proceed to the advertised demonstration across the river at the Palais Bourbon. Feminists could choose which portion of the day's activities suited their sense of dignity. Auclert hoped for 150 marchers; she got 50. When they arrived at the Place Vendôme, Auclert found almost as many policemen: the Prefecture of Police had kept an agent active in Suffrage des femmes for over twenty years and knew every detail of her plans. Her procession reached the southern mouth of the Place Vendôme on the rue Castiglione and stopped in surprise. Auclert exhorted them to complete their protest, but only three women followed her. When Auclert tore a few pages of the Code and struck a match, policemen descended on her quite roughly. Without a single memorial ash for the banquet but with bruises on her arms, Auclert and her followers were driven back to the rue de Rivoli. After regrouping and marching the short distance to the Palais Bourbon, Auclert found more gendarmes awaiting the protesters. The police prevented them from even raising a placard stating "The Code Crushes Women," and the demonstration collapsed.[13]

Shaken by her treatment and shocked by the apparent betrayal of feminism by some informer, Auclert withdrew from further gestures during the centenary. The Prefecture of Police possessed greater stamina. Reinforcements were summoned, and all women seeking to enter the state banquet were turned back lest they had procured ashes from another source to enact Kauffmann's demonstration. That did not deter Kauffmann from making an unannounced gesture at the ceremonies at the Sorbonne on October 30th. She released golden balloons imprinted with "The Code Crushes Women" as rapidly as her hired man could inflate them. When he ran out of breath, she shouted slogans until she was arrested and led away. Kauffmann was found innocent of a charge of "injurious disturbance" (*tapage injurieux*) a few weeks later when a judge ruled that there had been neither injury nor injurious intent.[14]

The acquittal of Caroline Kauffmann did not lessen the impact of the government's message to feminists in 1904: they would use all necessary force to protect the republic against its militant critics, and feminists could expect the iron fist as well as the velvet glove. For the militants to whom this warning was given, there were other lessons in 1904. They could compare the fifty demonstrators at the Place Vendôme with nearly twenty times that number at Durand's more sedate protest. They could note how few militants would actually step forward at the Vendôme column. Yet Auclert soon recovered from the shock of October 1904 and argued that those events were merely a step in the evolution of militant tactics. Whatever that evolution might bring, it had not yet made feminism persuasive: a month after the celebrations, Premier Combes named an extraparliamentary commission to study possible revisions of the Code; the minister of justice, Ernest Vallé (a president of the Radical Party), named an exclusively male commission.[15]

The question of appropriate tactics arose a year later during the preparations for the parliamentary elections of 1906. French suffragists had been relatively quiet during the parliamentary elections of 1902 and the municipal elections of 1900 and 1904, largely due to the frustration and disappointment deriving from their unsupported electoral efforts during the 1890s. The expense and defeat of Vincent's court case in 1893, plus the disillusionment when socialists refused to aid women's candidacies during the elections of 1893 and 1898, had left little enthusiasm for electoral activities. During the elections of

1900-1904 Auclert continued her habit of twenty years—pasting up the little green posters stating "Women Must Vote," which she had made a familiar part of the Parisian political landscape. But no one wished to join her in a larger effort. When she sought to revive enthusiasm for attempting to register to vote, exactly ten women, all members of Suffrage des femmes, were willing to try. When she considered another woman's candidacy, Schmahl wrote, "I cannot accept the renewal of fictional candidacies. It is no longer possible to ignore the legal conditions of eligibility."[16]

The events of 1904 changed many minds; by 1906, most feminist groups planned propaganda campaigns to coincide with the parliamentary elections. Their chief division remained the choice of behavior. Militants advocated taking their cause into the streets; moderates sought a plan more compatible with their sense of bourgeois propriety. Many moderates even agreed to support a suffrage coalition, if it were limited to a joint poster. Amélioration contributed the prestige of its name and the treasury that could finance printing costs. The tone of the poster suited its signatorees. Auclert's slogan remained—"Women must vote!"—but the text stressed conservative suffragist appeals such as the benefit of women electors working against alcoholism. So modest was the appeal that at the last minute Solidarité chose to put up its own supplementary poster. Lacking financial resources, they hung the posters themselves, an act that reintroduced suffragists to police harassment. Several members of the group were arrested outside a department store on the boulevard Bonne-Nouvelle while pasting up a poster reading "We want UNIVERSAL suffrage, not UNISEXUAL suffrage." They had complied with all legal technicalities, such as having a man's signature on the *affiche* as the candidate in whose behalf it was raised, but the novelty of women hanging a poster had attracted a curious crowd; hence, they were deemed guilty of disturbing the peace.[17]

Militants also ran into difficulties with the law when they planned a public demonstration. The clash with police in 1904 had persuaded Auclert and Kauffmann that they needed a completely legal way to dramatize their cause in the streets. Once again, they opted for two stages of their protest, in hopes of attracting less daring women to one portion. On the day of the runoff elections (March 18, 1906), they held a suffrage rally at the Musée Social, which was becoming a frequent meeting place for moderate feminists due to the connection of Jules Siegfried, one of its principle founders, and Julie Siegfried, the vice-president of the CNFF. After hearing suffrage speeches there, militants planned to lead the audience in a parade to several polling places and distribute literature. An ordinance of 1900, prompted by the Dreyfus affair, presented legal problems for this plan. A march of such size would require the prior approval of, and crowd control by, both the Ministry of the Interior and the Prefecture of Police. Considering their relations with the police, militants sought an alternative and discovered a loophole in the ordinance: they organized a cortège of banner-bedecked automobiles and taxicabs, led by a horse-drawn flatbed truck full of women distributing suffragist leaflets.

French feminists still resisted activity in the streets. Hundreds attended the rally at the Musée social, including a delegation of Christian feminists. Only fifty agreed to ride in the parade. Oddo-Deflou, Feresse-Deraismes, and Schmahl predictably withheld their support, but the militants received a much worse blow. Eliska Vincent also declined to join, marking a shift in her attitudes which culminated a few years later in her selection as president of a new moderate society. It was a premonitory sign that the expansion of suffragist militancy was severly limited. The reaction of the crowds in the streets of Paris also depressed suffragists: they heard less applause than shouts of "Back to your darning! Back to the kitchen!" Reflecting on the disappointments of the demonstrations, Auclert was moved to open the question of violence: "Will feminists be obliged to employ propaganda of the deed?"[18]

A few weeks after the electoral demonstrations, Pelletier and Kauffmann executed one of the most dramatic gestures suffragists had yet attempted. They obtained tickets to the spectator's gallery at the Palais Bourbon for the opening of the new legislature on June 3, 1906, from Adrien Meslier (socialist, Seine), whom Pelletier knew as a fellow physician. Pelletier and Kauffmann interrupted the proceedings by standing up in the gallery and showering the hemicycle with suffragist handbills. The deputies, many of whom had sat through a similar attack (but with a bomb) by Auguste Vaillant in December 1893, scattered in fear of an explosion. Other spectators, also thinking a terrorist attack was in progress, seized Pelletier and Kauffmann. They were not arrested, however. After interrogation and admonition, the government declined to prosecute them specifically because they did not want to make them suffragist martyrs or to give them the attention of the Parisian press. Meslier never forgave Pelletier, and the loss of his support was probably greater than any suffragist progress gained by the act, as most feminists were more horrified than the deputies had been.[19] Pelletier, however, continued to organize demonstrations in the streets. Twice she staged marches along the quays to the Chamber of Deputies, there to seek deputies in the lobby and to talk to them about women's suffrage. She especially sought out socialist deputies, whose newly unified party (hereafter, SFIO), she had joined. Her energetic participation in socialist politics ultimately led Pelletier to unusual prominence in the party for a woman, including appointment to the "permanent administrative commission" that governed the SFIO. Thus, Pelletier expected her marches to the Palais Bourbon in 1906 and 1907 to produce some results.[20]

In December 1906, Pelletier led about one hundred women to the chamber, found René Viviani, and hectored him into arranging for their admission to the regular meeting of the socialist deputies. After Pelletier, Kauffmann, and others outlined their grievances and asked the party to honor its promises by opening the debate on women's suffrage, Jean Jaurès gave a reassuring speech. He agreed that "the hour has come" for women to vote and stated that he thought the clerical peril was diminishing, particularly as more women joined the labor force. "The socialist party is going to occupy itself with the reform that you advocate," Jaurès promised. "Woman, the equal of man, must possess equal rights to those of man." *L'Humanité* reaffirmed that vow the next day. It was the sort of unequivocal promise that fell frequently from socialist lips but rarely led to suffragist action.[21]

Six months later, socialist deputies still had not raised women's suffrage in the chamber, and Pelletier led another march to parliament. She had arranged for a deputation of British militants from the Women's Social and Political Union (hereafter, WSPU) to meet with Solidarité to discuss tactics. These discussions led to the conclusions that it was important to keep pressure on socialist deputies and to encourage Premier Clemenceau to approve of the socialist suffrage bill when it was introduced. The whole group (the majority of whom were British suffragettes) assembled under a large white banner and set off to find Clemenceau. They got no closer than the adjunct chief of his cabinet for the Ministry of the Interior, who promised to transmit their concerns to Clemenceau. Jaurès did receive the protesters, informed them of the subcommittee of the SFIO that was working on their request of the previous December, and promised his continuing support. The demonstrators filled out the afternoon by distributing propaganda leaflets to the legislators and left confident that they were making progress.[22] That confidence was misplaced. Socialists made no serious effort to secure parliamentary discussion of women's suffrage. Moreover, Pelletier was certainly not making progress with other feminists, and gradually concluded that she would "never find grace among the bourgeoisie."[23] Even if they became more militant, few feminists wanted to march beside Pelletier. When she proposed a repeat performance of the leaflet-bombardment of the Chamber of Deputies, she found one woman willing to do so. If Pelletier were to lead French suffragism to militancy, it would be by setting a lonely example which somehow changed the situation. She accepted this: "I prefer suffering isolation to helping them to deny my dearest convictions."[24] So she determined to alter events with whatever little support she could find. And she increasingly considered violence to be the answer.

Maugeret and Suffragism on the Feminist Right, *1904-1907*

While militants took their cause into the streets, a very different suffragism was developing on the feminist right. Marie Maugeret had been attracted to women's suffrage in the late 1890s, but she realized that most Catholic women found her "decidedly too feminist." Her nationalism and religiosity reassured women of the right, but Maugeret held too many advanced ideas to be completely acceptable. She responded to her isolation by organizing an annual conference of the entire Catholic women's movement. The Congrès Jeanne d'Arc devoted considerable attention to the "feminine apostolate." It was unflinching in its criticism of the "Godless republic." Appropriate to its name, one of the congress's foremost aims was the canonization of Joan of Arc. It promoted unity among Catholic women's groups. And it provided Maugeret with a forum to advance some of her ideas among conservative women.[25]

Maugeret's first Congrès Jeanne d'Arc met in the spring of 1904. With the aid of Françoise Dorive and her monthly bulletin, *Le Devoir des femmes françaises*, she arranged several sessions touching upon liberal Catholic and feminist concerns, including one on the political rights of women. Many delegates reluctantly participated, but they were unwilling to adopt any feminist resolutions. Instead, the congress produced resolutions that reflected the outlook of the LPF and the LFF. Nonetheless, Maugeret was pleased to have established cooperation among such groups. The following year she created the Fédération Jeanne d'Arc to provide a permanent structure for organizing the annual assemblies. The spirit of collaboration grew in 1905, when Maugeret effected a reconciliation between the leaders of the LPF and the LFF, who had been fighting over monarchism since the LPF had joined in the rallying of Catholics to the republic. In the glow of this new mood, an officer of the LFF even addressed the 1905 Congrès Jeanne d'Arc with an exhortation to all Catholic women to become more active in social questions.[26]

Several members of the Catholic intelligentsia and the liberal Catholic movement were advancing ideas similar to Maugeret's at the time that she was organizing her annual congresses. The Abbé Henry Bolo's *La Femme et le clergé* (1902) and the Abbé Paul Naudet's *Pour la femme* (1903) both endorsed Christian feminism. A third priest, Jean Lagardère, founded a periodical, *La Femme contemporaine* (later, *La Femme catholique contemporaine*) in 1903, with the belief that "feminism is the order of the day" and the church must take a leading role in it. This mounting interest in Catholic feminism prompted the Abbé Antonin Sertillanges to deliver a series of lectures at the Institut Catholique, which were later published as *Féminisme et christianisme*. The most influential of these authors was Etienne Lamy, whose *La Femme de demain* (1901) went through more than twenty editions by the 1930s and became the best-selling book on French feminism before Simone de Beauvoir. Several of these authors advocated some version of political rights for women. Charles Turgeon devoted six chapters of his *Le Féminisme français* to defending women's suffrage, in a forceful argument that it was "illogical and unjust" to deny women the vote. They "must be electors on the same basis as men." Conservative authors often distrusted universal suffrage on principle, but generally agreed that if men voted, women should too. Jules Lemaître argued, for example, that women "are for the most part conservatives and traditionalists [and] they would vote in general better than men." Maugeret's Catholic feminism profited from such attitudes. She hailed Turgeon's book as "a monument, almost perfect and definitive," and in 1903 engaged him as a contributor to *Le Féminisme chrétien*. Brunetière, Lemaître, and Lamy helped to establish Action sociale and participated in the group's first series of lectures in 1904. Even the LPF urged its members to read Lamy's book.[27]

Even with such support, Maugeret was in a delicate position. Her advanced ideas separated her from traditional Catholics, but her strong defense of the church equally separated her from republican feminists. She dreamt of stating a program "an equal distance" between the avant-garde and reaction, but responses kept her firmly rooted in the Catholic women's movement. She briefly participated in Amélioration. In 1902 she proposed a joint campaign of Christian and republican feminists to support the Gautret Bill. In 1906, she tried to participate in the suffrage coalition. And in 1908 Maugeret was the only French participant on the program of the IWSA congress at Amsterdam, where she joined an American suffragist, the Reverend Anna Howard Shaw, in a session entitled "Woman Suffrage Presented from a Christian Point of View." French republican feminists, however, consistently rejected Maugeret's overtures. Only a handful of Christian feminists would have followed Maugeret in such cooperation, but they never received an opportunity. Considering the issues dividing the two groups, this is scarcely surprising. How could "the priest-ridden" meet with "masonic agents of Satan"? How could the defenders of the traditional family meet with women who advocated (and practiced) divorce or abortion? How could organizations with a significant Jewish membership ally with others given to anti-semitic rhetoric? Maugeret concluded that they could not. After 1906, she essentially confined her labors to Catholic women: they should support the vote in order to defend the church, reform the republic, and commence the regeneration of France.[28]

Maugeret directly confronted Catholic women with the suffrage question at the third Congrès Jeanne d'Arc in 1906. Most of the program concerned social problems and religious questions, but Maugeret scheduled for the last day a meeting on "women and politics." It became a skillfully produced triumph for Catholic suffragism, although it was clearly far ahead of the opinion of most Catholics. Many delegates did not attend the session: some provincial women left early, unaware of the significance of the meeting; others boycotted the session after learning the true issue. Those attending found that Maugeret had scheduled an array of pro-suffrage speakers. Lagardère spoke forcefully: "women have both the right and the duty to engage in politics." Another speaker read from the bulletin of the Grand Orient to illustrate the opposition of Freemasons to Catholic women voting. Eliska Vincent spoke effectively to her audience by reminding them that women's suffrage had existed under the monarchy and had been lost during the revolution: "If I were one of you, if I were born to your ranks, if I had faith like you, I would arouse the world with this question, which is a question of both tradition and justice." Maugeret herself defended women's suffrage with one of the well-established liberal arguments of the *ralliement*: "In order to clean up a house, it is first necessary to enter it. Let us enter this house." These speeches induced the delegates to adopt two motions. The four to five hundred women present called unanimously, if somewhat ambiguously, for the representation of women in politics. A more precise second motion, endorsing full political rights for women, passed by the narrow margin of 83-67, with the majority of delegates abstaining.[29]

The suffrage motion at the Congrès Jeanne d'Arc was heatedly debated in the following months. Maugeret invited representatives of various women's groups to present their opinions at the June 1906 meeting of her circle. She worried that Catholics might dismiss her as too militant, but she nonetheless reiterated her belief that Catholic women should claim the vote. The Baroness de Boury protested for the LPF against the "surprise" motion and delivered a conservative critique of women in politics. Such activities, she lamented, "would be a new breach in the constitution of the family, and a deviation from women's role such as it has been understood by Christian civilization." Others denied that women's suffrage would help the church. Some were disturbed that militants such as Vincent supported Maugeret. Maugeret adroitly claimed a centrist position, telling the right that she still wanted the vote and the left that she still planned to use the ballot "to combat whoever attacks religion." A majority of the women present agreed with her, and they adopted another motion in favor of women's suffrage.[30]

This did not convince the Catholic majority. The LPF and LFF ignored the suffrage debates in their reports of the Congrès Jeanne d'Arc; both excluded the subject from their own annual conventions. Their argument against women's suffrage was simple: the pope opposed it. Pius X approved of the education of women, "that women work, that they teach, that they be doctors or lawyers," especially that they be active in traditional spheres such as charity work. In April 1906, however, he had told an Austrian feminist that he opposed women in politics. "Women electors, women deputies? Oh, no!" he was reported to have said, raising his hands toward heaven. "Women in parliaments! That is all we need! The men there have already created enough confusion! Imagine what would happen if there were women there!" A report of this interview was picked up by *Le Temps* and widely circulated by French conservatives. Rumors even circulated that Pius had criticized Maugeret's efforts when she received an audience later in 1906. She denounced this "absolutely fanaticized account," and questioned the veracity of the other remarks attributed to the pope. The question was settled, however, when the leaders of the LPF and the LFF obtained their own papal audience and reported that Pius X had stated that it was an error for women to seek the same rights as men. This time, the pope's opposition to women's suffrage was reported in *L'Osservatore Romano* and reprinted in the French press.[31]

Maugeret's difficulties were reflected in the behavior of Dorive, her closest ally. Dorive derived as many of her ideas from Copin-Albancelli's obsessive anti-masonry as she did from Maugeret's liberalism; indeed, *Devoir des femmes* shared the same headquarters as Copin-Albancelli's Ligue de défense nationale contre la franc-maçonnerie. Reassured by Maugeret's hostility to the Freemasons, Dorive had supported her in 1904 and kept the women's suffrage debate alive through a yearlong study of the question in the pages of her *Devoir des femmes françaises*. That bulletin reprinted a pro-suffrage (but certainly not pro-feminist) article by Edouard Drumont; a speech by Lagardère urging Catholic women "to brandish the electoral sword"; and several articles by Maugeret defending her position. But Dorive remained personally unconvinced. She encouraged her readers to submit their own opinions, promising to reprint representative letters. Most of these were hostile, such as one by "the Baronness L. F." who argued that only a few women were prepared for the vote and that giving it to the masses would create great problems. Dorive concluded in April 1907 that Maugeret was wrong: a Catholic campaign for women's suffrage was inopportune. Instead, Catholic women should devote themselves to the defense of the family and the church, perhaps gradually approaching the notion of municipal suffrage because the communes had power over the churches.[32]

Why did most Catholic women in 1906-1907 reject Marie Maugeret's ideas? The most compelling answer was the LPF's: the pope had stated that suffragism was an error, and that settled the issue. A fuller explanation must include several other factors. The great preponderance of Catholic women did not challenge the assumption that woman's place was in the home. Insofar as they considered the subject, they perceived the participation of women in politics to be a threat to the home and the family, just as conservative anti-suffragists insisted. Their traditional conception of womanhood led to the conclusion that politics and feminism were "unfeminine." They associated suffragism with the Godless republic and suffragists with such repugnant ideas as divorce, free love, abortion, and socialism. They furthermore associated women's political rights with an unwanted (and Protestant) stress upon individualism; consistent with Catholic thought, they preferred doctrines that emphasized duties rather than rights. Catholicism also offered women an ideological and institutional home, which provided all with a sense of place and many with a career; in such ways, Catholic women were less likely to understand the need for enfranchisement than Protestant women. Suffragism was additionally a new and alien doctrine in most of France. If Catholic women perceived that the vote could benefit the church, or the family, they could become its most numerous supporters; indeed, it would be their duty to do so. That happened after World War I, but in 1906 Catholic women were far from persuaded. Maugeret had expanded the base of French suffragism to include an elite of liberal Catholic feminists, but she had a long way to go to bring the mass of Catholic women to such a conviction.[33]

The Conversion of the Feminist Center to Suffragism

Under pressure from both the left and the right, the French women's movement could no longer resist the call for political rights. One might try to ignore Auclert and Pelletier, but Maugeret was acutely embarrassing to moderates who thought of themselves as more advanced than Catholics. One might make snide remarks ("O, miracle! wrote Oddo-Deflou), but the fact remained that Catholic women had aired the suffrage question more thoroughly than they had.[34] Most moderates had gone no further than to sign the electoral poster of 1906. The CNFF had inscribed suffrage on its program but had never held public discussions of the right to vote. Even so advanced a feminist as Marguerite Durand still hesitated to embrace suffragism.[35] The majority of feminists desired to vote, but preferred to wait for the issue to become less controversial. After June 1906, they could no longer hold that opinion comfortably. If they were to be the vanguard of republican progress, they must be more advanced than the Catholics. Within two years the entire republican feminist movement accepted suffragism. The conversion of Oddo-Deflou was typical. She had long desired women's suffrage but declined to seek it, fearing to alienate some women or drain off energies needed to secure other civil rights. Although she had agreed to sign the suffrage poster of March 1906, Oddo-Deflou spent the electoral campaign seeking "the good will" of candidates. Maugeret's suffrage motions of the following June stung her. A few days after the vote at the Congrès Jeanne d'Arc, Oddo-Deflou informed Etudes that "henceforth a notable part of our activity will be devoted to obtaining the right to vote."[36] Within the next year, the group published a suffragist brochure and financed a book on the question. Oddo-Deflou maintained her belief in the primacy of re-forming the Napoleonic Code, but she became a vocal suffragist in addition. She explained that the new policy derived from the slow pace of feminist progress: the vote was "an implement to acquire civil rights."[37]

The most consequential change of the feminist center came with the passage of the CNFF to suffragism. The metamorphosis of the genteel philanthropists at Versailles into active participants in the search for political rights implied the fundamental alteration of the suffrage movement. The council numbered 73,000 members in 1906-1907. Here was the first harbinger of a mass movement rather than the campaign of a small elite. And with that possibility came the prospect of a campaign shaped by moderate, cautious women rather than the militant avant garde.

The transformation of CNFF policy was gradual. Feminist groups accounted for less than 10 percent of the organizations affiliated with the council (9 of 102) and less than 5 percent of the membership; charities (16), educational organizations (13), trade unions (8), and professional organizations (5) provided most of the adherents. Many of these societies were increasingly sympathetic to feminism, however, especially the members of bourgeois discussion circles (6) and the leagues (such as temperance or pacifist groups) that profited from association with social feminism. This permitted the council's legislative section to take a role in feminist campaigns for reformation of the Civil Code. The founders, however, had intentionally excluded women's suffrage from their initial program because political rights seemed "premature" to many people. Feminists within the council won a pro-suffrage resolution in 1902, but this was only an endorsement in principle; it recognized a need for the education of women as a preliminary step, and its authors refused to create a suffrage section to prepare for that development. The CNFF declined to take any further action until 1906. None of the annual national assemblies, nor the public meetings at the Musée Social, during the years 1901-1906 included a discussion of women's suffrage comparable to the 1906 Congrès Jeanne d'Arc. The CNFF even declined to sign the electoral poster of 1906.[38]

Three important elements explain the evolution of CNFF policy: pressure from the international feminist movement, the role of the CNFF's executive council, and the activity of Maugeret. The pressure from abroad resulted from the fact that France had no national suffrage association in the IWSA. As the only French group affiliated with international feminism, the CNFF was the logical body for foreign suffragists to approach. Furthermore, the International Council of Women had a suffrage section and urged the creation of a similar section by each national council.[39] The executive committee of the CNFF was sympathetic to this idea, having always been more feminist than the membership. Two members, Bonnevial and Maria Martin, had urged suffragism since the council's inception; two others, Oddo-Deflou and Marie Georges-Martin (a leader of mixed Freemasonry) were recent converts. The decisive voices came from two of the moderate founders, Sainte-Croix and Siegfried. Sainte-Croix concluded that she must make her private views public. In 1906 she wrote *Le Féminisme*, a book that proclaimed women's suffrage to be "the keystone of the feminist edifice."[40] With such pressures upon the executive committee, the suffrage vote at the Catholic congress had a tremendous impact. That meeting and the CNFF's national assembly had taken place almost simultaneously in June 1906. The contrast was inescapable. It was acutely embarrassing to advocates of steady republican progress that supposed reactionaries should seem more progressive. Hence the nucleus of suffragists in the executive committee persuaded the council to establish a suffrage section that would "study" the question of political rights.

The CNFF's suffrage section became a center of activity, rather than a study group, before it first met. The explanation was a matter of membership again. Everyone agreed that the council could not examine the vote without inviting Auclert, the elder stateswoman of that issue, to accept the presidency. Any other course would have been a breach of etiquette, to which the women of the CNFF were particularly sensitive. Auclert was a critic of the CNFF and not even a member, so it may be assumed that the offer was a *beau geste*. Auclert's acceptance must have been a considerable surprise. The adhesion of Suffrage des femmes and the creation of a suffrage section were announced simultaneously at a special meeting in November 1906 under the honorary presidency of Mme. Curie. The CNFF was certainly not hiding its new policy. Other members of the section showed how little it would be merely a discussion group: Bonnevial, Vérone, Sainte-Croix, Georges-Martin, and Julie Auberlet (of both Solidarité and Suffrage des femmes).[41]

Despite the auspicious signs surrounding the birth of the CNFF's suffrage section, Auclert and the council were fundamentally incompatible. Auclert tried to take hesitant women too far, too fast. Her presidency lasted four months. The initial plans of the section were quite suitable to co-existence: the CNFF would write to the head of every political group in parliament for support and would organize a huge petition campaign to impress politicans with the number of people supporting women's suffrage. Auclert could not stop there. She asked for a public demonstration, such as a rally paying homage to Maria Deraismes at her statue in the Square des Epinettes. This was simply too much for the ladies of the national council. Whereas the goal of enfranchisement previously divided feminists, tactics now did. The line separating them ran through the streets of Paris; the CNFF would not step across that line even at the strolling pace of a parade. Simultaneously, the suffrage section voted to devote its energies to the petition and Auclert resigned the presidency, citing reasons of health. The council immediately named her the "honorary president" of the section (which they had presumably wanted in the first place) and chose a moderate, Marie Georges-Martin, to succeed her.[42]

Auclert's short tenure was nonetheless important. Had a moderate led from the start, the section might have become the study group originally envisaged. Auclert, by urging her advanced position on the council, made moderate suffragism an acceptable compromise. Subsequent presidents built on this base, making the CNFF an integral part of moderate suffragism, which now claimed tens of thousands of adherents.

During the same years that the feminist center embraced the cause of political rights, France experienced the slow growth of provincial suffragism. Parisian feminist leagues began to establish provincial branches; when the parent organization joined the suffrage coalition, the issue was consequently discussed in other cities. By 1908 there were than two dozen provincial feminist organizations; in northern France, nearly half of all departments had such groups. (See Map 1.) The largest association of provincial feminists was in the lodges of mixed Freemasonry, such as Droit humain, although their connection with radicalism inhibited their suffragist potential. By 1908, feminist masons were active in Lyons, Le Havre, d'Evreux (Eure), Auray (Morbihan), Lille, Clermont-Ferrand, Angers, Nantes, Marseille, Le Mans, Nancy, and Nice, in addition to the four lodges in Paris.[43] The CNFF began to create chapters with the work of Gabrielle Alphen-Salvador at Tours in 1902. By 1908, branches at Le Havre (the Siegfried's summer home), Lyons (Pauline Kergomard), Bordeaux, and Rouen emulated the national council in creating suffrage sections. Similarly branches of Etudes at Sens and Orléans and a Burgundian group of Amélioration followed their Parisian leaders, although generally remaining more moderate. This pattern encouraged other activity. For example, Anne de Réal began publishing *Le Féministe* at Nice in November 1906 and linked her monthly with Etudes. Although very cautious and upper-class for its title, *Le Féministe* endorsed the vote in 1908.[44]

The principal feminist effort to expand outside Paris came through lecture tours, chiefly an annual circuit by Nelly Roussel during the years 1903-1913 which several Parisian groups and newspapers co-sponsored. Roussel (1878-1922) was born to the comfortable Parisian middle class of the liberal professions but broke with her family at age twenty to marry a struggling sculptor, Henri Godet, with whom she entered the freethinking and socialist movements. Like Madeleine Pelletier, Roussel developed a broad conception of the emancipation

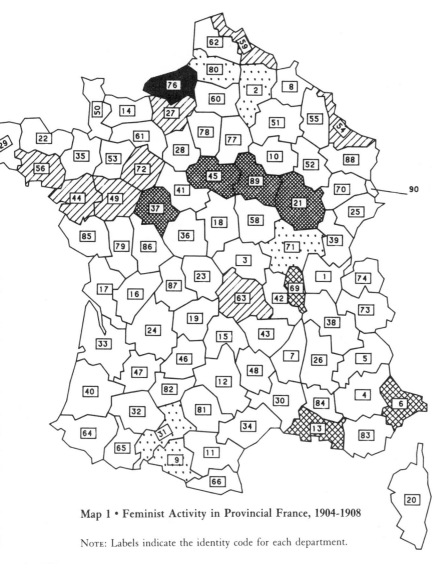

Map 1 • Feminist Activity in Provincial France, 1904-1908

NOTE: Labels indicate the identity code for each department.

 Departments with a branch of a Parisian feminist league *and* a mixed masonic lodge.

 Departments with a branch of a Parisian feminist league.

 Departments with a mixed masonic lodge *and* local feminist activity.

 Departments with a mixed masonic lodge only.

Departments with local or individual activity only.

Departments with no known feminist activity.

of women that included neo-Malthusian theories of sexuality, birth control, and abortion; unlike Pelletier, Roussel had an easygoing, extroverted personality which prevented her advanced ideas from leading to ostracism. Roussel cooperated with moderates and even served as an officer of the UFF, as a member of the executive committee of the CNFF, and as the Parisian representative of Darnaud's organization. It was her natural eloquence and her training as a diction teacher, however, that made her feminist career. Roussel organized her lecture tours to reach a variety of people. The socialist-sponsored "popular universities" created by Georges Deherme were the most frequent choice, but freethinker societies, neo-Malthusian and pacifist groups, teacher's unions, and mixed masonic lodges also collaborated in sponsoring the tour. Roussel was an eager speaker. *L'Action* advertised her forthcoming speeches and she invited interested organizations along her route to arrange another address. Thus her tour of April-June 1905, for example, included thirty-four speeches in fifteen departments. Her subsequent tours were smaller, but for the years 1906-1910 she averaged six provincial lectures per year. Her speeches were usually delivered in the larger towns and cities, where the feminist movement expected its expansion, but Roussel made an especial effort to arrange one or two addresses each year in smaller locales, such as to the workers at Oullins or to vineyard laborers at Bugey. Roussel spoke on a great range of feminist interests, but her stock speech was on woman as "the eternally sacrificed." For much of provincial France, this speech represented the first contact with the public argument of equal rights of women.[45]

The growth of provincial suffragism also owed much to a few exceptional women determined to labor for the vote single-handedly, such as Marie Denizard at Amiens and Arria Ly at Toulouse. Denizard (d. 1922?) was a woman of letters who contributed to several newspapers and reviews in northeastern France. The congresses of 1900 stimulated her to write and to lecture on feminism. Like others, she had ties to philanthropy; she became a local celebrity in Amiens during the smallpox epidemic of 1903-1904, when hospitals could not hold all of the afflicted, by organizing visits to the homes of victims. Her suffragism followed the tactics she observed in Paris, particularly those of Hubertine Auclert. Denizard personally financed and hand-posted thousands of *affiches* calling for women's suffrage throughout the department of the Somme during parliamentary elections. In 1907, she circulated a copy of an Auclert petition and submitted it to the *conseil général* of the Somme. Later she stood as a candidate during various elections, founded a feminist review (*Le Cri des femmes*), and refused to pay her taxes. Denizard, however, found few activists in Amiens who would challenge provincial opinion; like Roussel, her greatest contribution to the suffrage campaign was to introduce the subject to people for whom it was alien, facilitating later developments.[46]

Arria Ly (1881-1934), born Josephine Gondon, was one of the most extraordinary individualists of a movement that attracted many. Her biography almost invites posthumous psychoanalysis. She was extremely close to her mother (whom she called "my sister"). They lived together her entire life, including a long voluntary exile from France after World War I; shortly after her mother's death, Ly committed suicide. Her father died when she was twenty-two, and she caused a sensation by shooting the physician who had attended him. Ly's relations with other men were very poor and she developed the theory that a true feminist could never marry. In an article entitled "The Young Girl's Nightmare," she discussed the terrifying psychological impact of merely dreaming of being married, a "shameful compromise." Instead of marriage, Ly preached "virginal feminism" by which women should conduct a permanent strike against sexual relations because man's passions were the source of woman's subjection. She dressed as a man and cut her hair very short but still could not stop men from remarking that she was a very pretty woman. Her public stress upon her virginity, her interrogation of other feminists about their sex lives, and her discussion of lesbianism in her correspondence estranged her from most feminists, who accepted the larger portion of contemporary middle-class attitudes. Even less did Arria Ly fit comfortably into the southern France of the early twentieth century. After a series of controversies, such as bursting into a public meeting, slapping the speaker, and challenging him to a duel (for deriding her ideas), she fled to a small Pyrenees village. There she precipitated a torrent of anti-feminism—organized in all seventeen villages of the canton by the clergy—by preaching the strike of Lysistrata to local women; there she faced the constant harassment of a shivaree. Not long thereafter, she chose a life of exile.[47]

Arria Ly tried to establish suffragism at Toulouse with the determination, and with the acceptance, that this biography implies. She joined the more militant Parisian societies and corresponded with their leaders, but she frequently turned down invitations to join them in Paris. Like Denizard, Ly preferred to stay at home, however little acceptance she received; like Denizard, she imported the tactics of the capital. Many of her efforts did not germinate in the stony soil of the South. In some cases, however, her persistence and ability produced remarkable success. In a petition campaign of 1908, for example, Auclert and many supporters obtained 2,600 signatures in Paris; Ly and her mother alone obtained 1,400 at Toulouse. When she copied Auclert and Denizard by appealing to the *conseil général* of the Haute-Garonne, the radical presiding officer, Joseph Ruau (Clemenceau's minister of agriculture), summarily dismissed her request. Her chief contribution was to begin the education of a hostile public. Among her private papers there survives a sad and eloquent testimony to her difficulties in establishing suffragism at Toulouse. It is the receipt book recording the subscriptions that she sold to her short-lived *Combat féministe*. Including the subscriptions of Parisian militants, Arria Ly circulated her ideas to forty-four regular readers.[48]

The Dussaussoy Bill of 1906 and the Political Realities of the Suffrage Campaign

French suffragists were becoming optimistic by 1906-1907. In addition to the conversion of moderates and the interest of some Catholics, politicians seemed to be responding. In 1906, a new suffrage bill, the Dussaussoy Bill, was introduced in the Chamber of Deputies, and Henri Chéron (republican, Calvados) reorganized the group of deputies for women's rights. In 1907, the *conseil général* of the Seine adopted a motion, based on an Auclert petition, calling on the chamber to pass women's suffrage. Other feminist bills were succeeding, notably the "Schmahl Law" of 1907 which gave married women control of their earnings. Women were obtaining the right to vote in professional situations, culminating with their franchise for the trade arbitrators (*conseils des prud'hommes*) in 1907. Was this evidence that women's suffrage was at hand? Feminists thought so.

The Dussaussoy Bill illustrated the classic political tactic of taking a step backward in order to proceed forward. It was the work of Paul Dussaussoy (Action libérale, Pas-de-Calais), the scion of a family of wealthy industrialists which had produced two other deputies since the July Monarchy. Dussaussoy was a conservative republican whose principal parliamentary interest was financial affairs, but who had introduced other electoral reforms. He proposed to limit women's participation to local and regional elections, in contrast to Gautret's provision for parliamentary suffrage, because he believed that France was prepared to accept the former but not the latter. "The state of our manners and institutions does not currently seem to permit us to confer full political rights on women," he candidly told the chamber in introducing the bill. On the other hand, he believed that all women deserved political rights and that Gautret had erred in limiting them to certain groups of women. Although the feminist left disliked the deletion of the parliamentary franchise, most suffragists felt Dussaussoy's proposition made "perfect good sense." Their optimism grew when the Commission of Universal Suffrage named Ferdinand Buisson (Radical-Socialist, Seine) as the reporter for the bill; Buisson had feminist sympathies dating back to youthful association with Léon Richer.[49]

Similar optimism attended the apparent invigoration of the Groupe parlementaire de défense des droits de la femme which, it was hoped, would lobby for the formal debate of the Dussaussoy Bill. Such a grouping of supportive deputies had existed sporadically in each legislature since 1895, when it had reached a size of thirty-six members but contributed little to feminist legislation. Chéron reestablished the group for the legislature of 1906-1910 with a flourish of publicity in July 1906, describing their renewed commitment in an article in *Le Matin*. Previous efforts were "insufficient," making French legislation "quite behind," he wrote. "Can anyone reasonably explain how women, who must obey all of our laws, remain foreign to any control over the acts that bind them or affect their wealth?"[50] The new group had an initial membership of 96 and quickly grew to over 200 in a chamber of 586. In addition to Beauquier and Chéron, it included such prominent figures as Viviani, Buisson, Caillaux, Siegfried, Joseph Reinach, Camille Pelletan (Radical-Socialist, Bouches-du-Rhone), Paul Deschanel (republican, Eure-et-Loire), and Adolphe Messimy (Radical, Seine). Not only was nearly half of the Chamber of Deputies on record as sympathetic to feminism, but nearly half of the Clemenceau cabinet of 1906-1909 as well.[51] It was a long distance from vague sympathies to active support, but in 1906-1907 this seemed to be immense progress.

A third source of suffragist optimism was the most dramatic success of Auclert's twenty-nine years of petitioning. She originally asked the *conseil général* of the Seine to endorse women's suffrage in 1886, receiving for her effort scorn, clichés, and eleven votes. Twenty years and innumerable petitions later, she submitted another appeal calling for them to support the Dussaussoy Bill. The council debated this request in November 1907, following a favorable report by the Comte d'Aulan. While suffragists watched, d'Aulan concluded, "I believe that women, who manage the interests of property, industry, and commerce, have the right to give their opinion on the fashion in which we manage the city and the department." He could not resist adding the opinion that "the fair sex ought not to get mixed up in political struggles," but he led the motion to a surprising, unanimous adoption. Suffragists were so pleased that some became skeptical: Were the councilors actually snickering at Auclert?[52]

Parliament had also shown itself more sensitive to feminist appeals. In 1904, divorced women obtained the right to marry their adulterous lovers; in 1905, *juges de paix* received the power to limit the authority of a husband in marital disputes; in 1906, remarried women received some rights over their children by previous marriages; in 1907, women acquired the right to be named the legal guardians of their illegitimate children; and in 1907-1908, liberalizations of the divorce statutes gave women further rights over their children and made the dissolution of marriages easier. These small successes for the women's rights movement built confidence in parliament; when the married women's earnings bill became law in July 1907, confidence became optimism. The earnings law, known as the Schmahl Law, had been the most ardently sought feminist reform of the Civil Code after the reinstitution of divorce in 1884. It had assumed especial importance as a contrast between the status of women in France and other countries. American feminists had won a landmark Married Woman's Property Law in New York as early as 1848. English women won their first act in 1857 and a complete Married Women's Property Act in 1882. By the end of the century, representative governments from New Zealand (1860 and 1870) to Iceland (1899) had followed suit. France was not alone in resisting such legislation—Germany and all of Catholic Europe had none—but France was among the last Western societies to consider it. The Chamber of Deputies first passed a property bill in 1896, but a hostile Senate reporter for the bill, Théodore Cazot (a life senator born in 1821), almost single-handedly blocked it for a decade by refusing to deliver his report; the commission supported his obstinance by repeatedly adjourning all votes on the bill. Conservative opinion acclaimed this defeat as the defense of the family, fearing the effects of greater financial independence for women. The feminist campaign for an earnings bill thus produced an unusual feminist-radical alliance. Jeanne Schmahl finally won enough backing from republicans in 1907, when radical backing in the Senate, supported by Gustave Rivet on the front page of *Le Radical*, carried the day.[53]

Another source of suffragist optimism was the progress women were making in winning the vote in professional capacities and acceptance in some posts in the bureaucracy. Teachers had won limited enfranchisement during the educational reforms of the 1880s; a series of laws between 1901 and 1905 required two women on each department's primary education council and opened the *conseil supérieur* to them. In the decade between 1898 and 1908 women won such equality in almost all occupations. Tradeswomen won the right to vote for the merchant-judges of the *tribunaux de commerce*, businesswomen for *chambres de commerce*. Working class women won similar rights in the councils and superior council of labor. The most ardently sought professional vote for working-class women, for the *conseils des prud'hommes*, came in 1907, marked by exuberant feminist celebration. Was parliament recognizing women's political capacity?[54]

All of this evidence notwithstanding, there was no realistic possibility that the ninth legislature (1906-1910) would adopt women's suffrage. Indeed, there were compelling political reasons to doubt that the legislature to be elected in 1910 would do so. The Radical and Radical-Socialist Party, without whose support no government could stand and virtually no legislation be passed, remained fundamentally hostile to women's political rights. The SFIO, the only party willing to endorse the reform, did nothing to secure its passage. Given the nature of the French parliamentary committee system, it was imperative that a majority of the Commission of Universal Suffrage press for a suffrage bill, and that was highly unlikely in the near future. Finally, should some remarkable about-face conduct the Dussaussoy Bill through the Chamber of Deputies it would still have to pass the Senate, a conservative graveyard for feminist reforms.

The simplest reason why French women would not vote in 1910, and probably not in 1914, was the position of the Radical Party. It has been seen that their opposition to women's suffrage derived from the core of the party's ideology: women presented a clerical peril that threatened the republic. At the pragmatic level of politics, this was a peril of self-interest: if women did vote for the church, they might not destroy the republic but they would certainly return a lot of radical deputies to private life. The party was at its apogee during the ninth legislature, controlling 46 percent of all seats, one of the greatest pluralities in the history of the Third Republic. All three cabinets during this legislature were sustained by radical votes. During most of that term, it was Clemenceau's first government (October 1906-July 1909), and Clemenceau so opposed women's suffrage that there was no chance that his government would support such legislation.

Clemenceau illustrates the obstacles confronting suffragists and the dilemma facing radicals. He was imbued with the radical commitment to democracy; he believed that "The principle of universal suffrage does not permit any compromise; it gives the same right to the learned and the ignorant, and it gives it by virtue of natural right."[55] His declaration of policy at investiture has justly been labeled as the most advanced manifesto put forward by any incoming French government prior to Léon Blum's declaration of 1936.[56] Clemenceau also gave evidence of sympathy to feminism. While premier, he published a pamphlet proclaiming the absolute equality of men and women and the need "to institute the rights of the woman and give her the means to defend them."[57]

Such fine words obscured a dilemma with no apparent resolution: how could radicals reconcile their fear of clericalism with their feminist intentions? Most resolved this *crise de conscience* by concluding that clericalism presented the immediate problem and therefore feminism, whatever its intrinsic desirability, must be generally postponed. The problem ran deeper, however, because the party contained another major element that did not perceive this dilemma, a large group of radicals who did not accept feminism as a desirable objective even ultimately. The party, founded in 1901, was yet an infant when Clemenceau came to office. It had remarkably little central organization and was actually an alliance of local federations which exercised great influence in shaping the party and directing parliamentary behavior. These federations represented local interests and were more sensitive to provincial sentiment than to Parisian theory. Their electoral strength existed in provincial towns, especially among the petite bourgeoisie. From this source, French radicals drew deep draughts of social conservatism, long before this characteristic of the party became palpable in the later years of the Third Republic. Just as he eloquently expressed democratic radicalism, Clemenceau partook of the deeper instincts of many of his colleagues. He believed that women were the weaker sex, needing paternalistic protection. At times he acted with blatant prejudice—once admitting that he would have made a different administrative decision if the people involved had been men instead of women.[58] He did not deny his doubts about women: "Where I would terribly dread a woman, I admit it, would be on the judge's bench." And Clemenceau consigned political equality to some distant time when women were adequately prepared for it. On this point the great radical was adamant. Women might vote "one day, when they are rid of their atavistic prejudices." In the meantime, "The number of those who escape from the domination of the clergy is ridiculously low. If the right to vote were given to women tomorrow, France would all of a sudden jump backwards into the Middle Ages."[59] Ipso facto, Clemenceau was a formidable obstacle to woman's suffrage.

The radical amalgam of small-town conservatism and republican progress produced an ambivalent feminism. The party supported some specific reforms sought by the women's movement and endorsed the theory of eventual equality but stood firmly opposed to enfranchisement. Radicalism was large enough to accommodate a few suffragists (such as Buisson, Georges Martin, and Louis Andrieux) and several feminists (such as Beauquier, Godart, and Le Foyer), but it could not find a compromise with the women's movement. The fear of a priest-ridden female electorate need not have applied to female candidates sent to the Palais Bourbon by the existing masculine universal suffrage; nor would women have posed a great threat to the republic by voting in municipal elections. The Radical and Radical-Socialist Party, however, was unwilling to admit women to membership, although those who would have sought it could hardly be accused of being prisoners of the confessional.

The radical congresses revealed the party's ambivalence. They also demonstrated that no radical-dominated Chamber of Deputies would adopt women's suffrage. The first party congress, at Paris in 1901, killed the issue in a subcommittee which reported that "it is not possible to permit [women] to participate in the great works of social emanicaption."[60] Municipal suffrage, raised from the floor by Georges Martin, was overwhelmingly rejected. Auclert never abandoned her hope that radicals would accept full democracy and repeatedly petitioned the party; the congresses regularly spurned her. The program of the Nancy congress of 1907—arguably the cardinal document of prewar radicalism—is a dramatic illustration. The delegates considered her petition and responded with a program stating the intention "to revise the constitution in the most democratic sense possible" (Article 1) and proclaiming "the sovereignty of universal suffrage" (Article 2). The executive committee, however, refused to put women's suffrage on the agenda for debate. One motion called for "the gradual extension of the rights of women" but added the paternalistic qualification that "women must be protected by the law in all the circumstances of life."[61] Subsequent congresses concluded that this had settled the issue.

The effects of radical attitudes may be seen in the working of the Commission on Universal Suffrage. The ninth legislature doubled the size of the committee to twenty-two members, and dominance passed to moderate republicans. Suffragist confidence rose with election of Charles Benoist (republican, Seine) as the president and Buisson as the reporter for women's suffrage. It was a naive optimism. A majority of the committee endorsed women's suffrage, but they attached a very low priority to it. In July 1906, they postponed the question sine die to pursue a different electoral reform, proportional representation. The introduction of *"Le RP"* promised to provoke a huge battle in French politics; it was, in fact, not adopted until 1919. The committee considered women's suffrage too controversial to raise at the same time as proportional representation, fearing that any linkage might defeat *RP*. Women must wait. In fact, the committee's agenda listed the Dussaussoy Bill as waiting until resolution of the secret vote, voting by mail, and the system of elections (*scrutin de liste* versus *scrutin d'arrondissement*). Suffragists waited with high hopes, little knowing how negligible the attention their bill received. They knew that Buisson was preparing a favorable report; they did not know that the minutes of the commission showed scarcely a single discussion of women's suffrage in the years 1906-1908, except to note the regular arrival of new petitions from Auclert. The Dussaussoy Bill remained buried, almost as forgotten as the de Gasté or Gautret bills.[62]

Chapter Four

The Turning Point for Suffragist Tactics, 1908-1910

At the beginning of 1908 the prospects for unity within bourgeois suffragism seemed poor. Since 1904 the feminist left had called for an activism that offended moderates. Auclert had foreshadowed greater militancy following the 1906 elections when she asked if propoganda "of the deed" might not be necessary. She returned to that theme in the spring of 1908. In an angry article in *Le Radical*, she attacked parliament for not examining the petitions it received or debating the bills proposed. Auclert bluntly raised the prospect of violence: "For women to obtain the vote in France, are they going to be obliged to knock down the urns that contain only male votes?"[1] A few days later, during the Paris municipal elections of 1908, Auclert committed the first act of violence in the name of French suffragism. The suffragist response showed how far away unity remained: Auclert's behavior was overwhelmingly rejected in favor of a strategy of legalism. After 1908, those who could not stay within the laws could not stay within the movement. Unity came at the expense of the defeat of the most advanced militants.

Suffragists first became involved in the elections of 1908 through the candidacy of Jeanne Laloë, a young reporter for *Le Matin* who had not been active in any feminist organization. Accounts of the origins of her race differ, but it apparently started with an editorial meeting at *Le Matin* concerning the coverage of uninteresting elections.[2] Laloë volunteered to be a candidate and the editors decided to support her in an effort to enliven the elections. A press gimmick or not, Laloë's campaign became a feminist offensive and the candidate met with Maria Vérone for legal advice. Vérone urged her to run as a serious candidate, insisting (as Vincent had in 1893) that the Municipal Elections Law of 1884 contained no text directly excluding women from presenting their candidacy. Through Vérone's tenacity and knowledge of the law, Laloë obtained a school hall for an electoral meeting—the first time a woman had received such official recognition. Newspaper publicity and feminist support attracted more than two thousand people, including twenty press photographers, to that meeting. Militant suffragists, however, were disturbed by the "frivolous appearance" that *Le Matin* gave to women's rights. Auclert and Pelletier attended to speak on Laloë's behalf, but they were distressed by the results. The crowd was full of hecklers who interrupted their speeches with calls to see the pretty candidate; they greeted Laloë with questions such as "Are you going to talk about hats?" The meeting might have led to collaboration between moderate and militant suffragists on Laloë's behalf. It had the opposite result. Auclert and Pelletier concluded that such efforts would accomplish nothing, an opinion that Auclert immediately expressed in an article calling for more activism.[3]

Dissatisfied militants met on election day to organize a demonstration. Approximately fifty to one hundred members of Suffrage des femmes and Solidarité agreed to march to polling places on the right bank, but when Auclert proposed taking forceful action, such as breaking into the polls, many quit. Pelletier and Kauffmann joined her in storming into one voting hall, where they shouted "Long live the rights of women! We want to vote!" Auclert grabbed the voting urn, precipitating a scuffle in which officials tore it from her hands. Police expelled the demonstrators without making any arrests but followed the marchers to other polls. In the Ninth Arrondissement Laloë pleaded with the feminists not to try to enter. This dispiriting plea angered Auclert, who evaded the police and succeeded in entering two other polls. At one, she and Kauffmann discussed destroying the ballots with acid. At the other, in the town hall of the Fourth Arrondissement, Auclert smashed an urn to the ground, broke it open, and trampled on the ballots in front of scandalized poll workers. She was arrested and formal charges filed against her, but the police only detained her for the remaining few hours that the polls were open. The first result of Auclert's demonstration came that night. The Clemenceau government called out large numbers of police to guard the polls during the counting of the ballots. A force of twenty policemen barred the entry to Laloë and Vérone, despite their protests that this was illegal. When they persisted in agruing, reinforcements were ordered.[4]

French suffragism had reached a decisive moment. Would suffragists rally to support their great pioneer and endorse her angry action? Would Vérone, an adamant and influential leader poised between the militants and the moderates, react to the illegality or to the use of police force? Might others follow Auclert's example and commit small acts of violence against property? Auclert was hopeful. "I am enchanted," she told a reporter. "I have held an urn, that urn of lies which is an outrage to the equality of the sexes." The resort to violence was logical, she continued: "We have not obtained the vote by legal means, so we are taking revolutionary means; we shall obtain by noise and force that which has been refused, in spite of all justice and legality, to sweetness and reasoning."[5]

At the very moment she was talking to the press, French feminists were starting to turn against her. With very few exceptions, the entire suffrage movement soon opposed what she had done.[6] Laloë's success in the voting encouraged that reaction. It is impossible to know her precise count because the government issued instructions that "All ballots bearing the name of a woman must be considered as blank." Her probable total was 987, or 22 percent of the total votes cast.[7] Most feminists interpreted this as a great victory for the strategy of seeking enfranchisement by legal means; Vérone filed suit over the counting of the ballots and the denial of access to the polls; justice would come through the laws. There was no reason to risk the dangers of Auclert's behavior.

Exactly one suffragist emulated Auclert. Pelletier summoned the members of Solidarité to discuss a resumption of violence during the runoff elections scheduled for the following weekend. Just a few days before the elections, Pelletier had published a timely article on feminist tactics in the *Revue socialiste*. When suffragists encountered opposition, she argued, they must resolve to push with even more ardor. Pelletier thus proposed another march to the polls to seek admission; if denied, they would smash windows. Even the militants of Solidarité opposed such violence. Three-fourths of the group refused to march and the remainder agreed to go but not to throw stones. Indeed, the members of the most militant suffrage society in France tried to persuade Pelletier not to make her demonstration. After all, one of them said, she "could wound the electors." Pelletier, who believed that "if damage is necessary, one resigns oneself to it in advance," went through with her plans. She led a small protest on the left bank; denied entry to a poll, she threw stones through the window and was arrested.[8]

The reaction of feminists and the press was to praise Laloë and ignore Auclert and Pelletier. Even the *Journal des femmes* hailed the Laloë-Vérone effort as "the harbinger of definitive victory." On the day after the election, the candidate was the toast of a large feminist meeting arranged by the LFDF. Laloë stressed that she had intentionally limited her campaign to "the legal means at [my] disposal," winning the enthusiastic applause of the suffragists. The Parisian press sang the praises of the moderates who rejected an "imitation of the suffragettes of London." And Laloë, who chose not to remain active in the women's movement, immediately entered its hagiography as a model for the triumph of legalism.[9]

The response of the Clemenceau government was firm, yet judicious. Vérone's suit was quickly dismissed, but the trials of Auclert and Pelletier were postponed until it was clear that they had no support among suffragists. The government apparently preferred to avoid creating new publicity or martyrs. The only charge brought against the demonstrators was "creating a disturbance in a public place." Auclert told the court that she had acted for the publicity value of the incidents, "to draw the attention of the public powers to the situation of women." She now doubted that such tactics would work and told the judge "it was a great pity that we used this violent method." Pelletier was not so penitent. She stated in court that she wanted to teach women "the A-B-C of revolt." Yet she too acknowledged the ineffectuality of her lesson: "the means used by British suffragettes seems to our militants the final unseemliness." Neither trial lasted a full day, nor made a ripple in the news. Both women received the minimal fine of sixteen francs and no attention from the feminist movement, which was largely enjoying the summer vacation at the time of the trials.[10]

By the summer of 1908, therefore, there was no question about the course of French suffragism. Aggressive militancy attracted no support. The legalistic approach seemed successful. *La Française*, the feminist newspaper with the largest circulation, underscored these conclusions:

We are absolutely opposed to the Englishwomen's method of making their claims. The method of violent public demonstrations, which they have adopted, and which are perhaps justified there, seem to us essentially incompatible with French style and would be injurious rather than useful to our cause here.[11]

The newspaper was not alone in heralding the triumph of legalism. Six weeks after the elections, the first national congress of French feminists in eight years took place at Paris. It produced the greatest unity French suffragists had yet known, predicated on a unanimous vow to repudiate violence as a method of claiming the vote.

The Congrès national des droits civils et du suffrage des femmes (June 26-28,1908) was the idea of an absent leader. Maria Pognon had written to leading feminists from her retirement in Sydney, Australia, urging them to hold another congress that would unite the factions that had met in separate congresses in 1900. Oddo-Deflou, who maintained good relations across the political spectrum, agreed. She persuaded Eliska Vincent to accept the presidency of an organizing committee and Marguerite Durand to join them in uniting bourgeois feminism. "The disparate trio" (as feminists called them) surprised themselves with their success. Their call for a congress stressed the need for a synthesis of feminist thought, for concentrating on a limited number of issues such as the vote, and for the adoption of a "program of action." They convinced Anna Feresse-Deraismes (then eighty-six) and Isabelle Bogelot (seventy) to share the honorary presidency of the congress, ensuring the participation of moderates from Amélioration and the CNFF. Almost the entire feminist movement followed. Vincent had difficulties persuading Suffrage des femmes and Solidarité to adhere to the aims of the congress, largely because Auclert and Pelletier felt estranged from other feminists by their militancy. Pelletier accepted her status as a pariah. "I know I am too advanced," she wrote to Arria Ly, "ever to find grace among the bourgeoisie; so much the worse for them."[12] Auclert, however, had demonstrated throughout her career an impressive pragmatism. She was also deeply affected by the response to her behavior. Two weeks after her arrest, a fortnight in which the disapprobation of her associates jarred her, Auclert wrote to Oddo-Deflou to say that she could not remain outside the congress. Pelletier remained uncompromising, and Solidarité did not join, but Auclert's adhesion signaled the success of the congress and the triumph of the moderates.[13]

The congress of 1908 voted to call for a huge list of feminist reforms in the Napoleonic Code. The agreement among the 800 participants was impressive. Not surprisingly, the effort to obtain a feminist synthesis produced an amalgam of the radical (divorce by consent), the conservative (automatic retention of French nationality by women who married foreigners), and the broadly feminist: abolition of the legal incapacity of married women (already before parliament in a Beauquier Bill), legalization of paternity suits (close to adoption as a Viviani Bill), endorsement of the right of women to serve on all juries, expanded rights of women as guardians, and the abrogation of Article 373 giving the husband virtually total power over children. On most issues there was surprisingly little dissent, but the congress was not without division. The absence of most Catholic and socialist groups made it easy to ignore conservative arguments about the family or the differing needs of women of the working class. After feminists had angered syndicalists by voting down three of their proposals, Vincent precipitated the biggest rift in the congress with a report on domestic servants. It was an echo of the congress of women's rights of 1900 when Pognon and Renaud had shouted across the chasm separating middle-class and working-class attitudes. Once again, bourgeois hostility to the prospect of a union for servants triumphed. The debate did not threaten the unity of the feminists attending the congress, but it showed the dim prospects of a broader unity including socialist women.[14]

The central concern of the congress was to develop a suffrage policy that all groups could accept, in order to bring the maximum pressure on the Chamber of Deputies to proceed with the Dussaussoy Bill. Seventeen different speakers gave reports on women's suffrage. Vincent and Léon Abensour (Clemenceau's secretary and an early historian of feminism) spoke on the history of women's political rights. Vincent later gave a second report, on the success of women's suffrage in professional organizations. Marya Chéliga, the founder and president of an organization to maintain links with the international feminist movement (Congrès permanent du féminisme international), provided a survey of women's rights in other countries. Three delegates from Britain discussed the suffragette movement there, with especial attention to the issues of unity, militant tactics, public opinion, and government policy. Oddo-Deflou expressed the new opinion of moderates that the ballot was essential in order to overcome the slow rate of progress in obtaining other reforms that they desired. Durand analyzed the argument that enfranchised women would vote as a reactionary bloc and insisted that women would never adhere to any single party. Ferdinand Buisson, Paul Deschanel, and Louis Marin (republican, Meurthe-et-Moselle) reported on suffragism in the Chamber of Deputies and Maurice Faure spoke on the prospects in the Senate. Marin, who was to become one of the leading parliamentary proponents of women's suffrage, gave an especially close analysis: suffragists should be optimistic that they could triumph in the near future, but be realistic in their evaluation of the present legislature which was not feminist. Maria Vérone studied the question of receiving political rights in stages and reported in favor of accepting municipal suffrage first.[15]

These speeches were all secondary in importance to that delivered by Hubertine Auclert. It must have been a painfully difficult moment for the proud and imperious Auclert. She had to choose between defending her activism—thereby threatening the ability of the congress to advance the reform she held dear—or making some sort of public recantation. If she retreated, she would do so before an audience of women who had opposed suffragism for most of their lives, who had rejected her leadership, and who now presumed to speak for the movement she had founded. Auclert chose to abandon violence as a tactic, but she said *nolo contendere* rather than *mea culpa*. It was a brave and rousing speech that marked both the triumph of moderate legalism and the twilight of a career.

Auclert began her address by reviewing the tactics of the movement. "For a long time," she said, "we have limited ourselves to completely legal demonstrations, we have said it was necessary to act like men." But her legal efforts of thirty years, she reminded the audience, had produced nothing but frustrations. The Chamber of Deputies had ignored her dozens of petitions ("they are put in the wastebasket") and even the motion of the *conseil général* ("they cannot hear out of that ear"). Auclert then explained how she had concluded that if suffragists were going "to act like men" they should admit that "to obtain the vote men built barricades." This led to the violence of May. The militants who acted were "very determined women," she told the audience pointedly, but "unfortunately [they were] not numerous enough." Auclert then related the details of protest, arrest, and trial. Although some delegates applauded her description of smashing an urn, she repeated her apology to the court: "It was a great pity that we used this violent method." Moreover, Auclert admitted, violence had not worked. Too few women had followed her, too little publicity was received, and "having done all that" militants still could not get "our legislators to deign to pay attention to our interests." Auclert therefore told the congress that she proposed to return to legal tactics. Her vigorous imagination already had produced a new idea for doing so. French electoral law required a minimum population of 100,000 for the constituency of each deputy. Since the courts had ruled that a woman was not a *citoyen* in electoral laws, women should not be counted in determining electoral districts and the total number of seats in the chamber should accordingly be reduced by more than 50 percent. Perhaps deputies would pay attention to women when they saw something "linking their interests with ours."[16]

The congress greeted Auclert's speech with great relief, according her one of the few standing ovations of her life. Her new proposal received a unanimous endorsement without debate. And the brief moment of French suffragette violence was at an end. In their most momentous decision of the meeting, French suffragists voted explicitly to renounce violence as a means of seeking their goal.[17] On that basis, the delegates forged a compromise program: they would seek complete political equality as an ultimate goal, but concentrate on municipal suffrage as a practical first step. To that end, they called upon Buisson (in his presence) to deposit a favorable report on the Dussaussoy Bill without delay and upon the members of the parliamentary group for women's rights (many of whom were also present) to obtain a prompt debate of the bill. There was widespread optimism that success was now possible.

That rejection of violence remained a permanent characteristic of the French suffrage campaign, although the question was again opened in frustration after World War I. Auclert did not experience a personality change, nor renounce militancy; she simply abandoned violence as a solution, a decision she maintained for the balance of her life. It was a pragmatic decision. As Auclert told an interviewer a few months before her death in 1914, English style suffragette violence "would not have any success in France. We will arrive at our destination by mildness, by persuasion, by goodness. French women loathe to shed blood. But their faith is no less solid."[18] This became the credo of French suffragism. As Parrhisia worded it on another occasion, "The rights of man have triumphed by revolution. The superiority of feminism will be to secure the rights of woman by evolution, without appeal to brute force."[19] Subsequent congresses reiterated the vow of 1908. When the example of suffragette violence in England increasingly shaped French journalistic opinion about the women's rights movement, French women added regular vows to "disassociate themselves from their [Englishwomen's] violent methods."[20]

In the summer of 1908, while the French suffragists were preparing for their national congress, the moderate British suffragists of Millicent Fawcett's National Union of Women's Suffrage Societies organized the greatest public demonstration in the history of suffragism: a huge parade to Hyde Park culminating in a rally attended by a throng so immense that estimates of its size ranged up to 500,000. That parade capped a year in which British moderates had put 1,500 women into the streets of Edinburgh, 2,000 into a parade in Manchester, and thousands in various marches in London.[21] French suffragists found such activities utterly unacceptable for themselves. They were not alone, of course; Anita Augspurg, a leader of German suffragism, participated in the Hyde Park demonstration but wrote from London: "What is known here as moderate would still be the summit of outrageousness in Germany."[22] Fawcett invited the French to participate in the Hyde Park demonstration. They declined. The English suggested a simultaneous rally of all French suffragists at the Bois de Boulogne. That, too, was inconvenient. The French wanted to maintain an unmistakable distance from their notorious sisters. This policy became especially clear during Christabel Pankhurst's exile in Paris: French suffragists virtually ignored her presence, paying far less attention to her than the French police did. Pankhurst held a reciprocal attitude, as she later told a Parisian newspaper: French suffragists "do much good, I know, but I do not believe that they will ever create a great movement."[23] As Oddo-Deflou told the 1908 congress, "other countries, other manners."[24]

The Feminist Center and the Foundation of the UFSF

One of the most palpable signs of the triumph of moderation in the French suffrage movement was the emergence of a new newspaper, *La Française*, as the voice of bourgeois feminism. *La Fronde* disappeared in 1905 (merging with *L'Action*) after seven years of losing money, leaving the movement without a high circulation periodical that linked the factions. Vérone (*Le Droit des femmes*), Martin (*Le Journal des femmes*), Pelletier (*La Suffragiste*), and Héra Mirtel (*L'Entente*) could not fill the gap. In addition to limited ideological appeal, each faced such precarious financing that it was a struggle to maintain even monthly publication. Instead, it was Jane Misme who succeeded in establishing a general circulation feminist newspaper, with the appearance of *La Française* in late 1906. Misme (1865-1935) had begun a career in journalism with *Le Figaro* and *Le Matin* in the 1890s before Durand hired her as the drama critic for *La Fronde*. She was one of the first members of Avant-courrière, and Schmahl shaped her cautious feminism. Misme stayed with *L'Action* briefly when it absorbed *La Fronde* but soon opted to try to succeed Durand in publishing the official organ of French feminism. She began by organizing a discussion circle, largely drawn from the literary and artistic world—members financially able to help underwrite a newspaper. The feminism of the *cercle* was extremely moderate, and Misme made sure that it was scrupulously nonpartisan in questions of religion or national politics. Her contacts from Avant-courrière and her career as a drama critic, combined with this caution, enabled Misme to attract a remarkable membership which included the extremely wealthy Duchesse d'Uzès, the Duchesse de Rohan (the president of the group), and two countesses. Their contributions, plus the assistance of the Siegfrieds, who arranged the legal work for the newspaper, were sufficient to start publishing in 1906. After first preparing the feminist movement by the imaginative ploy of a "spoken newspaper" that delivered reports to all groups about the meetings of each of them, *La Française* appeared in October 1906.[25]

Misme tried to address the entire republican feminist movement but spoke for its conservative wing. It was a well-matched union when *La Française* became the official organ of the CNFF in 1921. Misme usually espoused reforms for which there was general feminist support, such as *recherche paternité*, and the campaigns of the social feminists. *La Française*, therefore, devoted considerable space to alcoholism, depopulation, prostitution, and pornography, plus retaining Misme's interest in the theater and cultural events. Catholics criticized the newspaper as dominated by freethinkers and some feminists complained that it gave little attention to advanced ideas, but *La Française* achieved a broader readership than the sectarian publications that characterized the feminist movement. It suffered their financial problems—losing 3,000 francs per year—but its breadth of support enabled it to survive periodic exigencies.

Misme and *La Française* were slow to call for political rights. As she later admitted, women's suffrage still seemed "terribly subversive" to many of her supporters in 1906. She preferred to build a large readership, educate them about political rights, and work for the vote later. *La Française* published an article sympathetic to suffragism as early as December 1906, reported the activities of suffragists, studied women's suffrage abroad, and surveyed the opinions of its readers on enfranchisement, but refrained from becoming an active participant in the May 1908 elections. When Misme subsequently became a suffragist, *La Française* emphatically stressed legalism. She did not hesitate to criticize Auclert or the English suffragettes, nor to insist that women act with the "innate caution of the French temperament." Yet despite such hesitancy, Misme and *La Française* played an instrumental role in the expansion of French suffragism—at the foundation of the Union française pour le suffrage des femmes (hereafter, UFSF).[26]

The origins of the UFSF date from the national congress of 1908 when suffragists discussed the continued absence of France from the International Woman Suffrage Alliance which was then preparing for its quinquennial assembly to be held in London in May 1909. After Auclert's quarrel with Catt at Berlin in 1904, no French group had sought affiliation in 1908. Jeanne Schmahl now took the lead. When she won her two-decade battle for a married women's earnings law in 1907, Schmahl dissolved Avant-courrière because it had fulfilled its purpose. The years of frustration leading to that reform convinced her that women must vote in order to facilitate the reforms they desired; Avant-courrière was not the best vehicle for reaching that goal, so Schmahl decided to create another. She was impressed by the IWSA's insistence upon making suffragism a non-partisan coalition which avoided extraneous political and religious stands. Avant-courrière had been such an organization, enabling her to attract members such as d'Uzès. French suffrage leagues, however, were all particularistic groups that could not embrace diversity nor hope to be truly national in scope. Schmahl envisioned a group that could accommodate women as different as d'Uzès, Siegfried, Vincent, and Auclert. This corresponded exactly with the editorial tone that Misme sought for *La Française*, and she gave her wholehearted support to her mentor's initiative. In January 1909, Misme introduced Schmahl as a columnist for *La Française* with the first of a series of articles outlining her theories, entitled *"Propos d'une Suffragiste."* The political rights of women, according to Misme's introduction, posed a question "so delicate" that a national movement had awaited both the right moment and the right leader: the congress of 1908 indicated the former, Schmahl was the latter.[27]

Schmahl's essays of early 1909 are among the foremost documents of French suffragism. With clarity and precision she summarized the movement. She first discussed the conversion of feminists to suffragism in recent years and the conclusion that she now shared with other moderates: "it is only by women's suffrage that we can succeed."[28] Subsequent articles discussed reasons why women wanted to vote and rebutted arguments against their doing so. The most important essays discussed the campaign to win that right. Schmahl identified and evaluated three different groups of women, labeling them the suffragists, the suffragettes, and the anti-suffragists. The suffragist and her strategy were "essentially bourgeois," characterized by patient legalism:

> [The suffragist] will seek by personal *démarches*, by patient proofs, and by persuasion, to make her cause triumphant with the competent powers. She will instinctively avoid everything that could shock or hurt those whom she hopes to win.[29]

The suffragette, in contrast, eschewed this middle-class caution, employing extreme and anti-social methods of claiming her rights. She was essentially proletarian in her attitudes, lacking the education of the "civilized" suffragist. One might praise the suffragette for her devotion to women's rights, but one could never approve of her behavior.[30] The anti-suffragist, according to Schmahl, was essentially an upper-class woman, unable to sympathize with either sort of feminist. She did not care for the vote because she did not understand any need to improve her life of idle comfort:

> [The anti-suffragist is], in general, neither a simple, active, moderate bourgeois like the suffragist; nor a working, expansive, energetic proletarian like the suffragette; on the contrary, she is ordinarily an idle person, sheltered by her situation from the pains of combat in life.[31]

Schmahl had drawn the lines with precision, albeit with some prejudice drawn from her own situation in life. There was no question where she and Misme stood. The French suffrage movement must be the work of the "active, moderate bourgeois." The national suffrage league that they would create to join the IWSA would fit that definition.

Three hundred women responded to Schmahl's summons to organize a national union in February 1909. Republican feminists from the CNFF to Egalité participated, leaving only the most militant suffragists outside. To neither the surprise nor the disappointment of Schmahl and Misme, Pelletier refused to join, as she would any grouping so profoundly bourgeois and unsympathetic to working women. Schmahl tried to woo Auclert, offering her the leadership of the federation. Auclert declined. She had gone to Canossa, but she would not take up residence there. She could not be what Schmahl and Misme had defined as the polite, patient suffragist of the future; she would not submit herself totally to the women who had denied her for years. The lesson of her presidency of the CNFF's suffrage section was sufficient. Auclert encouraged Schmahl, endorsed the union, and wrote a letter to be read at the organizational meeting, but she would go no further. She tactfully cited her age and her health to explain her refusal. Schmahl, herself a dominant personality accustomed to leading, and Misme, who never reconciled herself to Auclert's behavior, did not try to persuade Auclert to accept an honorary presidency.[32]

From its inception the UFSF represented the triumph of the feminist center. The cautious suffragists of the CNFF—Siegfried, Sainte-Croix, and even Monod—joined the union and endorsed it to the members of the national council. Other moderates followed. Vincent, who had frequently aligned herself with moderates since 1906, gave her strong support, as did the leaders of the LFDF. Thus, the UFSF could claim to be a national union that embraced the feminist left as well as the center. Schmahl, who had won the admiration of some Catholics for her work through Avant-courrière, even dreamt of the day when the union's non-partisanship could produce a rapprochement with right-wing feminists. To underscore the appeal to unity, Schmahl persuaded d'Uzès to join her in the leadership of the UFSF, and Misme proudly advertised their success at Nice in "cornering the clerical and royalist party." The initial leadership of the UFSF was symbolized by the election of two vice-presidents, one a duchess (d'Uzès) and the other the president of a women's trade union (Mme. Blanche-Schweig of the cashiers' union). Schmahl was unanimously chosen as president with Misme as her secretary-general, a position intended to be the president's amanuensis. In addition, the executive committee included Vincent and representatives of the LFDF, the UFF, and the CNFF.[33]

The statutes of the UFSF are eloquent testimony to the character of French suffragism. They were consistent with Schmahl's *modus operandi*, explicitly stating that suffrage was the sole aim of the union—a regulation often broken in the future. Several articles stressed the methods by which the UFSF would seek the vote, with emphasis upon establishing sections of the union in all departments of France. The statutes stressed moderate forms of propaganda (publications, posters, lectures) but acknowledged the possibility of demonstrations in the streets. Members were explicitly pledged to do nothing "of a nature to disturb the order nor to disturb anyone's legitimate suscep-tibility." They also had to keep "a general manner, in all forms of action, favorable to the cause," and by their example "prepare women to fulfill with dignity their duties."[34]

Schmahl's organizational efforts succeeded. The UFSF followed her non-partisan, non-sectarian formula (within the implied context of accepting the bourgeois republic) and grew rapidly. Within a year it was the largest suffrage organization in France (over a thousand members) and had attracted several wealthy supporters who joined as "founding members" (at a minimum contribution of 500 francs). This device permitted well-to-do women to support suffragism with-out participating in meetings or demonstrations—a category of "hon-orary suffragists" which included the wives of prominent politicians, scholars, and celebrities. Schmahl and Misme had equal success at the congress of the IWSA at London in April 1909, where the two-month-old union was accepted into the international alliance, which now numbered twenty-one countries.[35]

Bourgeois *Mentalitiés* and the Triumph of Legalism

What explains the complete victory of moderation and legalism in French suffragism in 1908-1909? Given the French revolutionary tra-dition, esteemed as the source of *liberté* and *égalité*; given the role of women in revolutionary violence from the bread rioters of 1789 to the *petroleuses* of 1871; given the acceptance of forceful collective action by non-feminist women of the Third Republic, such as the wine-growers' unrest of 1907 or the food price demonstrations of 1911; given the lesson of how men obtained universal suffrage in 1848; and given the contemporary example of the English suffragettes (whose window-smashing campaign began in June 1909), why did French suffragists define their strategy within such cautious limits?

The best answer to this question is found in the domination of the movement by women of the liberal middle classes and in several associated factors.[36] French suffragists shared similar backgrounds and the collective attitudes and values that accompanied them. Late nineteenth-century bourgeois *mentalités* predisposed them to gradual, lawful solutions and made them abhor violence (and many lesser forms of collective action) per se. These leaders then imposed compatible attitudes on their organizations, as illustrated by the statutes of the UFSF. Suffragist homogeneity tolerated latitude in ideas but not in behavior. Transgressions against the shared standard of "dignified means" meant ostracism, as befell Madeleine Pelletier.

The social origins of the suffragist leadership have been seen above. Although the middle-class identity of some suffragists was marginal (perhaps accentuating their attachment to bourgeois attitudes) few leaders came from completely outside the bourgeoisie. D'Uzès, the only great aristocrat prominent in suffragism, was a woman whose general behavior was quite atypical of her class; her noble friends were in the LPF and the LFF. No peasant women and surprisingly few working-class women worked for political rights. Politically active proletarian women preferred socialist organizations such as the GFS or worked in the syndicalist movement. There is little evidence that women of the small villages and countryside joined any political groups, excepting such Catholic and syndicalist organizations.

The few women from working-class backgrounds who became leading suffragists generally experienced embourgeoisement. Eliska Vincent, Marie Bonnevial, Madeleine Pelletier, Blanche Cremnitz, and Lydie Martial were daughters of the laboring class. Vincent and Martial married moderate wealth: by the early twentieth century Vincent was a prosperous landowner, while Martial's husband financed her periodical, *L'Heure de la femme*. Cremnitz's father rose to a managerial position and a life of middle-class values. Bonnevial returned from her exile to a life of respectability. Only Pelletier tried to maintain a working-class identity, but that was as ideological triumph over her middle-class education, her middle-class profession, and her two residences. And Pelletier, it must be remembered, was the great pariah of the movement. The general pattern was clear by 1908; daughters of workers among the suffragist leadership got there by entering the middle class. Some remained eloquent defenders of working-class women, speaking as Vincent did at the national congress of 1908. But they had adopted the general values and attitudes of the bourgeoisie, as Vincent showed in her break with militant behavior. The marginality of their social position probably increased their commitment to respectable behavior more than it challenged that standard.

Wealthy women of the upper-middle class far outnumbered the few women of aristocratic or working-class origins in the suffragist leadership. Most of this wealth was concentrated in the CNFF, prompting Héra Mirtel's remark about the density of millionaires there. Several other suffragists, notably Auclert and Mme. Remember (an editor of *La Suffragiste*), lived on inherited *rentes*. Durand, whatever the source of her wealth, personally financed a daily newspaper for six years. Cécile Brunschwicg (who succeeded Schmahl as the head of the UFSF) was the daughter of Arthur Kahn, a prosperous Alsatian industrialist. Many of these women were themselves in a marginal position in French society because they belonged to religious minorities, prompting Pettelier's remark about a "Judeo-Protestant coterie."

The largest group of suffragist leaders came from the liberal professions. By birth, marriage, and their own careers, their world was filled with lawyers, journalists, physicians, artists, professors, novelists, Protestant clergy, and teachers. Consider, for example, the LFDF in 1908-1914; the president was a teacher (Bonnevial), the secretary-general a lawyer (Vérone), the vice-presidents a lawyer (Lhermite) and a doctor (Edwards-Pilliet); the executive committee included two other lawyers. The quartet who dominated the CNFF at that time were the wife of an attorney (Bogelot), two daughters of Protestant pastors (Monod and Siegfried), and a weathly writer (Sainte-Croix). The UFSF, 1910-1914, was run by the wife of a professor (Brunschwicg) and a nine-member committee that included three lawyers.

The importance of middle-class homogeneity in French suffragism derives not from occupation or income but from collective attitudes. Suffragists graphically illustrate André Siegfried's assertion that the

French bourgeoisie could best be characterized by its attitudes, behavior, and mores.[37] Two pillars of bourgeois respectability dictated the limits of political behavior to them: the insistence upon maintaining dignity and upon avoiding ridicule. Suffragists candidly admitted their preoccupation with appearance and proper behavior, particularly when contemplating any form of direct action.

Illustrations of this attitude are legion. As *La Femme* said in 1910 on the subject of suffragette violence, "Our compatriots are not, unlike Englishwomen, impermeable to ridicule."[38] It was the danger of ridicule that Schmahl had cited in a 1902 letter to Auclert when she refused to support a woman candidate; Oddo-Deflou made exactly the same argument during the 1910 elections. Suffragette violence was impossible in France, according to Marguerite Durand, because it "would quickly be stopped by the ridicule."[39] It was not a casual remark when Misme insisted upon behavior compatible with French sensibilities, nor a trivial passage of the statutes of the UFSF when Schmahl inserted the word "dignity." French suffragists thoroughly agreed with a provincial leader of the UFSF, Marguerite Clément, who said in founding a chapter at Bordeaux, "We do not want to be seen as ridiculous, not in dress, in manners, or in claims."[40]

The great bulk of such evidence cannot be ignored: the chief reason why French suffragists rejected Auclert and Pelletier in 1908 and unanimously embraced moderation was the collective *mehtalités* of their social class. Taken alone, however, this is an insufficient explanation, as a comparative view of French suffragism in an international context suggests. Around the world, women's suffrage was a bourgeois phenomenon, led by women of education and leisure who recognized the gap between their socioeconomic status and their political position. All of the affiliated groups in the IWSA, such as Fawcett's National Union of Women's Suffrage Societies (NUWSS) in Britain, Catt's National American Woman Suffrage Association in the United States, Augspurg's Deutscher Verband für Frauenstimmrecht in Germany, or Zinaida Mirovich's Women's Union in Russia, were liberal, middle-class societies. A survey of the American suffragists listed in *Notable American Women*, for example, has shown that they came overwhelmingly from the well-educated middle class; similarly, a questionnaire completed by participants at the All-Russian Women's Congress of 1908 showed the movement there was thoroughly bourgeois. Nor were French suffrage groups the only ones led by lawyers.

Augspurg received a legal education at Zurich. Catt had some legal training, as did one of the most prominent American militants, Harriet Stanton Blatch. Blatch's co-founder of the Equality League (which popularized the very tactics French women rejected), Inez Milholland, held a law degree from New York University. Richard Pankhurst was a barrister and his militant daughter Christabel read the law at Victoria University in Manchester. The Pankhursts' WSPU also demonstrated that middle-class affluence was no barrier to militant behavior. Emmeline Pankhurst was the daughter of a well-to-do Manchester manufacturer, and the WSPU drew heavily upon the wealth of the Pethick-Lawrences for several years.[41]

Several other factors must be added to explain the triumph of bourgeois *mentalités* and the resultant limitation of collective action. First, the effect of middle-class values was especially pronounced in France (and continental Europe generally) because the suffrage campaign did not receive the leavening of working-class experience that it did in Britain (and, less directly, in the United States). The gulf between French feminists and socialist or syndicalist women prevented the development of collective attitudes that led in other countries (and in other circumstances in France) to more militant forms of collective action. Secondly, French feminism was at a stage of development by 1908 that the movements in Britain and America had reached a generation earlier. This meant that the era of women's militancy elsewhere coincided with a period of optimism in France. French suffragists believed that legalism was working and would succeed—there was no need to consider different forms of action. Finally, it is essential to appreciate the unique relationship between bourgeois feminism and the bourgeois republic in France—a variable that distinguishes French suffragists from those in other continental states as well as those in Britain, America, Canada, Australia, and New Zealand. They were deeply committed, both ideologically and personally, to a regime that appeared to be unstable. They could not automatically assume the survival of liberal democracy, as suffragists in English-speaking countries did; they could expect a better relationship with their government than other continental suffragists.

The first of these factors requires a closer look at militant suffragism outside France. An examination of British suffragism (and to some extent, American) reveals some differences in social composition and significant differences in the source of collective attitudes. The WSPU was unmistakably bourgeois during the period of its greatest notoriety (1906-1914). The origins of the union, however, were closely associated with working-class politics in Manchester, and a large share of the initial membership were workers. More important, the Pankhursts learned about collective action from their involvement in socialist politics. The early WSPU (1903-1906) duplicated the behavior that members had found necessary and effective while working in the Independent Labour Party (ILP). A strategy of public protest and demonstration was therefore well established before WSPU became a middle-class organization.

Emmeline and Richard Pankhurst were both ILP candidates for office in the 1890s, and Emmeline rose to the ILP's National Administrative Council by 1904. The first time that Emmeline Pankhurst was arrested had nothing to do with women's suffrage: in 1896 she participated in a Manchester ILP demonstration over the city council's decision to close a local park to ILP meetings. At a time when international suffragism was essentially a movement of salon and drawing room, with polite lectures in rented halls, the Pankhursts were learning the advantages of parades and outdoor assemblies—a natural form of protest in a movement that could not always afford rentals. The Pankhursts brought this working-class experience to suffragism, drawing upon very different group attitudes than French suffragists did. Indeed, the Pankhursts initially conceived of the WSPU as a working-class organization which they planned to name the Women's Labour Representation Committee. The majority of the founders of the WSPU were workers affiliated with the ILP. The principal speakers for the WSPU included Annie Kenney (a cotton factory worker), Hannah Webster Mitchell (a maid and a seamstress), Teresa Billington (a teacher and the daughter of an iron foundry clerk), and Flora Drummond (a Scottish worker). When the WSPU began its militant campaign in 1905-1906, it was still largely a working class organization. In the march of February 1906 that launched WSPU activity in London, the largest contingent of demonstrators was 300 workers recruited by Sylvia Pankhurst in the East End of London. Few workers remained when militancy turned to violence in 1909; but, as Sylvia Pankhurst always maintained, her work with laboring women in the East End resulted from the family tradition that Christabel abandoned.

It is even more important to note that collective action learned from working-class politics shaped the behavior of the moderate, middle-class suffragists of Fawcett's national union. An earlier generation of English moderates, typified by Lydia Becker, had followed the sedate program favored in France by the CNFF and the UFSF. Fawcett sought "to steer an even keel" between the unsuccessful tactics of Becker and the unacceptable extremism of the Pankhursts. The existence of the WSPU facilitated this effort by making some forms of action, such as huge but peaceful marches, seem moderate. Furthermore, the middle-class suffragists of the NUWSS themselves learned tactics from the English working class. An active group of "radical suffragists" in the Lancashire cotton towns also rejected Becker's traditional methods and the self-destructive means employed by the WSPU. Women such as Esther Roper and Eva Gore-Booth drew on working-class collective action to establish tactics such as factory-gate meetings, door-to-door petition campaigns, and peaceful outdoor rallies. This middle course led to the NUWSS campaign of marches and mass meetings—a tactic that still seemed too revolutionary in France.[42]

Militant suffragism in the United States did not have such direct roots in working-class politics, yet it had a closer connection than French suffragism did. American suffragists perceived direct action as a working-class tactic, as Catt testified to the Judiciary Committee of the House of Representatives. The source of this behavior in the United States, however, was chiefly a closer connection between American militants and the WSPU. Blatch introduced large suffrage demonstrations in America after returning from twenty years in England; Milholland embraced English tactics because they coincided with her experience as a socialist labor organizer—New York City strikes had taught her the value of activity in the streets. Both Alice Paul and Lucy Burns, whose Woman's Party staged the most dramatic demonstrations in the United States, belonged to the WSPU and served time in prison with the Pankhursts. Thus, the root of militant demonstrations in American suffragism was at least indirectly working-class politics. Militants recruited members who accepted such tactics. Blatch dedicated the Equality League (of Self-Supporting Women) to the "drawing of industrial women into the suffrage campaign"; the Woman's Party, although fundamentally middle class, had a large proportion of working-class women compared to French suffrage groups.[43]

Continental suffragism was significantly different. German suffragists avoided street demonstrations and parades precisely because these were socialist tactics. Did not Rosa Luxembourg say that activity in the streets was a rehearsal for the coming revolution? Simultaneously, the German socialist women's movement joined the French GFS in rejecting collaboration with bourgeois feminism; why should workers aid suffragists who merely wanted reforms to preserve their world? The same thing happened in Italy and Russia. "Between the emancipated woman of the intelligentsia and the toiling woman with calloused hands," wrote the prominent Bolshevik Alexandra Kollontai, "there was such an unbridgeable gulf that there could be no question of . . . agreement between them." Indeed, Bolshevik women were instructed not to participate in bourgeois feminist activities unless they could take control of them or disrupt them. Kollontai tried this tactic at the founding meeting of the Women's Union, provoking one feminist to respond "Strangling is too good for you!"[44]

The bourgeois character of international suffragism, therefore, clearly had national variations. In continental states, where the class struggle was more sharply perceived, suffragists faced a different situation than their colleagues in Britain and America. Middle-class insistence upon respectable behavior was indubitably a powerful factor in conditioning suffragist collective action everywhere. Yet it was doubly important for French women: it deprived them of a militant leavening and experience which British suffragists shared, and it prevented public demonstrations because they were too closely associated with revolutionaries.

The second factor need not be reexamined at such length. The slower evolution of suffragism in France meant that when a mass suffrage movement was beginning elsewhere, French feminists were preoccupied with campaigns others had already won or never faced; when militancy appeared elsewhere, French suffragism was just developing and still characterized by confidence in the political process. French optimists held that legalism provided an acceptable variety of tactics without unseemly behavior. This optimism continued to grow in France, before, during and immediately after World War I. In this, too, French women lacked the experience of others. Auclert was still seeking 5,000 signatures on a petition to the Chamber of Deputies forty years after British suffragists had inundated the House of Commons with 255 different petitions bearing 61,000 names—without breaching that masculine fortress. In another instance, Auclert's success in persuading the *Conseil général* of the Seine to endorse women's suffrage in 1907 led the UFSF to adopt the local appeal as its chief policy before the war. American suffragists had learned the dubious value of such campaigns. From 1870 to 1910, they staged 480 local campaigns in thirty-three states, seeking referenda on women's suffrage; they got the issue on the ballot in only seventeen cases and won just two of them.[45] The French remained optimistic and therefore prudent.

The third factor, the relationship between bourgeois feminists and the established regime, sets the French in particularly vivid relief. French suffragists were almost invariably devoted republicans. The majority supported the radical, anti-clerical government of the early twentieth century. Most were ardent Dreyfusards (as Durand and Séverine showed in *La Fronde*). Some moderate feminists, particularly in the CNFF, were more comfortable with the conservative republicanism of the *progressistes*, but all shared the vision of a laic, reformist republic that protected private property. The role of women in the Commune (which Richer and Deraismes had denounced) held no appeal for suffragists, despite the case of Eliska Vincent. Equally few shared the anti-republican sentiments of Boulangism, despite the early connection of Durand and d'Uzès with it. French suffragists, in short, considered themselves part of the established regime; they merely sought a direct role in it.

This attachment to the Third Republic was not soley ideological—it was intertwined with the personal lives of French suffragists. Louise Cruppi, for example, was a CNFF section president. She was also a Crémieux—born to the aristocracy of radicalism. Her husband was a deputy from the Haute-Garonne, Jean Cruppi, who served as Clemenceau's minister of commerce, Monis's minister of foreign affairs, and Caillaux's minister of justice. The Cruppis were not a unique couple. The suffragist collaboration of Julie and Jules Siegfried has already been seen. Jeanne Chauvin was the sister of Emile Chauvin, a Radical-Socialist deputy from Seine-et-Marne. Mme. Pichon-Landry, an officer of both the CNFF and the UFSF, was the wife of Stephen Pichon, the minister of foreign affairs in four prewar cabinets. Valentine Thomson, the editor of *La Vie féminine* and a leader of the UFSF, was the daughter of Gaston Thomson, who sat in six cabinets. A president of *Etudes* married Maurice Faure, Briand's minister of public instruction. Marie Georges-Martin married a radical senator from the Seine. Marguerite de Witt-Schlumberger, a president of the

UFSF, was the daughter of a deputy from Calvados. Alice Mollard, a member of the executive bureau of the UFF, was the daughter of Antoine Mollard, a deputy and senator from the Jura. Mme. Pierre Goujon was the daughter of Joseph Reinach. It is scarcely surprising that Avril de Sainte-Croix described French feminist groups as "essentially republican institutions."[46]

These political connections do not seem, prima facie, to distinguish French suffragists from others. A survey of eighty-nine prominent American suffragists, for example, has shown that more than half of the women came from families in which the men were active in politics. The 168 "suffrage prisoners" of the Woman's Party jailed by the Wilson administration included daughters of congressmen from Connecticut and Kansas, daughters of a state senator and a secretary of state, and the niece of Vice-President Stevenson. Similar ties to the governing elite existed in other countries.[47] These women, however, did not share the French fear that collective action might threaten the existence of the regime to which they were bound. Victory in the *fin de siècle* political crises had not bred an aggressive self-confidence in republicans; instead, it had given birth to the caution so characteristic of interwar France, and suffragists were no exception. Hence, they limited their appeals to the processes of formal politics, matching their style of action to the bourgeois republic that they supported.

One final aspect of the suffragist relationship with the republic must be stressed: that relationship was defined by the stick as well as the carrot. Violence in the political process is not merely a function of the conscious decision of a distressed group about what action to take; it may equally result from the response of the governing elite to the appeal of this group. Thus, it is important to note that when the WSPU was turning toward aggressive collective action in 1906-1909, the Clemenceau government was reminding French women of the repressive powers of the state by its treatment of labor unrest. Despite their closeness to the republic and the calculated caution of the government in 1908, French suffragists could not doubt that the government stood ready and willing to use force against them. Clemenceau enjoyed referring to himself as "the number one cop [*flic*] in France." Could feminists doubt him? In 1906, he mobilized 20,000 soldiers against the striking coal miners of Courrières-Lens; in 1907 he turned the army loose on demonstrating wine-growers in the Midi, with results such as those at Montpellier where troops fired on the crowd, killing several protesters; and in 1908 he arrested labor leaders during another strike and again called out troops who fired on a crowd at Villeneuve-Saint-Georges. Proletarian women participated in the collective action preceding Clemenceau's use of force, and the army shot demonstrators without regard to their sex—a fact that confronted French suffragists precisely in the years when Auclert, Pelletier, and others proposed aggressive tactics but found no followers.[48]

If Clemenceau's socialist minister of labor accepted troops firing on strikers, would feminist sympathizers in the cabinet hesitate to authorize force against a few violent suffragettes? The Prefecture of Police and the Ministry of the Interior were prepared. Their agents had infiltrated organizations and recorded suffragist plans. Large numbers of policemen had somehow awaited public demonstrations. Suffragists knew what was happening. The implications of police activities during the protests of 1904, 1906, and 1908 were unmistakable. It was a potent incentive to maintain their instinctive behavior.

Provincial Teachers and the Potential of Mass Suffragism

The recruitment of leadership from the liberal professions had tremendous implications for the expansion of the suffrage campaign across France. Where were such women to be found in the provincial towns? Suffragists took pride in signs of increasing vitality in the rights movement outside of Paris, but they still lacked a systematic approach that could compete with Catholicism or syndicalism in the organization of women. Feminists must find some key to the countryside—as a provincial leader chided them at the 1908 congress—or abandon it to hostile opinion.

One encouraging sign was the creation of the first women's suffrage society that was wholly independent of the Parisian leagues, the Société féministe du Havre. Interest in women's suffrage at Le Havre had been stimulated by Julie Siegfried, who resided there a few months each year because it was her husband's constituency. She founded a branch of the CNFF there, and a local feminist, Pauline Rebour, organized and led its suffrage section. That led to the inclusion of Le Havre on the provincial lecture circuit organized by Parisian feminists. After a vigorous suffrage speech by Camille Bélilon in that series in the spring of 1908, Pauline and Raoul Rebour organized the Société féministe du Havre. The Rebours were typical converts to suffragism from the educated middle class. Pauline (d. 1937) was a lawyer, a professor in a girls' school, and the daughter of a *collège* headmaster; Raoul was a senior civil servant in the Ministry of the Interior. Both were ardent but moderate suffragists. Although their society later affiliated with the UFSF, the LFDF, and the CNFF, the Rebours distinguished themselves and their small group (twenty to twenty-five members in 1909) by adopting suffrage activities without Parisian guidance. The society established its own lecture series and began publishing its own *Bulletin*. They adopted the passage of the Dussaussoy Bill as their single priority and undertook a letter-writing campaign in the spring of 1909 to persuade Buisson to deposit his report, even daring to call upon all Parisian groups to follow them in this campaign. The energy of the Rebours was a stimulating example to others; a few months later, Venise Pellat-Finet founded a similar Société féministe at Vienne.[49]

Such activity was encouraging, but it was not the key to the provinces. The greatest prospect for provincial suffragism lay in the politicization and organization of teachers. The expansion of public education after the reforms of the 1880s resulted in the feminization of public primary instruction as well as the laicization of the schools. The number of these *institutrices* quadrupled between 1876 and 1906, from 14,000 to 57,000; in 1906, nearly one-half of the public primary teachers in France were women. This was a feminization of *public* primary education, because *institutrices* were replacing nuns, whose number in primary education fell from 20,000 to under 1,000 in that same generation. This transformation had significant implications for the future of French feminism. Educated women, keenly aware of the disadvantages women faced due to their own struggle for equal treatment with male teachers, were being posted to every corner of France. As Madeleine Pelletier observed, this put a potential feminist leader in every community.[50]

This national army of teachers (as theorists of laic education perceived them) occupied an ambiguous borderland between the bourgeoisie and the proletariat. By family background, they came from both classes; teaching was a route of upward social mobility for daughters of the working class and a position of republican respectability for those of the middle class. By their training from the state, *institutrices* acquired a broad range of bourgeois-republican attitudes. Yet the niggardly salaries that the state paid them plus their professional grievances drove them toward alignment with the labor movement. The majority of these women were married; hence, despite the justness of their economic complaints, the two-income marriage produced a standard of living more characteristic of the bourgeoisie than the proletariat. By the strict regulations upon their behavior, they were expected to be models of bourgeois propriety. Yet by organizing to improve their lot, they were led toward socialism, syndicalism, and collective action atypical of middle-class women. By their roles as the infantrywomen of the national intelligentsia, they were drawn in both directions, some toward the life of middle-class intellectuals and some toward intellectual leadership of proletarian women.

Politically active *institutrices* devoted their energies to a range of feminist, syndicalist, and socialist organizations. Many teachers had already played roles in the establishment of republican feminism— Marie Bonnevial, Maria Vérone, Odette Laguerre, Marguerite Belmant, and Pauline Rebour for examples. Others, such as Elizabeth Renaud and Hélène Brion, had similarly important roles in the development of the socialist women's movement. Unified political activism by *institutrices* was often difficult because their economic interests pulled them toward syndicalism and socialism while their political attitudes often led them to bourgeois feminism. This was apparently resolved in most cases by a self-selecting process of class identity. Women who were most comfortable in bourgeois groups chose feminism; teachers who identified chiefly with the proletariat were less active there.[51]

In 1908, Marie Guerin of Nancy created the first feminist organization to unite provincial teachers, the Fédération féministe universitaire (FFU). Guerin had organized a study group of teachers in Nancy in 1903 which developed a large feminist interest by 1905. The growth (200 members by 1908) and vitality of Guerin's group of feminist teachers led her to aid other teachers in founding feminist organizations. In 1908 she united them in a federation which sponsored an annual meeting and published its own organ, *L'Action féministe*. The FFU found teachers eager for such organization and grew rapidly. By the end of 1909 there were thirty departmental groups of 100 to 150 members each, with ten more being organized. (See Map 2.)

Guerin was more sympathetic to bourgeois feminism than to so-

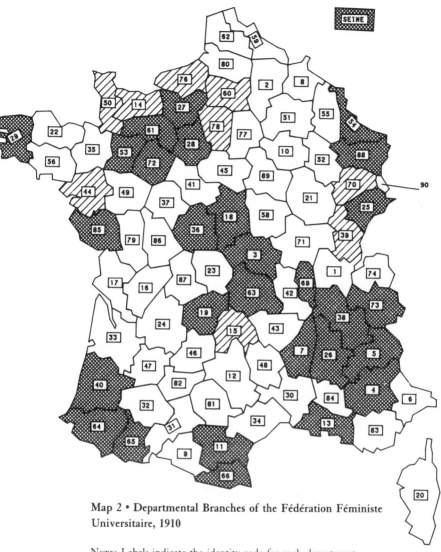

Map 2 • Departmental Branches of the Fédération Féministe Universitaire, 1910

NOTE: Labels indicate the identity code for each department.

 Branches active in January 1910.

 Branches being organized during 1910.

cialism and directed the FFU accordingly. Her statutes stated that the goal of the federation was "to search for and to employ the proper means to ameliorate the lot of women in general and women members of primary education in particular." There was no question about the first specific goal: to obtain equal treatment, especially in salaries, of *institutrices* and *instituteurs*. This economic and occupational focus enabled the FFU to accomodate the membership of militant teachers who had few initial sympathies with bourgeois feminism. That, in turn, divided the FFU when Guerin sought to make women's suffrage the foremost feminist aspiration of the federation. The leadership of the FFU included several other dedicated suffragists, such as Rebour and Pellat-Finet. A majority supported political rights, but the question remained controversial. Socialists within the federation argued that the vote had done little for workingmen and would do little for *institutrices* but bind them to the bourgeois republic. The debate raged at FFU congresses and in the pages of *L'Action féministe* and *L'Ecole émancipée* (the organ of the federation of teachers' unions). Suffragists carried the day, often by large margins: 197-3 in a vote at Grenoble in May 1909. The pressure of a militant, anti-parliamentary minority often made the FFU's suffrage motions more militant than the prevailing moderation of the Parisian movement; the Dussaussoy Bill, for example, was denounced as "notoriously insufficient" in one such vote. The future of the FFU in French suffragism was uncertain, but in 1909 it represented the greatest hope outside Paris.[52]

The Buisson Report of 1909 and Parliamentary Politics

The triumph of moderates in French suffragism coincided with increasing optimism that the vote would soon be won. The unity shown at the congress of 1908 and in the formation of the UFSF strengthened this belief. Foreign events also encouraged French suffragists. In the years 1906-1908 women won full political equality in Finland (1906) and Norway (1907), the right to stand for local offices in Britain (1907), and municipal suffrage in Denmark (1908) and Iceland (1908). It is doubtful that a single French suffragist believed her own enfranchisement was more than thirty-five years away.

The most compelling new reason for optimism was the submission of the Buisson Report, in favor of women's suffrage, to the Chamber of Deputies in July 1909. Ferdinand Buisson only gradually emerged as a hero to suffragists. He had a recognized feminist record, including youthful membership in the LFDF, participation in the congresses of 1900 and 1908, and repeated affirmations of support for women's political rights, but some suffragists had been skeptical due to his prominent position in French radicalism. Buisson was one of the principal authors of the laic education laws, a founder of the League of the Rights of Man, a founding member of the executive committee of the Radical and Radical-Socialist Party, and a frequent contributor to *Le Radical*. It seemed likely to some that his love of women's suffrage was more platonic than impassioned, that he would work for eventual rather than immediate enfranchisement. Certainly one could doubt that he was an ardent suffragist within the Commission of Universal Suffrage: three years after being named reporter for the Dussaussoy Bill he still had not deposited a report. He supported the committee's concentration on proportional representation and consistently resisted suffragist appeals to complete his report.[53]

Upon reading it, suffragists agreed that the Buisson Report had been worth some delay. It was not only the first parliamentary report in favor of women's suffrage; it was an entire book on the subject— a vigorous 400-page defense of that right. "The right to vote is the first right of the citizen in all free countries," Buisson told the chamber. "The idea [of women's suffrage] has left the period of theoretical debates. It is no longer permissible to speak of it as a dream." Suffragists were extremely pleased. They should have been—Maria Vérone wrote some of the critical passages of the report. Buisson had asked suffrage groups for assistance, and the CNFF responded with a vast amount of information. The suffrage section of the CNFF asked Vérone to draft a report on the Dussaussoy Bill in March 1909. She submitted it both to the council's general assembly (adopted June 6, 1909) and to Buisson, who incorporated much of her material in his report (submitted July 16, 1909). The Buisson Report praised the CNFF as "much the most important French feminist federation." In turn, suffragists adopted Buisson as their greatest parliamentary hero.[54]

Buisson's report was not the only reason why suffragists believed in 1909 that they would soon win the municipal vote. Clemenceau, their steady foe, fell from power in July 1909 just when it seemed certain that he would hold the premiership through the 1910 elections. His fall further encouraged suffragists because it resulted from a battle within the Radical Party—the reemergence of a longstanding feud between Clemenceau and Théophile Delcassé. Sixty-two radicals voted to bring down the government. Delcassé was also an implacable foe of women's suffrage, typical of the socially conservative Radical Party in the small towns of southwestern France. Suffragists, however, hoped that the schism might facilitate a faction of the party (the more feminist element in the Paris region) in following Buisson's lead (he reported four days before Clemenceau fell).[55]

A third reason for optimism was the choice of Aristide Briand as premier. He was an unknown quantity on women's rights, but suffragists perceived Briand as a defender of human rights and applauded the inclusion of such known feminists as Viviani and Chéron in his cabinet. Thus motivated, Schmahl requested and received a meeting with Briand in October 1909 to discuss women's suffrage. She urged him to support the Buisson Report and the Dussaussoy Bill. Briand avoided any commitment but assured Schmahl of his support for women's right to vote "in principle."[56] Such words were a dubious victory; even anti-suffragists used them. The optimistic insisted that they were another sign of progress. Was this not a vast improvement over Clemenceau's policy? Was it not especially auspicious when compared to the refusal of Prime Minister Asquith to meet with some leading British suffragists?

Attempts to get Briand to clarify his stand failed. Auclert, for example, wrote to him a few months later and got no response.[57] A decade later, Briand won suffragist praise for a vigorous speech on their behalf. In 1909, however, he was not ready to see them vote. He intended to postpone the question, as may be judged from his speech on electoral reform a few days after talking with Schmahl. The debate on proportional representation began in late October and Briand spoke in favor of adjourning the subject for further study. His reasoning suggests that he would have done the same had the Dussaussoy Bill come forward:

> It is not sufficient that a reform be just in principle, it is not even sufficient that it be voted with the support of a majority. ... For it to be viable and durable it must have had a large amount of collaboration of the nation in its elaboration ... to reflect upon its consequences.[58]

Women's suffrage, "just in principle," still lacked that collaboration of the country.

If Briand's speech cooled suffragist optimism, two other speeches during the proportional representation debate heated it up again. The day after Briand spoke, Marcel Sembat (SFIO, Seine) astonished the chamber by interrupting the discussions to call for women's suffrage. Sembat criticized the notion "that electoral reform is summed up by proportional representation." Charles Benoist, who feared that the linking of *le RP* with women's suffrage would defeat the former without advancing the latter, tried to quiet Sembat by talking of the commission's program for reforms. Sembat would not be silenced: "One cannot realize complete justice in electoral matters while the right to vote is denied to women."[59] This intervention did not change the scheduled debates, but it cheered suffragists who interpreted it as proof that socialists would insist upon debating the Dussaussoy Bill in the near future. Hopes for early discussion of that bill rose again a few days later when the president of the republic, Armand Fallières, declared his support for feminism in a speech to the Ligue de l'enseignement. "I have always thought," the president said, "that women must have the same rights in society as men have."[60] Those words meant that in the span of less than four months evidence of feminist sympathies had come from the Commission of Universal Suffrage, the premier, the socialist party, and the president of the republic. The support was actually shallow, but with backing accruing at that rate it is not surprising that suffragist confidence grew.

ⓧⓞ

Chapter Five

Suffragist Progress and Optimism, 1910-1914

The efforts to create suffragist unity in the years 1908-1909 resulted in the diminution of the small groups that once characterized the woman's rights movement. Most had faced problems of recruitment and financing throughout their history; now they had to cope with the advancing age of their founders and to compete with larger and more respectable leagues such as the UFSF and the CNFF. Avant-courrière disappeared completely. Suffrage des femmes, Egalité, and Etudes survived almost solely due to the personality and historic roles of Auclert, Vincent, and Oddo-Deflou. Their ever smaller numbers (see Table 5) meant the loss of their preeminence; they would last little longer than the women who were their animating spirits. In this way, *Le Journal des femmes* died with Martin in 1910 and Egalité with Vincent in 1914. Some groups, such as Amélioration, survived the loss of leadership (although their *Bulletin* disappeared with the death of Feresse-Deraismes in 1910) due to their financial or ideological strength, but they endured only as narrow constituencies of diminished influence.

The leadership of French suffragism in the years before World War I rested with the large leagues that expressed the consensus reached in 1908-1909. Their formula had noteworthy success. Whereas there had been fewer that two hundred suffragists in France in 1900-1901, there were perhaps fifteen thousand active suffragists by 1914.[1] The UFSF grew rapidly, numbering twelve thousand before the war. As Jean Finot wrote in his pro-suffrage *Préjuge et problème des sexes* in 1912, middle-class opinion was impressed with the new suffragism; women who had held themselves aloof from the movement of Auclert now joined the UFSF or CNFF with pride. "The crisis of the growth of feminism is ended," Oddo-Deflou triumphantly wrote in 1910. The conviction that suffragism was now a well-rooted political movement enhanced the widespread optimism of French suffragists. "I believe," wrote Anne Réal, "that feminists can envisage the future with serenity, given the certitude of their coming success."[2]

The salient element in the development of a large suffrage movement was the growth of the UFSF under the leadership of Cécile Brunschwicg. Brunschwicg (1877-1946) was a late recruit to feminism. The daughter of a prosperous Jewish industrialist, Arthur Kahn, and the wife of Léon Brunschwicg, an eminent philosopher at the Lycée Henri IV and later the Sorbonne, she had previously thought suffragism unimportant. The Dreyfus affair politicized her; subsequent work in the women's trade union movement converted her to a moderate feminism and led her to the CNFF. Brunschwicg later admitted that her husband's repeated insistence that women would achieve little without the vote led her to join the council's suffrage section, attend the 1908 IWSA congress in Amsterdam, and participate in the formation of the UFSF. Initially she was not a member of the UFSF central committee, but her energy and administrative ability soon brought her to prominence. At the December 1909 meeting of the executive committee, Brunschwicg and Pichon-Landry carried a motion to establish a membership and propaganda committee with Brunschwicg as its head. It quickly became the center of UFSF activity. Brunschwicg produced a membership of 700 before the first anniversary of the founding of the union—a number that made it larger than all women's rights groups except the CNFF. *La Française* immediately labeled her "a woman of action of the first order."[3]

Jeanne Schmahl resented Brunschwicg's activities, perceiving them as a threat to her leadership. Schmahl possessed an independent and imperious personality and she expected the members of the UFSF to follow her quietly. She was now sixty-six years old and unprepared for an unknown subordinate half her age to usurp the leadership of her organization. Schmahl's friends acknowledged that "the roughness [*aspérités*] of her character increased with age," ill-suiting her for the new suffragism of large organizations working through many committees.[4] Schmahl understood the dynamics of authority. Twenty years earlier she broke with Maria Deraismes, criticizing her for similar personality faults. "A leader," Schmahl had written, "who expects blind obedience from undisciplined troops must be in a position to enforce it."[5] In December 1910, Schmahl decided to enforce her own

Table 5 • Parisian Women's Rights Organizations, 1910-1914

Name	Founded	Leader(s)	Associated Publications	Estimated Membership 1900-01	Estimated Membership 1910-14
BOURGEOIS-REPUBLICAN					
(Militant [full suffrage])					
Suffrage des femmes	1876	Auclert	(none)	under 100	c. 25
LFDF	1882	Bonnevial (pres.) Vérone (s.-g.)	*Le Droit des femmes*	under 200	500-1,000
Solidarité	1891	Kauffmann Pelletier	*La Suffragiste*	under 100	c. 25
LNVF	1914	Ducret-Metsu (pres.) Tisserand (s.-g.)	(none)	—	c. 500
(Moderate [municipal suffrage])					
Amélioration	1876	Montaut, 1910-12 Martial, 1912-20	(none)	100-150	c. 50
Egalité	1888	Vincent	(none)	under 100	c. 25
Etudes	1898	Oddo-Deflou	*La Femme de demain,* 1913-14	c. 100	c. 50-100
UFF	1901	Hammer	*Bulletin*	under 100	c. 100
CNFF	1901	Monod (pres., 1901-12) Siegfried (pres, 1912-22) Sainte-Croix (s.g.)	*L'Action féminine*	21,000	90-100,000

Congrès permanente du féminisme international	1908	Chéliga	(none)	—	c. 50
UFSF	1909	Vincent (pres., 1911-14) Witt-Schlumberger (pres., 1914) Brunschwicg (s.-g.)	*La Française, Bulletin,* & *Jus suffragii*	—	12,000
CATHOLIC					
Féminisme chrétien	1897	Maugeret	*Le Féminisme chrétien*	under 100	
Action sociale	1900	Chenu	*L'Action sociale*	under 200	
Devoir des femmes françaises	1901	Dorive	*Devoir des femmes*	under 100	
SOCIALIST					
Groupe des femmes socialistes	1913	Saumoneau, Rauze, Renaud	*La Femme socialiste*	—	c. 50-100

NOTE: Precise data for the smaller groups are scarce. Estimates are based on fragmentary evidence such as: one of the last issues of Amélioration's *Bulletin* gave a membership of 46 (October 1908, p. 570); police reports on the meetings of Suffrage des femmes in 1910 and 1911 showed an attendance ranging between 13 and 26 (reports of October 11, 1910 and February 10, 1911, Dossier Vote des femmes, B^A 1651, APP); similar reports on the GdFS in 1915 estimated its membership in the department of the Seine at 50 (Dossier La Campagne féministe en faveur de la paix, F^7 13266, AN).

control of the UFSF. She called a meeting of the central committee and attacked the "personal propaganda" conducted by a member of the committee without the approval of the president. Schmahl claimed that Brunschwicg's recruitment directly contradicted the non-partisan basis of the union, giving it "a character hostile to conservative and religious ideas," a policy that should not be continued "at any price." Could the UFSF tolerate the republicanism of one member threatening Schmahl's overture toward Catholics? Could it survive "indiscipline and intolerable behavior"? If the committee permitted a member to act without the president's direction, Schmahl would resign. The confrontation resulted in a coup, Brunschwicg gaining control of the UFSF. The membership of the union was nearly two thousand, 90 percent of whom had been enrolled due to Brunschwicg's work. The central committee saw a brighter future in Brunschwicg's numbers than in Schmahl's non-partisanship and proceeded to elect Brunschwicg secretary-general of the UFSF with control of correspondence and all committees. The president would represent the UFSF at all official functions. Schmahl recognized "a purely honorary role" when she saw it and resigned. The UFSF maintained the polite fiction that she left because she was "ailing." D'Uzès reluctantly followed her friend, but the remainder of the leadership, including Schmahl's erstwhile protegé, Misme, backed Brunschwicg.[6] It must have been an exceptionally painful meeting for many people.

Under Brunschwicg, the UFSF adopted the openly republican philosophy that Schmahl sought to avoid. It was a moderate republicanism, consistent with the cautiousness of the group; the invitation to Catholic and conservative membership remained open, so long as they were not hostile to the regime. The presidency of the UFSF, reduced to a ceremonial role, was given to an unmistakable republican, the seventy-year-old Eliska Vincent, in recognition of her lengthy feminist career and her rallying to the side of the moderates. Two years later, the moderation of the UFSF was underscored by the election of Marguerite de Witt-Schlumberger to replace Vincent. De Witt-Schlumberger (1856-1924) was a social feminist, attracted to women's suffrage for its utility in fighting alcoholism and prostitution. Her feminist background came through the Protestantism of the Conférence de Versailles, *La Femme*, the CNFF, and philanthropic work as a leader of the Association pour la répression de la traité des blanches. She was the maternal granddaughter of Guizot, the daughter of a conservative deputy (Conrad de Witt, Calvados) and a successful writer (Henriette de Witt-Guizot), and the wife of a well-known Alsatian businessman, Paul Schlumberger. These family origins and contacts, plus her activities, made de Witt-Schlumberger an ideal president of a league eager for respectability. She was a feminist who could successfully deliver a speech entitled "How to Reach the Society Woman." And her feminism was not threatening. "We are wives and mothers," de Witt-Schlumberger said, "and we wish to remain wives and mothers."[7]

The policy of the UFSF matched the moderate republicanism of Brunschwicg and the social feminism of de Witt-Schlumberger. The union maintained close relations with parliamentary feminists such as Buisson and Marin, accepting their slow approach to enfranchisement. When the question of suffragist electoral activities arose in 1910 and 1912, the UFSF preferred to work for the election of sympathetic male candidates. Militant propaganda was repeatedly and explicitly rejected.[8] Instead, women of the union attempted to educate the republic, distributing 18,000 free brochures in March 1910 and placing copies of the Buisson Report and UFSF literature in public libraries around France. The conservative tone of the UFSF showed in its attention to social questions, such as alcoholism, despite the statutory insistence that the vote was their exclusive interest. This formula was extremely successful (for France) in recruiting suffragists from women of the urban, republican bourgeoisie (see Table 6). The UFSF doubled in size almost yearly, going from Schmahl's 300 to 12,000 in early 1914, with chapters in seventy-five departments. The union complemented the CNFF, whose suffrage section, under the presidencies of Georges-Martin (1910-1911), Bonnevial (1912, 1914), and Vérone (1913), endorsed the Vérone and Buisson Reports in favor of the Dussaussoy Bill—but only limited suffrage for the present. "In order to avoid too abrupt a shock to the state," the women of the council voted in 1913, "the congress is of the opinion that suffrage should be given in stages, beginning with municipal suffrage."[9] With the UFSF and the CNFF in close collaboration, the overwhelming majority of French feminists were commited to moderation.

The growth of the UFSF came in provincial France. The statutes of the union bound the executive committee to "intensive propaganda" in all regions of the country, and Brunschwicg followed this injunction with the same zeal that had won her control of the group. The creation

Table 6 • Growth of the UFSF, 1909-1914

Date	Membership	Departments
February 1909	300	n.a.
February 1910	700	n.a.
May 1910	1,000	n.a.
December 1910	2,000	n.a.
March 1911	2,600 (+5,000 affiliated)	9
March 1912	6,000 (+9,000 affiliated)	17
March 1913	9,000 (2,500 in Paris)	48
March 1914	12,000	75

NOTE: Figures are from the UFSF's *Bulletin*, usually the secretary-general's annual report. Cf. the analysis by Evans (*The Feminists*, pp. 133-34) finding the performance of the UFSF "far from impressive." Evans stresses the amount of the union's membership in affiliated societies, which are not included in the 12,000 membership given here. It is true, as Evans contends, that the UFSF had a large affiliated membership from the FFU, temperance societies, and unions of postal workers; it is also true that the provincial membership relied heavily on teachers and their students. Seen in the context of French suffragism, however, the size and importance of the UFSF was greater than Evans finds when viewing it in an international context, where it was certainly dwarfed. (The National American Women's Suffrage Association already had over 13,000 members in 1983 and surpassed 100,000 by the end of 1914.)

of a provincial branch required a minimum of twenty-five local members who would accept the orientation of the UFSF and the leadership of Paris. Brunschwicg devised a simple plan to attract them. She began by identifying a feminist of suitable attitudes in any provincial town. Just one would do. This woman became the local UFSF "delegate," and the union sent her brochures and posters to create local publicity. The delegate was to find a few prospective adherents—numbers were not critical—and constitute with them a committee. This committee would set an appropriate tone of respectability and avoid identification with any political faction. The UFSF instructed the local committees to establish cordial relations with the Hotel de Ville and the local newspaper, with the objective of obtaining a meeting place and reports on their existence. Whenever a delegate succeeded in these undertakings, the UFSF would finance the publicity for a meeting at which a prominent suffragist (usually Brunschwicg, Misme, or Rebour) would speak. With the financial support of the union and some backing from a local newspaper, the committee might attract enough people to enlist twenty-five members and become a branch of the union. If not, they would try the same strategy again the following year.[10]

This plan worked. Brunschwicg created a large, national suffrage union because her model was simple and her preparation excellent. She found local delegates by forging an entente with the suffragist wing of the FFU. Some delegates were found in the anti-alcoholism movement, or in charities, but the majority were teachers. Rebour, Pellat-Finet, and Guerin all contributed to the UFSF-FFU link, but the principal architect was the second secretary-general of the FFU, Jane Méo. Méo was an ardent feminist who believed that the worst obstacle faced by *institutrices* was the sexual prejudice of *instituteurs*; hence, it was more important to seek improvements through feminism rather than to cooperate with male teachers in trade unionism. Brunschwicg made Méo a member of the UFSF central committee and together they recruited teacher-delegates, including such future leaders as Marguerite Clément at Bordeaux, Mlle. Ancel at Saint-Etienne, and M.-L. Berot-Berger at Saint-Quentin.[11]

The UFSF turned to the pro-suffrage male organizations such as the Ligue des droits de l'homme and the Ligue des électeurs pour le suffrage des femmes for help in obtaining local political support. The union also undertook the task of helping to identify provincial newspapers that would publish notices of suffrage meetings. This effort was almost the single-handed accomplishment of "Djénane"—the pen name of Mme. Salonne-Le Gac—a reporter for *La Reveil* of Brest and a leading Breton suffragist. Beginning in 1910, Djénane (and later, Jane Misme) corresponded with regional newspapers and built a list of papers that would cooperate; by mid-1911, she had found forty-five, excluding Parisian or explicitly feminist periodicals. (See Map 3.)[12]

The result was the growth of the UFSF to 12,000 members, 75 percent of whom were outside the department of the Seine, by 1914. In the first year, branches were established at Nice (250 members), Clermont-Ferrand (25), Bordeaux (150), Rouen (150), Nîmes (55), Saint-Quentin (30), Boulogne (25), and Saint-Etienne (25). By the second year of the program, there were sixteen active provincial groups, twelve more applying to join the union, and committees active in forty-five departments. Brunschwicg already claimed "we are a truly national society." In early 1914 she was within sight of her goal of a chapter in every department: only ten departments lacked groups,

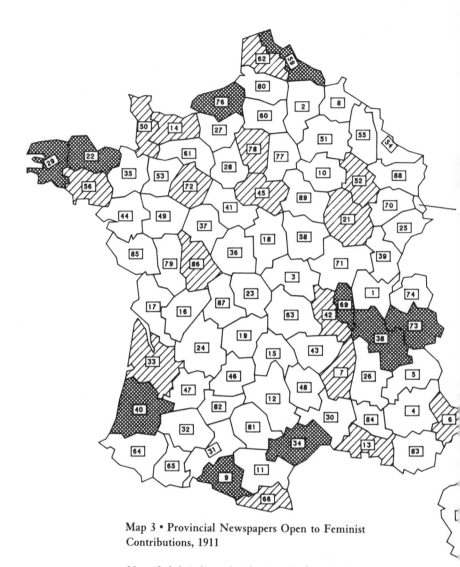

Map 3 • Provincial Newspapers Open to Feminist Contributions, 1911

NOTE: Labels indicate the identity code for each department.

 Departments with two or more newspapers open to feminist contributions, according to Djénane's survey.

 Departments with one newspaper open to feminist contributions.

Not shown: Parisian publications, expressly feminist papers, and papers not responding to the survey.

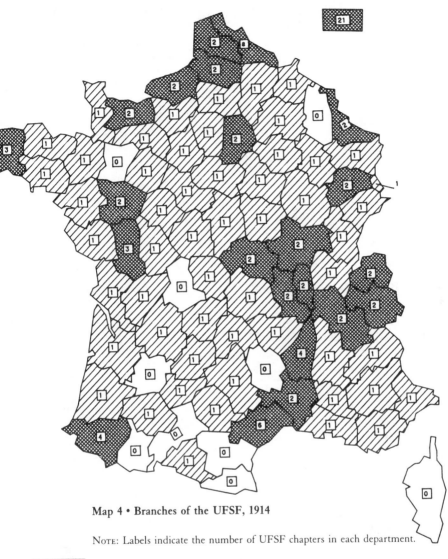

Map 4 • Branches of the UFSF, 1914

NOTE: Labels indicate the number of UFSF chapters in each department.

Departments with two or more branches of the UFSF in March 1914.

Departments with one branch of the UFSF.

Not shown: Chapters in London and Algiers.

almost all of them in the south. (See Map 4.) The union was especially strong in the north (with eight sections in the Nord, for example) and in the Rhône basin (with 1,200 members in Lyons alone). In twenty-four departments the central branch had a membership over 100, greater than most of the historic feminist groups of Paris. Some of these provincial chapters of the UFSF were surprising pockets of suffragist strength. Djénane's Finistère branch had three sections (Brest, Quimper, and Morlaix) and attracted 2,000 people to a single rally in 1913; the group in the Basses-Pyrénées had four sections (Pau, Bayonne, Orthez, and Oloron), a total of over 400 members, and the ability to launch their own series of brochures and regional lectures; Clément's Girondin branch published its own booklet in defense of women's suffrage; the oldest section, the group of the Riviera at Nice, proudly advertised its ability to attract members of the upper classes. In June 1914, the UFSF recognized its provincial base by holding its annual congress at Lyons.[13]

The provincial success of the UFSF stimulated many other feminist efforts there. By 1914, the CNFF, the LFDF, the UFF, and Etudes had more than two dozen branches in provincial cities, chiefly concentrated in northern France. At the same time, several independent, if evanescent, organizations appeared in cities like Amiens, Chalon-sur-Saône, Saintes, Mans, Lille, Bordeaux, La Rochelle, and Bayonne.

The clearest sign of a flourishing suffragism in the provinces, however, was the creation of regional federations of feminist groups that acted without the guidance of Paris and even aroused some trepidation there. This was the accomplishment of Venise Pellat-Finet and women of the FFU who organized the Fédération féministe du sud-est at Lyons in 1911, bringing together representatives from feminist groups in Ardèche, Rhône, and Isère—a region of considerable feminist activity. The federation soon included feminists from thirteen departments of the Rhône valley and Savoy. (See Map 5.) In addition to the FFU and independent organizations in Lyons, Vienne, and Chalon, the groups participating covered a considerable ideological range: from moderate republicans (UFSF chapters), through radical republicans (mixed masonic lodges) to socialists (one chapter of the Groupe des femmes socialistes). Six hundred feminists attended the congress held at Vienne in December 1911—quite comparable with the historic Parisian congresses of 1900. By 1912, the federation had 2,800 regional members; in early 1914, over 5,000. And it was energetically suffragist.

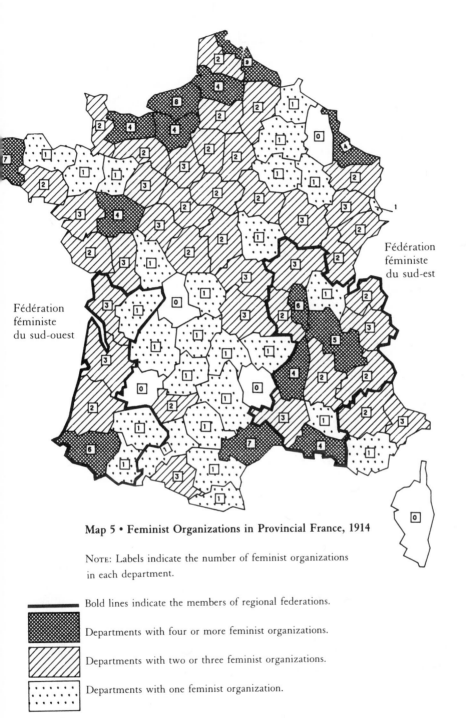

Fédération féministe du sud-est

Fédération féministe du sud-ouest

Map 5 • Feminist Organizations in Provincial France, 1914

NOTE: Labels indicate the number of feminist organizations in each department.

Bold lines indicate the members of regional federations.

Departments with four or more feminist organizations.

Departments with two or three feminist organizations.

Departments with one feminist organization.

The founding members adopted political rights as their "indispensable" goal and pledged "to undertake all possible action" to win the vote. Their activity prompted teachers at the June 1913 meeting of the Girondin chapter of the FFU to found a similar Fédération féministe du sud-ouest encompassing seven departments in which feminism had previously had little success. There was even talk of a Fédération féministe du sud to coordinate activities in the region between the two federations.[14]

The provincial suffragism launched by the UFSF was still in an early stage of organization. It was relatively small and essentially confined to urban, middle-class women. Its numbers were impressive when compared to French feminism at the turn of the century, but provincial opinion remained to be conquered. Conservative anti-suffragists were correct when they claimed that most French women did not ask for the vote; the majority of French women were not so much hostile to the reform as they were indifferent or uninformed. Five departments, three of which were in the unsympathetic southwestern quarter of France, had no feminist organization whatsoever. In twenty departments, the total membership in all feminist groups combined amounted to fewer than 100 persons. While the UFSF's 12,000 members, or the Fédération féministe du sud-est's 5,000, represented striking accomplishments, this stage of development may be understood by comparing membership with the Catholic women's movement. The conservative, anti-suffrage Ligue patriotique des françaises had 2,160 sections around France in early 1914 with 585,000 members, less than 7 percent of whom were from the department of the Seine.[15] It is also important to note that the newborn provincial suffrage movement possessed very little leverage on the French political system. How could they make politicians cognizant of, and responsive to, their grievances? Deputies who remained attentive to the party federation that nominated them and to the special interests of the constituency that elected them could ignore feminists in their district with impunity, because women were political ciphers.

To combat their political ineffectiveness, branches of the UFSF borrowed an idea from Hubertine Auclert. Deputies were somewhat responsive to the interests of their local councils, so feminists tried to convert their *conseils généraux*, or even *conseils municipaux*, to suffragism. In almost all departments where suffragists attempted this ploy they obtained the adoption of a motion calling on the Chamber of Deputies to pass the Dussaussoy Bill. Seventeen departments passed such vows before the war, fifteen of them in the years 1912-1914. (See Map 6.) Djénane won the support of eight Breton councils, including that of Finistère in 1912. The federation of the southwest obtained the backing of five councils in the Pyrenees; the federation of the southeast persuaded seven departmental and eight municipal councils. Pauline Rebour won over the council of Seine-inférieure, Marie Denizard that of the Somme, and Georges Martin that of Loir-et-Cher. This approach was indirect and not greatly influential. The importance attached to these motions may perhaps be judged from the lack of debate with which they succeeded. One is moved to wonder if the councillors did not recognize, as Auclert did, that such motions had little influence at the Palais Bourbon. Whatever the efficacy of the fifty-one vows adopted by 1914, they represented a small portion of the local governments of France; in sixty-five departments, no motions were passed on any level. Provincial suffragists remained optimistic, and a few more years of nationwide victories in the councils might indeed have forced the chamber to pay attention to what was happening. This did not happen because World War I truncated their campaign.[16]

Suffragist Activism and the Parliamentary Elections of 1910

The first test of the moderate consensus of 1908-1909 came during the parliamentary elections of 1910, when suffragists disagreed over tactics. Militants did not wish to duplicate the actions of Auclert and Pelletier in 1908, merely those of Laloë. Her success in winning 20 percent of the vote was an irresistible temptation. How much could that share be increased if an earnest feminist were the candidate? How much more publicity and public approval could a better organized campaign generate? Whatever the answers, the UFSF and the CNFF disapproved.

The idea for a women's candidacy in 1910 apparently originated with Marguerite Durand. After closing *La Fronde* in 1905, Durand had been more active in Parisian journalism (at *L'Action* and later *Les Nouvelles*) than in feminism. She had established an Office du travail féminin to help working women in 1907 and had been one of the organizers of the national congress of 1908, and a correspondence

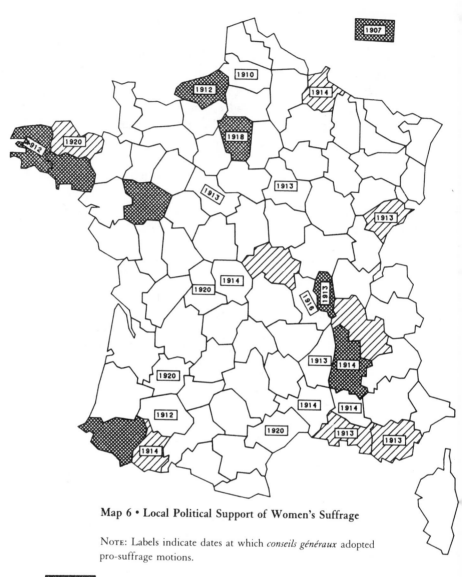

Map 6 • Local Political Support of Women's Suffrage

NOTE: Labels indicate dates at which *conseils généraux* adopted
pro-suffrage motions.

Departments in which two or more local councils (*conseils municipaux*
or *conseils d'arrondissements*) adopted pro-suffrage motions.

Departments in which one local council adopted a pro-suffrage motion.

in 1909 with Auclert about feminist aspirations seems to have reinvigorated her. During the winter of 1909-1910 she conceived the idea
of exploiting the 1910 elections to publicize their program. By early
1910, she was launching trial balloons in the press. In addition to
announcing her own candidacy, Durand proposed that Parisian suffragists enter a candidate in every *arrondissement* of the city. She
publicly appealed to Auclert and Roussel to join her; privately, she
urged Vérone and the LFDF to coordinate the twenty races. Throughout it all, Durand repeated in a series of newspaper interviews that
she envisioned candidates who would disdain the least rowdiness.[17]

Durand's proposal received a mixed response, generally supportive
from the feminist left and critical from the center. Auclert did not
need much persuasion to run, but Roussel was unable to do so for
personal reasons. Vérone organized a great rally to launch electoral
efforts. Moderates, however, were openly hostile. The UFSF announced that it would undertake "vast propaganda" during the elections, but added that those "who know its program will not even
suppose that this could be ... feminine candidates." Oddo-Deflou
stated in an interview that Durand's ideas were unrealistic—"denuded
not only of truth, but even of any likelihood." Laloë and Durand,
she argued, possessed bases of operation in Parisian journalism and
financial resources that others could not match; attempts to follow
them would fail. In this way, the UFSF, the CNFF, the UFF, and
Etudes all spurned Durand in favor of campaigning for their male
supporters. Anything more daring than posters and postcards was
branded "suffragette tactics."[18]

Vérone's rally of March 1910 was such a dramatic success that
feminists immediately dubbed it "the first great suffrage meeting."
She and Bonnevial had previously decided that an essential step in
developing French militancy within the law was to push attendance
at such events into the thousands, as women did in other countries.
The notion of assembling thousands of women for a protest was too
disturbing for the UFSF and the CNFF, neither of which would co-
sponsor it. Vérone secured the support of the smaller groups and a
long list of prominent politicians, including Buisson, Marin, Beauquier,
Godart, Deschanel, Sembat, Francis de Pressensé (socialist, Rhône),
Senator Paul d'Estournelles de Constant (republican, Sarthe), Eugène
Fournière (director of the *Revue socialiste*), and Joseph Menard (a
Parisian municipal councillor and leader of the Catholic Action libé-

rale). And she succeeded in her purpose: approximately two thousand people packed the great hall of the Sociétés savantes and hundreds more were turned away for want of space.[19]

Durand received less support for her slate of candidates. Auclert announced her own candidacy in the Eleventh Arrondissement (where she resided) and that of two of her lieutenants in the First and Third. Pelletier proposed to enter the lists in the Fifth, the treasurer of Solidarité in the Seventh, Kauffmann in the Eighth, and two editors of *La Suffragiste* in the Tenth and Seventeenth. With Durand's own race in the Ninth, her plan for suffragist candidates in all twenty *arrondissements* was almost half realized. In early April, two and a half weeks before the first round of elections, the LFDF completed the slate. It was an optimistic fiction. Despite the precedent of 1908 and the intervention of Viviani and Beauquier, the prefect of the Seine refused to accept the candidacies, denying them the free use of public facilities. As Oddo-Deflou had foreseen, it was financially impossible for most women to run. Durand was undeterred. She sent legal notification of her candidacy to Briand and the Ministry of the Interior, filed an appeal against the prefect's decision, and personally financed several meetings. Auclert financed a much smaller campaign and tried to help her friends. Pelletier and Kauffmann turned to the SFIO for aid; receiving little, both continued out of determination. Only nine of the twenty supposed candidates recorded their names at the Hôtel de Ville, and of those just four actively campaigned. The races were less eventful than Laloë's had been. The absolute insistence upon calm, peaceful behavior even convinced the Prefecture of Police, which seems to have paid scant attention to the races. The disapproval of the feminist center meant, as Héra Mirtel pointed out, no body of women turned out to help the candidates. And, as Oddo-Deflou had predicted, only Durand attracted the desired publicity.[20]

The greatest accomplishment of Durand's campaign was her articulation of a finely detailed program, perhaps the best summation of French feminism before World War I. This program, developed by Durand and Auclert in their correspondence of 1909, contained fourteen points "in the special interest of women" and nineteen points "in the general interest," plus the unifying commitment to women's suffrage. The former category of claims included a blanket demand that "all schools, careers, professions, and all public posts and functions" be opened to women, who must receive equal salaries for equal work. Other points reiterated the expected feminist reforms of the Civil Code, but the program went further than summarizing an old consensus. Perhaps the most radical points called for the payment of wives for household work and obligatory humanitarian service by all unmarried women, corresponding with the military obligation of men. Durand's demands "in the general interest" were a complicated mixture of conservative social feminism and left-wing national politics. The former included attacks upon regulated prostitution and absinthe, support for maternity insurance, and mandatory education of girls in child care. The latter produced attacks upon monopolies and the length of the working day. Thousands of copies of this program were printed on small cards and distributed at Durand's meetings.[21]

Durand's campaign itself also produced controversy. On April 8, 1910, the *Cour de cassation* handed down a remarkable ruling overturning the decision of a judge in Savoy which had held that idiots could not exercise political rights. Durand immediately scheduled a debate between herself and an alleged idiot. First Durand outlined her program with the skill of a trained actress, then he spoke. The contrast hardly needed Durand's summation: "That idiot has the right to be an elector and a candidate, and I, an intelligent woman, I can neither vote nor be elected!" The spectacle produced an angry audience, frequent interruptions ("You belong in the kitchen!"), and a good deal of newspaper discussion.[22]

The electoral meetings of Auclert, Pelletier, and Kauffman drew less attention. Auclert was embittered when the government refused public facilities. Why would the prefect give a meeting place to Laloë, "who made a joke," she asked an interviewer, but refuse one "to us who are serious?"[23] She financed a few meetings to give her cynical response: If the government expected feminists to spend their limited resources on the elections, women should do as men do—buy votes! Establish a party headquarters and practice "electoral hiring" (*embauchage électoral*). "We must do as men do. They give two, three, five, or ten francs to the electors who support them at the poll. That is why one can be a deputy if one is rich, even if one is stupid."[24] Pelletier received the free meeting place denied to Auclert, but that success entailed other problems. She originally inaugurated a race in the Fifth Arrondissement as a feminist, but as a socialist, she had no right to run for parliament without the party's approval. Summoned to defend her irregular behavior, Pelletier explained that the SFIO had offered her no race so she had chosen to stand outside it. Her numerous enemies within the SFIO engineered a trap: the party would offer Pelletier a socialist candidacy in a hopeless district. She would run there as a socialist or be driven from the party. Their choice fell upon one of the rockiest terrains for socialism (or feminism) available in Paris: the Madeleine quartier of the Eighth Arrondissement, the safe seat of the prominent monarchist Denys Cochin. In 1906 he had outpolled his socialist opponent by 7,058 to 263 and had received 75 percent of all votes cast. Pelletier accepted, reasoning that she must preserve her position within the party and that her official candidacy represented a feminist victory itself, wherever the constituency. Thus, the SFIO obtained meeting places for her through fictive male applications. The price, in Pelletier's words, was that she had to "leave feminism a little in the shadows." A single sentence summarizing her race in *L'Humanité* suggests the magnitude of the problem: "In this reactionary quartier, Citizeness M. Pelletier propagates socialist doctrines and *her* feminist theories."[25] Caroline Kauffmann had greater difficulties. The SFIO belatedly backed her but gave less assistance than Pelletier received. Kauffmann publicly praised the party for accepting women candidates, but she was privately furious with her treatment. Her financial situation must have been desperate because she asked Durand, whom she had disliked for several years, for help in renting a hall. Durand coolly responded that she was "absolutely opposed" to Kauffmann's extremism.[26]

Despite their brave assertions to the contrary, the vote totals of the 1910 feminist candidates must have been an acute disappointment. Precise totals are unknown because only Pelletier had a representative inside the polls during the counting; other had to estimate their votes from the totals of "blank ballots" reported. In addition to the government's policy of not counting votes cast for women, the totals were deflated by the repeated problems women had with the distribution of their ballots. Furthermore, Durand invited her supporters to feel free to vote for other candidates, as the race seemed to be close. Such facts notwithstanding, the results were dismal: about 4 percent of the poll in each case. Suffragists had to take succor from small victories—that the SFIO ran women candidates, that Pelletier outpolled her male predecessor, that so many women ran at one time, or that they scored victories over each other. Still, this must have been a bitter pill when everyone recalled that Jeanne Laloë, whom none of them admired, received 22 percent of the votes in 1908.[27]

Ironically, greater success came in the provinces; Marie Denizard ran at Amiens, Arria Ly at Toulouse, and Elisabeth Renaud at Vienne. Denizard made an astonishing, single-handed campaign throughout the entire department of the Somme, posting over 15,000 copies of her *affiche*, including one in every village of the department. Ly conducted the highly outspoken campaign that made her one of the most notorious feminists of France.[28] Neither of them surpassed the electoral success of the Parisians, but Renaud did so in resounding fashion. Renaud stood as the candidate of the SFIO (again under the fictive candidacy of a man) but with great advantages over the races run by Pelletier and Kauffmann. Her constituency, chiefly comprised of the suburbs and small villages near Vienne, was an improvement on the Eighth or Ninth Arrondissements of Paris. It contained a growing socialist minority under a local leadership unusually sympathetic to women's rights. The feminist movement in Isère was one of the best developed in the provinces, including both the Société féministe de Vienne and a very active branch of the FFU, both under the suffragist leadership of Venise Pellat-Finet. Due to the syndicalist orientation of the FFU, the bifurcation of feminism and socialism was far less severe at Vienne than at Paris. Renaud, an *institutrice*, belonged to the FFU. She also had the excellent credentials of her founding role in the GFS and membership in the LFDF. Renaud spent eight days campaigning in the Isère. Feminists (including the LFDF) and socialists combined to finance her adequately. She spoke daily, in two or three villages, and with ardor for both of her causes. The attendance and interest amazed even her backers: without her name once appearing in either Vienne newspaper, she drew 600 to 800 listeners in villages of 2,000 to 3,000 population. The final tally was equally surprising. She received 2,869 votes for 27.5 percent of the poll. This was taken as dramatic evidence of what feminist-socialist collaboration might achieve. And it was especially reassuring to militants who felt that they should do better than Laloë had done.[29]

Political Opinion and the Dussaussoy Bill, 1910-1914

During the tenth legislature (1910-1914), French suffragism was characterized by steadily increasing optimism. "No doubt, we will soon conquer the vote," said Marguerite Durand in 1910, and most suffragists sincerely believed her.[30] They enthusiastically subscribed to the summation of the international movement that Carrie Chapman Catt made in her presidential address to the IWSA congress at Stockholm in 1911:

> [The movement] pins its faith to the fact that in the long run man is logical. There may be a generation, or even a century, between the premise and conclusion, but when the premise is once stated clearly and truthfully the conclusion follows as certainly as the night the day. . . . Our premise has been stated. . . . Woman Suffrage is . . . a mighty incoming tide.[31]

Parisian feminists were confident that not only was their premise clearly stated, but that it had already won wide acceptance. Feminist novels, feminist plays, even feminist histories for children had intertwined the subject with the popular culture of the epoch. Lectures were heard on the woman question at the Sorbonne and an entire course devoted to it at the Collège de France; a steady stream of scholarly theses, especially in law, addressed the topic.[32] Prominent Parisian figures in politics and letters endorsed their aspirations. Large organizations followed. Feminism, in short, was no longer a novelty or curiosity in the capital; the educated public accepted it as a serious issue, worthy of attention. To be sure, jokes about feminists and the derisive treatment of their claims did not suddenly disappear, but they had ceased to be a common response in respectable discourse. Jean Finot, the editor of *La Revue* and one of many prominent intellectuals converted to feminism, summarized this situation in 1912 by asserting that the breaches made in Parisian opinion constituted a greater triumph than any of the legislative reforms achieved.[33]

A survey of Parisian newspaper treatment of women's suffrage illustrates this trend. At the beginning of the century, just four major papers, all on the political left—*L'Action, La Petite République, Le Rappel*, and *L'Humanité*—had stated their support, and they combined to reach fewer than 150,000 readers. *Le Figaro* still branded the equality of the sexes as "contrary to natural law," and *Le Temps* thought feminists "arouse the hostility and fear of even the most resolute partisans of reform." By 1914, however, more than a dozen daily newspapers with a combined circulation over 1,700,000 called for the vote; only half a dozen papers, printing fewer than 750,000 copies, remained expressly opposed (see Table 7). Support came from papers of all political views, from monarchism to socialism. *L'Autorité*, for

Table 7 · The Parisian Press and Women's Suffrage, 1906-1914

	Circulation	General Policy on Women's Suffrage
RIGHT		
Action française	23,000	Expressly anti-suffrage
Autorité	15,000	Limited feminism, but pro-suffrage
*Echo de Paris**	134,000	Occasional sympathy
Intransigeant	38,000	Strong pro-suffrage tradition
*Liberté**	75,000	Cautious interest in suffrage
*Libre parole**	48,000	Expressly non-feminist, but pro-suffrage
*Patrie**	42,000	Anti-feminist
Petit journal	725,000	Little interest in feminism
*Presse**	66,000	Feminist tradition of Naquet ended
*Soleil**	12,000	Very anti-feminist, anti-suffrage
*Univers**	8,000	Anti-suffrage
CONSERVATIVE		
*Croix**	140,000	Cautious acceptance of suffrage
Figaro	46,000	Cautious, but open to suffrage
*Gaulois**	20,000	Cautious, but some suffrage support
INDEPENDENT		
*Eclair**†	93,000	Cautious but early support
Excelsior†	125,000	Pro-suffrage, 1913-1914
Gil Blas	6,000	Cautious pro-feminism
Matin	645,000	Anti-feminist
Temps	36,000	Very cautious, uncommitted
REPUBLICAN		
Journal†	1,060,000	Vigorously pro-suffrage, esp. 1914
Journal des débats	26,000	Cautious support of municipal suffrage
Nouvelles†	3,000	Moderate feminism
Petit Parisien	1,375,000	Feminist tradition of Richer lost
Siècle†	5,000	Pro-suffrage, 1912-1914
LEFT REPUBLICAN		
Action†	20,000	Strongly pro-suffrage
Aurore	7,000	Pro-feminist, cautious on suffrage
Démocratie	15,000	Strongly pro-suffrage
Droits de l'homme	(weekly)	Strongly pro-suffrage
Homme libre	(est. 1913)	Anti-suffrage
Lanterne	28,000	Feminist tradition, cautious on suffrage

Table 7 • Continued

	Circulation	General Policy on Women's Suffrage
Petite république†	52,000	Pro-suffrage
Radical†	36,000	Ambivalent, but hesitant on suffrage
Rappel	16,000	Early suffragism lost
SOCIALIST		
Bonnet rouge	(weekly)	Pro-suffrage, 1913-1914
Humanité	70,000	Solidly pro-suffrage

* Indicates papers that the LPF circulated to Catholic women

† Indicates papers with a regular feminist column or contributor

NOTE: Circulation data from the Prefecture of Police file, Tirage des journaux, giving press runs for March 1, 1912, F7 12843; cf. the slightly different data for 1910 and 1912 in Bellanger et al., *Histoire générale de la presse française*, 3:296. Ideological groupings based on the papers' own identifications, given in Bluysen, ed., *Annuaire de la presse française, 1914*, pp. 907-953, and Bellanger, 3:239-405. Characterization of suffrage policy is based on clippings files at the BMD and the BHVP, plus spot-checkings of response to major suffrage activities in April-June 1908, April-May 1910, and 1914.

example, argued that suffragism and monarchism were not inconsistent by citing the case of Norway, where King Haakon VII personally championed the political rights of women. The reform was "so logical, so rational, so fair," that royalists should accept it. When readership of pro-suffrage newspapers increased more than tenfold in a decade, suffragists realized that some of this new support was shallow. Furthermore, many newspapers, including some with huge circulations and some with great prestige, remained noncommittal. But the trend was sufficiently clear to convince suffragists that their strategy would soon conquer Parisian opinion.[34]

Another source of suffragist optimism derived from their collaboration with social reform organizations. One of the most effective of these alliances was with the anti-alcoholism campaigners. Gaston Paris's Ligue nationale contre l'alcoolisme, the male-dominated union of temperance and anti-alcoholism societies, endorsed women's suffrage in 1903. When the CNFF showed increasing interest in temperance, the league created a "women's committee" charged with developing the liaison with the feminist movement. That committee joined the CNFF in 1907 and cooperated so closely with the UFSF that its head, Mme. Robert Mirabaud, was elected to the suffrage union's executive committee in 1912. The alliance between Paris's league and the UFSF resulted in a coordinated electoral program of sponsoring candidates in 1912. This connection enabled the women's movement to present its ideas to a new constituency. The membership of the Ligue nationale contre l'alcoolisme included businessmen and managerial personnel, who worried about the effects of alcoholism on their workers, and army officers (over 900 in 1913) with similar anxieties about the results of alcoholism on soldiers. Gradually they appreciated that women's suffrage might have powerful applications in social control, a point recognized much earlier in other countries, through the work of the WCTU. Joseph Reinach provides a good illustration of the link between suffragism and anti-alcoholism in the Chamber of Deputies. Reinach was sympathetic to the women's rights movements but, like many radical politicians, did not consider it urgent enough to list on his electoral program. After the Dreyfus affair, alcoholism became the great cause of Reinach's political career; by 1906, he was convinced that the French were "the most alcoholic people on earth." As president of both the national league and the parliamentary anti-alcoholism group, he came to appreciate that women's suffrage was desirable for the social consequences of enfranchisement. He was not alone in reaching this conclusion. A list of the politicians active in the anti-alcoholism campaign reads almost exactly like a list of parliamentary supporters of women's suffrage: Caillaux, Painlevé, Poincaré, Andrieux, Waddington, Buisson, Siegfried, Guyot.[35]

A more direct sign of the political progress of women's suffrage was its endorsement by the League of the Rights of Man. That league had impeccable credentials with left-wing republicanism due to its role in the Dreyfus affair. Under the presidency of Francis de Pressensé, the league grew to 90,000 members, emerging as one of the most influential extraparliamentary associations in France and attracting its membership from precisely that segment of the nation that feared women's suffrage would produce a clerical revolution. De Pressensé, however, opened the league (unlike the Radical Party) to women and affiliated it with the LFDF. Their first commitment to suffragism came in 1907 when Auclert proposed her great petition. The central committee of the league voted support and submitted it to the local sections, where it obtained the endorsement of 73,000 members. In 1908, the committee invited Vérone to deliver a suffrage report to the league's next congress. She urged the congress to support the Dussaussoy Bill; de Pressensé intervened, however, to call for full political rights for women, and he carried that motion with virtually no opposition. Thereafter, the League of the Rights of Man collaborated closely with the women's suffrage campaign. Vérone made de Pressensé one of the principal speakers at the first great suffrage meeting in 1910; she, in turn, was elected to the league's central committee. A few weeks later, the league's weekly newspaper, *Les Droits de l'homme*, published one of the most emphatic appeals for women's rights that the Parisian press had yet seen. And in 1911 the connection between the League of the Rights of Man and the suffrage campaign grew even stronger with the election of Buisson to succeed de Pressensé as president of the league.[36]

Suffragist optimism also derived from the creation in 1911 of the first masculine organization devoted solely to winning the vote for women, the Ligue d'électeurs pour le suffrage des femmes—a men's auxilliary. The statutes described it as grouping together all men who believed that women should have the same political rights as men. The program, however, was attuned to the predominant moderation of the women's movement: equality should come in stages and should be sought by calm propaganda as "permitted by the law." Buisson was the titular head of the League of Electors, but its guiding spirit was Jean du Breuil de Saint-Germain, the son of a deputy who had worked for women's rights in the late nineteenth century. The officers of the league reveal its close connection with suffragism: Léon Brunschwicg (the husband of Cécile) was a vice-president; Raoul Rebour (the husband of Pauline) edited the league's *Bulletin*; Wilfred Monod (a brother of Sarah) and Paul Gemahling (the husband of a UFSF executive committee member) both served on the *comité*, along with Victor Margueritte and Francis de Pressensé. The membership included such prominent politicians as Louis Marin (a vice-president of the league), Charles Benoist, Justin Godart, Paul Deschanel, René Viviani, Jean Jaurès, Marcel Sembat, and Albert Thomas.[37]

Thus, in many ways, suffragist confidence was a reasonable interpretation of the evidence: the existence of a moderate, compromise proposition in the Dussaussoy Bill; the favorable report of Buisson and the Commission of Universal Suffrage; the existence of a large group of deputies for women's suffrage; the backing of influential organizations such as the League of the Rights of Man and the pledged votes of the SFIO en bloc; the increasing approval of Parisian public opinion, especially in the daily press; the vows of local governments in favor of the Dussaussoy Bill; the significant penetration of the provinces by suffragist organizations; pledges of support from several barons of parliament.

This confidence, however, was premature, if not naive. Marin was closer to the truth when he told suffragists that parliament remained essentially hostile to the reform despite signs to the contrary.[38] Opponents of women's suffrage outnumbered its advocates in the Chamber of Deputies by a three-to-two margin during the legislature of 1910-1914—a coalition of approximately 330 deputies who declined to co-sponsor the Dussaussoy Bill. Their resistance was more complicated than the misogyny of Emile Combes and the anti-clericalism of Clemenceau. Such antagonism remained typical of the Radical and Radical-Socialist Party, but it provides only a necessary, not a sufficient, explanation of the postponement of women's suffrage. Radicals, it is true, still dominated the chamber, holding 42 percent of the seats during the Tenth Legislature and 66 percent of all ministerial appointments. The next largest bloc, the republicans of the right-center, counted only 26 percent of the chamber and 25 percent of the ministries. This would seem to suggest that radical anti-suffragism accounts for the continuing delay. But radicals did not oppose women's suffrage by a greater margin than any of the parties to their right (see Table 8). They were divided on this as on so many other issues; seventy-seven radicals, nearly a third of their deputation, publicly endorsed the Dussaussoy Bill. As the anti-suffrage radicals accounted

Table 8 • **Support for Women's Suffrage during the Tenth Legislature, 1910-1914**

	Deputation	Pro-Suffrage	Suffragist %
Socialists	103	85	82.5
Radicals	248	77	31.0
Republicans	152	50	32.9
Right	88	26	29.5
Total	591	238	40.3

NOTE: Based on those deputies who signed the joint feminist appeal for women's suffrage, 1910-1914, as listed in the joint feminist letter to all deputies, June 1, 1914, contained in the Dossier Vote des femmes, 1914, BMD.

for barely half of the opposition, one must look beyond that party to understand the parliamentary position of the Dussaussoy Bill.

Suffragists believed that many of the silent deputies would vote for the bill if it were ever debated. They did not need many. By the end of the Tenth Legislature, suffragists claimed 261 deputies (44.2 percent of the chamber) had stated their support. (See Map 7.) If their sympathizers would only bring forward the Buisson Report and inscribe a suffrage debate on the order of the day, suffragists believed, the anti-suffrage margin of 330-261 would soon disappear. Part of the explanation for the continuing disenfranchisement of women must therefore be traced to the behavior of pro-suffrage politicians. Why did the allies of the women's movement hesitate? Some of them, it appears, supported suffragism only *pro forma*: they admitted the justice of the idea and associated their names with it, but they were in no rush to achieve the reform. Suffragists were appalled to discover, for example, that the parliamentary group for women's rights was only a false façade, a political Potemkin Village: it never even met, much less adopted a program or lobbied for it.[39]

For most pro-suffrage deputies, the delay was a matter of priorities. Women must wait their turn, after the resolution of more important matters. As a result of this feeling—or perhaps rationalization—the fate of the Dussaussoy Bill became intertwined with other political struggles and suffered constant postponement. The primary concern remained proportional representation. Until some version of this reform became law, women's suffrage had few parliamentary supporters—far below 261—and would remain undebated. The Commission of Universal Suffrage remained adamant on this point, with the expressed approval of virtually all parliamentary suffragists, Ferdinand Buisson included.[40] Pressed by Auclert, Louis Andrieux and a few other maverick pro-suffrage deputies tried to link the questions of proportional representation and women's suffrage in 1913. Andrieux's amendment to that effect was utterly swamped. The number of parliamentary suffragists willing to support him declined by over half, to 117. And even that number is misleadingly high because it included some conservative opponents of both *le RP* and women's suffrage who hoped to doom the former by uniting it with the latter. Among the well-known feminist deputies who defected on this amendment were Buisson, Viviani, Chéron, Reinach, Poincaré, Jaurès, and even Jules

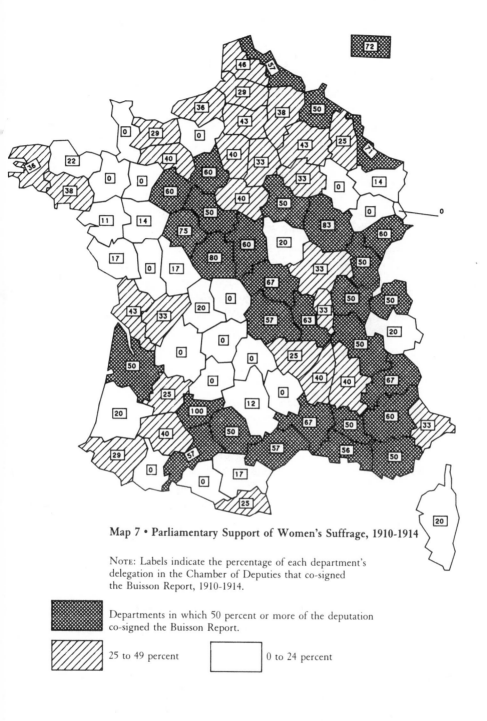

Map 7 • Parliamentary Support of Women's Suffrage, 1910-1914

NOTE: Labels indicate the percentage of each department's delegation in the Chamber of Deputies that co-signed the Buisson Report, 1910-1914.

Departments in which 50 percent or more of the deputation co-signed the Buisson Report.

25 to 49 percent   0 to 24 percent

Siegfried. Those who stood beside Andrieux included Beauquier, Cruppi, Godart, and Marin.[41]

Women's suffrage would wait, therefore, until its advocates were ready. The complexity of the proportional representation debate meant that the delay could be (and was) many years. It had already preoccupied the Commission of Universal Suffrage throughout the Eighth Legislature (1902-1906) and the Ninth Legislature (1906-1910).[42] Would, for example, proportional representation entail the abandonment of single-member constituencies (*scrutin d'arrondissement*), lambasted by Briand as "stagnant pools"? Did "proportional" mean an equitable distribution of seats among the established parties or the first representation of smaller minorities? Was the reform to include the elimination of runoff elections with their notorious bargaining among allied factions? Were measures against electoral corruption, such as vote-buying, or the introduction of the secret ballot appropriate parts of the package?[43] Radicals were understandably ambivalent. As did women's suffrage, *le RP* divided them between democratic ideals and the politics of self-interest. The existing system favored radicals, and they knew it. In the elections of 1910, more than one hundred radicals had been sent to the Palais Bourbon despite being the first choice of less than one-third of their electors. The average radical candidate in that election needed slightly over 11,000 votes to win the election; his successful socialist colleague had to find an average of 20 percent more votes—a total of 14,000.[44] Consequently, the Radical Party split and procrastinated, and delay for proportional representation was delay for women's suffrage. Furthermore, the barons of the chamber exploited the issue of electoral reform to conduct the open brokerage of support so characteristic of the Third Republic's multiparty coalitions. Could *le RP* be passed if some backers agreed to Caillaux's income tax bill? or to the bill to institute three years of military service instead of two?

Such political maneuvering caused women's suffrage to remain undebated throughout the Tenth Legislature. Suffragist hopes suffered particularly in 1913. The Chamber of Deputies had finally agreed on a proportional representation bill in 1912, but in March 1913, the Senate rejected the bill because it contained proportional representation for small minorities. In June, the Senate adopted its own version, but the chamber refused to back down. After hectic bargaining in the lobbies, which in July produced the Law of Three Years, the deputies

again voted their original form of proportional representation in November; the Senate remained unswayed. This demonstration of senatorial power to stop reform legislation should have, per se, curbed
suffragist optimism. They had never counted their votes in the Senate;
had they reflected upon the Senate's record on the woman question
the conclusion could only have sobered them. In the years immediately
prior to World War I, for example, the Senate gave no signs of interest
in women's suffrage but three times discussed the need for women
to stay at home and raise families in order to combat depopulation.[45]

Trouble on the Left and the Right: Socialists, Catholics, and the Political Rights of Women

The parliamentary strength of suffragism depended a great deal on
the support of the socialist party. When suffragists reckoned that they
had 261 votes in the Tenth Legislature, they were counting on the
unanimous backing of the SFIO and independent socialists to provide
103 votes. In contrast, suffragists expected the backing of less than
one-third of all 488 non-socialist deputies. Socialism and suffragism
would seem, prima facie, to have been intimate allies. They were not.
Upon investigation, the feminism of French socialists seems almost
as shallow as that of their radical colleagues.

The public position of the socialist party was unequivocally pro-
suffrage. The Second International placed the right to vote on the
socialist agenda as early as the Brussels Congress of 1871, a commitment Auclert won from French socialists at Marseille in 1879. Subsequent assemblies reiterated this pledge, as, for example, did the
congresses of Tours (1902) and Rheims (1903). The rise of Pelletier
in the socialist party coincided with other explicit renewals of this
policy. She raised women's suffrage at the Limoges Congress (1906)
and obtained its unanimous ratification. At Nancy the following year,
she carried a motion to take suffragism to the meeting of the international at Stuttgart in 1907, where socialists again repeated their
pledge. Individual leaders of the SFIO never hesitated to repeat their
vow, as Jaurès did at a feminist meeting in October 1909 or Albert
Thomas did in announcing to the Chamber of Deputies in June 1910,
that the SFIO supported the Buisson Report en bloc. Similarly, the
socialist press regularly reminded the world of the party's stand, as

the *Revue socialiste* did in a special issue in 1906, Marcel Sembat did in a major article in 1907, and Bracke repeated in *L'Humanité* in 1912.[46]

The SFIO offered many words and little action. Pelletier and others began to question the party and then to doubt it.[47] The career of Albert Thomas provides a clear illustration of the problem. There is no reason to doubt that he believed in the justice of equal political rights for women, but his behavior puts that belief in perspective. Thomas attended the congresses of Limoges, Stuttgart, and Amiens and reported on them for *La Revue syndicaliste*; not once in his summaries of events did he mention women's rights. His electoral program and *"profession de foi"* stressed democratic electoral reforms in detail but omitted women's suffrage. The avoidance of the question can be seen vividly in his personal papers. Thomas kept records of a vast array of social issues, but not women's suffrage. It simply was not a question in his active political life.[48] Jaurès—who held conventional middle-class ideas about women—provides a similar example. During the proportional representation debates of 1912 Jaurès became the target of considerable pressure to honor his pledges and introduce the issue in the chamber. He discussed the idea with his parliamentary colleagues and gave his answer in *L'Humanité* in December 1912, pronouncing it "essential that the question be posed, and that it be posed without delay." Yet when Louis Andrieux did so for him a few months later, Jaurès actually voted against the idea. As for many republicans, saving proportional representation was more important to him than debating women's suffrage.[49]

Had the socialist party desired to establish women's political rights, the elections of 1910 provided a great opportunity. The SFIO held thirteen safe seats in Paris, St. Denis, and Sceaux, four of which were awarded to new candidates in 1910. Had Pelletier been the official candidate in one of these constituencies, and had socialists actually voted for a woman, Pelletier would have won. If so, the prefecture would doubtless have nullified the results and conducted a by-election. Had Pelletier won a second time, the issue would be joined quite dramatically. "You are sovereign," Auclert once told electors in proposing such a candidacy; "your will has the force of law." Pelletier propounded this idea in 1910, but the Madeleine quarter was scarcely likely to present the government with such a *fait accompli*.[50]

Most suffragists concluded that the SFIO was insincere. By 1912

Pelletier believed that socialists simply were not feminist; worse, "they will be ... the last [party] to take our ideas seriously." For a person who had served on the Permanent Administrative Council of the SFIO and still proclaimed herself a socialist, Pelletier was quite outspoken in her disillusionment: "What party to choose? In general I think that feminism has more to hope for from the republican parties than from the parties of the extreme right or left."[51] The plangent feminism of Pelletier had no home among those republican parties, nor could she find a comfortable life among moderate feminists "more monied than I." Just as earlier disappointments had led her away from Freemasonry, she drifted to the extreme left of socialism, briefly finding a home with the Hervists and anarchism. Later she found new hope and new disillusionment with the Communist Party. Her ardor for women's equality did not diminish, but she learned to accept insincere professions of support with a certain fatalism. As she once wrote Arria Ly, in a mood of such depression, "it serves nothing to recriminate; that which is, is."[52] If Pelletier could be driven to that point, it is hardly surprising that bourgeois feminists found it very easy to doubt the left.[53] Recent research has demonstrated just how justified this skepticism about socialist feminism was.[54]

Why did French socialists not take a more active role in seeking women's suffrage? Part of the answer was a function of socialist beliefs. On the right of the party, reformist socialists such as Jaurès essentially accepted the republic and sought to reshape it. Their republicanism made them susceptible to the arguments of republican anti-suffragism: the insufficient education of women, the dangers of a reactionary vote by priest-ridden women, or the primacy of other democratic reforms such as proportional representation. Hence, Jaurèsian socialists could speak of the need for a "brief delay" before actually enfranchising women. Guesdists and more orthodox Marxists had a direct ideological reason for not working for suffragism: reformist campaigns were seen as diversions that detracted from preparation for the proletarian revolution which would produce complete equality, including between the sexes. They believed, as Marx had written in the *Economic and Philosophic Manuscripts of 1844*, that "the emancipation of the workers contains universal human emancipation." On the socialist left, revolutionaries and anarchists such as the Hervists also had a simple doctrinal answer for not working for women's suffrage: they were anti-parliamentarian and saw no virtue in the republican electoral regime, regardless of the definition of the electorate. Instead of seeking to vote, women should press men not to participate in politics.[55]

Another essential factor in understanding why the SFIO was not actively suffragist is the conflicting social bases of the two movements. Suffragists were chiefly recruited from social groups that feared a proletarian revolution. Socialist workers were not greatly sympathetic to the pleas of middle-class women, just as bourgeois suffragists were not greatly sensitive to the plight of workers. The theory of the class war put suffragists and socialists on different sides of the barricades. Militant suffragists might denounce this characterization of feminist-socialist relations, but the gulf between the classes remained. The socialist response could be blunt: bourgeois feminists failed "to extricate themselves from the organic egoism of the privileged" and therefore could not appreciate how feminism was "an insufficient palliative to the misery of the workers."[56]

A third explanation for the socialist hesitancy on suffragism derives from the nature of the socialist constituency. Working-class men were not merely uninterested in women's rights, they were often openly hostile. Such hostility had many roots—the fear that "disloyal competition" from women for jobs would produce lower wages and greater unemployment; the psychological compensation for being the slave of an employer by becoming the master of a wife; the traditional family orientation of France, whether peasant or proletarian; the doctrinal cachet given to working-class misogyny by Proudhonist theories; the often open anti-feminism of the CGT. "The working class will be the last to come to feminism," Pelletier concluded. "It is in the nature of things; the ignorant respect only brute force. ... I am a socialist, because I passionately love justice. But to love the working class such as it is now—no!"[57]

A final important factor in shaping socialist behavior on the suffrage question was the anti-suffragist orientation of the socialist women's movement. In the GFS of 1899-1905, there had been a delicate balance between the anti-feminism of Louise Saumoneau and the feminism of Elisabeth Renaud. The reconstituted group of 1912—significantly renamed the Groupe des femmes socialistes (GdFS)—initially seemed likely to adopt an active suffragism but soon bore the unmistakable imprint of Saumoneau's ideas. The GdFS had been established upon the initiative of Marianne Rauze (the witty pseudonym of Marie Comignan). Rauze previously wrote for *La Française* and participated in the UFSF, only joining the SFIO in 1912. At her invitation, the founding members of the GdFS included mostly socialist women connected with the suffrage movement—Renaud, Vérone, Bonnevial, Kauffmann, Pellat-Finet, and two young socialists who had recently joined the UFSF, Hélène Brion and Marguerite Martin. Pelletier declined an invitation. Her disillusionment with socialism convinced her that feminists must not place any party above their aspirations as women. This new group, Pelletier argued, would result in the subordination of feminism to socialism: "I fear that the socialist women's group will be only the kindergarten of the socialist party and that it will leave feminism behind to please the men in the party." Initially it seemed that Pelletier was wrong. Saumoneau, whose rivalry with Renaud continued, was intentionally excluded from the foundation of the GdFS. Renaud was chosen as the first secretary-general, with Vérone, Bonnevial, Brion, and Martin elected to the executive committee. One of the first meetings of the group was devoted to a suffragist lecture by Vérone. The group openly collaborated with the UFSF, including the co-sponsorship of a suffragist rally at Brest, where both Rauze and Martin spoke in favor of the vote.[58]

The suffragist orientation of the GdFS lasted less than a year. Saumoneau assaulted socialist feminism, both in the meetings of the group and in the pages of her newspaper, *La Femme socialiste*, which she had reestablished in 1912. By the winter of 1913-1914, Saumoneau had succeeded in a coup against the suffragists, resulting in the ouster of Renaud, Brion, Vérone, and Bonnevial from the leadership of the GdFS and her own election as the secretary-general. Thereafter, there was no question of collaboration between the group and bourgeois feminists, whom Saumoneau branded "that amalgam of intriguing, naive, deranged, and hysterical women." The struggle for the direction of the GdFS was conducted publicly in the pages of Rauze's *L'Equité* (founded 1913) and Saumoneau's *La Femme socialiste*. Suzanne Lacore (later to join Cécile Brunschwicg and Irène Joliot-Curie as the first women to sit in a French cabinet) fired the opening salvo in an article in *L'Equité*, aimed squarely at "the boat of bourgeois feminism." Socialist women must accept, she insisted, the fact that their liberation would come only through that of the entire working class. Rauze immediately opened *L'Equité* to a debate on this subject while Saumoneau launched a series of articles praising Lacore's position and denouncing those who rebutted her. Saumoneau especially directed her vituperation toward Brion ("a scatterbrain"), who had the temerity to claim that their suffering primarily resulted from sexual, not class, inequality. The victory of Louise Saumoneau in this struggle was a significant setback for French suffragism. She drove women such as Vérone and Bonnevial out of the GdFS, perpetuated the division of the women's movement, helped deprive suffragism of support from working-class women, and facilitated the parliamentary inaction of the SFIO.[59] Why should the party act forcefully on women's suffrage when women within the party believed that they should not?

The estrangement of bourgeois suffragists from the socialist women's movement was duplicated on the right by the continued anti-suffragism of the Catholic women's movement. Despite the efforts of Maugeret, suffragism simply did not take root in Catholic soil before World War I. The events of 1906-1907 taught Maugeret that even her friends thought that she was going too fast. She retreated to the slightly more acceptable socioeconomic concerns of liberal Catholicism—such as working with the Count de Mun in 1908 to secure Catholic support for a minimum wage for seamstresses who worked at home. *Le Féminisme chrétien* became silent on the suffrage question. The issue did not appear on the program of the Congrès Jeanne d'Arc for several years. The ultramontane orientation of the conservative women of the LPF and the LFF, buttressed by papal opposition to women's suffrage, quieted Maugeret for half a decade.

Maugeret was equally separate from republican feminists. She won the admiration of some moderates, such as Jane Misme, but her beliefs were as unacceptable to the UFSF as they were to the LPF. So long as fundamental disagreements such as the status of religious associations, the control of education, the ownership of church property, the law of divorce, and many aspects of the degeneration debate split Catholics and radical republicans, no rapprochement of the two women's movements was possible. Even Cécile Brunschwicg, who claimed that she wanted a "truly national" UFSF, was uninterested in such cooperation. As she told a feminist congress in 1912, Catholic women were welcomed into the union, but not those who took an active part in Catholic politics.[60] It was an argument little different from Saumoneau's.

Maugeret made another attempt at building Catholic suffragism at the Congrès Jeanne d'Arc of 1910. To avoid the criticism she encountered in 1906, Maugeret carefully advertised the session on political rights. She relied on well-known conservatives to present her position. A member of the Institut argued that women's suffrage was both just and expedient; a theologian insisted that nothing in Catholic doctrine prohibited the vote; a journalist from *La Croix* analyzed the recent elections to the Norwegian parliament and attributed the conservative victory there to newly enfranchised women. Maugeret read letters of support from prominent figures. The response of Catholic women to this appeal remained unchanged. The delegates still perceived political rights as a threat to the family. All knew that the Vatican did not approve. Anti-suffragists, led by the Countess Lecointre, prevented the adoption of any suffrage motion. This defeat was Maugeret's last major effort. She was sixty-six years old in 1910; although she lived until 1928 and still gave suffrage speeches in her late seventies, the acceptance of her ideas had to await younger champions and a different climate of opinion.[61]

Despite this rejection, there were some signs that opinion could change. Chenu led Action sociale in occasional discussions of women's rights and the league's bulletin published some sympathetic articles. *La Femme contemporaine* continued to publish reports for Catholic women on the activities of republican feminists, culminating in a 1913 article endorsing the vote. Even the LPF gave a hint of considering political rights. The death of the Baroness Reille in 1910 briefly led to the withdrawal of the LPF from any form of political activity. Her successor as president, the Vicountess Vélard, began in 1911 to conduct a series of "study groups" on women and politics. The league's official policy was neither to approve, nor to disapprove, of women's suffrage. It did, however, encourage Catholic women to take an interest and an active role in politics. The LPF had the support of the church in this. Cardinal Amette, the archbishop of Paris, told the women of the LPF in 1914 that it was their duty to seek political influence because all votes "have consequences for the church." He urged Catholic women to attend to local politics, where mayors had considerable powers, such as the ability to prevent public processions. Amette's talk of duty, defense of the church, and local matters was a position that could easily lead to a Catholic reconsideration of the Dussaussoy Bill. Cardinal Amette also touched upon the sine qua non for the development of Catholic suffragism by suggesting that the pope approved of women seeking political influence. He quoted Pius X as saying "When religion or the state are in peril, it is not permissible for *anyone* to remain inactive." The LPF simultaneously received a modest pro-suffrage stimulus from the Action libérale populaire, the political party with which they were closely associated. One-third of the party's deputies in the legislature of 1910 (five of fifteen) publicly endorsed the Buisson Report. This was a small minority, but it was a level of support that compared favorably with the backing that suffragists received from republican parties.[62]

Chapter Six

OXOXOXOXOXOXOXOXOXOXOXOXOXOXOXOXOXOXOXOXOXOXOXOXOXOXOXOXOXOXOXOXOXOXO

The Apogee of Suffragist Activity:
The Campaign of 1914

Although the majority of French suffragists were optimistic about their prospects at the beginning of 1914, a few dissenting voices could be heard. Some militants and skeptical realists wondered if the conversion of opinion was not too slow, if the calm suffragism of the UFSF would actually succeed. Foremost in this group of skeptics stood Maria Vérone, who began to argue that French suffragism must enter "a new phase." Violence was still out of the question, but surely, she concluded, a nonviolent activism could be found to launch a final push for victory. Vérone launched her new activism during the holiday season of December 1913 by violating the suffragist taboo against activity in the streets. Her action, although cautious, opened both a seven-month period of great suffragist activity and the old split between moderate and militant republican feminists. Vérone operated a "suffragist kiosk," on the boulevard de Sébastopol near the rue Réamur. For over two weeks in late December and early January 1914 she and a few supporters sold small holiday gifts wrapped with feminist literature and accompanied by proselytizing conversation. Vérone intended this activity to confront anti-suffragist opinion yet to maintain respectable behavior. She summarized her ambitions by relating the story of one confrontation in the streets: "Nothing from suffragettes," one browser told her. "Pardon, ... suffragists," Vérone corrected. "The former burn chateaux, the latter sell New Year's gifts."[1]

The publicity provoked by Vérone's little kiosk reinforced her determination to find some means to awaken the suffrage movement. At the January meeting of the LFDF she introduced a plan to sponsor the registration of women during the annual revision of electoral lists. This was not a novel idea; both Vincent and Auclert had attempted it repeatedly. The LFDF, however, proposed to sponsor registration efforts in all twenty *arrondissements* of Paris and then to challenge all refusals in court, relying on the legal talents of the league's own leadership. At the very least, Vérone reasoned, this should engender considerable press coverage and inaugurate an active campaign during the legislative elections scheduled for the spring of 1914; at best, perhaps the courts would find a new definition of *citoyen*. Vérone won the cooperation of a few individuals from the GdFS whom she had impressed during her brief membership there, plus the help of some dissatisfied militants within the UFSF, but her campaign had very limited success. Sympathetic municipal officials registered women in three *arrondissements*, taking a total of twelve names for the electoral lists. Bonnevial and Suzanne Grinberg (an officer of the UFSF) registered without incident in the Seventeenth Arrondissement, although they were informed that they could only use their registration as permitted by the law. In the Nineteenth, the secretary of the LFDF and five working women from the GdFS were registered when a group of socialist men said that they would not leave the *mairie* until the women were accepted too. On the other hand, officials in three *arrondissements* summoned the police to eject all women from the *mairie*. Small scuffles occurred in the Fourth (where Auclert had seized an urn in 1908) and in the Ninth (where Vérone had confronted a squad of police in 1908). Some officials insisted that they supported the cause but were powerless to act, as Renaud was told in the Fifth Arrondissement. Others responded facetiously: the clerk in the Eleventh demanded first to see a military *livret* proving service in the army; an official in the Sixteenth wanted a letter of permission from Ferdinand Buisson. The most common reaction was bureaucratic caution. Officials in several *arrondissements* decided to take the names and addresses of all applicants and then refer the matter to the prefecture of the Seine. That solution quickly ended the LFDF efforts to register women: within twenty-four hours of receiving notification, the prefecture delivered a formal order against registering women. Copies of this order were the only answer that subsequent LFDF delegations received.[2]

Maria Vérone and her husband, Georges Lhermite, undertook litigation on behalf of the women denied registration. Such cases went first to a special commission for matters of electoral registration; negative decisions there could then be appealed before a *juge de paix* for the appropriate *arrondissement*. The LFDF filed such appeals in five different districts. Vérone based her case on the contradictory interpretation of the words *français* and *citoyen* in the law, despite the explicit ruling of 1893. She coupled this argument with a plea to the judge to recognize the difference between French suffragists and English suffragettes, stressing that French women were strictly adhering to the law and believed that it already provided for them.

Among the court cases filed by Vérone and Lhermite, most attention focused on the appeal of a socialist student in the Thirteenth Arrondissement, Jeanne Halbwachs, who later became a well-known pacifist under her married name of Halbwachs-Alexandre. The Halbwachs case went poorly from the start. The judge interrogated Halbwachs with undisguised condescension, reproach, and irony. He delayed handing down his ruling until feminist attendance at court diminished and then abruptly concluded that women could not be inscribed. Gustave Téry, a suffragist covering the case for *Le Journal*, was astonished to hear the verdict delivered "like a scene by Beaumarchais." The words that shocked Téry, however, were essentially a paraphrase of the ruling of 1893:

> The quality of *"citoyen"* does not belong indistinctly to both men and women like the term *"français"*; men alone can become *"citoyens,"* while women remain *"françaises."* In consequence, they are not capable of exercising political rights.[3]

Vérone and Lhermite immediately appealed this judgment to the *Cour de cassation*. They lost again. Once more they heard that French women were not, and could not be, citizens. That opinion, handed down in April 1914, effectively foreclosed the pending cases and ended the LFDF campaign. Nothing had changed in the generation since Eliska Vincent's case, and Vérone had to find a different route to greater suffragist activism.[4]

Vérone was not alone in the belief that French suffragism needed reinvigoration. A number of younger members had begun to chafe under the endless patience of the leadership of the UFSF and the CNFF and to question the effectiveness of their apparent reconciliation to the political situation. It was a young member of the UFSF's executive committee, Thérèse Belle, who originally conceived the idea of a suffragist kiosk; she took the idea to Vérone only after her colleagues at the union found it to be inappropriate. Another member of that executive committee (Grinberg) defied the union in collaborating with Vérone's registration campaign; some provincial activists, inspired by Jeanne Mélin, did the same. This strife within the UFSF occurred at the same time that several young militants—Marguerite Martin, Hélène Brion, Marianne Rauze—were leaving the union for the GdFS in hopes of making that group a home for more advanced suffragists. As one old militant put it, the leaders of the UFSF liked to pretend that they had invented feminism but in fact would only follow a feminist course when the path had been swept clean in front of them.[5] This dissatisfaction with the established suffragist leadership was not endemic to the UFSF. Madame Remember (the pseudonym of Louise Deverly-Dupont) broke with Vérone to seek her own way to invigorate the movement. Remember (1845-1925) had followed the well-trodden route from middle-class comfort, through philanthropy and *La Fronde*, to feminism, winding up a member of the LFDF and one of the editors of *La Suffragiste*. In mid-1913 Remember founded her own newspaper, *Le Féminisme intégral*; appropriately for a period of militant revival, she subtitled it "an organ of combat." The newspaper offered a mixture of the ideas of Pelletier, the Bélilon sisters, Arria Ly, and Auclert rather than a new course, but her dissatisfaction was typical of many militants by 1914.[6]

The most important expression of discontent on the feminist left was the creation of a new militant society, the Ligue nationale pour le vote des femmes (LNVF) in January 1914. The leadership of the league came from young militants in the UFSF—"zealots," according to Jane Misme—and socialist suffragists driven from the GdFS by Louise Saumoneau. The secretary-general of the LNVF, Fabienne Tisserand, and three other officers (Mme. Ducret-Metsu, president; Anne Léal, secretary; Caroline Kauffmann, vice-president) all left the GdFS together. Their statutes for the league announced that membership would be open to any supporter of women's suffrage but that recruitment would primarily be among working-class women whom the UFSF and the CNFF overlooked. "It is the league of democracy," Ducret-Metsu proclaimed, "which extends its propaganda and its influence among the workers, and in general among women of the proletariat." That aspiration appealed to several well-known feminists—Vérone, Roussel, Durand, Pelletier, Séverine—who joined the league and gave lectures to attract more members. It also attracted the director of *Le Journal*, M. Letellier, a friend of Ducret-Metsu, who provided the LNVF with considerable publicity and free meeting facilities at the great hall of the newspaper. With such advantages, the league grew rapidly from 25 founding members to 250 dues-paying members within six weeks.[7]

The LNVF provoked suffragist controversy by challenging the moderation of the UFSF. Indeed, the rivalry between the two organizations became a leitmotif to the campaign of 1914, producing acrimony on both sides. Their argument was not the old battle over appropriate collective behavior, although that was on the minds of many women. Instead, the LNVF challenged the policy of working for the Dussaussoy Bill. From their very first meeting, the founders of the new league agreed to work for nothing less than integral suffrage. Municipal suffrage was just "a bone to gnaw on"; they would not spurn it if parliament offered it, but they would not devote their energies to so small a target.[8]

The clash of the LNVF with the UFSF encouraged other militants to challenge the moderate consensus. Vérone and the LFDF had been drifting further from the UFSF, and the appearance of the new militant league made their disagreement public. Vérone first rethought her position on the Dussaussoy Bill after the congress of the League of the Rights of Man in 1909 called for full rights for women. A campaign for integral suffrage was implicit in her voter registration work of 1914 and in the search for new answers that led her to join both the GdFS and the LNVF at their creation. Vérone, however, was a little uncomfortable with the militancy of the LNVF and concentrated her energies on her own league. That meant, in turn, a more outspoken position for the LFDF and open disagreement with the UFSF.[9] The assertive policy of the LNVF also attracted individuals who had drifted away from suffragism in dissatisfaction with the hegemony of the UFSF. Nelly Roussel had tried for years to make the suffrage union take a more forceful stand. Failing in that, Roussel emphasized her disagreement in one of her most often requested speeches, "Let Us Create the Citizeness":

> Some will say that the conquest of municipal suffrage is a necessary first step; that one must not be too hard to please at the start; that prudence and moderation are the conditions of success. I hold an absolutely contrary opinion and believe that in order to obtain a little, it is necessary to demand a lot.[10]

Roussel's candor, in combination with new programs of the LFDF and the LNVF, threatened to divide the suffrage campaign. The LNVF, for example, seemed to take pleasure in criticizing Ferdinand Buisson for his dilatory politics and insistence upon municipal rights; the UFSF, in response, readied the first place in the suffragist pantheon for him.

The new militancy soon reopened the question of appropriate forms of collective action. Some change in tactics was implied in Vérone's term, "a new phase," and the wide popularity that it enjoyed. Hubertine Auclert, now sixty-six and in poor health, was among the first to respond. At a meeting of Suffrage des femmes in mid-March, she gave her support to those who called for full enfranchisement. To this encouragement Auclert added her belief that it was now time to pass from words to acts, "and to act vigorously." Suffragists must go into the streets in great numbers. It was time, Auclert proclaimed, for "a monster demonstration."[11] This was to be Auclert's last contribution to French suffragism. In early April 1914 she died, leaving behind a movement that had grown uncomfortable with her guidance. Less than three months after Auclert's death, however, the new phase saw more than five thousand women step into the streets.

The first attempt to follow Auclert's advice resulted in a dismal failure. Fabienne Tisserand of the LNVF, in collaboration with a pro-suffrage publicity specialist, M. Gabert, hastily drafted a plan to protest the court ruling against Jeanne Halbwachs with a "descent into the streets" in late March. Gabert proposed to hang a huge banner, decrying judicial hypocrisy, on the balcony of his offices at the Carrefour Feydeau, on rue Montmartre. Prominent militants would speak from the balcony, then descend to the street to lead a cortège in a procession past the banner. Skillful advance advertising could attract thousands of women, demonstrating that women's suffrage had the backing of more than a feminist elite. Gabert would secure the cooperation of the Prefecture of the Police to cordon off the street and protect the orderly assembly by repeating the pledge that he gave to moderate suffragists: the march would remain absolutely within the limits of the law.[12]

The Feydeau demonstration bore little resemblance to the plans of Tisserand and Gabert. Only one other feminist organization, Solidarité, agreed to participate. All of the large leagues—the UFSF, the CNFF, and even the hesitant LFDF—disavowed it and did not even send observers. The opposition of the UFSF and the CNFF derived from their well-known policy concerning respectable behavior; the refusal of Vérone to participate appears to have resulted from her anger at the unauthorized use of her name and from her unwillingness to denounce the courts in which she still had voter registration cases pending. Jane Misme and *La Française* initially expressed support for the rally but quickly retreated to criticism of all such demonstrations. "French suffragists are not ready for these gigantic parades that England and America constantly see," Misme wrote. "They will not be ready for a long time." She attributed this to "an innate caution in the French temperament" that had become a "second nature" for French women. Even if suffragists were capable of such behavior, Misme added, they realized that it was neither necessary nor desirable: "I believe that among us marches and processions are not at all necessary for the success of the cause and perhaps are harmful to it." In the face of such hostility from their colleagues, the LNVF could only attract approximately two dozen suffragists and perhaps two hundred Sunday pedestrians. Alone among the militants who participated, Pelletier understood what it meant to be a pariah even to fellow feminists. Most participants shared the sense of betrayal and bewilderment that Camille Bélilon expressed in a letter: "Most feminist societies ... even protested! I do not understand it at all."[13]

The LNVF's ill-fated descent into the streets provided further evidence of the distance French suffragists had yet to go. The response of both the Parisian press and the Prefecture of Police justified Bélilon's depression. Sensing that the aloofness of "well-behaved" feminists meant that the participants were fair game, the press amused itself with the sort of feminist-baiting that had almost disappeared from French journalism. *Le Soleil*, which had a long anti-suffrage record, explained to its readers how to identify feminists in such a crowd: look for women with very short hair and men with very long hair. *L'Intransigeant*, with an equivalent pro-suffrage record, joked that militant suffragettes should be permitted "to make noise" if they caused no trouble, because it would provide "a few minutes of joy" for children watching the spectacle. "What did this demonstration prove?" *Le Radical* asked. "Perhaps we'll read it tomorrow on other posters." Even *L'Action* labeled the event "completely grotesque." As for Gabert's agreement with the Prefecture of Police, nothing had changed since the feminist encounters with the police in 1904, 1906, and 1908. The police arrived in great numbers, not to control traffic and permit a demonstration but to control the demonstrators. "Perfidious!" recounted one participant. "We were forbidden to gather, even for a second and even beneath the banner unfurled on the balcony. They forced us to keep moving, with an arrogant air, as if we were some sort of malefactors."[14]

The best that could be said for the LNVF rally at the Carrefour Feydeau was that it had reopened the question of public demonstrations. Within a few weeks this would prove to be a significant contribution to the suffragist campaign of 1914.

The Feminist Center and the Dussaussoy Bill

Even before the fiasco of the Carrefour Feydeau, the moderates of the UFSF, the CNFF, and *La Française* saw no reason to seek a new phase for the suffrage campaign. Their optimism remained undiluted. The steady evolution of parliamentary suffragism had brought them within a few deputies of a majority in favor of the Dussaussoy Bill. The most optimistic now reckoned that as many as three hundred deputies might support it.[15] Surely, they reasoned, this progress would continue with the 1914 parliamentary elections: just a few more deputies and "In 1916 Women Will Vote!" announced the UFSF's 1914 poster. With victory at hand, abandonment of municipal suffrage as a goal or extreme caution as a strategy was unthinkable.[16]

Even while the militant rebellion of 1914 developed, attendance at the meetings of the moderates had grown enormously. The CNFF and the UFSF regularly attracted between 1,000 and 2,000 people to suffrage lectures; even the UFF drew 500. The message they heard was easy to follow: be patient, support parliamentary suffragists, and you will soon vote. In March 1914, for example, Julie Siegfried spoke to the largest meeting the CNFF had ever sponsored. Over 1,800 women heard her summarize the situation: "These women wait with confidence for the day when men will call them to work with them to make humanity better."[17] If this patient optimism widened a few of the fissures in the suffragist unity, or even produced some arguments with old friends, the moderate majority remained certain that it was the proper course.

Moderates possessed important new evidence to sustain their optimism. On February 2, 1914, the Commission of Universal Suffrage bowed to years of suffragist pressure and formally requested that the Chamber of Deputies inscribe the Dussaussoy Bill on the order of the day. And the chamber calmly agreed to do so. It was the furthest that a suffrage bill had ever gotten. No chance whatsoever existed that the chamber would actually debate the bill, because the Tenth Legislature would end in a few weeks for elections to the Eleventh, and the chamber's calendar was far too crowded for a new bill of such magnitude to wend its way to the floor. Suffragists had scored only a symbolic victory; politicians had made only a *beau geste*. Realists might wonder if this were a hollow gesture; republican suffragists entertained few such doubts—the new chamber would not retreat, women's suffrage would again be inscribed on the order of the day in January 1915. For these optimists, therefore, the spring of 1914 meant not the search for a new beginning but dedication to aiding the electoral campaigns of men likely to vote for municipal suffrage in the new Chamber of Deputies. The UFSF, in collaboration with the League of Electors, adopted this strategy. Candidates were polled to determine their attitudes and publicity was undertaken on behalf of the sympathetic.[18]

The elections of 1914 sharply changed the parliamentary situation for the Dussaussoy Bill. Eighty-nine deputies from the outgoing legislature who had backed the Buisson Report did not return to sit in the Eleventh Legislature—ninety, if one adds Jaurès, assassinated in the early days of the session. Of those losses, ten were socialist deputies replaced by other socialists; they were joined by thirty-eight socialists who won seats previously held by other parties. Assuming that the new socialists honored the party's commitment, suffragists suffered a net loss of forty-two votes. However, some feminists claimed, but did not name, 291 incoming deputies favorable to the Dussaussoy Bill. If this were so, suffragists had scored a net gain of thirty votes with the election of seventy-two new, non-socialist deputies sympathetic to their cause. As the Chamber of Deputies for the Eleventh Legislature would have 601 total members, suffragists were counting on starting with the support of 48.4 percent of it, compared to 44.2 percent for the outgoing legislature. This claim meant that moderates believed they were only ten votes away from an absolute majority. This may have been overly optimistic. In the opening days of the new legislature, when bills and reports inherited from their predecessors had to be returned to the commissions or abandoned, only 236 deputies co-signed the Buisson Report. There were presumably more pro-suffrage votes in the chamber than that, but it may be doubted that fifty-five strong supporters were silent.[19]

Several other new factors complicated the prospects for passage of the Dussaussoy Bill. Among the missing in the new legislature were two pioneers of the chamber's women's rights group, Henry Chéron (who died in 1913) and Charles Beauquier (who retired at age eighty), and two other influential suffragists, Joseph Reinach (defeated) and Théodore Steeg (elevated to the Senate). Worst of all for the cause, Ferdinand Buisson lost his seat representing the Thirteenth Arrondissement of Paris when a socialist candidate outpolled him on the first ballot and he withdrew from the runoff election, adhering to the traditional pact of "republican solidarity." Buisson's position as the *rapporteur* of the Dussaussoy Bill had been the greatest strength suffragists held in the Ninth and Tenth Legislatures, so women's groups carefully studied the new Commission of Universal Suffrage. They were satisfied with the results. Due to the continuing preoccupation with proportional representation, the commission had been expanded to forty-four members. Whereas the most optimistic suffragists claimed about 48 percent of the chamber supported them, they were confident of a majority in the commission: twenty-two of the members had co-signed the Buisson Report, two others had previously supported the Dussaussoy Bill, and four more were socialists whose backing was expected. With twenty-two to twenty-eight votes in hand, suffragists expected a prompt report. The new reporter was Pierre-Etienne Flandin (republican, Yonne), the youngest deputy in parliament at twenty-five, a future premier and foreign minister, and an announced supporter of the Dussaussoy Bill. Flandin lacked both Buisson's political influence and feminist ardor, but suffragists were satisfied that their interests were well-represented. The president of the commission was still Charles Benoist, who continued to back women's suffrage as a secondary question after *le RP*, yet suffragists believed that their cause would not be forgotten since the outspoken Louis Andrieux had also been named to the commission.[20]

Moderate suffragists had further reasons for their optimism when they considered the new legislature. With the defeat of Buisson, the strongest suffragist at the Palais Bourbon was unquestionably René Viviani who, on June 13, 1914, became the head of the government.

Among other sympathetic voices in his cabinet was Gaston Thomson, whose daughter Valentine had just established a new suffragist periodical (*La Vie féminine*) in collaboration with the UFSF. At the same time, the Chamber of Deputies elected Paul Deschanel—a longtime suffragist and the son of one of the earliest members of the LFDF—as its presiding officer. The leaders of the UFSF surveyed this evidence and concluded that their cause progressed toward victory. They were within ten votes of a majority in the chamber, had solid support in the committee, had good friends as premier and president of the chamber, and had seen the willingness of the chamber to put women's suffrage on the order of the day. Assembling for their annual congress at Lyons in June 1914, they told the press that they had "all confidence" that they would be voting in the municipal elections of 1916.[21]

The "New Phase": April-June 1914

While the UFSF was aiding the election of pro-suffrage deputies, other suffragists found the dramatic action with which to inaugurate their desired new phase. The device chosen was a poll. Throughout the parliamentary elections, suffragists would persuade women to sign "blank ballots" stating whether or not they wished to vote. The UFSF had briefly considered this idea in 1912 but rejected it in the belief that French suffragism was insufficiently advanced to produce the dramatic numbers needed to have any effect. The proposal to conduct such a poll during the elections came from Gustave Téry, now an editor at *Le Journal*. Both Téry and his newspaper had strong pro-suffrage records. Téry had been one of the strongest advocates at *Le Matin* of the Laloë race in 1908; in 1910 he had worked with Durand's election campaign, personally filing a protest when her ballots were not counted. *Le Journal* had been the most important pro-suffrage newspaper in Paris for several years. As early as 1906 it had begun publishing sympathetic articles; by 1908 feminists recognized it as their best ally in the mass press; in 1914 many of the larger groups held their meetings in the paper's meeting hall, including both the LFDF and the LNVF. Although most closely associated with the more militant suffrage groups, *Le Journal* also hosted UFSF meetings and published the union's proposals for the 1914 elections.[22]

Militant suffragists, and many moderates, enthusiastically embraced

Téry's plan for *Le Journal*'s poll. Beginning in mid-March, *Le Journal* showed this support by publishing letters from dozens of suffragists, ranging from Auclert to d'Uzès, endorsing the poll and recapitulating their justifications for women's suffrage. Roussel, for example, called for tens of thousands of women to participate because the poll had "the immense advantage of fixing public attention on our claims." Even Séverine, who had remained aloof from the suffrage campaign for years, ardently backed the plan. By the beginning of April, the LFDF had decided to co-sponsor the poll; other groups rapidly followed. With some hesitation, *La Française* and the UFSF decided to add their support to a plan that the majority of suffragists clearly desired. Jane Misme urged her readers to participate, but used the same article to reiterate her ideas about seeking the vote cautiously; she worried that a mass poll was "still premature." The UFSF agreed to endorse the poll without working for it because that might distract from their parliamentary campaign. Pauline Rebour, however, led several individuals from the union to work with the poll's organizers.[23]

To reach the maximum number of women, suffragists planned to maintain a continuous poll throughout the electoral period, from April 26th to May 5th. *Le Journal* agreed to print a ballot in each edition, thus putting it into more than one million hands daily; women need only sign the ballot and mail it to the newspaper. Parisian women who desired to vote in person, in a mock election, could fill out ballots at nineteen different polling places in the city—two established by *Le Journal*, eleven by the LFDF, and six by individuals. Militants from the LNVF did not even wait for voters to come to them. Members followed Auclert's old petitioning strategy and took blank ballots to women in cafes, les Halles, the Luxembourg gardens, and even into factories.[24]

Nearly 17,000 French women voted on April 26, 1914, proclaiming with near unanimity their desire to be enfranchised. On its first day, the *Journal* poll had thus become the largest demonstration in the history of French feminism—the largest by a factor of almost ten. Even if one excludes the 3,000 votes accumulated by the LNVF's roving pollsters as possibly collected from passive sympathizers, 14,000 women had taken the initiative to go to a polling place. On the second day, 6,700 more women voted at the polls, and the first mails brought in an astonishing total of 60,000 ballots clipped from *Le Journal*. After three days of voting, the total number of participants crested 100,000 and other Parisian newspapers began to urge women to express themselves. Had 100,000 French women ever before participated in a single political event of any sort? Whatever the previous record, *Le Journal*'s poll soon eclipsed it. In ten days of balloting, 505,972 women called for their political rights. According to *Le Journal*, only 114 women submitted ballots opposed to the right to vote.[25]

"The 500,000 of the avant-garde," as suffragists quickly labeled them, brought the women's suffrage campaign in France to its apogee in the months of April to July 1914. For many years, French suffragists had both suffered and profited from comparisons to the women's rights movements in other countries—suffering because the contrast to England or America showed the French campaign was smaller and less active, profiting because French public opinion appreciated the greater moderation that such contrasts highlighted. The *Journal* poll suggested that the comparison was not so simple. French suffragism retained its reputation for calm behavior that pleased the press so much.[26] Moderates such as Misme were palpably relieved that French women had made "a magnificent demonstration" without compromising their reputation for caution. At the same time, everyone realized that what had occurred was "a fact without precedent."[27] Perhaps anti-suffragists could still claim that suffragism was not yet a mass movement, but the participants in the demonstration represented nearly 4 percent of the adult female population of France—a rate of activity not often exceeded in modern politics. To be sure, the "poll" was in no way a scientific sampling of opinion—it was artful propaganda which obscured the numbers of women still opposed to, or indifferent to, the right to vote.[28] Yet no contrast with foreign suffragists could now dismiss the French movement as small or insignificant; it was different, the natural result of different national histories and contemporary problems, but it had arrived as a large political campaign. At 500,000 voices, politicians would soon have to pay attention. After all, suffragists gloated, the theoreticians of proportional representation said that 14,000 votes should give any minority a seat in the Chamber of Deputies.

The euphoria produced by the *Journal* poll engendered suffragist enthusiasm for pursuing the new phase by creating a federation of all suffragists for concerted action. Despite the events of 1908-1910, the suffrage movement was still fragmented. A few large leagues dominated activities, but there remained more than a dozen independent societies in Paris alone. To stress the dichotomy between moderates and militants correctly identifies the most severe division of the movement, but it also oversimplifies the factionalism among women separated by personal rivalries, different social origins, partisan politics, and conflicting attitudes about a variety of issues ranging from free love to foreign policy. The nuances within French suffragism, in short, were as finely defined as the multiparty factionalism of French parliamentary politics.

Only a woman who had not been active in the suffrage campaign, yet had sufficient prestige to believe that feminists would listen to her, could have thought a federation was possible. Only the mood derived from an event such as the *Journal* poll could have made it plausible. The proposal came from Séverine, one of the most respected women of letters in France and a well-known left-wing activist, but a woman with little record of feminism and none of suffragism. Séverine (1855-1929) had been a close associate of Jules Vallès in the 1880s, directing for several years his socialist newspaper, *Le Cri du peuple*. Her career in journalism included the contribution of a column to *La Fronde*, "Notes d'une frondeuse," in addition to writing for many influential Parisian papers, from the conservative *Le Figaro* to the mass circulation *Le Journal*. In the years before World War I, she collaborated closely with *L'Oeuvre* (1908-1911) and *L'Intransigeant* (1909-1914), developing her reputation as a zealous defender of the rights of the underdog. Throughout this career Séverine had remained outside the feminist movement, although she collaborated with feminists on behalf of women strikers. Socialists had twice offered her parliamentary candidacies (1885 and 1906), and she had twice refused. According to her biographer, Séverine strongly believed in the equality of the sexes but concentrated her feminism in her own life rather than in organizations. It is clear that she opposed women's suffrage early in her career, on the argument that women were insufficiently educated. And she had been an outspoken critic of androgynous feminism: "Women fancy that they support their cause by smoking like sappers, by clipping their hair, and by imitating men. None of that *chez moi!*" She had, however, often contributed to the feminist cause as an individual, as when she served in 1905 on the extraparliamentary Comité de la réforme du mariage which recommended reforms in the Napoleonic Code. When she occasionally turned her pen to questions of women's rights, few in the feminist movement could match the excoriating prose with which she imprecated masculine injustice. Nonetheless, it greatly surprised some suffragists when Séverine took an active role in the suffrage campaign of 1914.[29]

Séverine first proposed an entente, to link all suffrage organizations, during the excitement of the *Journal's* poll. She had joined the LNVF at one of its first meetings and participated in the poll with that group. Not content merely to propose suffragist unity, she took her idea to meetings of the LFDF, Amélioration, and the UFSF in search of support. To avoid threatening the particularism of any established group, Séverine outlined a suffragist understanding that would not create a new, separate organization—just an entente by which all groups pledged to try to work together. Any society subscribing to the entente could convoke a meeting to seek coordinated action on any pro-suffrage idea. Each league would retain its individual identity and the right to oppose any controversial program of the others. This minimalist version of unity was persuasive. Amélioration, whose members had been holding discussions on feminist disunity since January, immediately backed the plan. The LFDF, in which Séverine had occasionally participated, voted to sponsor the plan upon the enthusiastic seconding of it by Lhermite. Vérone thereupon invited representatives from all pro-suffrage groups to a meeting to draft an agreement for the federation. The executive committee of the UFSF approved of the meeting but cautiously agreed only to propose the entente at the union's annual congress at Lyons in June. The congress later voted unanimously to support any entente that did not hinder the autonomy of the partners.[30]

The organizational meetings in May-June 1914 immediately produced disagreements between militants and moderates. Seventeen pro-suffrage organizations participated, including the LFDF, the UFSF, the CNFF, the LNVF, the UFF, Amélioration, Etudes, and Suffrage des femmes (led after Auclert's death by her sister, Marie Chaumont, and by Gabrielle Chapuis). Moderate republican, radical republican, and socialist youth organizations all sent delegates. The League of Electors, the League of the Rights of Man, the mixed masonic lodges, and the Fédération de la libre-pensée, plus anti-alcoholism, laic education, and pacifist groups joined. Their disagreement centered on a few specific problems. Were they creating a "federation," as the LFDF considered it, or a much looser "entente," as the UFSF held? Would this body have any continuing existence through a standing central committee, as the LFDF asked? Would all members retain veto powers, as the UFSF demanded? Buoyed with confidence from the *Journal*'s poll, they found compromises. They agreed to a "federal entente" which would not have any "personality" of its own and would serve only as a "center of common action." There would be a permanent committee, comprised of two delegates from each group; if it reached a consensus, it would convoke a general meeting. Séverine would preside over this committee; its other leaders would be Vérone for the LFDF, Grinberg for the UFSF, and Tisserand for the LNVF. They had no powers except the right to call meetings. This was an extremely tenuous form of unity, yet it, too, convinced suffragists that they were nearing their goal. The next step was to celebrate their new unity by agreeing upon some dramatic action that would publicize suffragist strength.[31]

The Condorcet Demonstration, July 1914

If an entente uniting all suffrage groups had seemed unlikely before the spring of 1914, an agreement of those groups to put several thousand women into the streets of Paris seemed wildly improbable. The great majority of French suffragists had steadfastly opposed such demonstrations. Approximately fifty women had marched with Auclert to the Vendôme Column in 1904. The same number was willing to join the suffragist cortège during the 1906 parliamentary elections. Fewer than one hundred women, many of them British suffragettes, joined Pelletier's marches to the Palais Bourbon in 1906 and 1907. Participation was even scantier—perhaps forty—in the parade that preceded Auclert's violence in 1908. The triumph of moderate tactics at the congress of 1908 caused a hiatus of six years during which not even fifty suffragists took their cause to the streets. When Pelletier and the LNVF broke the taboo at the Carrefour Feydeau in 1914, fewer suffragists stood in the street than had done so with Auclert a decade earlier. The pattern was unmistakable. Yet on July 5, 1914, between 5,000 and 6,000 suffragists assembled in the Tuileries Gardens for the *"manifestation Condorcet"* and proceeded to march to the left bank. If the *Journal* poll and the federal entente were insufficient evidence, the Condorcet demonstration left no doubt that French suffragism had entered a new phase.

The idea for the Condorcet demonstration originated with Séverine. She proposed at the March 1914 meeting of the LFDF that the group sponsor a public rally to honor the pioneer of political rights for women. Séverine owed her inspiration to Hubertine Auclert. A few days before Séverine's suggestion to the LFDF, Auclert had suggested that it was time to return to the streets; a few years earlier, on the occasion of the centennial of the Lycée Condorcet, Auclert had also proposed feminist celebrations to honor Condorcet. Séverine's plan to link these two ideas did not initially attract great attention or interest. A few militants discussed the notion without reaching any conclusion, and then the hectic activities of the spring of 1914 eclipsed it. When Séverine returned to her idea in late May, she had the advantages of the new mood and greater experience in suffragism which taught her some of the political realities of the movement.[32]

Séverine's initiative was tactically brilliant: She took her idea directly to the UFSF. Speaking to the annual congress of the union in early June, Séverine suggested the celebration of an annual "feminist day"—which the UFSF had contemplated in the past—to publicize the campaign for political rights. An ideal day, she continued, would be the anniversary of Condorcet's death each spring, although for 1914 the feminist day festivities would have to occur in early summer. The choice of Condorcet was especially appropriate for this audience. Not only was Condorcet one of the first advocates of women's suffrage, not only was he a respectable male political figure, but his philosophy of steady progress was the irreducible core of the liberal beliefs of the women of the union. Séverine was addressing an audience of Condorcetiennes who profoundly believed in a linear historical progression that would inevitably bring them the ballot. Séverine shrewdly refrained from explicating upon the scope of the celebration she had conceived, and the congress had no difficulty in deciding to sponsor her plan.[33]

Having won the general backing of the UFSF for a Condorcet fête, Séverine continued to court moderate opinion. Avril de Sainte-Croix, who had devoted a section of her 1907 book on feminism to praising the role of Condorcet, readily subscribed to the plan; where the secretary-general went, the CNFF was likely to follow. Assiduously avoiding any linkage between her plan and the militants, Séverine next suggested a Condorcet demonstration to the new federal entente. It would be, she claimed, the perfect event to highlight the new strength and unity of French suffragism. An outdoor meeting could be held that would carefully follow the formula for indoor lectures. A large, but scrupulously planned, parade could proceed to the statue of Condorcet on the left bank, there to deposit memorial garlands. Séverine's shrewd maneuver carried the day. Moderates were already committed to sponsoring the feminist day; militants had no trouble in rallying to the plan; and neither faction was willing to see the entente collapse in the month of its construction. With minimal trepidation, the leaders of the federal entente named a committee to prepare for a *manifestation Condorcet*; moderates from Amélioration, the UFSF, the UFF, and *La Vie féminine* all agreed to sit on it.[34]

The about-face of UFSF moderates in accepting a public demonstration can only partially be explained by Séverine's adroit politics. The ebullience of the moment, with 500,000 ballots fresh in mind, certainly helped, as did the UFSF's desire to maintain unity. The disassociation of the demonstration from previous advocates of such behavior, plus the interest of women like Sainte-Croix and Fonséque facilitated the decision. A slight shift of opinion in the inner councils of the UFSF was also emerging, perhaps stimulated by the defection of such young members as Rauze, Brion, and Marguerite Martin. New voices in the union's leadership were somewhat more willing to consider actions that Brunschwicg, de Witt-Schlumberger, and Misme might otherwise brush aside. For example, Pauline Rebour, now the assistant secretary-general, had induced the executive committee to accept her cooperation with *Le Journal*'s poll, against the judgment of other leaders—and the results had strengthened her position. Suzanne Grinberg, the head of the UFSF section in the Fifth Arrondissement and an executive committee member, had personally participated in Vérone's voter registration campaign, against the union's policy. Thérèse Belle, the treasurer and executive committee member, had backed Rebour and Grinberg in these activities. The UFSF did not abandon its traditional orientation, nor did Rebour, Grinberg, and Belle wish to do so. Jane Misme still had mixed feelings and did not hesitate to express them, even as others were being swept up by the excitement of the moment.[35] But insofar as a demonstration could be presented as respectable and utterly lawful, the union was now willing to consider it. In the final analysis, UFSF participation depended upon Séverine's ability to present the *manifestation Condorcet* as a calm, moderate event and upon the belief that the arrangements were appropriate to UFSF attitudes.

Séverine succeeded in persuading moderates that participation in the Condorcet rally was actually a conservative act. She argued that they were paying homage to a man, thereby showing their critics that feminism did not mean war between the sexes. Indeed, suffragists were assembling in great numbers precisely to show the world how pacific the movement was, how deeply committed to conciliation. According to Séverine, the demonstration would thus prove that:

> One can claim one's rights without gnashing one's teeth; one can desire justice without preaching hate. Our feminism includes keeping our smiles, our senses of humour, and our good manners. ... We will arrive at our rights without reprehensible actions, with hands untouched by violence, with hearts not filled with resentment.[36]

This feat of ratiocination transformed at a single stroke the demonstration of which Auclert had dreamt into a proof that the UFSF had been correct in opposing her. The UFSF accepted Séverine's reasoning. Rebour became the head of the federal entente's arrangements committee as a sign of this approval and as a way to guarantee a suitable demonstration.[37]

Séverine undertook careful negotiations with the government to obtain permission to hold a meeting in the Tuileries Gardens and to conduct a parade across the Seine to the statue of Condorcet near the Institut de France. The advantage of having a lifelong feminist as premier quickly became apparent. Viviani personally endorsed the proposal, expediting negotiations with the Ministry of the Interior, the Ministry of Education (whose under-secretariat for fine arts contained the department responsible for the gardens), and the Prefecture of Police. The Ministry of the Interior approved of the demonstration, contingent upon the suffragist acceptance of all appropriate restrictions imposed by the prefecture; the Ministry of Education agreed to accept whatever stipulations the prefecture determined. Séverine, in turn, readily accepted all conditions that the police desired. Hence, it was agreed that the demonstration would be scheduled for a Sunday, to create minimal interference with traffic, and that it would be limited to a total duration of three hours; that there would be no speeches on the streets, or halting of the parade en route, although speeches could be planned on the terrace of the Orangerie and at the statue; and that all participants would obtain in advance and wear visibly some distinctive insignia that would permit the police to keep any spectators from joining the demonstration. All parties agreeing, the government granted permission four days before the demonstration.[38]

The result was the largest demonstration that French suffragists ever staged. Estimates of the crowd ranged from 2,000 (by non-suffragists) to 10,000 (the maximum size permitted by the agreement with the government). Most newspapers and suffrage groups claimed a figure of 5,000 to 6,000.[39] "This is the first demonstration in the streets that French suffragists have organized," Jane Misme claimed on the eve of the rally. "It is essential that they maintain great dignity. The feminist cause will be judged by public opinion according to its supporters." She need not have worried. It was a model for well-regulated, peaceful demonstrations. The wall of the Orangerie and the speakers' podium were ornamented with olive branches to symbolize the pacific intentions of the movement; several groups had their members carry branches. Speakers stressed the contributions of Condorcet and other men to the cause of women's rights. Marguerite Durand spoke—for Suffrage des femmes!—explicitly on the need for peaceful behavior. The most controversial act of the afternoon was the decision of some marchers to distribute handbills to spectators along the one-mile parade route. More passed out flowers as they marched across the Pont de Solferino and along the quays to the statue of Condorcet, where Séverine laid a memorial wreath of flowers. The mood was so euphoric that one participant even described the police as courteous and charming. Celebrating continued into the evening, as the LFDF hosted a feminist banquet for 600, where there were champagne toasts to demonstrations in the streets. An immense distance had been traveled to cover the few hundred yards between the Place Vendôme in 1904 and the Orangerie in 1914.[40]

The campaign to win the right to vote for French women reached its apogee with the Condorcet demonstration of July 5, 1914. The movement had grown steadily and optimistically for over a decade. Whereas most feminists had believed that a call for enfranchisement was premature in 1900, the ballot had become their unquestioned first priority. From only a few dozen suffragists as late as 1904, their numbers had grown to the claimed "500,000 of the avant-garde." Tiny organizations such as Auclert's Suffrage des femmes and Vincent's

Egalité had been superseded by large suffrage leagues, such as the 12,000-member UFSF with its branches reaching into almost every department of France. Instead of the derision of the turn-of-the-century press, suffragism had won a hearing in public opinion and the support of many masculine organizations. An age when the Gautret Bill of 1901 could disappear without a hearing had given way before the growth of parliamentary suffragism; 261 deputies had backed Buisson's pro-suffrage report to the chamber and suffragists believed that the elections of 1914 had brought them within ten votes of winning the municipal franchise. René Viviani, a man who had been a suffragist before most of the women in the movement, occupied the premiership. And then, in 1914, French suffragism had entered "the new phase" with one dramatic success following another, culminating in the Condorcet demonstration. Little wonder that so many women believed that they would vote in 1916.

On the terrace of the Orangerie, on that confident Sunday afternoon, Séverine read an ode by Raoul Rebour entitled "The Sermon of July Fifth." It proclaimed the oath of the federal entente "not to cease to raise our voices" until they had seen women's suffrage "graven in the marble of the laws!" That oath lasted for four weeks; it was shattered by gunfire on the northern frontier. The excited weeks in which French suffragism had reached its apogee coincided with the better-known narrative of the Balkan crisis that preceded World War I. French suffragists had agreed upon the statutes of the federal entente on June 29th, a few hours after the assassination of Archduke Franz-Ferdinand at Sarajevo. On July 5th, while French suffragists gazed through the trees of the Tuileries at their target across the river at the Palais Bourbon, another historic meeting was taking place. On that same day, an envoy of the Habsburg government took lunch at Potsdam and received assurances of German support for Austria-Hungary in the Balkan crisis—the so-called "blank check." Long before the leaves fell from the trees in the Tuileries, France was at war.

The beginning of the war absolutely stopped the suffrage campaign in France, as it did in the other belligerent states. Without hesitation, suffragists rallied to the tricolor. Pacificism had been a prominent feature of French feminism, but so had devotion to *la patrie*. The women at the LFDF banquet after the Condorcet demonstration were aware of the international crisis, and patriotic talk was intertwined with their suffragist pride. As one feminist reported, their champagne toasts to their success were no more vigorous than their high-spirited cries of "*Vive la France!*"[41] Those women would have no doubts about abandoning their campaign in favor of supporting a "sacred union" to defend France. The war would truncate their campaign at its apogee.

XO

The World War
and the Suffragist Truce

French suffragists wholeheartedly supported the government and its war effort in August 1914. With no apparent hesitation, they abandoned their pacifism and their efforts to win the vote. Periodicals disappeared, congresses were canceled, lectures and demonstrations no longer scheduled. Instead, feminists sought ways to participate in the war—through the Red Cross, through organizations to aid refugees, through the recruitment of women to replace men called to the colors. "We will claim our rights," the LFDF proclaimed, "when the triumph of Right is assured."[1] Only late in the war did suffragism reappear in France.

Premier Viviani directly appealed to the women of France shortly after the Chamber of Deputies declared war. He summoned peasant women to become "soldiers of the harvest," and proletarian women to "replace on the field of labor those who are on the field of battle."[2] Within a week, Margueritte de Witt-Schlumberger wrote to all members of the UFSF, exhorting compliance. Bourgeois women might not go to the fields or factories, but they could support the government by joining charitable associations. A few days later, the UFSF distributed a handbill calling on women of all classes to join the feminist *ralliement*: "We are all sisters in the love of our country and in our duties toward the national defense." The CNFF quickly followed suit. Siegfried and Sainte-Croix sent a letter to the membership urging them to undertake war work. Siegfried then embarked on a lecture tour to persuade women to do their duty.[3]

Suffragists hastened to prove their patriotism by dismantling the instruments of their campaign. Denizard closed the *Cri des femmes*. Misme ceased publishing *La Française*, then resumed printing (without feminist columns) to boost morale. She reiterated the call for a suffragist moratorium: "while the ordeal that our country is suffering continues, it will not be proper for anyone to speak of her rights."[4] The LFDF likewise suspended *Le Droit des femmes* for nine months, reviving it only to help the war effort. The UFSF went further, abandoning its *Bulletin*, its regular meetings, and the annual congress that united its provincial chapters. Many branches simply dissolved. The union published its program in late 1915 but made no reference whatsoever to women's suffrage—by statute, the union's sole raison d'être. When the UFSF finally held a national congress in April 1916, de Witt-Schlumberger stated in the presidential address, "It goes without saying that this is not the proper time for suffragist lectures."[5] This attitude endured for most of World War I. As late as March 1917, Siegfried (who had three sons in uniform) reassured political and religious leaders that the truce continued: "Women of our land and our race, we consent to all sacrifices that are asked of us."[6]

Virtually all French feminists agreed. The women of Etudes, always champions of nationalist feminism, abandoned reform agitation with a statement that they must do nothing to unsettle the army. Marguerite Durand revived *La Fronde* in August 1914, stating that she did so "not to claim the political rights of women, but to help them accomplish their social duties." Even the socialist women of the GdFS rallied to support the government, following the SFIO. If Jules Guesde could sit in the "ministry of sacred union," if Albert Thomas could take an under-secretariat beneath Alexandre Millerand, the course for socialist women was unmistakable. Saumoneau had inextricably linked the GdFS to the party; she now disagreed, but her organization did not hesitate to follow it.[7]

Feminist patriotism meant relinquishing the pacifism that had characterized the women's movement. All of the large suffrage leagues held explicit commitments to pacifism in 1914. The statutory connection of the CNFF and the peace movement, the Christian pacifism of leaders such as Monod, and the council's association with The Hague Conference of 1906 had led in 1912 to the creation of a seventh administrative section, to coordinate women's work for peace. The LFDF's pacifism dated from the nineteenth century; as recently as May 1914, Vérone had attended an international feminist congress at Rome and protested that pacifism was not inscribed on their program. The UFSF congress that assembled at Lyons a few days later did not

make that omission: one of the principal speakers, Marguerite Clément, stressed the union's commitment to pacifism.[8]

A few feminists could not accept this abrupt change. Jeanne Halbwachs refused to follow her friends in the LFDF and became a leader
of the international women's movement for peace. Gabrielle Duchêne,
the head of the CNFF's labor section, broke with the council to remain
a pacifist. When Duchêne went to Switzerland to meet with Romain
Rolland and other pacifists, the CNFF responded by closing its peace
section. Pelletier, who had argued in a pamphlet that feminists must
oppose war both intrinsically and as an instrument of men's power
over women, briefly spoke against the war in August 1914. Pelletier,
however, quickly became disillusioned with feminist chauvinism. Cynical about the future, she chose to abandon all politics and enroll as
a chemistry student at the Sorbonne for her *license ès sciences*. Saumoneau left the GdFS rather than accept its patriotic socialism when
the group refused to send a delegation to Clara Zetkin's peace conference at Berne in 1915. After trying to organize meetings against
the war and to persuade workers not to fight, Saumoneau was arrested
for circulating the Berne Manifesto. Many members of the GdFS,
notably the new secretary-general, Alice Jouenne, and Marianne Rauze
sharply criticized Saumoneau. Hélène Brion initially spoke against
the war, then rallied to the SFIO position. In 1917, she again opposed
the war and was sentenced to three years in prison by the *Conseil de
guerre* as part of Clemenceau's repression of "defeatist" propaganda.
A few militants—Durand, Roussel, Séverine—testified on Brion's
behalf, but most feminists believed that the sentence was justified.
Misme publicly supported it in *La Française*.[9]

These feminist pacifists during World War I remained a small
minority surrounded by nationalists. There was not a single prominent
defection from the sacred union among bourgeois suffragists. The
same women who had planned to go to Berlin for the IWSA congress
in 1915 fervently hoped that the French army would arrive there
instead. Feminists who pledged in July 1914 not to break ranks until
they had won the vote called suffragist demonstrations unpatriotic a
month later. "Duty," said Marie Bonnevial, "called more loudly than
rights."[10]

That sense of duty led feminists to the conclusion that women could
best aid the war effort by replacing men in military and civilian
capacities, thereby releasing more men for the front. Neither the

military, the government, nor the trade unions accepted feminist offers to organize such a conscription. At the outset, they preferred a more restrained feminine contribution to the war—filling such traditional roles as keeping morale high, organizing charities, preparing for peace, or serving in the Red Cross.[11] Army chiefs considered the supply of men sufficient for their auxiliary services, although they later accepted large numbers of women as nurses, cooks, accountants, secretaries, and draftswomen. Similarly, the government declined to employ feminists to direct the mobilization of women in the labor force, creating its own placement office in 1915.

Feminists persisted. A coalition formed the Union pour l'enrôlement des françaises in August 1914 to do unofficial recruitment and to find work for women. Léon Abensour, Clemenceau's secretary, later admitted that this came too early in the war to be appreciated; the indifference of the public and the press, the uninterestedness of the government doomed the union. As the war changed needs and attitudes, feminists did obtain a collaborative role. The largest employer of women, the Ministry of Armament, created a Commission du travail féminin and named moderate feminists such as Sainte-Croix to serve on it. This encouraged feminists to establish a new coalition for the recruitment of women, the Office central de l'activité féminine, with an executive committee drawn from the CNFF, LFDF, UFSF, UFF, Amélioration, and the feminist press. Other members suggest the approval of the government: Mmes. Loubet, Carnot, Cruppi, Pichon, Waddington. Their office accounted for a tiny share of women recruited to the labor force (8,600 were placed, December 1916 to December 1917), but even this suggests the advantage that the government had lost through reluctance to deal with feminists.[12]

Most feminists thus turned to war-related charity projects. Public opinion was more comfortable with this traditional role for women and it won feminists more praise than their efforts to collaborate with the government. Feminists as different as the Duchess d'Uzès and Madeleine Pelletier turned to the Red Cross. D'Uzès received great publicity for touring the front with the Red Cross and then converting her Chateau de Bonnelles into a hospital; Pelletier, criticism for insisting on equal treatment for casualties from both sides. Many groups developed programs to aid the suffering *poilu*. Amélioration organized artistic and recreational programs in military hospitals; the LFDF financed cantines, and the CNFF *"Foyers du soldat,"* to aid soldiers on leave; the UFSF organized a campaign to send packages to the front and to prisoners of war.[13] As the war expanded, they turned this philanthropic effort to civilian problems. Two projects were especially successful: UFSF aid for refugees and evacuees from northeastern France and CNFF efforts to reunite dispersed families. By 1918, the union had housed over 25,000 refugees. The CNFF's Office de renseignements pour les familles dispersées, created in December 1914 by Pichon-Landry, maintained a card file on the location of refugees which reached 1,400,000 names by April 1916.[14]

The reformist aspiration of feminists did not stay suppressed. Having vowed not to importune the government about women's rights, most organizations turned to social feminism, to that cluster of problems ("threats to the race") portending the degeneration of France—depopulation and alcoholism foremost among them. If the trend of French natality seemed foreboding in the 1890s, the war made it appear alarming. The birth rate dropped sharply following the mobilization of young men; *pari passu*, the death rate soared as those young men perished in the fighting. Birth rates over the entire following generation would be skewed. The importance of comparative Franco-German demographic curves was obvious. French feminists had always been sensitive to arguments of natalism and held that women should have children as well as advanced ideas. As the war highlighted the issue of depopulation, such attitudes were expressed more candidly. *La Française* published a banner headline in May 1916 exhorting women to have children. Grinberg wrote a report insisting that the first duty of women was to reproduce. Brunschwicg, Buisson, Siegfried, and de Witt-Schlumberger helped co-found in 1916 a league entitled Pour la vie to seek ways to raise the birth rate. The 1916 congress of the UFSF did not discuss the vote at all, but considered depopulation in detail; resolutions called for state aid to large families, benefits for pregnant women, and a campaign to reduce infant mortality.[15]

A second illustration of wartime social feminism may be seen in the campaign against "the social plague" of alcoholism. "Guardian of the home, and of the race, woman must see in alcohol her worst enemy," insisted one leader of the LFDF. Alcohol, UFSF literature stated, was "more terrible than the German" in destroying the nation. "All French women must combat alcoholism!" proclaimed a banner headline in *La Française*. Misme followed her own advice by establishing a regular column under the rubric "War on Alcohol."[16] Such zeal produced anti-alcohol rallies at the Sorbonne in April 1915 and April 1916, the second being the largest feminist meeting held during the war. Old allies, such as Joseph Reinach, were already active in the fight; together they advanced the theory that "anti-alcoholism is one of the forms of patriotism." Among the victories in this campaign were a decree of January 1915 and a law of March 1915 forbidding the manufacture or sale of absinthe, a military decree of March 1915 forbidding the sale or gift of alcohol to soldiers in the war zone, and a bill adopted by the Chamber of Deputies in July 1915 to suppress public drunkenness.[17]

The nationalism inherent in such concerns was typical of wartime feminism. Some groups succumbed to the temptations of exaggerated chauvinist rhetoric; all demonstrated strong patriotism.[18] Whatever suffrage group police agents infiltrated—the LNVF, the UFSF, the LFDF, Suffrage des femmes—reports came back the same: suffragists opposed the peace movement and strongly supported the government.[19] The best illustration of suffragist patriotism came during the Hague Conference of 1915. That meeting resulted from the cancellation of the IWSA congress scheduled for Berlin in June 1915. Feminists from neutral states, led by Aletta Jacobs of the Netherlands and Jane Addams of the United States, decided to organize the international women's movement to work for peace. Their congress received the support of both the IWSA and the International Council of Women, so their French affiliates were automatically invited. Affiliated societies in Belgium, Britain, and Germany agreed to participate but the UFSF and the CNFF drafted a manifesto flatly refusing:

> Our feminine and feminist societies have unanimously decided that they cannot participate in an international congress, nor accept the program that you propose. How would it be possible for us, at the present time, to meet with the women of enemy countries ... ? Have they disavowed the political crimes ... of their government?

Leaders of the French leagues sent personal letters to reiterate their opposition. Other feminist groups backed them with resolutions and articles. Some asserted with Sainte-Croix that they remained sincere pacifists, obliged to defend their invaded homeland. Most preferred categorical rejections: "French women ... united with those who battle and die, ... do not know how to talk of peace."[20]

The War and the Position of Women in France

There is substantial evidence that suggests, prima facie, that the war was a decisive experience in altering the position of women in Western societies. Some historians surveying such evidence have concluded that women had "thrown off their age-old shackles of inferiority and gained a new and respected status."[21] In support of this, one can point out that women entered the war economy in greater numbers and new capacities, that women obtained legal rights previously withheld, that attitudes about the role of women in society shifted and a new climate of opinion developed in which women could expect full political equality. "In three years," wrote one French author at the end of the war, "women realized more progress than in fifty years of struggle."[22] Feminists may not have overstated the case so much, but during the war they certainly agreed that their cause was making progress. They had good reasons to think so. By mid-war, there were palpable differences in the role of French women. Women were seen serving as mayors of small villages and sitting on municipal councils! Furthermore, women were contributing directly to the war effort; without their labor in the munitions industry, for example, the army could not long have continued the fight. Feminists, therefore, simply could not believe that on the morrow of the victory that women helped to win, a grateful nation would do other than accept them as equals.

There are many reasons to doubt that the war years constituted such a climacteric period. Much of women's progress was illusory, many of the changes evanescent. Women mobilized to serve in an extraordinary situation found themselves demobilized rapidly in a postwar rush back to normalcy. The *poilu* returned to his job, his wartime replacement to her home. For what did we endure such suffering, veterans might ask, if not the preservation of the prewar France? Both economic and legal gains of French women fell to this attitude. To be sure, some important changes endured and others followed the war. This, however, must in part be attributed to gradual trends in France. The steady growth of an educated class of women, for example, would have meant alterations in occupations and attitudes, war or no. At the very least, the war could not have produced change without the simultaneous existence of such trends. Furthermore, attributing to the war an altered position of women ignores the contribution of the prewar feminist movement.

The medical profession provides a good illustration of this situation. It is hardly surprising to read that female physicians obtained wider acceptance during four years of fighting when casualty rates averaged over one thousand per diem. The important fact is not that the French public accepted *doctoresses* as replacements, or that women received new appointments at hospitals and clinics. Rather, it is the gradual education of women in medicine during the previous forty years and the campaigns of feminists to open the profession to them. The trend that saw 357 female medical students enrolled at Paris in 1912 is more important than the wartime use of women doctors, many of whom were deprived of their occupations after the armistice. A woman (Dr. Long-Landry) had already become the head of a clinic in 1911; that others followed during the war only to be demoted afterwards hardly marks a turning point in women's rights.

Working women certainly found new jobs open to them during World War I. Before the war, the state railways employed 6,000 women (85 percent of them as barrier guards); by 1918, 57,000 women worked for the railroads. Similarly, the Paris Metro went from 124 women workers to 3,037. The Ministry of Posts had been the second largest source of state jobs for women (18,000 in 1911) yet still had to replace over 20,000 men who were drafted. The Ministry of Education, which already employed 71,000 women (96 percent of them in primary education), had to open 30,000 positions (chiefly in secondary education) due to conscription. Banks, businesses, and government alike desperately needed women to replace men on clerical and secretarial staffs. The greatest need, of course, occurred in the munitions factories, where women workers increased from 15,000 in 1915 to 684,000 in 1917.[23]

Such illustrations convey misleading impressions about the extent and nature of the progress that French women made during the war. This is partly a function of inadequate data—the government did not conduct the quinquennial census scheduled for 1916. It is also a result of misreading the evidence that does exist. First of all, many women sought jobs less as a matter of patriotism or feminism than of simple survival. Any woman who had been dependent solely on the weekly wage of a working man was immediately in trouble if that man was drafted. The government provided the wives of mobilized men with a daily allotment of 1.25 francs; dependent mothers, sisters, or lovers received nothing. Secondly, if one views the situation of women as the war unfolded—not from the end of the war—the story of working women is very different. The beginning of the war caused a broad range of business closings and curtailments. For 1914-1915, the chief effect of the war was to drive women out of work. Female unemployment reached enormous proportions—61 percent of those in textiles and 67 percent in the garment industries were put out of work.[24]

The employment of French women during World War I must therefore first be understood as a process of redistribution of the labor force, based as much on the need of women to survive as on governmental policy. According to Clemenceau's secretary, half a million women entered the industrial work force during the war. That total is far less than the number employed in munitions work alone. What was happening was the arrival of women from other sectors of the economy, women left unemployed, and women in straitened circumstances. The war took women from domestic services or traditionally feminized segments of the economy, such as textiles, and put them in wartime jobs as male replacements.[25]

Women, whether they came from other occupations or newly entered the labor force, did not retain their wartime jobs. According to census data there were 8.6 million women in the working population in 1921, compared to 7.7 million in 1911. The number of working women declined, however, to 7.8 million in 1926, a drop that meant that women actually constituted a smaller percentage of the national labor force in 1926 than they had in 1911. Furthermore, when one considers only industrial occupations, the number of women employed in 1921 was already lower (2 million) than it had been in 1906 (2.1 million)! By 1926, women accounted for only 28.6 percent of industrial workers, whereas they had held 34.4 percent of the jobs in 1906. The sharp decline occurred despite the fact that 1.4 million men died during the war. Obviously, postwar governments and employers made a tremendous effort to hire demobilized soldiers and to demobilize working women. Only in the agricultural sector did the effect of the war endure for a decade, hardly a great turning point in the economic history of French women.[26]

Similar doubts appear when one examines the legal and political rights that French women obtained during the war. It is true that the extraordinary wartime circumstances resulted in a few cases of women performing the functions of mayors and adjunct-mayors or sitting in municipal councils. Some wartime agencies, such as the agricultural committees established in each rural commune in 1916, made provisions for women's suffrage. Women also obtained legal release in 1915 from some provisions of the Civil Code, permitting them to exercise rights previously limited to men. After July 3, 1915, for example, mothers could exercise the paternal authority defined by the code. In March 1917, the Senate finally gave women the right to become legal guardians, accepting a bill that had passed the chamber years before the war. French feminists were understandably proud of these accomplishments, but a closer look shows how meager were the actual victories. The few cases where women held political office were in desperate circumstances, usually rural communes denuded of educated males. In most cases, the commune turned to the local *institutrice* to study and to sign documents. Her powers were strictly limited and her career expectancy clearly understood. In cases where women sat on municipal councils, they did so explicitly as non-voting members. The right to vote in agencies, restricted to begin with, ended with the war. The law providing paternal authority to women was also valid only for the duration of hostilities, only in urgent cases, and only with individual judicial approval. It was necessary for the orderly continuation of business and was adopted as such, not as a feminist landmark. And it was no improvement over the same temporary rights that the Government of National Defense had granted women in December 1870. As a detailed legal thesis demonstrated in 1919, the war government had only extended the rights of women during "the non-presence" of the men in whom those rights actually reposed. The return of the army meant the disappearance of such rights.[27]

French women certainly won some permanent rights during World War I. The only major right to survive, however, was that of guardianship. That was important, but it scarcely made the years 1914-1918 a period of feminist legislative triumph to overshadow the prewar years. Instead, the war slowed the pace of lasting reform. Of course, it is also necessary to consider women's rights acquired after the war, on the argument that it prompted subsequent change. This issue is taken up later; it will be seen there that there was no great wave of feminist legislation in France.

The most difficult argument to assess about the war and the position of women in France concerns attitudes. A strong case can be stated to show that attitudes about the public role of women changed, that new behavior was socially acceptable. By necessity, women had acquired a freedom of action that was not entirely respectable in the antediluvian world of 1914. Women had to go out in public unchaperoned, had to work alongside men, had to live alone on their own wages. Thousands of nurses and clerical workers in the masculine world of warfare, business, and government plus tens of thousands of female factory workers had to affect attitudes. Women alone on the streets in 1917 were a common sight; a generation earlier, the police might have detained them. The world in which Hubertine Auclert had once been denied a hotel room while on a trip to visit her family, on the argument that no respectable young woman would seek such lodgings, was gone. A freedom, born of necessity, could even be seen in the clothing that women wore—shorter, less form-fitting, more practical. Many contemporaries commented on the change. Charles Bouglé, a Sorbonne sociologist, summarized their view in 1923: "a hundred thousand of the surviving barriers to women fell at a single blow."[28] Nor have historians hesitated to ascribe great changes to the war. One of the most vigorous recent versions of this theory stresses a shift in attitudes and behavior:

> What women had gained during the four years of war was much more important than the right to vote. ... This was all of the changes in manners and habits, ... the most important change that the war of 1914 introduced into the history of women was not, as has been believed, the replacement of men by women, but the conquest of total freedom of circulation and communication with men. ...[29]

It is probably correct that the war adjusted attitudes, but one wonders if this new mood was so far-reaching or long-lasting.[30] Many of these changes were temporary, enduring as long as the unusual circumstances that produced them. It is probably more correct to see the war as only one factor in a longer and slower evolution of attitudes than as a momentous change. Can one imagine that millions of veterans returned from the front, having thrown off their traditional prejudices? Could any society with deeply ingrained feelings about the importance of the family and of women's position within it suddenly embrace the idea of the emancipated woman? Is it not a probable human reaction, after so great a tragedy, to seek to revive the *status quo ante bellum*—to "return to normalcy," in the language of the 1920s? Does not the evidence of the ephemeral and limited nature of women's economic and legal gains suggest modulating claims about new *mentalités*? Perhaps a clear perspective on the postwar situation of women in France—amended but not fundamentally changed—was implied by an observer for *The Times* of London who noted "to be unmarried is no longer a disgrace; it is merely a misfortune."[31]

World War I as a Setback for the Women's Suffrage Campaign

The perception that the war had permanently altered the position of women induced the conclusion that they would soon obtain political rights. When women were soon enfranchised in many countries, the Great War seemed to explain it. Historians have generally accepted this convenient, but facile, theory. It is an interpretation nurtured by the luxuriant growths of *post hoc, ergo propter hoc* logic that great events seem to produce. At its best, it is an insufficient explanation; at its worst, simply wrong. To attribute suffragist victories to the war derogates the generations of feminist labor that made enfranchisement possible by posing the question and winning opinion to accept it. If the war were the independent variable in the extension of women's rights, why did many neutrals, such as the Netherlands and the Scandinavian states, lead the way? Why did such major combatants as France and Italy deny women the vote? Even in such frequently cited cases as Great Britain, a reconsideration of the politics of women's suffrage suggests that the direct importance of the war is vastly overstated.[32]

In France, World War I was actually a setback for the women's suffrage movement.[33] There are many important reasons for this assertion. The war truncated a political campaign that had apparently reached its takeoff stage in 1914 but could not recover so well in 1919. During the hiatus in suffrage activities, leaders, organizations, and periodicals disappeared. Much of the disbanded movement could not be reconstituted in time to participate in the debate of 1919. Those

1. Marguerite Durand

2. (*above*) Hubertine Auclert, c. 1910
3. (*right*) Eliska Vincent

4. The members of Solidarité, c. 1900. Caroline Kauffmann is in the front row, holding the book

5. Caroline Kauffmann

6. Madeleine Pelletier

7. Maria Vérone

8. Jeanne Oddo-Deflou

9. (*right*) Marie Maugeret
10. (*below*) Nelly Roussel, 1910

11. Jeanne Laloë addressing her electoral meeting, May 1908

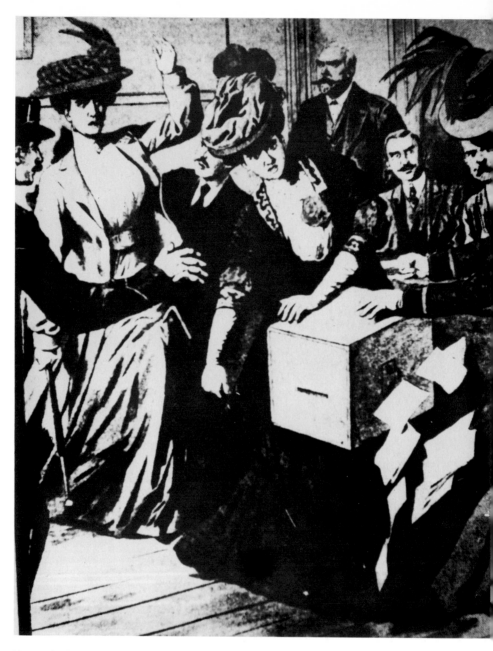

12. Auclert's demonstration, May 1908, as imagined by a newspaper artist. Among other errors, the drawing depicts Pelletier as knocking over the urn and Auclert (arm raised) watching.

13. Jeanne Schmahl, 1909

14. (*right*) Cecile Brunschwicg

15. (*below*) An LFDF polling place in Paris during *Le Journal*'s poll, April 1914

16. Séverine

17. Suffragist marchers at the statue of Condorcet, July 1914.

18. Members of Amélioration before a march, c. 1920, with placards typical of the group's moderate social feminism

19. The LFDF's "assault tank" for electoral propaganda, 1920s. Maria Vérone is third from the left, wearing a light hat

who returned to suffragism often did so with less single-mindedness—
their wartime interests now took more of their time. Some social
problems affecting suffragism, notably depopulation, were exacerbated
by the war, demanding a more vigorous feminist response but simultaneously driving away potential support. The success of the Russian revolution of 1917 also weakened French suffragism. Communism siphoned off some activists from the feminist left, fragmented
the women's movement anew, and led to a "Red Scare" against the
advocates of any egalitarian reform. The war also buried women's
rights under a host of other problems to which politicians accorded
primacy, such as economic recovery or the diplomacy of French security. Such problems created a national mood in which the foremost
desire seemed to be a return to the halcyon days of a lost *belle époque*
rather than to further the transformation of French society. In response, many feminists became more conservative, both in what they
asked and how they did so. Simultaneously, however, suffragists became overconfident, believing that the government would reward
them for their contribution to the war. All of this added up to a
suffrage campaign weaker in 1919-1922 than it had been in 1908-
1914.

Most of the small suffrage societies disappeared during the war. In
some cases this was only indirectly related to the war. Egalité, for
example, ceased operation following the death of Vincent; none of
the members were energetic or imaginative enough to overcome wartime inhibitions. In other instances, the effects of the war were more
direct. Jeanne Oddo-Deflou lost most of her family and her income
during the hostilities; poor and demoralized, she retired. The collapse
of the stock values on which she lived reduced Mme. Remember to
penury; she survived by selling flowers in the streets. Along with
leaders and organizations, the war took a severe toll of feminist publications. The costs of paper and manual labor increased dramatically,
forcing some publications to fold and others to curtail sharply their
size or frequency. Such problems forced *La Française* from weekly to
monthly publication in 1919, at which rate it was difficult to be the
Journal officiel of feminism. *Le Féminisme intégral* slowly evaporated:
first a monthly, then irregularly published, it became a quarterly in
1917, suffering until "exhorbitant costs" converted it to a pamphlet
series. Pelletier tried to revive *La Suffragiste* in 1919, but it soon folded.
As she explained to Arria Ly: "printers are extravagantly expensive;

they want 600 francs for what I formerly paid 50. Impossible!" The same crisis afflicted the Parisian daily press, of course; even *Le Radical* shrank to a two-page paper in 1919. This also hurt the suffragist cause. Old supporters almost disappeared: *L'Action* lost 95 percent of its circulation between March 1912 and November 1917; *La Petite république*, 87 percent. And smaller newspapers were much less willing to insert items submitted by the feminist societies.[34]   Other parts of the suffrage movement, particularly provincial organizations, suffered from their patriotic disbandment and were only slowly reestablished. Local commissariats of the police and several prefectures surveyed feminist efforts to rebuild provincial suffragism in 1918; several reported to the Sûreté générale, as the prefect of the Loire did, that a few militants were trying but having no success. While the larger chapters of the UFSF had continued to meet during the war, and the union's total membership was up, smaller groups disappeared completely. Several, such as the branch for Hérault, had to be recreated following the slow pattern that Brunschwicg had developed in 1910-1912. Some of these groups were still not active in 1920, when the union claimed eighty branches—a dozen fewer than in 1914.[35]

The war also impeded suffragist activity by drawing away supporters to non-suffrage enterprises. The individuals who had ceased their campaign in 1914 could not abandon the interests that had taken their time in 1914-1917; social feminism thus consumed more of the efforts by suffragists in 1918 than it had in 1914. The UFSF, for example, never returned to its statutory concentration solely upon the vote. Pacifists who had chosen patriotism in 1914 now felt conscience-bound to give some of their time to the League of Nations. Marguerite de Witt-Schlumberger, for example, presided over a Union féminine pour la Société des Nations. The most important instance of this diffusion of suffragist activity was their response to the question of depopulation. Conservative opponents of women's suffrage found the birth rate to be a forceful argument against any change in the position of women: more than ever, women owed France motherhood. "France has more need of children than of electors," ran a typical article of 1919. "The fate of France, its existence, depends on the family." The suffragist response to this situation combined a sincere agreement that patriotic women must be mothers, and a feminist argument that women could still contribute more to France if enfranchised. More conservative suffragists, such as Brunschwicg, even considered accepting familial suffrage if it addressed both problems; whatever their perspective, all feminists had to devote more attention to depopulation after the war.[36]

Many other issues inundated the woman question—issues that politicians, pressure groups, and journalists considered more urgent. The list was staggering. Economic matters included the reconstruction of the war zone, the resettlement of refugees, the reparations and war-debt problems, the transformation of production to peacetime manufacture, the demobilization and economic reintegration of hundreds of thousands of veterans, widespread labor unrest, and the stabilization of supply and prices. Diplomatic matters included the general issue of security against Germany, the negotiation and application of the Versailles Treaty, troubled relations with wartime allies, exceptionally complicated financial diplomacy, and the international politics of anti-Bolshevism. Feminist reforms appeared less critical in this context and accordingly received short shrift. Some women saw all of this adding up to a new basis of anti-feminism.[37]

Among the many French national concerns of 1918-1919 that obscured feminism, one had an especially strong impact on the women's movement: the repercussions of the Russian revolution. The response to Bolshevism enlarged the disagreements between bourgeois feminists and socialist women, driving each group away from conciliation. Furthermore, many militant suffragists defected to communism during the revolutionary enthusiasm of 1917-1921: the feminist left lost Pelletier, Kauffmann, Séverine, Roussel, Rauze, Brion, and Léal for varying periods. Pelletier was so enraptured that she undertook a trip to see Russia under communism and to contemplate permanent residence there. The rump organization of Solidarité left Paris for suburban Montreuil where it became a non-feminist association of proletarian women. French revolutionary socialism, and later French communism, did not welcome this influx of former suffragists by adopting their program. Communist women felt, as Saumoneau had taught, that political emancipation within bourgeois society was "a sham." Repubican socialists such as Vérone attacked Bolshevism as a threat to both their suffragism and their republicanism, but this was insufficient to spare feminism another ill effect of the Russian revolution, the ensuing wave of anti-communism. Fearful conservatives had little difficulty in connecting the feminist threat to the family and to traditional French society with an international communist conspiracy, especially when so many prominent feminists became communists. Hence, police surveillance increased and governmental cooperation decreased.[38]

One final, and ironic, result of the war must be noted. While it may seem contradictory in view of the preceding evidence, French suffragists left the war overconfident. They perceived many of the problems discussed here, but they underestimated them. The women who were optimistic in 1914 believed as an article of faith in 1919 that they would soon be voting. As early as 1916, leaders of the UFSF claimed that women would participate in the next elections. When peace came, the UFSF even participated in discussions about dissolving the International Women's Suffrage Alliance because it was no longer needed. Some suffragists, particularly in the UFF, were so confident that they devoted their time to teaching women about the political process rather than lobbying for enfranchisement. Could French politicians possibly refuse? Valentine Thomson asked the readers of *La Vie féminine* in 1919. "For my part, I cannot believe it," she answered.[39]

French suffragists might have profited from a reading of the history of the women's movement in the United States. Elizabeth Cady Stanton and Susan B. Anthony had similarly suspended their suffrage campaign during the Civil War and formed a National Woman's Loyal League in support of the union. The victors acknowledged the contributions of women by refusing to include them in the constitutional amendment that enfranchised emancipated male slaves. This lesson went unnoted in 1919; French suffragists understandably chose a comparison to the postwar adoption of women's suffrage in Britain and America.

The Resumption of the Political Rights Debate

The suspension of the women's suffrage campaign lasted until mid-1916, and the majority of French suffragists did not resume activities until 1917. In January 1916, Camille Bélilon could still write to the exiled Arria Ly, "As for feminism, there is nothing happening."[40] A few days after Bélilon's letter, Valentine Thomson published an editorial in *La Vie féminine* stating that "At an hour when everyone living must be in mourning for the dead, ... the claims of feminism must impose silence upon themselves."[41] De Witt-Schlumberger expressed the same sentiment to the UFSF congress of 1916. How could it be proper for women to ask for the vote when the masculine franchise had been suspended for the duration of the war? When less patient women questioned this policy, Jane Misme replied with a stinging article in *La Française*: "The great feminist associations persist in believing that they have had better things to do for the past two years than to absorb themselves in a sterile propaganda."[42] A sterile propaganda! Misme reported news of suffragism abroad—in the United States, Great Britain, Canada, and even Russia—but nothing more.

The stimulus to resume suffragism came from an unlikely source: Maurice Barrès, the nationalist deputy from Paris. In early 1916, Barrès adopted and embellished an idea previously suggested by another deputy, Jean Hennessy (republican, Charente). Hennessy proposed to give the vote in local elections to widowed mothers. Barrès dressed this notion with the catchy name of "suffrage for the dead" (*suffrage des morts*) and with patriotic rhetoric: "The right to vote of every soldier who dies for France passes to his widow, if he was married; to his father, if he was a bachelor; in the case of the prior death of his father, to his mother." Barrès's reputation made it difficult for suffragists to remain mute; when he raised the idea a second time and a similar plan appeared in the Senate, suffragists began to speak out.[43]

Feminists initially gave "suffrage for the dead" a mixed response. Some moderates—whom Roussel labeled "the opportunists, the timid ones"—started to rally to the Barrès plan in late 1916. *L'Action féminine*, the organ of the CNFF, praised the combination of a moving gesture and an acceptable first step toward fuller suffrage. The central committee of the UFSF, led by de Witt-Schlumberger, even entered negotiations with their supporters in the Chamber of Deputies to see if they could help to advance such a bill. These actions shocked other suffragists. Marie Bonnevial attacked the UFSF by name at a meeting of the LFDF; two consecutive meetings of the league passed resolutions disapproving of *suffrage des morts*. As Vérone later put it, "Does the bullet that kills the man create intelligence in the woman?" The most astringent rejection came from Roussel, writing in *L'Equité*: "No, M. Barrès, we women of conscience do not want your injurious generosity. We do not want to think for another, to speak for another."[44]

The Barrès plan received little consideration in the Chamber of

Deputies, but it stimulated reconsideration of women's suffrage. The Commission of Universal Suffrage decided to support a modified version of the Dussaussoy Bill but had instructed the new *rapporteur*, Pierre-Etienne Flandin, not to deposit a report until the end of the war. Flandin supported this moratorium. He candidly stated his belief that it would be "criminal" for the chamber to devote time to women's suffrage during the hostilities. A new president, Alexandre Varenne (socialist, Puy-de-Dôme), however, convinced the commission to reverse itself. In addition to the Barrès plan, Varenne was reacting to the consideration of women's rights in other countries.[45]

There were many indications of a revival of international suffragism in the years 1915-1917. Women in Denmark and Iceland received the vote in June 1915. That same year, the British House of Commons began a study of electoral reform to facilitate the participation of the army; the committee that considered this issue was chaired by a suffragist who linked the questions of female and military franchise, resulting in a report favorable to both. In Canada, the western provinces of Alberta, Manitoba, and Saskatchewan gave women the vote in local elections in 1916; British Columbia and Ontario followed in 1917. The national government adopted an expanded version of the Barrès plan. A Military Voters Act granted the ballot to female subjects—chiefly nurses—who participated in the Canadian military; a Wartime Elections Act enfranchised an additional 500,000 to 1,000,000 women who had close relatives under arms.[46]

None of these events attracted as much attention in Paris as did the suffrage politics of the United States, due to the issues of U.S. neutrality and the 1916 presidential election. Women voted in twelve of the forty-eight states (all in the West and Midwest) and their role was the subject of careful scrutiny in France. Furthermore, the United States produced suffragist activism. Carrie Chapman Catt assumed the presidency of the National American Woman Suffrage Association in 1915 and increased its membership in little more than a year from 100,000 to a staggering 2,000,000. By 1917, five more states had adopted versions of woman's suffrage—including the first victories in the East—and the first woman, Jeanette Rankin of Montana, had been elected to Congress. That same year, Alice Paul, Lucy Burns, and their Woman's Party brought demonstrations to the streets of Washington, D.C.[47]

The final, dramatic foreign stimuli to French suffragism came from

Petrograd and London. The revolution of February 1917 reawakened Russian feminism. Demonstrations led by revolutionaries such as Anna Milyukova, won the assurance of Prince Lvov that women would vote; in mid-April the Provisional Government granted full political equality to women at age twenty. Meanwhile, in London, it had become clear by early 1917 that the House of Commons would approve of women's suffrage. In June, the house endorsed "the general principle" by a vote of 385-55. Lest the denizens of the Palais Bourbon miss these trends, Marguerite Durand mordantly called them to Flandin's attention: "to occupy themselves with such questions in the middle of war, to encourage women in their noble effort! What 'criminals' these English must be!"[48]

The Commission of Universal Suffrage began reconsideration of women's suffrage in early 1917. Varenne met with leaders of the UFSF in January to determine their reaction to a conservative modification of the Dussaussoy Bill. Learning that they would consent to a lesser bill, Varenne held committee meetings in February. According to one commission member, the UFSF's "sensible attitude" improved suffragist prospects from "very chilly" to "quite warm." Flandin presented the rewritten bill to the commission on February 15, 1917. He proposed to amend the Municipal Elections Law of 1884 by following the term *français* with the clarification "of both sexes, without reservation." Flandin went on, however, to ask for two major changes in the Dussaussoy-Buisson texts: 1) women would not obtain the vote at age twenty-one, like men, but at age twenty-five; 2) women elected to municipal councils would not be permitted to participate in the electoral colleges which named senators. The commission approved these amendments, re-endorsed women's suffrage, and again bade Flandin not to deliver his report until the end of hostilities.[49] Report or not, the question was open again.

The reopening of the political rights debate found the women's movement unprepared, their enthusiastic entente of 1914 only a memory. Séverine, president of its "permanent committee," attempted to resume activities with a speech to the UFSF congress of April 1916. She received an expected rejection—an especially cold rejection because she called for the vote to enable women to work against war. Séverine promptly abandoned bourgeois feminism, returning to the more familiar milieu of syndicalism and working-class politics. A few months later, the October revolution converted Séverine to communism, ending both her work for women's suffrage and any prospect that middle-class suffragists would listen to her.[50] Even if the federal entente had been resuscitated, the Flandin Bill would have killed it. The UFSF had angered militants by considering the Barrès plan, then supporting Flandin. De Witt-Schlumberger told the press that the union feared "too hasty developments" and believed "we must limit our desires." The union's *Bulletin* insisted that "it is wise to proceed in France by stages." The entire feminist center copied this caution, holding, as Siegfried did, that they should "speak less of our rights and more of our duties."[51]

The LFDF took the lead in challenging the UFSF. Vérone argued that others had reopened the suffrage question, and suffragists could not tolerate discussion limited to the ideas of Barrès and Flandin. A delegation of militants carried this message to Alexandre Varenne and sympathetic deputies like Louis Andrieux. When the Commission of Universal Suffrage adopted Flandin's plan, Vérone took her criticism to the press. A few weeks later, Vérone and Durand led another deputation to meet with Flandin, whom they bluntly told of their dissatisfaction. The LFDF resistance to suffragist self-effacement received the backing of the feminist left. Andrieux—now the honorary president of Suffrage des femmes—urged feminists to press for fuller rights. Somewhat more surprisingly, Louis Marin added a conservative voice to the militant protest. Finding "very little talk of women's suffrage" at the 1917 UFSF congress, Marin chided the union for not bringing pressure to bear on the commission.[52]

Militants also won the backing of two newly created suffrage organizations, Action des femmes and the Comité d'action suffragiste, whose very names suggest growing feminist dissatisfaction with inaction. Action des femmes appeared in 1915—with a program stressing education and philanthropy. The group grew to over 150 members and underwent radicalization, apparently resulting from an influx of members from the LNVF, a group badly enervated by the suffragist moratorium. Anne Léal and Irma Perrot, both former LNVF activists, gave Action des femmes its militant orientation. Their statutes, adopted in 1917, denounced the government's inaction on women's rights. Jeanne Mélin established the Comité d'action suffragiste in December 1917 with similar intentions. She also attracted a membership of about 150 women, largely from the LNVF and the dissatisfied minority in the UFSF. Mélin sought a socialist position distinct from revolutionary

Bolshevism, open to all feminists who accepted the republic but desired major reforms in it. In her view, Flandin's plan was merely a paraphrase of radical anti-suffragism.[53]

The suffragist bifurcation of 1917 revived many prewar debates, such as municipal suffrage versus integral suffrage. The spirit of the 1914 compromise was lost. The militants of Action des femmes, for example, published a pamphlet denouncing municipal suffrage as "a humiliation, an indignity, an injustice." In return, Misme excoriated these women as "suffragist maximalists" who should listen to those leaders of the UFSF and the CNFF who had labored for the vote "for long years." The Chamber of Deputies would accept municipal suffrage but would reject integral suffrage for many years. By mid-1918, the debate was acrimonious, and the end of the war found the movement more divided than it had been since the elections of 1908.[54]

ⓍⓄⓍⓄⓍⓄⓍⓄⓍⓄⓍⓄⓍⓄⓍⓄⓍⓄⓍⓄⓍⓄⓍⓄⓍⓄⓍⓄⓍⓄⓍⓄⓍⓄⓍⓄⓍⓄ

Chapter Eight

Short-Lived Victory and
Long-Lived Defeat, 1918-1922

The old suffrage leagues emerged from World War I more conservative than they had entered it. Whether one looks at their rhetoric, objectives, or tactics, they were more restrained in the winter of 1918-1919 than they had been in the summer of 1914. The leaders of the movement shared the mood of the bourgeoise—exhausted but patriotic, nervously anti-Bolshevik, eager for reconstruction, anxious about perceived "threats to the race." Marguerite de Witt-Schlumberger, for example, wrote to the members of the UFSF in late 1918 to reopen their campaign, but her letter stressed the postwar problems of France. Feminists, she insisted, "must not consider the suffrage as a prerogative to obtain, nor as a compensation for our tireless devotion to France, but as the only means possible of responding to the needs of the country." Even the women of the LFDF, although more forceful in calling for the rights of women, shared the conservative social arguments of the UFSF. This cautious mood enabled the prewar suffrage leagues still active (see Table 9) to agree upon a collaborative manifesto in December 1918. This document called for the chamber to debate the Flandin Report and grant women's suffrage before the first postwar elections, but it omitted any reference to the specific rights—municipal or integral—expected because feminists could not agree. Thereafter, each suffrage organization chose its own means of seeking the vote; no effort to recreate the entente of 1914 was made.[1]

The most energetic revival was in the LFDF. After the death of Marie Bonnevial in an automobile accident in 1918, Vérone assumed the presidency and total direction of the league; instead of naming a new secretary-general, the office was split into a secretariat of several women. Vérone drafted new statutes declaring the LFDF to be a national federation and then sought to make this a reality. This made

Table 9 • Principal Suffrage Organizations, 1919-1922

	Founded	Leader(s)	Associated Publication(s)	Estimated Membership
FEMINIST LEFT				
Suffrage des femmes	1876	Chaumont	(none)	c. 25
LFDF	1882	Vérone	*Le Droit des femmes*	c. 1000
FFU	1908	Méo		
Action des femmes	1915	Perrot (s.-g.) Léal (pres.)	*La République intégrale*	c. 200
Comité d'action suffragiste	1917	Mélin	(none)	c. 200
FEMINIST CENTER				
Amélioration	1876	Martial	*L'Heure de la femme*	
CNFF	1901	Sainte-Croix (s.-g.) Siegfried (pres.)	*La Française* (from 1921)	125,000
UFF	1901	Raspail (s.-g.) Hammer (pres.)	(none)	c. 200
UFSF	1909	Brunschwicg (s.-g.) Witt-Schlumberger (pres.)	*Bulletin* *Jus Suffragii* (IWSA) *La Française* (to 1921) *La Vie féminine* (to 1919)	20,000
Société nationale du féminisme français	1915	Remember	*Le Féminisme intégral*	
Comité de propagande féministe	1919	Brunet	*Les Forces nouvelles*	c. 350
FEMINIST RIGHT				
Action sociale de la femme	1901	Chenu	*L'Action sociale*	c. 1000
LPF	1901	Frossard (s.-g.)	*L'Echo du LPF*	600,000
CESC	1919	Chenu		1,000,000
UNVF	1920	LeVert-Chotard		

the league a rival to the UFSF in the departments as well as in Paris, exacerbating the traditional split between the feminist left and center. Largely due to her efforts on the lecture circuit, Vérone's plan succeeded. By 1920, the LFDF counted chapters in twenty-three departments. (See Map 8.) Like many other feminist societies, the LFDF found its greatest strength in the north—72 percent of its branches.[2] In contrast, Suffrage des femmes left the war as a tiny society under the direction of Auclert's sister, Marie Chaumont, who chiefly devoted herself to completing the publication of Auclert's final book, *Les Femmes au gouvernail* (1923).

The old societies of the feminist center undertook no comparable new initiatives. The UFSF, drawing on the energies of a younger generation of leaders such as Suzanne Grinberg (born 1890), Germaine Malaterre-Sellier (born 1889), and Marcelle Kraemer-Bach, concentrated on reviving its provincial base in competition with the LFDF. The CNFF organized large public meetings with prestigious speakers in an effort to attract press attention. The typical propaganda of the center was devised by Lydie Martial, the postwar president of Amélioration. Her poster advanced nine reasons why women should vote: to avoid war, to protect children, to improve hygiene, to eliminate slums, to combat alcoholism, to increase production, to reform the Civil Code, to reduce inflation, and to conquer contagious diseases. (See Illus. 18.) The postwar bourgeois feminism is also well illustrated by the most successful new organization, Louise Brunet's Comité de propagande féministe, which attracted 350 members. Brunet envisioned her society as a circle of literary and artistic feminism which would publicize the cause within the middle-class chiefly through feminist "galas"—concerts, banquets, theater parties. Her program was revealing: 1) to contribute to the evolution of feminist claims, 2) to instruct proletarian women in their duties outside the home; 3) to prepare women to become responsible citizens; and 4) to publicize women's claims. This won the support of conservatives, such as Louis Marin and Paul Painlevé, and it dramatized the gap between bourgeois feminism and socialist feminism.[3]

On the far left of the women's movement, socialist women were again sharply divided. Some of the groups of the GdFS, such as Gabrielle Yung's at Pantin, resisted the efforts of Saumoneau to lead the party into Lenin's Third International and fought to develop feminism within the party. Saumoneau soon broke with French com-

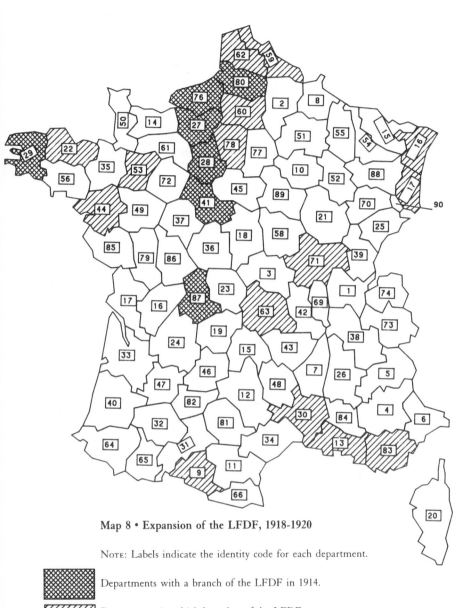

Map 8 • Expansion of the LFDF, 1918-1920

NOTE: Labels indicate the identity code for each department.

Departments with a branch of the LFDF in 1914.

Departments in which branches of the LFDF were established, 1918-1920.

munists, however, and reasserted her non-feminist policy in the GdFS, so these groups remained relatively powerless. The locus of the suffrage debate on the left thus became the active socialist women's press which appeared at the end of the war. (See Table 10.) The most energetic feminism came from Louise Bodin's *La Voix des femmes*. It was established as a weekly paper in 1917 and soon approached a

Table 10 • Principal Feminist Periodicals, 1919-1922

	Founded	Editor	Frequency
BOURGEOIS-REPUBLICAN			
(Feminist Left)			
Le Droit des femmes	1906	Vérone	Monthly
Action féministe	1908	Méo	Monthly
La République intégrale	1915	Perrot	Monthly
(Feminist Center)			
La Française	1906	Misme	Weekly 1919, 1922 Monthly, 1919-1921
Jus suffragii	1906	IWSA (Geneva)	Monthly
Le Parthenon	1911	Brault	Monthly
UFSF Bulletin	1911	Brunschwicg	Annual
Le Féminisme intégral	1913	Remember	Quarterly, 1919-1921
La Vie féminine	1914	Thomson	Fortnightly, 1919
La France féminine	1917	Martinot	Monthly
L'Heure de la femme	1919	Martial	Monthly
CATHOLIC			
Action sociale	1901	Chenu	Monthly
L'Echo du LPF	1903	Frossard	Monthly
SOCIALIST-COMMUNIST			
Les Travailleuses	1907	Berot-Berger	Monthly to 1919
La Femme socialiste	1912	Saumoneau	Monthly
La Voix des femmes	1917	Bodin	Weekly, 1917-1919 Fortnightly, 1919-1922
La Vague	1918	Capy	Weekly
La Lutte féministe	1919	Brion	Weekly
La Suffragiste	1919	Pelletier	Monthly, to 1920

circulation of 5,000; the financial exigencies of 1919 made it a fortnightly, but recovery permitted daily publication in 1922. Its editorial policies followed similar shifts. In its first phase, *La Voix des femmes* combined militant suffragism with socialism, pacifism, and internationalism. But in the months following the Congress of Tours (December 1920), the paper turned away from feminism and toward communism. By March 1921, the editors had dropped all ties to bourgeois feminist groups and began to deride those groups, particularly the CNFF. Bodin then adopted Saumoneau's program, insisting that socialist women must not separate the emancipation of women from the emancipation of the proletariat. This communist phase too was short-lived, and in 1922 *La Voix des femmes* again proclaimed itself the voice of "independent feminism." In the interim, however, the loudest voice on the women's left contributed nothing to the parliamentary campaign for enfranchisement. Bodin's policy was challenged by two smaller papers, Marcelle Capy's *La Vague* and Hélène Brion's *La Lutte féministe*, but they too found collaboration with bourgeois suffragists difficult.[4]

These developments among bourgeois feminists and socialist women were all reminiscent of their prewar behavior; dramatic change occurred only on the Catholic right wing of the women's movement, which now endorsed women's suffrage. There are several reasons for the transformation of Catholic opinion, beginning in Rome. In early 1919, Pope Benedict XV reversed the Vatican's attitude to women's political rights in an audience with several Englishwomen. Annie Christitch of the Catholic Women's Society directly asked his opinion. Benedict responded: "Yes, we approve! We would like to see women electors everywhere."[5] The greatest barrier which Maugeret encountered had thereby fallen. Indeed, the pope's attitude was considered so important that French feminists have erroneously attributed the birth of Christian feminism to it.[6] This is an exaggeration for two reasons: it ignores the arduous ground-breaking of women like Maugeret, and it overstates the strength of Benedict's suffragism. He acknowledged the inevitability of women's suffrage, "counting on 'the devout female sex' to defend the cause of religion and of Catholic morality."[7] Conservative Catholics, like Cardinal James Gibbons of Baltimore, disputed the feminist claim that Benedict was a suffragist, and the pope did not take the opportunity to clarify his feelings. Other papal pronouncements of 1919 on the woman question amplified his conservative social intentions. In a discourse in reply to the Italian Catholic Women's Union, Sono avventurati, Benedict agreed that "the conditions of the times have enlarged the field of woman's activity." He stressed, however, that "no change in the opinions of man, no novelty of circumstances and events, will ever remove woman, conscious of her mission, from her natural center, which is the family."[8] Some ambiguity thus remained about papal intentions, but this did not alter the conclusion that French Catholic women could now support women's suffrage.

Postwar Catholic suffragism was similarly facilitated by the conversion of prominent conservatives such as Charles Maurras and René Bazin. Their motivation was often the Russian revolution. Women's suffrage might be "the grain of sand that will stop the formidable collectivist machine." For other Catholic intellectuals, the decisive fact was that the republic would adopt the reform, and Catholics must accept that fact. Hence, the question was not to judge the merits of enfranchising women, but to understand the instrument that the republic was creating. Most based their attitude on the traditional Catholic concept of duty. Catholic women should prepare to vote, not because it was their right as individuals to do so, but their responsibility to defend the family, church, and *patrie*. By voting in accordance with the church's teachings, they might better protect children, undo divorce legislation, combat neo-Malthusian sex education, liberate the church's schools and associations, lash out against vice and alcoholism, support legislation on behalf of the family, and generally confront the enemies of Christianity. This line of reasoning, developed by the Jesuit advisor to the LPF and circulated through the league's *Echo*, did not call for an active pursuit of the vote, but it made it wrong for Catholic women to abstain from using their political powers. The battle between church and state had receded sufficiently in memory by 1919 to allow more Catholics to accept the republic and its institutions, with hopes of changing them. The war had done much to establish this new attitude. The activities of Catholic women during the war stimulated their sense of civic responsibility, producing the conclusion that women did not have the right to hold themselves above the political process, and providing the argument that women had earned the vote. The war also stirred their national pride, leading them to claim the rights that other nations (including defeated Germany) were granting their women.[9]

Although Maugeret staged another Congrès Jeanne d'Arc in 1919, it was Jeanne Chenu and the women of Action sociale who led the way to the new Catholic suffragism. In March 1918, the members decided that political rights were "a necessity"; before the end of the year, they had published a book entitled *La Femme devant les urnes* and persuaded the diocesan congress to consider political rights for women. Their foremost argument was duty: women, for example, had to protect the families of war dead which now had no electoral voice. In January 1919 Chenu organized a new federation of Catholic women to unite all of the leagues for common action—the Commission d'éducation sociale civique de la femme (CESC). Representatives of fifteen different Catholic groups participated; the LPF, the LFF, and a dozen charities and labor unions all joined. Another leader of Action sociale, Mme. Levert-Chotard, organized a committee devoted to women's suffrage and persuaded the CESC congress of April 1920 to support enfranchisement. So widespread was the new mood that the motion to endorse women's suffrage came from the leader of a philanthropic society of upper-class women who stated, "Women *do not have the right* to distance themselves from events." Other conservative women who had opposed Maugeret now supported Chenu and Levert-Chotard, notably the leaders of the LPF. The Marquise de Moustier, president of the LPF and wife of a deputy who supported integral suffrage in the Chamber of Deputies, proclaimed the Ligue's patriotique's new policy: "I enthusiastically rally to the support of . . . Mme. Chenu," she wrote. "I am quite content from a Catholic point of view (which is the one that interests us) to see that women's suffrage has made enormous progress . . . from a point of view of all that is good, of all that can reinforce the life of the family . . . it will be desirable that all Catholic women take part in this necessary campaign."[10]

This new Catholic consensus on the vote promoted the establishment of the first Catholic organization devoted solely to women's suffrage. In the autumn of 1920, Levert-Chotard, Chenu, and de Moustier founded the Union nationale pour le vote des femmes (UNVF), under the presidency of Levert-Chotard. The prospectus for the UNVF and its statutes clearly distinguished Catholic suffragism from the feminist mainstream. The union's objective was to use the vote for "the preservation of the highest tradition of the family, the established order in society, and the old conception of the duties of wife and mother." Use of the ballot was not seen as an individual right but as a collective duty; the sexes were seen as "equivalent," not "absolutely equal."[11] With this conservative basis established, with the concepts of duty and family foremost, the UNVF took strong suffragist stands. By 1921, Levert-Chotard was even willing to reject any formula of familial suffrage that deprived women of the right to vote: "The woman is a human being, married or not. Why should her position as a wife or mother deprive her of her political rights?"[12] It remained to be seen if this provided an adequate basis for collaboration with republican suffragists, or if the decision of the leadership coincided with the sentiments of the hundreds of thousands of members who were certainly not the monolithic phalanx that radicals saw.

Whatever the varied intentions of feminist organizations in 1919, they faced extraordinary difficulties in reorganizing a women's suffrage campaign. Their conflicting aspirations made collaboration unlikely; the public mood made the conquest of opinion difficult; but a larger problem confronted them—France was still in a state of siege, in accordance with the laws of 1849 and 1878. This legislation permitted the government to establish an extraordinary regime that curtailed civil liberties such as the freedom of the press or of assembly, at the discretion of military authorities. Pre-war statutes had made protest difficult enough, particularly the ordinance of 1900 and the Law of Public and Private Meetings of 1907 which empowered the government to regulate dissent. Civil liberties were much more sharply curtailed, however, by the decree of August 1914 that placed all departments in a state of siege. As the armistice of November 1918 did not lead to the immediate rescinding of these restrictions, suffragists were at the mercy of the government. Neither the cabinet, nor the prefects, nor the police were in merciful mood. Their greatest anxieties concerned labor agitation, pacifism, and Bolshevism rather than feminism per se, but they found sufficient correlation between feminist organizations and these activities to justify the continued curtailment of women's demonstrations. The Sûreté générale compiled a list of fourteen women's groups to watch in October 1918, including such thoroughly moderate groups as the UFSF, Amélioration, and the UFF. The Prefecture of Police added surveillance of several others. And the director of the Sûreté sent explicit instructions to the prefects: "Keep me very closely informed on feminist agitation in your department."[13]

The enforcement of martial law impeded many suffragist plans. Military authorities rejected a request to stage a second feminist day on the model of the Condorcet demonstration of 1914. Permission was denied many other meetings; those ruled acceptable generally required every participant to possess an individual invitation. Such prohibitions so infuriated Vérone that she devoted almost an entire page of *L'Oeuvre* to protesting them. Her essay there echoed the frustration and the contemplation of violence that Auclert had expressed in *Le Radical* in 1906-1908. Public meetings and demonstrations in the streets being forbidden, Vérone asked, what are we to do? "We recognize perfectly the means that most often succeed ... threats, violence, blackmail—but we desire to employ other means." Vérone reflected on the prewar tactics of English suffragettes—slashing paintings, pouring acid in mailboxes, breaking windows—and insisted that French women did not want to try them. But she left the implication that this was possible. No such campaign occurred in 1919; indeed, very little suffragist activity of any sort took place. Due to the state of siege, suffragists held small meetings and published multiple appeals but were more dependent than ever upon their allies in parliament and the press.[14]

Short-Lived Victory: The Chamber of Deputies, 1918-1919

Even without a major campaign in the months following the armistice, feminists expected an early victory in the Chamber of Deputies. In 1917, Viviani (then the minister of justice) had given the UFSF a promise that the government would support municipal suffrage after the war. Jules Siegfried, nearing his eighty-first birthday, delivered the *doyen d'âge's* speech at the opening of the 1918 session and declared that women must be given the vote in recognition of "their admirable attitude during the war." Such support from old friends was reassuring, but suffragists were more excited by the apparent conversion of new, powerful supporters. A few days after Siegfried's speech, a reporter for *La Renaissance* interviewed ten politicians and found that they all approved of some form of women's suffrage. Those speaking out included Senator Edouard Herriot, the mayor of Lyons and rising star of the Radical Party; Senator Charles Debierre of the Nord, who was a president of both the Grand Orient and of the Radical Party;

and the Comte de Las Cazes, a conservative senator from Lozère. Unquestionably the most encouraging sign, however, was a public statement by Georges Clemenceau in February 1919 that women deserved municipal rights. After that astonishing shift, it was almost anticlimactic when Maurras wrote a leader in *L'Action française* supporting women's suffrage.[15]

The issue of women's suffrage consequently made quick progress through the Chamber of Deputies in late 1918 and early 1919. The Commission of Universal Suffrage held two formal proposals, the conservative Flandin plan of February 1917 and a bill deposited by Emile Magniez of the Somme in January 1918. The Magniez Bill called for integral suffrage with one exception: prostitutes and the keepers of bawdyhouses would be disenfranchised. "The war has fully revealed," he stated, "the immense value of feminine cooperation to the national life . . . they can be our precious collaborators; let us not treat them as slaves!" Three weeks before the armistice, the commission voted to deposit the Flandin Report, unaltered. Flandin alluded to the Magniez Bill but announced that the committee rejected it. Indeed, he told feminists that he was pessimistic that the chamber would accept even his regressive report. The committee intended to keep the Flandin Report off the order of the day until the chamber completed its consideration of proportional representation, which seemed likely to be adopted. In December 1918, however, Louis Andrieux introduced an amendment to apply *le RP* "without distinction of sex." A month later, Bracke (Alexandre Desrousseaux), a socialist deputy from Paris, added another amendment, for integral suffrage. Before those amendments could be disjoined from the proportional representation bill, two additional versions of women's suffrage reached the chamber. At the end of January 1919, Andrieux reported, for the local government committee, a proposal to give the vote in all elections to women at age twenty-one, if they were widows, mothers, or heads of families (e.g., the sister who served as guardian for her deceased brother's children). Andrieux then disassociated himself from the committee report and introduced another amendment for integral suffrage. "The reporter has the disgrace not to be fully in agreement with either commission," he said, deriding their plans. "Since the Buisson Report, ten years have passed under the bridges of the Seine. Gentlemen, judge the progress made! . . . [we] refuse to women the eligibility to sit . . . even on the modest little *conseil d'arrondissement*, whose powers scarcely go beyond the adoption of inoffensive motions." Altogether, that totaled six versions of women's suffrage afloat in the Chamber of Deputies.[16]

Parliamentary opinion was as hostile to the connection of women's suffrage and proportional representation in 1919 as it had been ten years earlier. Even Ferdinand Buisson, now an honorary president of the Radical Party, counseled against it. When debate began on electoral reform in March 1919, Alexandre Varenne easily got all encumbering amendments disjoined from the bill and tabled. The problem arose again when the Baron Henri Roulleaux-Dugage (Union républicaine, Orne) intervened in debate to propose familial suffrage, and Andrieux seized the moment to propose integral suffrage. The deputies had diminishing patience for such tactics and beat back all efforts for women's suffrage by steadily increasing margins. On the last vote, Andrieux lost by 325-116—one vote less than he had obtained on the same motion in 1913. The Chamber of Deputies thereupon adopted proportional representation.[17]

In May 1919, the Chamber of Deputies honored the longstanding promise to debate women's suffrage after other electoral reforms had been adopted. Discussion, the first in the history of the chamber, began on May 8 with Pierre Flandin presenting the commission's bill before a packed gallery which included the presidents of all major suffrage groups. Flandin spoke briefly, but forcefully, in favor of his limited plan, asking if France would be the last advanced state to admit women to political life. Subsequent speakers quickly turned consideration toward integral suffrage. Bracke announced that the socialists would introduce an amendment to that effect, but it was a conservative, Siegfried, who most forcefully insisted that women be given the vote as "a gesture of justice."[18]

The anti-suffrage counterattack began a week later. Victor Augagneur (Republican Socialist, Rhône), once a feminist hero for his campaign against regulated prostitution, briefly expressed the republican anti-suffrage argument—women were still insufficiently prepared for political responsibility. The greatest attack came on May 15 from Edmond Lefebvre du Prey, a conservative landed proprietor with a considerable reputation for parliamentary eloquence. He combined a panegyric, eulogizing abstract Woman, and a broadside, assailing all forms of women's suffrage. It was a comprehensive recapitulation of conservative arguments against feminism: political life is outside the natural function and the true role of women—women are neither physically nor morally prepared for the task—the emancipation of women is a threat to the authority of the husband and the stability of the family—woman's place is in the home—France must not be swayed by the behavior in alien cultures—French women do not want to vote. If revolutionaries succeed in this drastic alteration of society, Lefebvre du Prey concluded in a passionate summary, "So much the worse for the children! So much the worse for the French family!" The Chamber of Deputies nonetheless voted by a large margin (330-218) to pass from general consideration to a discussion of the articles.[19]

Baron Roulleaux-Dugage posed the next threat with a substitute bill calling for familial suffrage. It had much greater support than its previous rejections suggested. The Ligue des familles nombreuses strongly supported it as partial cure for depopulation, and the chamber's group affiliated with the league lobbied for it, bringing support from the left as well as the right. Louis Breton (Republican Socialist, Cher) led the defense of familial suffrage. He had been the leading socialist advocate of natalism for twenty years, working for benefits for pregnant women, the Law of Large Families in 1913, and leaves for conjugal visits by soldiers at the front. Such efforts soon won Breton the portfolio for health in the Millerand cabinet (January 1920) and the nickname "Minister of Natality." French deputies were acutely sensitive to the natalist arguments of Roulleaux-Dugage and Breton. Many found familial suffrage a convenient response to two great issues. Some, doubtless, liked the idea as a way to vote for women's rights yet retain male political superiority; many who disliked it were too intimidated by the population question to vote against it. As a result, Varenne and Flandin had an unexpectedly difficult time in defending the commission's bill against the substitute; a motion to disjoin the issue of familial suffrage carried by only 281-200, with more than a quarter of the chamber not voting.[20]

Following that narrow victory, the advocates of integral suffrage resumed the offensive on the final day of debate, May 20. Other socialists reintroduced Bracke's proposal. Andrieux added his own substitute wording, with a passionate call for "justice for women." Varenne and Flandin defended the theory of limited suffrage, granted in stages. Others, with Augagneur the most strenuous, reiterated the arguments of republican anti-suffragism, "the inherent danger" for

France of these new proposals. "You are setting off on an adventure," Augagneur warned, "and whatever it leads to, you will be obliged to accept the consequences." The turning point of the women's suffrage debate occurred when Viviani intervened to support integral suffrage. It was one of the most effective speeches of his thirty-year parliamentary career, a 5,000-word peroration rebutting every objection raised in the debate. Invoking the spirit of the French revolution and pride in the war effort, Viviani summoned all "sons of the revolution" to show "the permanent idealism that reposes in the republican tradition." The chamber erupted in prolonged applause and Viviani had difficulty regaining his bench due to the crowd that sought to congratulate him. Varenne briefly tried to hold back the flow of sentiment, but he had lost his audience. That became especially clear when Aristide Briand rose to laud the eloquence of Viviani and announced, "I am voting for the equality of the rights of men and women." Women's suffrage won by the incredible margin of 329-95.[21]

At first glance, the adoption of women's suffrage by the Chamber of Deputies in May 1919 is stunning. The margin of victory was greater than three to one. Those voting for full political equality included Maurice Barrès, Jacques Piou, Baron Roulleaux-Dugage, and even Victor Augagneur. *La République française* spoke for many when they called the vote "un coup de théâtre."[22]

Hindsight suggests that the vote was less of a victory than it seemed. An examination of the roll call tabulation first shows that 104 deputies did not cast a vote. (See Table 11.) The percentage of the chamber voting for women's suffrage thus falls from an apparent 78 percent to an actual 62 percent—a big victory, but much less dramatic. Furthermore, it must remembered that 200 deputies had just demonstrated that they preferred familial suffrage. Vote switching clearly occurred and it raises difficult questions. How many of the 329 actively desired integral suffrage? How many, therefore, would press for it (or any suffrage bill) in a struggle with the Senate? Might not a significant share of the majority have voted with ulterior motives? If precise answers could have been put to such questions in 1919, suffragist joy would probably have diminished.

Several other characteristics of this ballot detracted from the great victory. Radicals remained the predominant bloc in French politics, and they were clearly still hostile to women's suffrage. Less than 40 percent of the radical deputies voted for the suffrage bill; nearly 70

Table 11 • Voting for Women's Suffrage in the Chamber of Deputies, May 1919

	Yes	No	Not Voting	No, plus Not Voting
Entire Chamber of Deputies	329 (62.3%)	95 (18.0%)	104 (19.7%)	199 (37.7%)
Socialists	104 (87.7%)	2 (1.7%)	10 (8.6%)	12 (10.3%)
Radicals and Radical-Socialists	75 (39.7%)	65 (34.4%)	49 (25.9%)	114 (60.3%)
Conservative Republicans	102 (66.7%)	22 (14.4%)	29 (19.0%)	51 (33.3%)
Parties of the Right	48 (78.7%)	6 (9.8%)	7 (11.5%)	13 (21.3%)
Members of the Clemenceau Cabinet	1 (5.3%)	0	18 (94.7%)	18 (94.7%)
Members of the Commission of Universal Suffrage	26 (59.1%)	8 (18.2%)	10 (22.7%)	18 (40.9%)

percent of all negative votes were cast by radicals. Such results might have been expected, but they hid an alarming fact: of the thirty-three radical deputies who announced their support of women's suffrage between 1910 and 1914 and then remained in the chamber to vote in 1919, more than one-third (36.4 percent) did not vote for the bill. This certainly boded ill for the difficult task of winning over the Senate. Worse yet, the Clemenceau government gave absolutely no support to the bill. Despite Clemenceau's pronouncement of February 1919, he did nothing to help women's suffrage, even in the modest version reported by Flandin. No member of the cabinet spoke in favor of the bill. Not one of the seven ministers who sat in the Chamber of Deputies voted; of Clemenceau's ten under-secretaries, only one (Alexandre Millerand) defied the obviously conscious policy to abstain. If the cabinet was not even willing to support the bill, they clearly would not use the instruments of state to press the Senate. Indeed, anti-suffragists in the Senate immediately noted the government's silence.[23]

Another serious problem lay hidden in the geographic distribution of support and opposition. French suffragists considered this issue briefly, but they were misled by the size of the favorable vote. They calculated that there were only six anti-suffragist departments in France and therefore erroneously concluded that they need not concentrate their efforts somewhere for the final push to win in the Senate.[24] Reasoning in this way, suffragists failed to appreciate how strongly their support was concentrated in the Paris region, the east, and the Rhône basin. (See Map 9.) More importantly, they failed to appreciate how solidly their opposition was located in the west and especially in the southwest. Five of the six departments with an anti-suffrage majority in the Chamber of Deputies (Aude, Charente-Inférieure, Gironde, Haute-Loire, and Basses Pyrénées) plus two of the three departments with complete abstention (Cantal, Lot-et-Garonne) were in that region. The opposition concentrated in the southwest should have suggested the persistence of traditional attitudes about women and the family in that region. This well-known fact should have, in turn, suggested the strong likelihood of senatorial opposition from this region. Hence, suffragists should have perceived the need to concentrate their subsequent efforts where they were most needed. They drew no such conclusions, and they paid for that oversight when the Senate voted.

Perhaps the worst problem obscured by the 329-95 vote was the insincerity of those who voted yes. Some evidence suggests an intentional effort by deputies to sabotage women's suffrage by voting for integral rights. Some deputies reasoned that the Senate might grudgingly accede to a municipal suffrage bill overwhelmingly adopted in the chamber, but never to equal suffrage. Once they were convinced that the Chamber of Deputies would adopt some version, they backed the most extreme in order to secure the defeat of all versions. Others voted with the majority because they believed the Senate would balk; hence, a vote in the chamber was an empty gesture without risk. It is impossible to calculate the number who actually opposed women's suffrage, but it is clear that this behavior existed. Charles Maurras, whose mind turned readily to conspiracy theories, reached this conclusion in *L'Action française* on the morrow of victory: the Chamber of Deputies acted on "the well-developed idea" that integral suffrage "would be interred in the Senate." *Le Temps* offered the same hypothesis about "perfidious" parliamentarians finding "in the bouquet

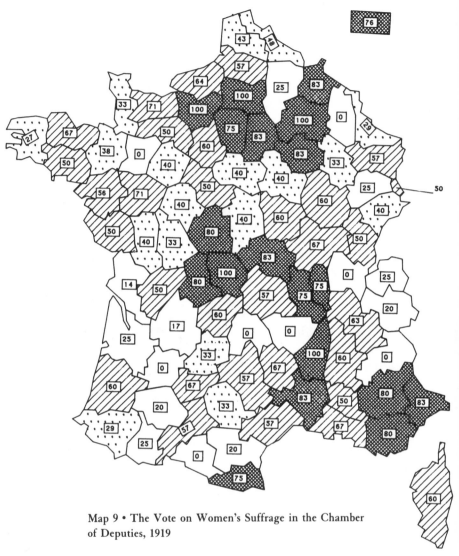

Map 9 • The Vote on Women's Suffrage in the Chamber of Deputies, 1919

NOTE: Labels indicate the percentage of each department's deputation that voted in favor of the Bon *contre-projet* (for integral suffrage) on May 20, 1919.

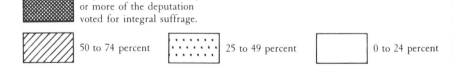

Departments in which 75 percent or more of the deputation voted for integral suffrage.

50 to 74 percent   25 to 49 percent   0 to 24 percent

of flowers offered to French women a few poisoned roses on which the reform will wither and die." *La Croix* agreed. Adversaries of the bill had voted with its partisans in order to provoke the Senate.[25]

What evidence sustains this cynical interpretation of the suffragist victory? One principal factor is the behavior of the Senate, analyzed below; it will be seen that many deputies who voted for the bill in 1919 were subsequently elevated to the Senate and there voted against any form of women's suffrage in 1922! The debates of May 1919 also provide evidence. Varenne, one of two socialists who voted against the bill, saw what was happening and bluntly warned that enemies of women's rights were trying "to compromise the result before the Senate." Georges Bonnefous, a conservative republican (Seine-et-Oise) who ultimately voted for the bill, made the same point on the floor: anti-suffragists were trying to frighten the conscript-fathers of the Luxembourg. Direct evidence came from the mouths of admitted anti-suffragists, especially Augagneur. He and Flandin engaged in a lengthy dialogue in which Augagneur opposed even municipal suffrage because women in politics constituted an unknown threat to the republic. Flandin accused him of being a "disguised adversary" of women's rights; Augagneur responded, "I am not disguising myself." A few minutes later, he reiterated his opposition to suffragism yet endorsed the sentiment in favor of converting the bill to integral suffrage. "It is preferable," he said, "to go all the way [*jusqu' au bout*]." Augagneur then voted in favor of integral suffrage. He was not alone. At least two radicals (those who spoke out) opposed women's suffrage yet encouraged deputies to vote for integral rights. No case could be clearer than that of Fernand Rabier (Radical-Socialist, Loiret). After several days of objecting to women's rights, he suddenly voted for integral suffrage; elected to the Senate in 1920, he continued to work against any form of women's suffrage and voted against municipal enfranchisement. The leading suffragists in the Chamber of Deputies saw what was happening but refused to capitulate to the tactic. Andrieux insisted that deputies must not compromise their sense of justice by voting in fear of the upper house. Viviani was more adamant: "It is necessary to proclaim some principles!" Briand even asserted that a show of conviction at the Palais Bourbon would advance the suffragist cause at the Luxembourg. Their eloquence carried the day and won an important victory, but that victory was a mixed blessing.[26]

The Final Push, 1919-1922

The optimism of French suffragists reached its peak in 1919. It now derived from four great sources: their interpretation of the effects of World War I, an international pattern of suffrage victories, the conversion of the Catholic women's movement to the cause, and the vote in the Chamber of Deputies. Then, the state of siege ended in October 1919, permitting the resumption of a vigorous campaign to win the vote. Maria Vérone exhorted feminists not to be overconfident, "We cannot stop now; we must continue more actively than before ... [and] establish a methodical and active siege of the Senate."[27] This did not happen. There was a good deal of feminist activity during the next three years—while the Senate procrastinated—but no organized or dramatic final push.

The fragmentation of the women's movement remained a severe problem. The new Catholic suffragism, for example, did not promote collaboration between the UNVF and the UFSF. The president of the UFSF could now attend a congress of Catholic women, applaud their attitude, and speak of her agreement with them. The women of the Catholic union might discuss cooperation, just as some of them had talked about the vote a decade earlier. But the gulf was still deep. As Levert-Chotard told the UFSF, republican feminists still understood the ballot as an individual right rather than a collective duty and thus were insensitive to Catholic attitudes about the role of women.[28] Simultaneously, bourgeois feminists found relations on their left even more strained. As women like Alice Jouenne and Marianne Rauze turned to the Communist Party as "the only party in which women are the equal of men," they lost all interest in the suffrage bill. Their answer to their former allies was Lenin's distinction between "real equality" and "formal equality": bourgeois reforms such as women's suffrage might produce a formal equality in the law, but there could be no true equality of rights while economic inequality still existed. There would be only "an equality between the well-fed and the hungry, between the property-owner and the propertyless." *L'Ouvrière*, a newspaper for communist women founded in early 1922, put it simply: "We know that it [the vote] will not be the weapon of our emancipation."[29]

The republican feminist leagues also remained internally divided. Should they press for the chamber's integral suffrage bill? "Too handsome," said Jane Misme; insistence upon it would lead to utter defeat.[30] Most provincial feminists and the Parisian center applauded this restraint. Should they settle for municipal suffrage, or even some version of familial suffrage? "I have never believed in the efficacy of partial reforms," chided Nelly Roussel, but Vérone only narrowed persuaded the CNFF not to endorse familial suffrage.[31] And how should feminists react to the array of new suffrage proposals? Senator Louis Martin (Radical, Var) suggested compromising by giving the vote to mothers and *institutrices*; a veterans' association with over 300,000 members offered to support the enfranchisement of all war widows who had not remarried; *La Dépêche de Toulouse* proposed the arbitrary selection of some future date, such as 1930, at which women would vote, thereby providing time for their civic education; another newspaper championed the idea of women's eligibility for office without the ballot. To the dismay of the feminist left, the UFSF seriously considered even the enfranchisement of war widows.[32] Should feminists consider the suffrage battle essentially won and concentrate their attention on other targets? Some militants, particularly at *La Voix des femmes*, thought it more important to campaign against the "villainous legislation" of 1920 which outlawed "provocation to abortion" and "contraceptional propaganda."[33]

The fragmentation of the women's movement naturally weakened the final push to win the vote. The old leagues, especially the LFDF, were active, and some new groups, particularly Louise Brunet's Comité de propagande féministe, contributed great energy. Most of their efforts, however, were directed to separate activities; these amounted chiefly to the same tactics employed for the past generation. Brunet achieved one imaginative new gesture—raining suffragist handbills on Paris from an airplane; Vérone had a potentially powerful idea that she could not execute—a national chain letter to inundate the Senate; but none of the groups found an effective means of leverage on the upper house.[34] The consensus seemed to be that the suffrage leagues should seek to duplicate their greatest prewar successes: new versions of the Laloë race of 1908, the *Journal* poll of 1914, and the Condorcet demonstration. All were tried. All turned out to be pale shades of the past, a fact that opponents of women's suffrage seized upon to bolster their argument that most women still did not want to vote. Worse, the concentration on old methods distracted feminists from capitalizing upon their greatest strength against the Senate: the political clout that they held through such senior statesmen as Presidents Deschanel (1920) and Millerand (1920-1924), Premiers Briand (1921-1922) and Poincaré (1922-1924), President of the Senate Léon Bourgeois (1920-1923), and former Premiers Viviani and Painlevé—all public advocates of women's political rights.

It was symptomatic of suffragist disunity that there were two separate efforts to emulate the *Journal* poll during the fall elections for the Chamber of Deputies in 1919. Both ventures combined attracted a small fraction of participants of the 1914 poll. Gustave Téry, the author of the original poll, was in 1919 the director of the left republican *L'Oeuvre*, for which Maria Vérone wrote a regular suffragist column; in October 1919 they announced their sponsorship of a new poll. Simultaneously, a group of moderate suffragists and the editors of *L'Excelsior* proposed their own. Both groups soon decided that they lacked the time and resources to match *Le Journal*'s success, so they restricted their polls—*L'Oeuvre* conducting a mock election in seven left-bank *arrondissements* and *L'Excelsior* confining its activities to the department of the Seine. Bad luck further curtailed their ambitions when a strike briefly closed down all Parisian newspapers during the elections. Both newspapers solicited mail balloting before election day and appealed to feminist societies to help collect votes. *L'Excelsior* publicized mobile voting places in a fleet of cars. The feminist response to the 1919 polls was poor. The LFDF backed *L'Oeuvre*'s poll but had to recruit *lycée* students to handle tasks in place of feminist volunteers who did not materialize. *La Française* mentioned the polls but did little to aid them. The CNFF and the UFSF ignored the efforts, preferring their own electoral programs. Socialist groups declined to participate. Some feminists even refused to vote, making the remarkable argument that they could not express their political preferences while parliament refused to recognize their right to do so. The result was that only 12,688 women cast ballots in *L'Oeuvre*'s mock election and 34,952 in *L'Excelsior*'s—a total of 47,640, or less than 10 percent of the participants in 1914.[35]

Suffragists tried to put a brave face on these events. Grinberg claimed that the results of 1914 and 1919 were similar. Vérone tried to shift the focus from numbers to the interpretation of the ballots cast in the mock election. They were said to demonstrate that women voted chiefly for republican candidates, or voted almost the same as men did, or voted solidly against right-wing candidates. Anti-suffragists, who pointed out that only an educated feminine elite had voted, were unimpressed. Indeed, senatorial opponents found the polls to be good illustrations of their contention that most women did not support feminist aspirations. "Where are they, all of these women wishing to vote?" asked one. So successfully did their enemies exploit this point that suffragists chose to stage yet another poll in 1922 to demonstrate that women truly desired to vote. *Le Journal* again sponsored the effort, and this time *La Française* urged moderates to join in the work. The number of participants was impressive: 224,155 claimed the vote. Unfortunately this still compared unfavorably with the 505,972 of 1914 and hence convinced no one in the Senate.[36]

A second reprise of prewar ideas occurred during the same elections. While the LFDF touted its poll, while the UFSF, the CNFF, and Amélioration concentrated upon aid of sympathetic men in their campaigns, another group of feminists promoted a woman's candidacy for parliament. The dissident minority in the UFSF, now concentrated in some of the Parisian branches, decided to sponsor a Laloë-style candidacy. Alice La Mazière, the vice-president of the Paris group of the UFSF and the leader of this faction, announced her own campaign in the St. Georges quarter of the Ninth Arrondissement, where Laloë had run in 1908 and Durand in 1910. La Mazière conducted a one-week campaign, based on posters and two electoral meetings, in which she concentrated on the conservative justifications of women's suffrage—the work that enfranchised women could do to combat tuberculosis, alcoholism, or depopulation. Most moderates ignored her efforts.[37]

Socialist suffragists conducted a separate race. Hélène Brion, a few sections of the GdFS, and *La Lutte féministe* began organizing for the elections months ahead. Brion first urged a campaign to register to vote, but that faltered after one success, when the mayor of Pantin refused to inscribe Brion herself. Brion next turned to the Socialist Party, but she had little success in persuading socialist women to demand their rights at the congress of 1919 and even less in convincing the party to adopt a strong suffragist stand during the elections. Undaunted, Brion tried to persuade socialists to adopt women candidates, as they had in the past, but this time in constituencies where they might win. She found little backing and an old answer: "the hour is too grave!" The party might lose a seat. Even if it did, Brion retorted, that would be better than losing the trust of socialist women: "You are up against the wall, comrade socialists! ... We will judge your attitude severely." The Pantin group of the GdFS picked up this theme and carried it to the meeting of the Federation of the Seine, where socialist candidates were to be named. Their motion in favor of women candidates failed. Still unbowed, the dissident socialist feminists prevailed upon Rauze to run, whatever the party thought. She agreed to campaign in the Sixteenth Arrondissement.[38]

The results of the suffragist electoral campaign of 1919 were mixed. The number of women who worked for enfranchisement and the variety of demonstrations they staged showed that the desire to vote had not slackened in the Parisian women's movement. Their efforts at electoral meetings persuaded several groups, such as Sangnier's La Jeune République, to inscribe women's suffrage on their programs. The division of their efforts, however, produced disappointing results in most cases. Just as the newspaper polls compared unfavorably with the previous success, women candidates fared less well than their predecessors had. Accounts vary, but La Mazière and Rauze seem to have garnered a combined total of only a few hundred votes, perhaps half of Laloë's total in 1908 or one-fourth of Renaud's in 1910.[39]

Unfavorable comparisons to the *manifestation Condorcet* also eclipsed postwar suffragist assemblies. In the summer of 1919 Fonséque tried to persuade moderates to return to the streets to celebrate their victory in the Chamber of Deputies and demonstrate their numbers to the Senate. The Prefecture of Police approved a parade but not public speeches. Amélioration therefore proposed a march from the Place de Clichy to the statue of Maria Deraismes in the Square des Epinettes (Seventeenth Arrondissement) on the twentieth anniversary of its erection. Virtually the same coalition of republican feminists who had staged the meeting in the Tuileries in 1914 agreed; several new organizations joined them: Perrot's Action des femmes, Brunet's Comité de propagande féministe, Remember's Société nationale du féminisme français. They paraded with banners, posters, and sandwich boards to lay wreaths at the statue, just as they had done for Condorcet, almost five years earlier to the day. Unfortunately, only 500 women agreed to march—ten times Auclert's number for 1904, but one-tenth the turnout of 1914. Subsequent rallies improved upon the participation in the Deraismes demonstration. The UFSF sponsored a meeting at *Le Journal* in early 1921 which drew over 1,000. Two separate CNFF suffrage meetings at the Sorbonne in 1922 each exceeded that total. The LFDF celebrated its fiftieth anniversary in March 1921 with a banquet which filled the largest meeting room in Paris, the grand hall of the Palais du Trocadéro. That assembly attracted thousands of diners (exaggerated estimates reached 5,000) and considerable press attention. It also induced Vérone to attempt another rally, because the guest of honor at the banquet, Raymond Poincaré, had been unable to attend.[40]

Vérone's *"fête féministe"* at the Trocadéro in December 1921 was one of the greatest successes in the campaign to win the Senate and, at the same time, an indication of the weakness of other suffragist activities. It was designed to be another bourgeois gala, with entertainment and dancing, rather than a militant demonstration, but the meeting had significant political implications. The theme of the evening was a celebration of the first anniversary of women's suffrage in Belgium. Belgian feminists and politicians testified, to an audience that included several senators, that women had produced neither a clerical reaction nor great gains for revolutionary parties. Poincaré then delivered an ardently suffragist speech drawing out this point. It was a "calumny against women," he asserted, for anti-suffragists to claim that they would vote against the republic that they had labored mightily to defend during the war: "Where has one seen that this was the case in other countries?" Belgian women had proven, according to Poincaré, that it was not just in Anglo-Saxon countries that women could join in political life. And he promised to use his influence to win the same rights for French women. Had Raymond Poincaré truly committed himself to securing a suffrage law, this banquet would have been the greatest accomplishment of the women's campaign of 1919-1922, as Vérone claimed. Poincaré had returned to the Senate (and a unanimous motion of praise from that body) in 1920, upon the completion of his septennate in the presidency of France. Barely a month after his Trocadéro speech, he formed his second cabinet and retained the premiership for over two years, during which time the Senate debated women's suffrage. No other member of the Senate could be expected to exercise the influence on that body that he could. However large or unified their demonstrations were, what suffragists needed was for Poincaré to make good his promises. If he did, women's suffrage might soon be fact.[41]

Long-Lived Defeat: The Senate, 1918-1922

Throughout the Third Republic, the French Senate stood as a conservative bulwark against precipitous change. Senatorial wisdom held that any reform that seemed brusque be blocked or delayed until times were more suitable.[42] In no area of legislation was this more evident than women's rights. The Senate defended the family as the fundamental social unit and warded off efforts to alter the position of women. The upper house had opposed and delayed the reintroduction of divorce, the diminution of paternal authority, women's rights as guardians, and the independent control of their wages by married women. Before the war, only one women's suffrage bill had ever reached the Senate: a plan for familial suffrage deposited by Louis Martin in 1914. Not a single senatorial voice had ever called for equal political rights from the podium of the Luxembourg Palace.

The Senate could not ignore the suffrage question in 1919: by the end of that year there were four different senatorial proposals for enfranchisement plus the bill transmitted by the Chamber of Deputies. Martin twice transformed his 1914 bill, finally proposing in June 1918 to give all women the right to vote, but not stand for office, at age twenty-five. When the Senate continued to ignore his bills, Martin obtained the creation of a special eighteen-member commission to consider them. In early 1919 that ad hoc committee also received a bill when Senator Dominique Delahaye (Right, Maine-et-Loire) submitted a plan similar to Barrès's *suffrage des morts*. President Deschanel transmitted the chamber's bill to the Luxembourg in late May 1919. A few days later that provoked another senatorial bill, from Eugène Beauvisage (Radical, Rhône), who pronounced the chamber's version "a premature measure" and asked women's eligibility for political office at age thirty (forty for the senate), but no right to vote. Finally, in July 1919, the special commission received its fifth proposal when the Comte de Las Cazes introduced familial suffrage.[43]

The commission that received these bills was unsympathetic from the start. The members elected as president Paul Régismanset (Union républicane, Seine-et-Marne), a seventy-year-old attorney opposed to enfranchisement. With virtually no deliberation, they voted eight to five to reject the Martin Bill for integral suffrage and charged the most notorious anti-suffragist in their midst, Alexandre Bérard, to write their report. Feminists protested that they had not even been called to testify, but Régismanset declined even to discuss the subject. Upon receipt of the bill from the Chamber of Deputies, the Senate decided to expand the commission to twenty-seven members. Most of those added came from the Radical and Radical-Socialist Party (the Gauche démocratique in the Senate), which had followed the advice of their president, Emile Combes, and nominated anti-suffragists. The new committee, with only seven or eight suffragists, agreed to listen to a deputation from the suffrage leagues but declined to question them; Régismanset and several others boycotted the meeting. Acting with dispatch, but no great examination, the commission rejected the suffrage bill from the lower house, ten to three, in July 1919, the fourteen absences being indicative of the Senate's interest in women's suffrage. By early October of that year, all other bills before it had been similarly dismissed. That left only the delivery of the Bérard Report to bring the matter to the floor of the Senate.[44]

With women's suffrage behind the *cordon sanitaire* of the committee, Bérard put on a remarkable display of the Fabian tactics that characterized the upper house. Almost single-handedly (although requiring the support of his colleagues), he prevented the subject from reaching the docket for more than three years. Bérard commenced his obstructionism after the commission voted against the chamber's bill in July 1919 by announcing that the members were too tired to prepare their report; it must wait until after the summer recess. When the second session assembled in October, Bérard was still dawdling. His report was ready, but he was not. While he delayed, suffragist protests were in vain: the president of the Senate could not inscribe the issue on the agenda until the commission was ready. Fierce attacks in the feminist press, such as Juliette Raspail's denunciation of "the narrow and brutal mentality" of some senators, did not move Bérard. Even a resolution introduced in the Chamber of Deputies by Bracke and adopted by 340-95, calling on the Clemenceau government to use its influence to obtain a Senate vote "in the briefest possible delay" produced no movement. Only with the session coming to an end did Bérard deposit the commission's verdict, and it did not appear in the *Journal officiel* (a step necessary for debate) until after adjournment.[45]

The Bérard Report of 1919 was a landmark of French anti-suffragism, a synthesis of 150 years of arguments against political rights for women. Its author expressed "stupefaction" at the chamber's rash proposal and proceeded to catalogue the reasons why the Senate should not concur, a list that won immediate notoriety as "Bérard's Fourteen Points":

1. The Chamber of Deputies surpassed its mandate in proposing such far-reaching legislation because it continued to sit past its scheduled termination in 1918 only to conduct the war effort.

2. Any legislation subversive of the established order must be thoroughly studied, and the country must be first consulted in an electoral campaign based on the issue.

3. French opinion does not approve of the change, not even in the large provincial cities; there is no trace of support in the small towns, much less in the villages.

4. The immense majority of French women, "so full of good sense," do not want to vote, do not want to leave home for the political arena: they know that their families would suffer as a result.

5. While women did give immense service to France during the war, they did so for love of the *patrie*, not in the expectation of a reward: it would be an insult to pay them for their patriotism.

6. Women have insufficient civic education for political rights; their uninformed participation would pose a grave threat to the republic.

7. Some women do claim the vote, but they are only "an infinitesimal minority . . . a handful of incoherent feminists."

8. The assertion that women are needed in politics to secure major social reforms is contradicted by parliament's record of twenty years of attention to these matters: the Senate and the Chamber of Deputies do not need help in drafting legislation.

9. Feminists are beginning to threaten "an uproar in the streets, even violent revolution" like the Bolsheviks, and the Senate must not capitulate to their threats.

10. France has always guided other people toward liberty and is great enough to decide for herself, on reasoned argument and not on foreign examples, what legislation to adopt.

11. The "Catholic mentality" of the majority of French women, combined with the hostility of the church toward the republic and liberty, mean that women's suffrage would lead to clerical reaction.

12. Women's suffrage would be "a formidable leap into the unknown" that might produce the election of a new Bonaparte as universal suffrage did in 1848, and might thereby lead to a new Sedan.

13. Nature has given women "a different role than men . . . a primordial role" to attend to the "incomparable grandeur" of maternity and to the family, which is the basis of French society.

14. Women are different creatures than men, filled with sentiment and tears rather than hard political reason: their hands are not for political pugilism or holding ballots, but for kisses.

All of these factors being considered, Bérard concluded, the Senate must repulse the ill-considered proposition of the Chamber of Deputies and not even pass to a discussion of its articles.[46]

The publication of the Bérard Report in December 1919 did not mean that the senatorial commission had lost the power to stave off debate. Bérard continued his dilatory tactics, repeatedly deferring debate by contending that the committee was not yet prepared for discussion. He and Régismanset stalled throughout the Senate's regular session of 1920 by the simple ploy of not filling vacancies on the commission and not calling meetings. No pressure seemed to affect this procrastination. Jules Guesde, Ferdinand Buisson (returned to the Chamber of Deputies in the elections of 1919), Bracke, Léon Blum, and sixty-three other deputies (mostly socialists) raised the stakes with a new bill to grant complete civil equality to women. The chamber voted Bracke's motion demanding action for a second time. The League of the Rights of Man called for enactment of a suffrage law. Sympathetic senators formed a *groupe* to concentrate their efforts. A few local councils adopted resolutions in favor of women's suffrage. Feminist groups rained letters on the Luxembourg. By the time that Bérard's adroitness at lingering had consumed most of the Senate's session of 1921, a group of pro-suffrage senators rebelled. Louis Martin promised suffragists that the Senate would begin discussion after the summer vacation; Antonin Gourju (Gauche radicale, Rhône) introduced a motion to place women's suffrage on the calendar. The commission ignored Martin and vigorously opposed Gourju. Bérard argued that senators were not yet adequately prepared for debate: the overturning of the regime was in question. Municipal, legislative, and senatorial elections had all taken place since the vote in the Chamber of Deputies, he pointed out, and virtually no candidate for office had put women's suffrage on his program or discussed the issue in electoral meetings. Clearly, Bérard concluded, France was not interested in debating the matter. Faithful to their traditional caution and deference to the commissions, the Senate voted by more than two-to-one to postpone consideration of the suffrage bill sine die.

Suffragists did not relent in seeking ways to convince the Senate to act. Justin Godart and the chamber's group for women's rights made a démarche to the Briand government. The UFSF sent a deputation to the premier asking him to use the influence of his office on behalf of his convictions. Joseph Barthélemy (Union républicaine,

Gers), a lawyer who entered the chamber in 1919 after a brilliant academic career, presented a new report for the Commission of Universal Suffrage, advancing the argument for women's suffrage more forcefully than the Flandin Report had. Even the president of the republic, Alexandre Millerand, was persuaded to make a cautious statement on behalf of limited suffrage in stages. The leadership of the Senate capitulated at the opening of the 1922 session and placed women's suffrage on the agenda for February 28. A few weeks later, however, Bérard suffered a minor accident and sympathetic senators accepted his request to postpone debate once again. His recuperation took longer than expected and each time a date was set it had to be changed. A leisurely recovery enabled Bérard to keep the suffrage bill in committee until the approach of the summer vacation, so the Senate rescheduled debate for October. Suffragists, convinced that the reporter was temporizing, alternately protested and lamented. De Witt-Schlumberger summarized the situation: "We are expecting a judgment on the Day of Judgment."[47]

At long last, the suffrage report reached the floor of the Senate in November 1922, after Bérard finally announced his readiness for discussion. The debate, stretched out over two weeks, dramatically revealed how deep the opposition of the upper house to women's rights remained. The galleries were packed with leading feminists, as their advocates, especially Martin and Gourju, began. Things went badly from the start. Hecklers interrupted pro-suffrage speakers. A large part of the Senate intentionally ignored these speakers and engaged in loud conversations and other distractions. The scene was so chaotic that the usher repeatedly tried to clear the floor. President Bourgeois called for order so often that he finally rebuked his colleagues for their cynical demonstration. Behavior only altered when the opponents of women's suffrage took the rostrum. There ensued, for four days, a vigorous senatorial competition for the laurels as the greatest scourge of feminism. Régismanset assured his colleagues that "poor woman" does not want to drink from the "bitter chalice of politics." Hugues Le Roux (Union républicaine, Seine-et-Oise) reminded the Senate that he was the author of over fifty works on such social questions, then derided the first woman in the House of Commons, Lady Astor. Bérard invoked the clerical peril: women's suffrage would be "sealing the tombstone of the Republic."

The unrivaled foe of women's rights was undoubtedly Senator François Labrousse. He characterized women as "impressionable and suggestible" and pronounced his judgment that "since woman's appearance, her role in history has always been deplorable." To support this claim, Labrousse advanced a remarkable string of assertions: women's suffrage in Sweden had led to female celibacy and the need for Swedish men to find German brides; in the United States, the ballot had precipitated a vast increase in the divorce rate, with the result that "marriage is only the preliminary ceremony to divorce." Labrousse added to this assault a barrage of anti-female epigrams, culled from authors from Juvenal to Schopenhauer. Along the way, he invoked the authority of numerous Frenchmen, particularly Proudhon, Comte, and Fouillée. At the end of Labrousse's offensive, one senator (François Saint-Maur) announced that he had been persuaded to vote for women's rights, but no oratorical equal rose to counter Labrousse's tirade. Feminists claimed that he was a great advocate for their cause, or called him a plesiosaurus, but it was difficult for them to be optimistic.

As the Senate's debates neared their conclusion, suffragists held to two hopes: that some senior statesman would turn the tide, as Viviani and Briand did in 1919, or that the government would intervene on their behalf. In the first instance, they relied again on Viviani who had come to the Luxembourg Palace as the result of a by-election in mid-October; in the second, upon Poincaré, who had been premier since January. Both men disappointed them. Viviani had not yet made his maiden speech and entered his name on the lists for the final day of the suffrage debate. At the last minute, he withdrew. Friends accepted the explanation that he was too ill to speak, although he attended the session; opponents hinted that he intentionally chose not to make his debut in a losing cause. Poincaré also failed to keep his promise. During much of November 1922 he was in Lausanne for negotiations as minister of foreign affairs. He made no public comment on the bill before the Senate, however, and it took repeated requests from the floor before a spokesman for the cabinet (Maurice Maunoury, the minister of the interior) stated tersely that it was the government's policy not to oppose proceeding to a discussion of the individual articles of the chamber's bill. Bérard recognized the strength of his position. He moved that the Senate not pass to the consideration of the articles and that the bill be returned to the special commission. On November 21, 1922, the Senate followed Bérard's recommendation by a vote of 156-134.[48] Women's suffrage was beaten, and it was to be a long-lived defeat; so long as the Senate of the Third Republic continued to exist, French women were not going to vote.

Considering the tremendous disparity between the votes in the Chamber of Deputies in 1919 and in the Senate in 1922, one must ask what happened in the Senate. The accepted explanation of this, and subsequent, Senate votes has been the opposition of radicals, based on a perceived clerical peril.[49] Many feminists subscribed to this theory. Alice La Mazière insisted that most of the arguments in the Senate "were only on the surface" and that "the real reason . . . is the fear of the priest." The UFSF cited the same explanation in its description of the defeat for *Jus suffragii*, the organ of the IWSA. Marguerite Durand did likewise when she resumed publication of *La Fronde* in 1926: "It is simply a question of convincing some senators that the vote for women will not involve any risk to republican institutions, will not mark a return to obscurantism and toward reaction."[50]

There are good reasons for the persistence of this interpretation. Although the Radical and Radical-Socialist Party was by no means unanimous, its opposition was unmistakable. The radical congress of November 1918 reaffirmed the party's opposition to enfranchisement. Combes led a caucus of the radical senators to do so again in May 1919. *Le Radical* reiterated the anti-suffrage theory. And at the same moment that the Senate debated women's suffrage, the radical congress of November 1922 refused to change the party's stand.[51] Thus, a breakdown of the vote in the Senate by parties (see Table 12) comes as no surprise: the Radical Party was the only party to vote against women's suffrage, and it did so by greater than a three-to-one margin. Indeed, more than 70 percent of all negative votes came from Radicals. No other bloc in the Senate gave women's suffrage less that 70 percent of its votes.[52]

Nonetheless, the opposition of radicals still does not adquately explain what happened in November 1922; it is necessary, but not sufficient. Even if one leaves aside such long-range issues as strength of traditional attitudes about the family or the anxiety about depopulation, other factors deserve attention. First, one must consider the difference between the votes in the Chamber of Deputies and in the Senate. How does a vote of 329-95 in 1919 become a vote of 134-156 in 1922? If one continues to focus on the Radical Party, how does a vote of 75-65 shift to 28-112? It is true that radical senators were often more conservative than their counterparts in the lower house, but

Table 12 • Voting for Women's Suffrage in the Senate, November 1922

	Yes	No	Not Voting	No, plus Not Voting
Full Senate	134 (43.4%)	156 (50.5%)	19 (6.1%)	175 (56.5%)
Socialists	3 (100%)	0	0	0
Radicals and Radical-Socialists	28 (18.2%)	112 (72.7%)	14 (9.1%)	116 (81.1%)
Conservative Republicans	90 (71.4%)	32 (25.4%)	4 (3.2%)	36 (28.6%)
Parties of the Right	13 (81.3%)	2 (12.5%)	1 (6.3%)	3 (18.8%)
Members of the Poincaré Cabinet	4 (66.7%)	0	2 (33.3%)	2 (33.3%)
Members of Previous Cabinets	13 (32.5%)	19 (47.5%)	8 (20.0%)	27 (67.5%)

they were a single party. Although an unusually large number of new senators were elected in 1920-1921, due to the wartime postponement of the elections, a majority of radical senators had first served in the Chamber of Deputies. Despite the assumption by suffragists that "old, tired senators" were the problem, the youngest senators (ages forty to forty-nine) were significantly more opposed to women's suffrage than were the oldest (seventy-five or older).

To maintain the focus on radicals, one is driven to acknowledge the conspiracy theory advanced by Maurras and others. Did radical deputies vote in 1919 for a bill that they actually opposed? There is some evidence to support this assertion. If one examines the behavior of the twelve radicals who voted for integral suffrage in 1919 and then entered the Senate before 1922, one finds that only five of them voted to consider the articles of that same bill. If the same held true for all radical votes in 1919, then more than two-thirds of the party's deputation opposed women's suffrage in the chamber; hence radical behavior can be seen as consistent in 1919 and 1922. This argument gains further plausibility when one recalls that those radicals who had signed the prewar suffrage petition included many who voted against the bill in 1919. One can sustain the focus on radicalism, therefore, by adding the factor of cynical political machination.

The focus on the radicals, however, obscures the importance of conservative opposition to women's suffrage. The roll call vote in the Senate is misleading because it was a procedural vote, not a vote to adopt a law granting political rights to women. Many conservative republicans and senators of the right voted "yes" because that was the only way in which they could obtain familial suffrage or even the *suffrage des morts* . . . as three senators admitted in the final debates. Thus, conservative opponents of equal rights seemed sympathetic while radical opponents did not. The simple truth is that only a minority of French senators—possibly politicians at any level—accepted the equality of women. Explaining the vote of 1922 in terms of the radicals, whatever their share of political responsibility, misdirects our understanding of French society because conservative opposition was equally strong and perhaps more fundamental. If Maurras's conspiracy theory is true for radicals, it must also apply to conservatives: several of them, led by Jules Delahaye, voted against women's suffrage in 1922 who did not do so in 1919.

The Poincaré government and the political elite also contributed to the defeat. Feminists relied upon the aid of powerful men to sway the truculent Senate, but they did not receive support when it counted. The Clemenceau cabinet abstained from influencing the chamber in 1919, but feminists expected little from them. Clemenceau still opposed integral suffrage. Even if the chamber had voted on a limited franchise, no one anticipated suffragist activism from a longtime opponent. Instead, suffragists in 1919 counted upon decisive support from their most influential allies. Three ex-premiers—Viviani, Briand, and Painlevé—helped carry the day. Thereafter, political support seemed to grow steadily at the highest levels of French politics. Suffragist politicians were in the right places to give aid; feminists realized that their fate depended upon these "most sincere friends of our cause." The leaders of the UFSF, for example, believed that they had an explicit promise from Poincaré to intervene. If the premier and the president used their influence, if Senators Chéron (who also sat in the cabinet), Viviani, Barthou, and Pichon spoke out in debate, a suffrage bill might win.

The exact opposite of suffragist expectations occurred. Poincaré did not help. Contemporaries believed that he tried to persuade the cabinet to act but could not do so. There are some problems with this view. Six members of the government sat in the senate; four voted in favor

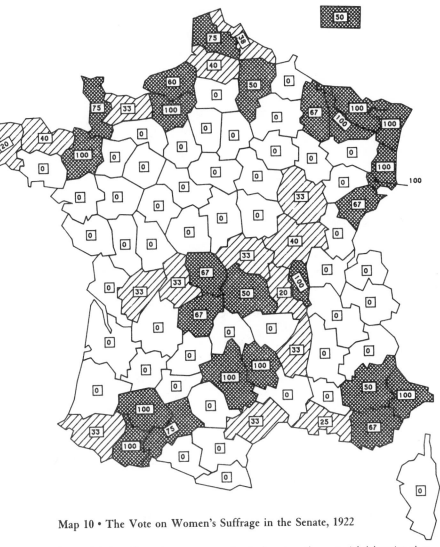

Map 10 • The Vote on Women's Suffrage in the Senate, 1922

NOTE: Labels indicate the percentage of each department's senatorial delegation that voted to proceed with consideration of the women's suffrage bill on November 21, 1922.

 Departments in which 50 percent or more of the senators voted to continue consideration.

 25 to 49 percent   0 to 24 percent

of passing to the reading of the articles and two did not vote; of the two, Barthou had stated his support for limited suffrage. It would seem, therefore, that Poincaré's cabinet was sympathetic to some form of women's rights. If one adds the deputies in the cabinet and examines their votes in 1919, the margin becomes closer (six to four) but remains pro-suffrage. One must ask why a moderately sympathetic cabinet, led by a strongly committed man of great prestige, did not intervene. Why did they evade direct requests for guidance from the Senate? Why did they designate the strongest anti-suffragist among them (Maunoury had voted against the 1919 bill) to speak for them in the Senate? And why did Barthou take his vacation during the final week of debate?[53]

One is pressed toward the conclusion that Poincaré and other ministerial suffragists were unwilling to treat women's rights as a matter of confidence. They might risk their offices on a matter of foreign policy, but not for equality of the sexes. They may have sincerely desired women's suffrage, but it was less important to them than other considerations. Hence they voted for it but did not champion it. Similarly, one may wonder why Viviani was well enough to attend the final session and vote for women's suffrage, but too ill to speak up. Or why Pichon abstained in the vote. Whatever the explanation, feminist backing at the highest levels of French politics seemed to evaporate. Of that elite group of senators with previous ministerial experience, barely one-third voted to pass to the reading of the articles. The abstention rate in that career-conscious group more than tripled the rate for the Senate as a whole. The message to senators must have been clear: women's suffrage was not an issue of great political strength, so individuals could vote their feelings without consequence.[54]

Another aspect of the vote that deserves attention is political geography. The behavior of the Chamber of Deputies in 1919 has suggested that there were strong regional variations in the acceptance of women's suffrage. Voting in the Senate confirmed this. (See Map 10.) Northern France, especially the northeast, solidly favored enfranchisement; southern France, especially the southwest, strongly opposed it. When one breaks down the roll call by regions, these distinctions become dramatic. (See Table 13.) Northern support was more than twice as strong as southern; the northeast was almost four times more favorable than the southwest. If the fifty-four senators of southwestern France had only split evenly, suffragists would have carried the vote,

Table 13 • Voting in the Senate by Regions

	Yes	No
NORTHERN FRANCE	74 (66.1%)	38 (33.9%)
Northeast	26 (96.3%)	1 (3.7%)
CENTRAL FRANCE	22 (40.7%)	32 (59.3%)
SOUTHERN FRANCE	36 (30.0%)	84 (70.0%)
Southwest	14 (25.9%)	40 (74.1%)
OVERSEAS	2 (50.0%)	2 (50.0%)

NOTE: Northern France is here defined as those departments entirely to the north of the Loire River (extending eastward to the Swiss frontier), the northeast as the departments of Moselle, Haut Rhin, Bas Rhin, Belfort, Meurthe-et-Moselle, Vosges, Meuse, and Haute Marne. Southern France is defined as all departments from a line between the mouth of the Gironde to Geneva, the southwest as the departments of Basses Pyrénées, Hautes Pyrénées, Pyrénées Orientales, Ariège, Aude, Haute Garonne, Gers, Landes, Gironde, Lot-et-Garonne, Tarn-et-Garonne, Tarn, Hérault, Aveyron, Lot, Dordogne, Charente, and Charente Inférieure.

147-143. Such interpretations of roll call data are speculative but suggestive. Repeated over time, they leave little doubt that local attitudes were very important in shaping the final result.

As one ponders the vote in the Senate, it becomes increasingly difficult to single out the role of the Radical Party. Even if this variable is deemed the most important, its explanation must be adjusted. Can it still be maintained that radical opposition derived from their obsession with the church? Might it not also derive from the same meridional attitudes about women most conservatives held? Furthermore, one must add the human factor. It has already been seen that radicals, as the party of a parliamentary plurality and the frequent party of government, had the most to lose by electoral reform. The addition of a new group in politics would mean the subtraction of power from someone; as the radicals held a disproportionate share of this power, it seemed in their self-interest to block that addition.

Chapter Nine

France and the Political Rights
of Women

The action of the Senate in November 1922 marked a major turning point in the history of French suffragism. The long ordeal of the parliamentary campaign had been completed. It was forty years since the Commission of Petitions had considered and rejected Auclert's first petition (1882), thirty-two years after Joseph de Gasté had introduced the first suffrage bill in the Chamber of Deputies, thirteen years after Buisson had presented parliament with its first full report on the subject. The defeat in the Senate did not close the question, of course. It merely started another sequence, leading to another rejection by the conscript fathers. The Third Republic lasted long enough for two repetitions of the cycle. And when the National Assembly transferred power to Marshal Pétain in 1940, the Senate still blocked women's suffrage.

Nothing summarizes the suffragist reaction to defeat better than the behavior of Maria Vérone. She sat in the gallery of the Luxembourg Palace with other leading suffragists and watched as the Senate dismissed the subject to which she had devoted her life. She heard the humiliating speech by Senator Labrousse and witnessed the contemptuous behavior of anti-suffragists; she sat silently as Viviani and Poincaré, men with whom she had worked closely, made no public effort to aid her cause; she attended the roll call vote and saw senator after senator switch the votes they had cast as deputies in 1919. When the tally was announced, Vérone stood up and shouted at the floor of the Senate. Did she summon the myrmidons to a campaign of suffragette violence at long last? No. Her words were "Long live the Republic all the same!" (*"Vive la République, quand même!"*) Thereafter she carried the nickname of "Madame Quand-même," a sobriquet that could as easily have applied to the entire bourgeois suffrage movement. The moment of the vote was typical in another way. As Vérone expressed feminist fidelity to the regime that denied her, authority responded in a predictable way: ushers immediately pounced on her and ejected her from the meeting, lest she provoke a violent scene.[1]

Militancy certainly did not disappear from French suffragism, nor did Vérone herself disavow it. When a reporter asked her in May 1919 what she would do if the Senate repulsed women's suffrage, Vérone answered without hesitation, "*Les Suffragettes!*" In a meeting with senators that same year, one of them asked Vérone if she was a suffragette; she answered, "No, monsieur, not yet." In the aftermath of the Senate vote, Vérone again spoke with passion: "Women of France, you have been calm and patient ... you have believed that you would be able to obtain everything by reason and persuasion. ... You were mistaken, we were mistaken!" She continued to talk in this way throughout the decade. When the Senate again blocked enfranchisement in 1928, Vérone proclaimed: "The feminist associations have agreed to declare that they will not recoil before any means to achieve women's suffrage." This was frustration and political rhetoric rather than a program. Even moderates could speak that way when exasperated. A UFSF letter to all senators, in response to the Bérard Report, had done so: "Are we truly living in an epoch when only the possibility of a revolt can lead to just laws and progress? ... We have, until now, repulsed all movements of violence or agitation; we have devoted our efforts to social reforms, to works of philanthropy. Will it now be necessary to abandon this activity which has motivated us, in order to create throughout France an agitation which is repugnant to us ... ?"[2]

There were militant demonstrations after 1922. Vérone organized parades, demonstrations before the Luxembourg Palace, even an invasion of the floor of the Senate. She and others paid for them by spending the night in accommodations provided by the police. But these actions remained small, rare, and ineffective; they produced more police harassment than political support. The LFDF talked of "direct action" but found few feminists interested: bourgeois reticence remained unchanged. The greatest militancy during the interwar years came from a new recruit to suffragism, Louise Weiss. Weiss joined the suffrage campaign, after years of working for pacifism, at the direct request of several members of the UFSF, especially Kraemer-

Bach and Malaterre-Sellier. Weiss founded a new group, La Femme nouvelle, established headquarters on the Champs Elysées, and launched an intensive publicity campaign through militant demonstrations. Between 1934 and 1939, La Femme nouvelle (with limited help from Vérone and Brunschwicg) staged demonstrations before parliament and at the Place de l'Opéra, occupied the column at the Place de la Bastille with a phalanx of women chained together (1935), and interrupted major sporting events such as the national soccer championship and the Grand Prix at Longchamps (1936).[3]

Most of the older suffrage leagues continued to grow and campaign for the vote in the 1920s and 1930s. The CNFF reached 150,000 members by 1929 and 200,000 before the war; the UFSF grew rapidly after 1922 and reached 100,000 members in 1928. Both their activities and tactics changed little. They supported an occasional woman candidate (Weiss, for example, ran in the Parisian municipal elections of 1935), but more often disagreed among themselves over the proper course to follow (Weiss and Brunschwicg conducted a small feud in the late 1930s). Perhaps the most innovative suffragist tactic of these years was the convocation of Estates General of Feminism, complete with *cahiers* of grievances. Such estates assembled in 1929, 1931, and 1937 to great publicity, albeit little progress toward winning the vote.

Subsequent research on the feminist movement of the 1920s and 1930s will amplify and clarify these efforts after the defeat of 1922. But the cardinal fact of those years is abundantly clear: suffragists still could not move the Senate. The Chamber of Deputies, led by Justin Godart, Joseph Barthélemy, and Louis Marin, readopted women's suffrage in April 1925. The Senate, with new anti-feminists and old arguments, stalled again. A new report, by Pierre Marraud (Radical, Lot-et-Garonne) in May 1927, opposed enfranchisement and the Senate declined even to discuss it by steadily increasing anti-suffrage margins (June 1928, 168-118; March 1929, 174-120). Despite continuing pressure from the chamber, including a vote of 319-1 in 1931, the Senate procrastinated further and then voted against extending the suffrage in November 1933. The Chamber of Deputies returned yet another suffrage bill in July 1936, but the upper house easily held it off. The most important suffragist victory before World War II came with the election of the Popular Front in 1936. Léon Blum named three women under-secretaries to his cabinet, as Viviani, Briand, or Poincaré might have done: Brunschwicg for national education, Irène

Joliot-Curie (who shared the Nobel Prize in chemistry for 1935 with her husband, Frédéric, just as her parents had shared the prize for physics in 1903) for scientific research, and Suzanne Lacore for child care.[4] And in February 1938 Popular Front legislation finally ended the civil incapacity of women embodied in Article 215 of the Napoleonic Code—the article that had required a husband's authorization before his wife could do such things as enroll in school, establish a bank account, or obtain a passport.

The enfranchisement of women waited until 1944. It came, like other fundamental alterations of French politics, from Charles de Gaulle. On April 21, 1944, with France still under German occupation, the Committee of National Liberation at Algiers announced that women would vote in postwar elections. The muse of irony must have smiled to see women's suffrage come in the decree of a provisional government, just as manhood suffrage had arrived in 1848. De Gaulle's war memoirs are silent on his reasoning, noting only that "this tremendous reform . . . put an end to controversies that had lasted for fifty years." The diminished influence of the Radical and Radical-Socialist Party, the appearance of a Catholic party that hoped to win the votes of women, the role of women during the occupation, and the fear of communist strength deriving from their role in the resistance surely all contributed. Whatever his reasoning, de Gaulle was determined: on the day of his arrival in Paris, August 25, 1944, he reiterated this decision. Within a month, the provisional government included over one hundred women serving as municipal councillors in the Paris region alone. And when a Provisional Consultative Assembly met at the Luxembourg Palace, a dozen women delegates sat in the seats formerly occupied by hostile senators.[5]

French women first voted in the municipal elections of April-May 1945. More than 10,000 women won council seats, a number that reached 14,899 in 1947 before declining for the remainder of the Fourth Republic. Elections in September 1945 named 39 women to the *conseils généraux*; legislative elections in October sent 33 women (17 communists, 6 socialists, 1 union républicaine, and 9 members of the Christian democratic MRP) to the 545-member National Constituent Assembly. Robert Schuman soon named the first French woman to head a ministry, Mme. Poinso-Chapuis (MRP, Bouches-du-Rhône). She held the portfolio for public health, devoted especial efforts to a campaign against alcoholism, and was the only female minister of the

Fourth Republic. French women did not make great political progress over the next generation, however. After the sweeping socialist victories of 1981, only 28 women sat in the National Assembly (5.5 percent of the seats)—fewer than had been elected in 1945. Not surprisingly, women were even less numerous in the Senate, obtaining only nine seats at the Luxembourg Palace (2.9 percent). At the lowest level of French politics, the story was hardly different: 2.3 percent of all mayors and 8.3 percent of all municipal councillors were women.[6]

As anti-suffragists had feared, there were more women electors than men in 1945, approximately thirteen million to twelve million, although in these initial elections men apparently participated at a higher rate than women. Public opinion polls and commentators produced contradictory data on the effect of women's suffrage. Feminists like André Lehmann, the postwar president of the LFDF, stressed that the parties of the right were routed. Others have argued that initially women showed a preference for the Catholic conservative candidates—60 percent of the vote obtained by the MRP came from women, according to one poll. The significance of this division, if true, is immense: without women's suffrage, a socialist-communist alliance would have held a solid majority in the late 1940s. More recent polls, however, have shown that there is less disparity between the votes cast by men and women.[7]

Few of the leaders of the suffrage campaign of the early twentieth century survived to vote in 1945. Julie Siegfried died in 1922, believing that the Senate would soon ratify the chamber's bill; Marguerite de Witt-Schlumberger followed in 1924. Before World War II, most of the old leaders were gone: Jane Misme (1935), Marguerite Durand (1936), Maria Vérone (1938), Avril de Sainte-Croix (1939). For most of them, the greatest recognition that the Third Republic ever awarded was the Legion of Honor, bestowed not for championing human rights but for their philanthropic work. Many militants perished in sadder circumstances. Caroline Kauffman died in obscurity, with only six people to attend her cremation. Oddo-Deflou passed her final years devoted only to spiritualism. Madame Remember survived briefly selling flowers on the street for a meager existence. Héra Mirtel murdered her second husband and died in prison after a theatrical trial known to the press as "the corpse-in-the-trunk case." Arria Ly committed suicide. And Madeleine Pelletier, in a tragic echo of the fate of Théroigne de Méricourt, died in an asylum where she was confined after a court found her mentally unfit to stand trial for performing abortions.

France and the Comparative History of Women's Suffrage

The rejection of women's suffrage by the French Third Republic is an important episode in the history of individual human rights. The subject assumes a broader importance when France is compared to other states and seen to be an unusual case. It has already been seen that women in more than two dozen states had obtained partial enfranchisement by 1914. (See Table 1.) In three of these countries, women also obtained integral rights before World War I—Australia in 1901, Norway in 1907, and New Zealand in 1910. Women's suffrage was still the exception rather than the rule before the war, but a trend was already evident. Then, in the few years between the beginning of the war and the vote in the French Senate, the overwhelming majority of Western countries enfranchised women. (See Table 14.) Of the five European "great powers" that went to war in August 1914, only France had not given women the vote by 1919. With the enactment of integral suffrage laws in the United States and Canada

Table 14 • States Granting Women's Suffrage in National Elections, 1915–1922

State	Year	State	Year
Denmark	1915	Lithuania	1918
Iceland	1915	Czechoslovakia	1918
Netherlands	1917	Hungary	1918
Soviet Union	1917	Rhodesia	1919
Finland	1917	Luxembourg	1919
Sweden	1918	British East Africa	1919
Great Britain	1918	India	1919
China (6 provinces)	1918	United States	1920
Austria	1918	Canada	1920
Germany	1918	Belgium	1920
Estonia	1918	Palestine	1921
Latvia	1918	Ireland	1922
Poland	1918		

in 1920, the equal political rights of women (at least in the law) had become an unmistakable characteristic of Western civilization. Indeed, Western imperialism exported this equality. The British soon implanted it in East Africa and South Asia. Ataturk encompassed it in his westernization of Turkey. By the 1930s, while the French Senate stood intransigent, women were voting in Palestine, parts of China, and several Latin American republics. Women voted in Estonia, Azerbaijan, Trans-Jordan, and Kenya but not in the land of Jeanne d'Arc and the Declaration of the Rights of Man. This contrast was widely noted in France. The Buisson Report covered it in detail and the Barthélemy Report reiterated the argument. By 1919, suffragists found it "humiliating to think that a daughter of the country of the Revolution" still had to beg rights granted to women in "backward" countries.[8]

This bothered French anti-suffragists not at all. Their France, as Alexandre Bérard reminded the Senate, was a leader, not a follower. No nation need tell France about democracy and human rights; no Frenchman need ask foreign advice. France may stand alone, but she had done so before in defense of the ideal society. Furthermore, anti-suffragists probed into the results of women's suffrage in other places and found all manner of horrors hidden there. Senator Labrousse's claims about female celibacy in Sweden and the divorce rate in the United States were merely the most *outré* expressions of an argument that won widespread approbation: Look at Norway, where women's suffrage produced a conservative victory! Look at the United States, where the only vote cast against entering the Great War came from the only woman in congress (Jeanette Rankin)! And look at Weimar Germany, where impeccable data show that women prefer clerical parties! There, during the elections to the Prussian diet in 1921, ballots of men and women were segregated ("for statistical reasons") in the districts of Cologne and Hagen (Westphalia). The four German left-wing parties (from democrats through communists) received a slight majority of men's ballots in these two constituencies but less than one-third of women's votes. Conversely, the Catholic party (center) received nearly half of women's ballots but less than a third of men's.

The fundamental anti-suffragist response to the trend of international suffragism was that France was different. Or, as more often stated, the "Latin nations" were different. These men kept their own list, showing the European states that did not accept the political rights of women. There, alongside France, they named Italy, Spain,

Table 15 • Voting in Cologne for the Prussian Diet, by Sex, 1921

Party	Men	Women	Total
Communists	10.9%	5.6%	8.3%
Independent Socialists	2.5%	1.1%	1.9%
Majority Socialists	30.5%	20.3%	25.6%
Democrats	4.9%	4.0%	4.4%
Center (Catholic)	31.7%	49.6%	40.4%
Populists	14.7%	14.2%	14.4%
Nationalists	4.8%	5.3%	5.0%

NOTE: Computed from vote totals reported in "Les Elections prussiens et les femmes," *La Voix des femmes*, March 10, 1921.

Portugal. They concluded that there existed a dichotomy between Latin and Anglo-Saxon peoples; hence, arguments from London, Washington, Stockholm, and Melbourne were irrelevant. Look instead, French anti-suffragists argued, at the understanding of the primordial role of women held in Naples, Madrid, and Mexico City.[9] There was some validity to this comparison. From the perspective of French feminists, for example, comparing their movement to Spain rather than Britain revealed its size and militancy more accurately. By the 1930s, however, the anti-suffrage comparison was losing its meaning: women received some form of political rights everywhere in Europe except France, Switzerland, Bulgaria, and Yugoslavia.

The assertion of differences leads to the crux of the matter: What made France different? What does one learn about France by seeing her in the context of international suffragism? The simplest answer was widely voiced in France: the Latin/Anglo-Saxon dichotomy was essentially a Catholic/Protestant division. For the pioneering states granting women limited suffrage before 1914, this argument seems irresistable. Almost all of them represented predominantly Protestant populations. Catholic states did not accept women voters. In many of them, anti-clerical governments thought much like the French radicals. In Mexico, for example, the government of President Plutarcho Elias Calles feared the potent role of women, particularly the League of Catholic Women, and resisted the postwar trend toward granting them suffrage.[10]

Why should such a difference exist between Protestant and Catholic states? Radical anti-suffragists felt that they knew: politicians in non-Catholic countries did not have to fear "a government of priests," as

Emile Darnaud explained to Jane Misme in 1914.[11] A more subtle interpretation of this fear of the confessional might add other factors, such as a masculine rivalry between husband and priest for the direction of women's lives, with a common fear that churchmen were more influential. If a man thought that he could not be the master of his home, could not even live a private and uncensored conjugal sex life because of the power of the curé in the confessional, he might well redouble his determination to prevent the female-priestly alliance he perceived from breaking his mastery of public affairs. In short, concern about the clerical peril to government may have been only part of the fears held by anti-clerical republicans. Whatever its psychological and social components, hostility to the confessional certainly conditioned different political behavior in France than existed in Protestant countries.[12]

The inverse of that situation also distinguished Protestant countries from Catholic. Whereas Catholicism contributed to masculine hostility toward women's suffrage, Protestantism contributed to feminine interest in enfranchisement. The effect of their religion on young women in the United States, compared to France, made a deep impression on Alexis de Tocqueville:

> Amongst almost all Protestant nations young women are far more the mistresses of their own actions than they are in Catholic countries. This independence is still greater in Protestant countries like England, which have retained or acquired the right of self-government; the spirit of freedom is then infused into the domestic circle by political habits and by religious opinions. In the United States the doctrines of Protestantism are combined with great political freedom and a most democratic state of society; and nowhere are young women surrendered so early or so completely to their own guidance.[13]

The independence of women in America that struck de Tocqueville contrasted vividly with the situation in France; in the former, home, religion, and political system all conditioned women in ways scarcely tolerable in the latter. The theological root of this difference was the stress that Protestantism, especially its Calvinistic varieties, placed upon the individual. All individuals, acting independently, might find salvation; all must learn to direct their own lives. Hence, it is not astonishing that Protestantism proved the more fertile soil for secular doctrines that focused upon the individual, including those of individual political liberty. Women's suffrage was such a doctrine, par excellence. Once again, de Tocqueville noted this correlation:

> Every religion is to be found in juxtaposition to a political opinion, which is connected with it by affinity. . . . . The greatest part of British America was peopled by men who, after having shaken off the authority of the Pope, acknowledged no other religious supremacy: they brought with them into the New World a form of Christianity, which I cannot better describe, than by styling it a democratic and republican religion. This sect contributed powerfully to the establishment of a democracy and a republic. . . .[14]

De Tocqueville did not lead this argument to the conclusion of French radicals—that Catholicism was anti-democratic—but to the view that Protestantism tends to make people independent.

An excellent illustration of Protestantism leading women to independent action may be seen in the development of women's reform and social control leagues, such as the Women's Christian Temperance Union (WCTU) in Protestant countries. In the United States, the WCTU brought to the suffrage campaign a membership of 200,000 to 250,000 women plus a branch in every state; in Australia, some of the most important suffrage organizations, such as the Victorian Women's Franchise League, were directly founded by the WCTU; in New Zealand, suffrage was essentially won by the WCTU, in the absence of effective suffrage leagues; similar alliances developed in Sweden and Canada.[15] The religiously motivated desire to impose puritan standards led to other, well-organized women's campaigns in many countries: to impose "blue laws," to end prostitution, to abolish slavery, to regulate immigration. Such efforts were conducive to women's suffrage in many ways. They taught women about their ability to effect change, gave practical lessons in how to succeed at politics, recruited moderate women to political activism, shaped public opinion about the capacity of women in public affairs, showed men the political benefits of accepting women in such roles, and provided the women's movement with well-established organizations that might be employed in a suffrage campaign.

French women had no such advantage. They certainly shared the concerns of social control movements in Protestant countries. Anti-alcoholism (not prohibition) became an important factor in French feminism, but it produced no analogous grouping of tens of thousands of women, nor the associated political experience. This comparative disadvantage can also be seen in the campaigns that women organized to oppose officially tolerated, "regulated" prostitution. Josephine Butler's association for the repeal of the Contagious Diseases Acts in Britain provided great advantages to nascent suffrage groups there. A study of the similar, but smaller, abolitionist campaign in late nineteenth-century France shows that it aided the development of feminism in a weaker way. Instead of organizing women for other campaigns, the French movement aided feminism by declining: activists from an unsuccessful crusade turned their energies to larger issues.[16] The correlation between such organizations and Protestantism was clear even in France, where groups such as the Conférence de Versailles and the CNFF played a sharply disproportionate role. Compared to countries such as the United States, however, these organizations appeared relatively late, were less organized, and were significantly less active. A French WCTU, with tens of thousands of women seeking to prohibit the consumption of all forms of alcoholic beverages, is scarcely conceivable. And the history of the women's rights movement in France was much different as a result.

This comparative disadvantage for French feminists underscored their relative inexperience in reformist collective action. In many countries, women obtained an apprenticeship in agitation through participation in national political movements. British women, for example, learned from working with the Anti-Corn Law League; American women, from abolitionist politics before the Civil War. In some countries, such political involvement led to the enfranchisement of women: Finnish and Norwegian suffragists profited from their association with the national-constitutional struggle with Russia and Sweden respectively; Bohemian women from a similar collaboration with the liberal-national movement within the Austrian Empire; Russian women from the post-Crimean War Alexandrine reforms; Australian suffragists won the national franchise through cooperation with the federalist movement.[17] French women had no comparable experience that they could convert to the suffrage campaign. They had a tradition of participation in revolutionary politics or labor actions, but they had virtually no experience in the organized, legalistic agitation of democratic politics. As this was the mode of change suited to the Third

Republic, and as it was precisely the tactic adopted by French suffragists, they had to learn on the job.

This French difference must be seen partly as a function of differing
philanthropic traditions. The women's philanthropy movement was
smaller and less political in France than in Britain or America. It has
been estimated that 500,000 women engaged in volunteer charity work
in late nineteenth-century England; for France, the number was probably a fraction of that. This contrast returns the focus of comparison
to the differences between Protestant and Catholic states. In France,
those highly motivated women who sought to dedicate their lives to
aiding others might choose to enter a convent; approximately 150,000
women did so in the last half of the century. Laywomen of the Catholic
bourgeoisie were, of course, active in charitable works. Their activities,
however, were rarely channeled into activist programs that undertook
political campaigns for social reform.[18] That remained more characteristic of the individualistic orientation of Protestant philanthropy.
Catholicism had a very different effect on French women. The church
provided a home for many women—in a literal sense for the thousands
who took the vows, but in a broader sense for all Catholic women.
The church gave many women a greater sense of their worth and
importance than the republic did. It provided a greater sense of equality, a clearer ideological identity, earlier access to esteemed professions,
and in some instances a political role. Thus, Catholicism, particularly
through the convent and service associations which had no parallel
in Protestant states, siphoned women off from desiring roles in the
secular republic. Furthermore, the church taught an obedience that
left most women, such as those of the LPF and the LFF, with no
hesitation in opposing women's suffrage because the pope did. Just
as Protestant theology led to a focus upon the independent individual,
Catholic theology produced a society that perceived the family as the
primary social unit. Women did not seek to fulfill rights as individuals,
but duties as part of the family. This fundamentally different attitude
and orientation was so powerful that even when the French Catholic
women's movement accepted suffragism, Catholics found themselves
unable to collaborate with most republican feminists. Nowhere was
the religious factor more dramatically illustrated than in Canada: with
the active help of Protestant clergymen, women won the provincial
franchise in all English-speaking provinces between 1916 and 1922,
the right to vote in federal elections in 1918. In French Québec, where

the Catholic church under Cardinal Villeneuve vigorously opposed women's suffrage, fewer women sought enfranchisement; women there could vote in national elections but were denied the provincial ballot until 1940.[19]

Does religion therefore explain the difference between France and the suffrage states? Certainly not alone. After all, Catholic Austria, Poland, Belgium, and Ireland all adopted women's suffrage in the years 1918-1922. Extraordinary circumstances existed—three of the four were adopting the first constitutions of new states, and the fourth, Belgium, granted only partial enfranchisement and did not extend integral rights until 1946.

The concept of Latin nations provides some additional understanding. There persisted other traditions received from centuries of Roman government, most notably the Roman law, which firmly established the principle of male dominance. In many ways, the treatment of women in the Napoleonic Code was merely a forceful recapitulation of millennia-old attitudes received through Roman law. The famous Twelve Tables of the Law, erected in the Roman forum in the fifth century BC, which were the basis of Roman legal development thereafter, devoted an entire table to *pater potestas*—the rights of the father as head of the family. That table established many of the principles that French feminists were seeking to excise from the Civil Code twenty-four centuries later. Another table of the law stated the doctrine that "females shall remain in guardianship even when they have attained their majority," a point of law with which Napoleon did not quibble. Roman law equally established the family, rather than the individual, as the fundamental social unit.[20] Considering that the single most common route to a political career during the Third Republic led through the law schools and the study of a legal regime that had shackled womem for more than two millennia, the term "Latin nations" has considerable significance.[21] English lawmakers, on the other hand, learned the principles of common law, usually from texts such as Blackstone's *Commentaries on the Laws of England*. Although the patriarchal principle, and many others objectionable to feminists, are to be found in Blackstone, there is a vast distinction between it and Roman law. It starts with Book One, Chapter One of the *Commentaries* which bears the heading, "Of the Absolute Rights of Individuals." French feminists recognized the significance of their legal tradition. When Jeanne Chauvin became the first woman to complete legal

studies in France, she did so with a thesis on the professions open to
women under Roman law and its correlation with French law.[22]

Were the republican anti-suffragists correct, therefore, in distinguishing a Latin nation built on Roman law and Roman Catholicism
from those states that embraced women's suffrage? Partly. France
was indisputably a different milieu. The Latin traditions were probably the most important facet of that uniqueness. But comparative
suffragism provides other rich contrasts, including some that differ-
entiated France from Spain or Italy. French women, after all, were
much more assertive in taking collective action in pursuit of their
rights than Spanish women were. Thus, one must add many modern
factors to the centuries of Latin traditions. One must recall the remarkable demography of France and the social politics associated with
depopulation; the unusual modernization of France, seen in an industrialization differing from Spain as well as from Britain; the strength
and nature of French socialism, so different from that in Britain or
the United States; the role of state violence in modern France; and
the weight of French political history.

French Political Geography and Women's Rights

French suffragists realized that the traditions of Roman law still
shaped French opinion about women. This clarified for them the
contrast between France and other countries, but it also conveyed an
understanding of the regions of France—for the Roman tradition was
much stronger in the south than in the north. In 1901, for example,
Parrhisia wrote an article for *La Fronde* on the possibilities of political
rights for women; she pointed to the Roman attitudes of the south
as the foremost obstacle. Hubertine Auclert noted the same point on
several occasions. In *Le Vote des femmes*, she stressed the reverse point:
suffragist hopes were highest in the north and northeast of France,
where the *loy et coutume de Beaumont* of 1182 had established a
countervailing legal tradition permitting women to participate in the
political process. The geography of women's rights had become clearer
by 1919, when the UFSF undertook its survey of regional opinion.
Juliette Raspail, who produced the union's report on women's suffrage
in small towns and rural France, found the most significant variation
to be between northern and southern opinion. It was her analysis that

the areas with a strong tradition of Roman law were the most hostile to enfranchisement.[23]

If one reconsiders the regional support that French suffragism received, the emphasis on Latin traditions gains further credibility. Several sets of data can be combined and weighted to show a general geography of political support for women's suffrage between 1907 and 1922. (See Map 11.) This evidence shows a significant difference between northern and southern responses, particularly between the northeast and the southwest. (See Table 16.) Two southern departments, Ariège and Cantal, never gave a single sign of accepting women's political rights! Nine others, from Charente-Inférieure to Savoie, gave only trivial support (less than 20 percent of the possible votes); only two northern departments (Mayenne and Haute-Saone) displayed the hostility of these southern eleven. This sharp regional difference in support for women's suffrage is even stronger than the correlation between Protestant population and support. A breakdown of departments by their percentage of Protestant population (see Table 17) shows that the larger that minority, the greater the support for women's political rights; yet the variation in support is not so great as it was between the northeast and the southwest. No department had a Protestant majority (or near to it), but five had minorities greater than 20 percent (Gard, Lozère, Drôme, Ardèche, and Deux-sèvres); four of these departments gave women's suffrage strong support. In contrast, barely a quarter of the departments with negligible Protestant population did so.

Protestantism may help to clarify the political geography of Alsace-Lorraine or the Rhône basin, but if one reflects upon the geography of French support for women's suffrage, it becomes clear that factors other than the Latin traditions of the south or pockets of Protestantism were operative. The comparative strength of support in the Paris region, in the northeast, in the Rhône basin, and along the southeastern coast suggests a logical correlation between urbanization or industrialization and that support. Such a correlation was not characteristic of the early triumphs of international suffragism. If it had been, victories should have come quickly in Britain, Germany, and the northeastern states of the United States; instead, the list is dominated by agricultural or lightly industrialized states—Australia, New Zealand, and the western states of the United States. In France, however, there was a significant correlation between support for the enfran-

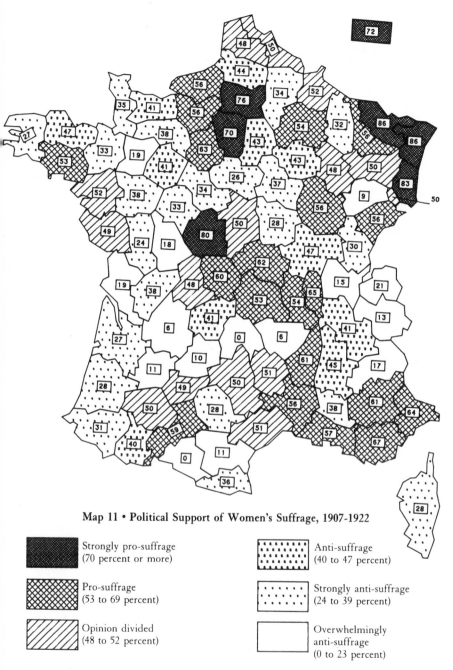

Map 11 • Political Support of Women's Suffrage, 1907-1922

Strongly pro-suffrage
(70 percent or more)

Anti-suffrage
(40 to 47 percent)

Pro-suffrage
(53 to 69 percent)

Strongly anti-suffrage
(24 to 39 percent)

Opinion divided
(48 to 52 percent)

Overwhelmingly
anti-suffrage
(0 to 23 percent)

NOTE: Labels indicate the percentage of possible support that women's suffrage obtained in each department. Four sets of data, previously expressed in Maps 6 (votes of local *conseils*), 7 (co-sponsorship of the Buisson Report), 9 (the vote in Chamber of Deputies), and 10 (the vote in the Senate) are combined here; these data were weighted in ascending order.

Table 16 • **Regional Support for Women's Suffrage, 1907-1922**

	Departments	Pro-Suffrage Departments	Mean Support for Suffrage
NORTHERN FRANCE			
(North of the Loire)	31	16 (52.6%)	52.6%
NORTHEAST	25	17 (68.0%)	53.3%
SOUTHERN FRANCE			
(Charente-Switzerland)	34	11 (32.4%)	32.7%
SOUTHWEST	18	4 (22.2%)	30.9%

NOTE: Data summarize the information displayed in Map 11.

Table 17 • **Protestantism and Support for Women's Suffrage, 1907-1922**

	Departments	Pro-Suffrage Departments	Mean Support for Suffrage
Large Protestant Minority (10% of population)	5	4 (80%)	47.4%
Small Protestant Minority (1% to 10% of population)	21	11 (52.3%)	44.7%
Negligible Protestant Minority (below .1% of population)	35	9 (25.7%)	39.6%

NOTE: Data on Protestantism from Paul-M. Bouju et al., *Atlas historique de la France contemporaine, 1800-1965* (Paris, 1966), Map 288, p. 144.

chisement of women and the urbanization or industrialization of a department. This suggests a simple interpretation: In northern France, where traditions were more predisposed to accept a public role of women, industrialization accelerated a prior pattern, resulting in the greatest support coming from the northeast; in southern France, where traditions mitigated against such roles for women, it began to break down tradition in the southeast and its absence left tradition strong in the southwest.

If one compares the most densely populated departments of France with the sparsely populated, the relative support for women's suffrage is strikingly different. (See Table 18.) Support was almost twice as strong in urbanized departments, even in the south; the more rural departments, even in the northeast (Meuse, Haute-Marne) were relatively unsympathetic. A list of highly industrialized departments gave women's suffrage 62 percent of all possible votes between 1907 and 1922.[24] Another way to reveal the urban basis of the political backing for women suffrage is to reexamine the roll call vote in the Chamber of Deputies in 1919 for the behavior of deputies from the great cities. (See Table 19.) The result is unmistakable. Paris voted 33-0; deputies from the ten largest cities, 64-5. And, significantly, radical deputies

Table 18 • Urbanization and Support for Women's Suffrage

Department	Population per Square Mile (1921)	Support for Women's Suffrage
Seine	23,864.4	72%
Rhône	866.5	65%
Nord	802.5	50%
Seine-et-Oise	422.0	70%
Bouches-du-Rhône	415.8	57%
Belfort	401.4	50%
Pas-de-Calais	379.9	48%
Seine-Inférieure	359.8	56%
Bas-Rhin	352.6	86%
Haut-Rhin	346.3	83%
Ten Most Densely Populated Departments		62%
Cantal	89.5	0%
Lot	87.7	10%
Meuse	86.1	32%
Corse	83.7	28%
Haute-Marne	82.2	48%
Gers	80.1	50%
Landes	73.2	28%
Lozère	54.5	51%
Hautes-Alpes	41.0	17%
Basses-Alpes	34.1	61%
Ten Least Densely Populated Departments		33%

Table 19 • **Voting by Deputies from Major Cities, 1919**

City	1921 Population	Yes	No	Not Voting
Paris (Seine)	2,906,472	33 (94.3%)	0	2 (5.7%)
Marseille (Bouches-du-Rhône)	586,341	4	0	0
Lyons (Rhône)	561,592	6	0	3
Bordeaux (Gironde)	267,409	3	1	2
Lille (Nord)	200,952	6	0	0
Nantes (Loire-Inférieure)	183,704	1	3	0
Toulouse (Haute-Garonne)	175,434	3	0	0
St. Etienne (Loire)	167,967	4	0	0
Le Havre (Seine-Inférieure)	163,374	2	1	0
Nice (Alpes-Maritimes)	155,839	2	0	1
Ten Largest Cities		64 (83.1%)	5 (6.5%)	8 (10.4%)
All Other Constituencies		265 (58.5%)	90 (20%)	96 (21.2%)
Radicals from Ten Largest Cities		8 (72.2%)	3 (27.3%)	0
All Other Radical Deputies		67 (37.6%)	62 (34.8%)	49 (27.5%)

from these same cities voted like their urban colleagues, not like their fellow party members.

Such evidence does more than reconfirm the obvious point that suffragism was a big-city phenonmenon. By adding urban pockets of support for women's suffrage to the geography of the Roman tradition and Protestantism, one obtains a clearer image of the political geography that feminists faced. Instead of a monolithic south opposed to them, they found considerable support in the populous Rhône basin—hence the pattern of southern opposition being most heavily concentrated in the southwest. Similarly the greater sympathy of industrialized regions for women's suffrage reinforced the greater willingness of northern France to accept the idea. Put differently, urbanization and industrialization tended to break down the traditional feelings about women. While the perception of the family as the fundamental social unit remained strong throughout France, those regions where the Roman tradition was weakest and/or urbanization strongest were more amenable to altering notions about limiting women to the household. In this way, attitudes in southwestern France were closer to those in Spain than in Paris; in the northeast, attitudes were more comparable to those held in neighboring states.

French Feminism and the Campaign for Political Rights

French feminists also considered the possibility that endogenous factors contributed to their difficulties in obtaining the vote. Was part of the explanation of 1922 contained in the nature of the women's movement and the campaign that they staged for the vote? Politicians certainly told them so. If suffragists complained that prominent men did too little to help them, they faced the response that French women had done too little to help themselves. Aristide Briand was particularly candid in this respect. When Jeanne Schmahl, as president of the UFSF, asked him to use his premiership of 1912 to press the chamber on women's suffrage, he answered, "It is up to you ... to create a situation worthy of the government's interest." When Briand was again premier in 1921 and leaders of the union visited him once more to appeal for help with the Senate, he repeated his criticism of the suffrage campaign. He chided Brunschwicg for letting the favorable moment of 1919 pass without exploiting it; he spoke of his disappointment that women's demonstrations had not been numerous, nor large, nor spread around France. Why did women not show that they wanted to vote? Léon Abensour, another friend of the movement, told feminists the same thing and later wrote that the defeat of 1922 was partly due to women not truly fighting for the ballot. This was not merely a masculine response. Militant suffragists, particularly Auclert and Pelletier, had complained that feminists were too timid in taking collective action.[25]

The first issue that such assertions raise is the size and scope of French suffragism. Few people on either side of the question doubted that the suffrage organizations drew their support from a minority of French women—generally an urban, bourgeois elite with the adherence of young, educated working women such as *institutrices*. And even in the capital, militants often despaired over feminine indifference. "Young women of Paris," Auclert wrote in 1909, "only think of pleasing men, of changing their dresses and appearing as *gamines*."[26] Caroline Kauffmann echoed her a few days later: "Their ideal, on the whole, is to be ... a very amiable, very refined, and very much courted woman.[27] Such militants agreed with the assessment of their opponents: "French women," said *Le Soleil* in 1910, "remain for the moment quite indifferent to the conquest of their political rights."[28] This theme is almost constant in the history of French feminism, whether stated as an accusation by anti-suffragists or as a lament by feminist activists: most women were apparently indifferent to winning the vote. There had not been a great change between Olympe de Gouges's cry in 1791 ("Oh, women, women! When will you cease to be blind?") and Louise Weiss's description of the response she received in the 1930s: "Peasant women kept their mouths tightly closed when I spoke to them about the vote. Working women laughed, shopkeepers shrugged their shoulders, and the *bourgeoises* pushed away horrified." The discouragement of Maria Deraismes when women did not respond to her feminist congress of 1878 and the taunt of Senator Albert in 1922 ("Where are they, all of these women who want to vote?") derived from the same truth. The majority of women did not seek their rights.[29]

Apathy produced a corollary problem for suffragists: recurring financial worries. French women, Avril de Sainte-Croix lamented, "have not yet learned to give for an idea."[30] Young women had little money, married women had no control over their income until 1907 (and restricted freedom thereafter), and the habit of giving by women was almost exclusively directed toward the church or favored charities rather than a political campaign. Although a few monied women supported feminism while not actively participating, as Mme. Elie Halévy did, little aid came from outside the ranks of the feminist leadership.[31] Auclert, Durand, Sainte-Croix, d'Uzès, and many others contributed much of the financing of their undertakings. Durand, for example, not only underwrote *La Fronde*, her 1907 Office du travail féminin, and her 1910 parliamentary campaign, but she also made frequent donations, such as 1,000 francs in 1899 to help establish a woman's typographers union, or paying the costs for thirty-one provincial *institutrices* to participate in the 1900 congress on women's rights. She was in a good position to complain about the relative poverty of French feminism (as she did in some 1914 reflections), but many others noted a sad comparison between French finances and those in Britain or the United States. The treasurer of the UFSF, Thérèse Belle, regularly pointed out this contrast in her annual report. English commentators on the French movement also noted it. And in the final hours of the 1922 campaign, Maria Vérone cried out, "If only we had a fraction of the funds that the British or Americans have!"[32]

Feminist periodicals particularly suffered from underfunding, compounded by often tiny circulation figures. Pauline Savari's feminist-syndicalist *L'Abeille* survived for only two issues before running out of money in February 1901. Arria Ly's *Le Combat féministe* produced a total revenue of 132 francs before folding. Efforts to found a French edition of *Jus suffragii* repeatedly foundered on the fact that the international publication barely attracted 100 French subscribers. Héra Mirtel poured more than 12,000 francs into publishing *L'Entente*. She started out in 1905 with a press run of 10,000 copies and brave hopes of replacing *La Fronde*; within two years she was writing to individual feminists to implore their help in reaching her break-even point . . . 200 copies. This was not just a problem of ephemeral publications. *La Fronde* sold a daily average of 12,000 copies, but that was insufficient to meet editorial costs of 40,000 francs. *La Française* encountered serious financial problems on several occasions, forcing Misme to appeal to her readers; only gifts from Julie Siegfried and Sarah Monod saved the paper in 1911. *La Voix des femmes* faced the same crisis in 1920 and 1921.[33]

The membership problems and financial crises that resulted from feminine lack of interest, however, obscure an equally important fact: *France did have a large, organized, and active women's suffrage movement.* Historians who write, "In France the issue of female suffrage scarcely rippled the political waters," have missed a major phenomenon.[34] Dozens of groups, with hundreds of provincial chapters, combining tens of thousands of members, conducting daily activities, publishing thousands of grievances and dozens of periodicals certainly splashed the political waters for over a generation. French suffragism indisputably existed on a lesser scale than Anglo-American versions, but it was a large movement. Suffrage organizations in France, for example, had more female adherents in 1914 (over 100,000 if one counts the CNFF) than trade unions (89,000) did.³⁵ French feminism was certainly less vigorous in its collective action than Anglo-American versions; few women had the courage of Auclert to scorn *déclassement*. But they did take collective action that must be appreciated as militant when seen in the French context rather than the Anglo-American. How many of the well-studied protest movements of pre-1914 France exceeded 5,000 marchers in the streets of Paris and 500,000 signatures for their demands? How many famous political movements of modern history could also be dismissed because a majority did not join in their aspirations?

When one appreciates the size and activity of French suffragism, it becomes important to explore the internal problems hindering the movement while it confronted so many external obstacles. One problem was certainly the regional maldistribution of suffrage activities— their concentration in Paris and the cities. Leaders of the movement recognized the need to develop their provincial base; many attempts to do so have been seen already. Individuals made tremendous efforts to build provincial suffragism, such as Nelly Roussel's years on the lecture circuit or Marie Denizard's visits to every commune in the Somme. Organizations, particularly the UFSF and the LFDF, certainly sought provincial chapters. Yet it seems clear that some of the obstacles of the suffragist penetration of the provinces came from within the movement.

Parisian feminism contributed to this problem by summoning its most active converts to the capital—a female version of the deracination that Barrès lamented in other forms. Pauline Rebour of Le Havre and Marguerite Clément of Bordeaux, for example, left the local movements they had founded in favor of joining the battle in Paris. Hubertine Auclert, who had herself left Allier to work at the heart of the movement, revealed this problem in a letter to Arria Ly: Auclert urged her to leave the south, where she met scorn and derision, for Paris, where she would find supportive kindred spirits and the excitement of daily feminist activities.³⁶ It must have been an extraordinary temptation for the women who felt isolated in unsympathetic surroundings. The trend was certainly understandable, but it tended to undermine the movement where dedicated leaders were most needed.

The UFSF made the greatest contribution to the spread of suffragism around France, but it also kept provincial groups weak. It did so in a way congruent with the French tendency toward the centralized dominance of Paris. The statutes of the union explicitly stated that no chapter outside Paris could undertake its own initiatives. They could not approach their deputies or senators, could not appeal to their municipal council, and certainly could not organize a demonstration—all of these decisions were reserved to the Parisian Central Committee. The annual congress of the union, which elected the committee and ratified its policies, was composed according to a formula that guaranteed the dominance of Parisian members. And provincial women elevated to this leadership were precisely those who, like Rebour and Clément, uprooted themselves.[37]

It is also arresting to examine the regions of France where feminists devoted their greatest energies. By combining the data already presented, one can obtain a general portrait of feminist activity on a department-by-department basis. (See Map 12.) In only three departments (Seine, Seine-Inférieure, and Rhône) can feminist activity be called frequent; in eight others (Aisne, Alpes-Maritimes, Bouches-du-Rhône, Finistère, Gironde, Isère, Pas-de-Calais, and Basses-Pyrénées) a feminist presence was apparently well-established, if often small. In contrast to these eleven departments there were ten in which virtually no trace of early twentieth-century feminism has been found (Aude, Belfort, Corse, Haute-Garone, Haute-Vienne, Lot-et-Garonne, Lozère, Mayenne, Meuse, and Pyrénées-Orientales). If one then compares these departments with the data on provincial political support of women's suffrage (see Map 11), it becomes clear that political support is associated with feminist activity. The three departments where feminism was relatively strong gave women's suffrage 68 percent of all possible votes; the eleven departments with a significant feminist presence, 53 percent. Standing in vivid contrast, the ten departments without a feminist movement overwhelmingly opposed women's suffrage—giving barely one-third of the possible votes.

One cannot infer causation from such correlations, but they certainly suggest a line of inquiry. Did suffragists direct their energies where they were most needed? The greater opposition of southwestern France to feminine enfranchisement has already been shown; feminists perceived this before 1914 and statistically demonstrated it themselves in the LFDF study of the chamber's vote in 1919. Yet this was precisely the region where feminists undertook the least action. Seven of the ten departments with no apparent feminist movement were in the

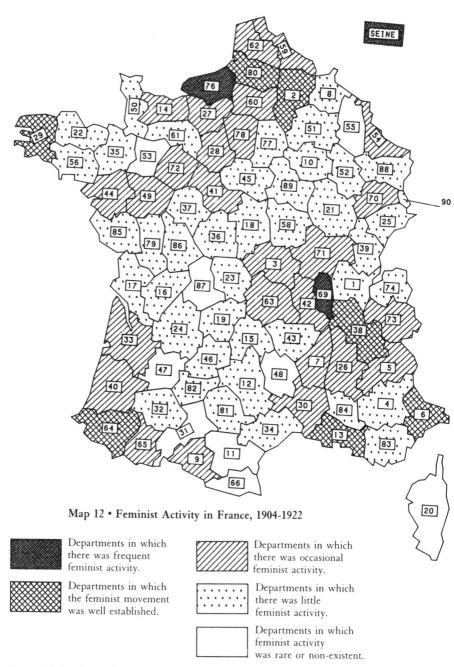

Map 12 • Feminist Activity in France, 1904-1922

Departments in which there was frequent feminist activity.

Departments in which the feminist movement was well established.

Departments in which there was occasional feminist activity.

Departments in which there was little feminist activity.

Departments in which feminist activity was rare or non-existent.

NOTE: Labels indicate the identity code for each department. The data previously expressed in Maps 1 to 5 and 8 are combined here. They cover individual activity; branches of the UFSF, LFDF, CNFF, and the smaller Parisian leagues; chapters of the FFU; lodges of mixed masonry; independent local feminist organizations or periodicals; membership in regional federations.

south, and six of those seven were in the southwestern quadrant of the country. The LFDF was actively building provincial chapters at the same time that it published the analysis of the 1919 vote. (See Map 8.) The league created fifteen provincial chapters in the years 1918-1920, but only one of those was in the southwest. And that single branch (in Ariège) was in a department that already had an active women's movement in 1914 (see Map 5), instead of one of the departments in which the movement was virtually nonexistent such as Pyrénées-Orientales, Aude, or Lot-et-Garonne. An analogous problem existed in the expansion of the LFDF in northern France. The league's own data revealed four departments in the north (Meuse, Aisne, Haute-Saone, and Mayenne) where deputies were hostile to enfranchisement. (See Map 9.) Most of the new branches of the league were opened in the north, yet only one of these (in Mayenne) was in the four departments that they had identified as trouble spots. It seems reasonable to suggest, therefore, that the suffrage movement was slow to expand where it was most needed.

The problem of provincial expansion is clearly related to the social composition of the women's movement, just as the matter of acceptable behavior has been shown to be. The well-educated, well-dressed, well-behaved *bourgeoises* of the UFSF, the CNFF, or Amélioration had little contact with the life of most French women. They had a strong philanthropic instinct to help the less advantaged, they had a sincere concern for the rights and welfare of women of different social classes, but the gulf between their worlds was immense. Recent research in French social history provides a wealth of illustrations of the gap between the bourgeois feminist movement and the women of France. The female day laborers of the vineyards of lower Languedoc, most unmarried or widowed, recognized the disparity between their two francs per diem and the wages of men, but they turned to revolutionary syndicalism, not feminism. The *bobineuses* of the textile mills of Roubaix knew that 98 percent of the higher paying spinning jobs went to men, but they were drawn not to the women's movement but to the Marxism of Jules Guesde or to nativist ethnic conflict with Belgian migrant workers rather than to one of the nine feminist groups active in the department of the Nord. The transformation of garment-making at Toulouse into an urban putting-out system of home production based on sweated female labor, rather than male artisans, did not produce a wave of recruits for the local campaigns of Arria Ly.

The fervently religious butchers of Limoges, who defended their fourteenth-century statue of the Virgin Mary during the violence of 1905, had no wives or daughters on the roster of a Limousin chapter of the UFSF.[38]

Bourgeois feminists contended that the class difference separating them from other French women should not make any difference. Instead, women of all classes should collaborate in feminine solidarity against all forms of masculine oppression—a feminist version of "solidarism" that reiterates how republican the women's movement was. Class war, as Maria Martin wrote in one of her last articles, was an intolerable doctrine; class cooperation was needed. Cécile Brunschwicg similarly argued that the UFSF must reach out to proletarian women; it should not matter, she insisted, that middle-class women led the suffrage campaign:

> If some *bourgeoises* are at the head [of the UFSF], it is because they are freer. It is also because they are not very bourgeois in consciousness [*de sentiments*], and at bottom that is what counts ... when one is conscious of the injustices and the suffering of others, when one gives their life to their ideas because that is worth the pain of doing it, I believe that the consciousness of class disappears completely. ...

Many feminists subscribed to this sentiment: members of the privileged class, it was their duty to improve the lot of working women; then, the two groups could work together to ameliorate the condition of their sex. Class consciousness was an obstacle to this great work.[39] Such solidarity rarely existed. So rarely, that one can hardly escape the conclusion that disunity was among the more severe problems confronting advocates of women's rights.

Feminist disunity paralleled the divisions in masculine politics. Just as republican and socialist men split along class lines, so did republican and socialist women. Brunschwicg's appeal to put aside differences provoked an immediate rejection by a leading syndicalist in the same periodical where it appeared. According to her, Brunschwicg's idea justified workers' "fears of interference by groups of the bourgeois party in trade union affairs," so she called for them to leave syndicalist women alone:

> I say to the feminist groups, let us act, us, the unionists, in our trade unions. Do not come to spoil our work with your untimely

enthusiasm. Stay on your own terrain and do not get in the way on ours.[40]

There was an enormous difference between those who concentrated on the problems of class and those who focused on sex, between those who stressed political equality and those most concerned with economic equality, between those who sought to reform the radical republic and those who wished to create the social republic. Working-class women often found middle-class feminists to be condescending "handmaidens of capital," as Durand was dubbed for her efforts to create the Office of Women Workers in 1907. The socialists of *L'Humanité*, the anarchists of Herve's *La Guerre sociale*, and the syndicalists of the CGT's *La Voix du peuple* joined in denouncing the devisiveness of bourgeois interference.[41] Similar differences blocked collaboration between feminists and Catholic women. On one side stood women speaking of rights; on the other, of duties. Feminists sought greater female autonomy, an idea repugnant to Catholic women. Thus, *La Française* was too revolutionary for Catholics and Marie Maugeret too traditionalist for feminists. Catholic women, said Sainte-Croix, preferred "to live in cloisters, ignoring all that passes around them." Revolutionary feminism, said Maugeret, was "the supreme artifice for tearing women away from the church, and through women, the entire society."[42]

Divisions within the women's movement—again, like national politics—went deeper than the rift with socialists on one side and Catholics on the other. Bourgeois feminists were not unified themselves. Until the early twentieth century, they disagreed about seeking political rights, thereafter, about the version of enfranchisement they sought. Throughout the Third Republic, they found no common program for collective action. Durand summarized their situation quite well in 1903 when she discussed the death of the daily publication of *La Fronde*: militants were "judged too bourgeois by socialist women and too revolutionary by bourgeois women."[43] One might add the corollary: bourgeois moderates were judged too revolutionary by Catholic women and too retrograde by militants. Feminist disunity, however, was more complicated and subtle than a simple split into moderate and militant factions. The women's rights movement was fragmented into approximately two dozen different groups and riven by the individual (sometimes idiosyncratic) ideas of several dozen leaders. "Every feminist," as Madeleine Pelletier wrote in 1908, "has their own private feminism."[44] The inequality of French women being so extreme, individual feminists had an immense range of targets upon which to concentrate. Some preferred to emphasize economic equality, and follow Durand or Eliska Vincent; some, civil rights and follow Jeanne Oddo-Deflou; some, sexual rights and follow Nelly Roussel; some, political rights and follow Hubertine Auclert. Feminists were also divided—and their efforts for enfranchisement limited—by their involvement in social problems tangential to women's rights. The members of Amélioration, for example, voted a new program in 1912. Its first objective was "to struggle against the social disorders" of alcoholism, tuberculosis, and the demoralization of youth.[45] For others, particularly in the CNFF, feminism was almost an extension of philanthropy. Indeed, working-class women sometimes perceived bourgeois feminism and bourgeois philanthropy as essentially the same thing.[46]

Social questions often found feminists on opposite sides of the debate. The members of the CNFF were not unanimous in supporting the Naquet Law and certainly disputed the militants who wanted easier divorces: this was the route to dreaded "trial marriage." Such arguments did not create a simple dichotomy between left-wing and conservative feminists. On sexual questions, for example, many prominent militants such as the Bélilons and Arria Ly were appalled by "free love feminists." Abortion and sex education produced similar divisions.[47] Naturally, the debate on depopulation compounded these disagreements. Many saw depopulation as a grave problem and carefully portrayed themselves as *mères de familles*. One of the founders of the UFSF could even say, "Women who reject maternity are like men who put down their weapons in battle—both are cowards and traitors to their race."[48] Yet others applauded depopulation: smaller families would reduce misery in the working class. And some feminists simply saw natalist arguments as a conservative, anti-feminist ploy to keep women in the home. Many such issues divided the women's movement and weakened the campaign for the vote. Should, for example, feminists accept paternalistic legislation to protect women? The Nancy Program offered it. *La Française* responded, "Bravo!" Others considered such legislation to be "anti-feminist maneuvers." "In my opinion," wrote Pelletier, "feminism must avoid anything in its program that tends to put women in a special place in society, even when that place appears to constitute an advantage for her."[49] Most of the CNFF could not accept that statement. This dilemma reappeared in many forms. Should special legislation restrict the hours of work for women more than for men? Should women be excluded from capital punishment? Should women serve in the military? There was no consensus on any of these questions.

Finally, it must be noted that feminist fragmentation also resulted from internecine personal rivalries. Pelletier surveyed the animosity within the movement in 1913 and concluded: "It is deplorable that feminists only know how to cut off their noses to spite their own faces."[50] The women of Amélioration and those of the LFDF fought incessantly over which group was the oldest feminist league; so they rarely cooperated. Leaders of the UFSF and the LFDF attacked each other in print. Eliska Vincent and Jeanne Schmahl were both bitter about their treatment by Cécile Brunschwicg; so their friends left the UFSF. Such facts led unsympathetic observers to facile stereotypes about women in politics; for example, that feminine bitchiness made women less effective politicians than men. No one familiar with the masculine politics of the Third Republic should draw such conclusions. The personal rivalries within the women's movement, like the ideological divisions, were merely typical of the political environment. Men, after all, so detested each other that they still fought duels over politics. And if anyone in French political life was bitchy, it was probably Georges Clemenceau, but if he made savage remarks about a rival, he was merely being a "tiger." Seen in this context, feminist rivalries are put into perspective: they were simply an important political problem that reduced effectiveness.

French Social Politics and the Collective Mentality

Finally, one must seek understanding from that political system which French women sought to enter. Many political answers have already been suggested. The hostility of the predominant Radical and Radical-Socialist Party, including such important leaders as Clemenceau and Combes. The unwillingness of allies, such as the SFIO, to press the issue; of friends in the political elite, such as Poincaré, to use (risk?) their position on behalf of women. The traditional priorities of politicians, such as proportional representation, behind which women's rights were made to wait. The slowness of the parliamentary committee system and the political calendar, which facilitated the burial of unwanted reforms while conveying the impression of serious consideration; the ease with which adroit opponents, such as Bérard, could manipulate procedures for years. The utter lack of leverage by which outsiders, such as women, could affect deliberations; the ineffectiveness of the few democratic instruments available to them, such as petitions and vows from local councils. The psychology and calculus of electoral politics, by which the election of one woman meant the rejection of a present male officeholder.

The accumulation of such factors sustains a powerful political explanation for the continuing rejection of women's suffrage in France, but it is also helpful to reconsider French politics in larger terms. The machinery of the Third Republic worked adequately at those tasks that journeymen politicians understood: the glamorous endeavors of foreign affairs, empire-building, and military preparedness; the annual bargaining over the budget; the attention to special interests, such as ensuring that the railroad reached the proper towns in one's department; the ideological passions of the regime, such as laicization or national education; and even the reforms demanded by sufficiently powerful groups. The *Journal officiel*, and many political histories, record this in fine detail.

The machine of state functioned somewhat less smoothly with social issues like the woman question. When the large political blocs confronted such social politics, they generally fell back upon their ideology, their theoretical identity, to produce some policy. This was a disaster for women's suffrage because the great blocs of the right, the left, and the center each turned to doctrines that were incompatible with that legislation. Indeed, there was a startling similarity to the theories of Catholics, socialists, and radicals—far more than contemporaries or historians have acknowledged. Each of the groups rejected the individualistic liberalism that had dominated European political thought; each concentrated instead upon a vision of the collective. And that collective mentality, whichever its variety, was not congruent with the demand for a new individual right.

The response of the Catholic right to social politics, whether the woman question or the degeneration debate, was to redouble their traditional beliefs. French ills would cease when the nation returned to its former strengths. Return to the family as the fundamental cell of French life. Return from appalling dechristianization, recorded in the republic's registry of civil ceremonies. Return to *la terre* and its simple inspiration—to the meadow as well as the chapel, as Barrès put it in his *Colline inspirée* in 1913. Come back to order, authority, and duty. This answer was deeply satisfying to millions of people. It reaffirmed their values and justified the inherited patterns of their lives. It also buttressed their ancient attitudes about the roles of women. An English audience at the Lyceum Club in 1906 laughed when Paul Cambon told them French women generally accepted the laws that put them under their husbands' protection.[51] The French Senate would not have laughed if Cambon had spoken there. Those chuckling English gentlemen failed to appreciate how deeply traditionalist France remained, how prevalent the conservative view of order and duty. Subsequent commentators may find those attitudes retrograde, but that does not advance one's understanding of France.

The socialist left had an equally comprehensive prescription for France's national ills: social revolution. Her malaise would last as long as the bourgeois republic did, and it would worsen. Reforms directed at specific problems were humanly desirable, but they were only palliatives that masked some symptoms of the affliction. Catholic reactionaries only created a different problem by seeking to return to an antiquated social order. Their formula was discredited in the past and unworkable in the present; and it lacked even the meager virtue of ameliorative reforms. Instead, the logic of historical change, the inevitable working out of the dialectic demanded an entirely new social order. With that revolution would come a world of equality in which the social causes of alcoholism, or the oppression of women, would be gone. That brave vision must not obscure the fact that a large percentage of the working class still clung to the same conservative ideas about women. Socialists and syndicalists might dismiss suffragism as a bourgeois phenomenon or an inapprorpriate route to a desired end. Beyond such factors of ideology, however, workingmen shared many attitudes more often associated with conservative classes, as the passions of the Couriau affair of 1912 demonstrated. The unwillingness of the Syndicat du Livre to accept the membership of a female typographer and their belligerence in expelling her husband for promoting her membership were not isolated incidents. Although women constituted more than a third of the industrial work force between the 1890s and 1914, women never accounted for 10 percent of the trade union membership, and, in part, this was because men did not want them. Some women complained that the workers' *bourses du travail* treated them worse than bourgeois managers did—at least in the finding of a CNFF study. It was not just bourgeois feminists who observed the deep conservatism about women among male workers. Pelletier, for example, wrote to Arria Ly in 1921 to complain that most socialists still thought that women belonged at home: "The majority is for the home; it is the working class, as you know, that is the least feminist."[52]

French radicals faced social politics by groping toward an ideological center without either Christ or Marx. For a century their solution had been the republic, whose institutions would usher in liberty, equality, fraternity. When the republic itself confronted troublesome social problems, their response became lists of reform legislation such as Clemenceau's electoral program of 1881 or the resolutions of the Nancy Congress of 1907. For less tractable problems the republican answer was education—vigorous secular education that would ingrain republican widsom (in women, for example). Few regimes have been more fond of educational legislation, more determined to reshape society through the schools. Thus would France follow the vision of progress sketched by Condorcet.

Radicals realized that their program lacked the philosophic coherence of Catholicism or socialism: compiling lists of liberal-democratic reforms was not so majestic as revealed religious truth or the inexorable unfolding of the dialectic of history. The resultant search for a theoretical definition of a third way produced "solidarism." True to the traditions of the Radical Party, it was a doctrine of left-wing rhetoric; faithful to attitudes in the small constituency committees which were the heart of the party, it was an essentially conservative doctrine to defend the bourgeois republic against the menace on the left. Above all, this neo-Jacobinism was a justification of the program of "reformist sociology." Solidarism sought fraternity through greater equality which was to be obtained by guaranteeing yet restricting liberty. Such diverse advocates of solidarism as Léon Bourgeois, Alfred Fouillée, Charles Gide, and Emile Durkheim all embraced some version of this theory. Radicals consequently defended private property but denounced the selfishness of laissez-faire liberalism. The individual must have democratic rights and liberties, but the government must concentrate on the collective interest. Hence, a powerful government must intervene in social problems, must continue on the course of reform legislation; it must act on behalf of the solidarity of all classes, against those who sought either class interest or class war. Seeking to defend and amend the bourgeois-republican society, radicals were, in the words of Lucien Herr, "conservatives who did not attend Mass."[53]

Conservative attitudes about the woman question girded radical ideology just as it did Catholic and socialist thought. The persistence of their traditional attitudes can be seen by comparing the report on the political rights of women that André Amar delivered to the Convention in 1793 with the Bérard Report of 1919. A century and a quarter altered very little: Was it the man of the eighteenth century or the twentieth century who asked his colleagues, "Are women capable of these cares and of the qualities they call for? In general, we can answer no. Very few examples would contradict this evaluation."[54]

How, then, were these three blocs alike in their social politics? Each championed *collective* interests against *individual* rights. To the right, the fundamental collectivity was the family, extended to a collectivity of families, the *patrie*. The collectivity of the left was the working class, which in turn was merely the vanguard of a larger collectivity, the classless society. Radical republicans, who traditionally had the greatest affinity with liberalism, were late in refining their collective mentality. By the early twentieth century, however, they were earnestly trying to jettison the individual in favor of a new collectivity, the republican solidarity of all classes.

The emancipation of women threatened the collectivist visions of Catholics, socialists, and radicals alike. To Catholics, it threatened the family; to socialists, it impeded the revolution; to radicals it implied the clerical dismantling of the republic. No aspect of that emancipation was more threatening than the political rights of women. Suffrage was a classical liberal cause, emphasizing the rights of the individual; it had little chance because it faced three different corporative theories that rejected liberal individualism. Put differently, one of the reasons why France, so often a textbook illustration of liberal society, rejected women's suffrage was that there were few classical liberals in French politics.

Whether the political explanation is more persuasive as a detailed study of parliamentary maneuvering or as an interpretation of French political thought, it must be drawn with many nuances. Cécile Brunschwicg provided a fine reminder of this. She alone among leading pre-1914 suffragists lived to vote in 1945. And Brunschwicg voted, with public enthusiasm, for the Radical Party.[55]

Notes

Chapter One

1. Léon Abensour, *La Femme et le féminisme avant la révolution* (Paris, 1923), pp. 335-37; Hubertine Auclert, *Le Vote des femmes* (Paris, 1908), p. 15.

2. Paul Viollet, *Histoire des institutions politiques et administratives de la France*, 3 vols. (Paris, 1890-1903), 2:3, 86-87; 3:188, 190; Maïte Albistur and Daniel Armogathe, *Histoire du féminisme français*, 2 vols (Paris, 1977), 1:25; Abensour, *La Femme et le féminisme*, pp. 340-45.

3. Viollet, *Histoire des institutions*, 3:306-308; Abensour, *La Femme et le féminisme*, pp. 326-35; Albistur and Armogathe, *Histoire du féminisme français*, 1:22.

4. Jane Abray, "Feminism and the French Revolution," *AHR* 80 (1975): 43-62; Alphonse Aulard, "Le Féminisme pendant la révolution française," *Revue bleue*, ser. 4, 9 (1898); Jeanne Bouvier, *Les Femmes pendant la révolution* (Paris, 1931); Elisabeth Racz, "The Women's Rights Movement in the French Revolution," *Science and Society* 161 (1951-1952): 151-68; Owen Hufton, "Women in the Revolution, 1789-1796," *Past and Present* 53 (1971): 90-108; Scott H. Lytle, "Second Sex (September 1793)," *JMH* 27 (1955): 14-26; Paul-Marie Duhet, *Les Femmes et la révolution, 1789-1794* (Paris, 1971); Ruth Graham, "Loaves and Liberty: Women in the French Revolution," in *Becoming Visible: Women in European History* ed. Renate Bridenthal and Claudia Koonz (Boston, 1977), pp. 236-54.

5. Marie-Jean-Antoine-Nicolas Caritat, Marquis de Condorcet, *Selected Writings*, ed. Keith M. Baker (Indianapolis, 1976), p. 103. The argument is from Condorcet's "Sur l'admission des femmes au droit de cité." See also his *Lettres d'un bourgeois de New-Haven à un citoyen de Virginie, sur l'inutilité de partager le pouvoir législatif entre plusieurs corps* (Paris, 1788).

6. For some of the documents involved, see: Frank M. Anderson, ed., *The Constitutions and Other Select Documents Illustrative of the History of France, 1789-1907* (Minneapolis, 1908); Darline G. Levy, Harriet B. Applewhite, and Mary D. Johnson, eds., *Women in Revolutionary Paris, 1789-1795* (Urbana, Ill., 1979).

7. Duhet, *Les Femmes et la révolution*, p. 34; Evelyne Sullerot, *Histoire de la presse féminine en France, des origines à 1848* (Paris, 1966), p. 42; Levy et

al., *Women in Revolutionary Paris*, pp. 87-96, 123.   8. *Feuille du salut public*, as quoted by Abray, "Feminism and the French Revolution," p. 50.

9. Claire G. Moses, "The Evolution of Feminist Thought in France, 1829-1889" (Ph.D. diss., George Washington University, 1978); Moses, 'Saint-Simonian Men/Saint-Simonian Women: The Transformation of Feminist Thought in 1830s France," *JMH* 54 (1982): 240-67; Léon Abensour, *Le Féminisme sous le règne de Louis-Philippe* (Paris, 1918); Marguerite Thibert, *Le Féminisme dans le socialisme français de 1830 à 1850* (Thèse de doctorat, Paris, 1926); Edith Thomas, *Pauline Roland: Socialisme et féminisme au XIXᵉ siècle* (Paris, 1956); Laure Adler, *L'Aube du féminisme: Les Premières journalistes, 1830-1850* (Paris, 1979); S. Joan Moon, "The Saint-Simonian Association of Working Class Women, 1830-1850," *PWSFH* 5 (1977): 274-81; Albistur and Armogathe, *Histoire du féminisme français* 1:405-416.

10. S. Joan Moon, "Feminism and Socialism: The Utopian Synthesis of Flora Tristan," in *Socialist Women: European Socialist Feminism in the Nineteenth and Early Twentieth Centuries*, ed. Marilyn J. Boxer and Jean H. Quataert (New York, 1978), pp. 21-50; Marie Collins and Sylvie W. Sayre, "Flora Tristan: Forgotten Feminist and Socialist," *Nineteenth Century French Studies* 1 (1973): 229-34; Moses, "The Evolution of Feminist Thought in France," pp. 136-49; Albistur and Armogathe, *Histoire du féminisme français*, 2:435.

11. Albistur and Armogathe, *Histoire du féminisme français*, 1:188-90; 2:436.

12. Jules Tixerant, *Le Féminisme à l'époque de 1848 dans l'ordre politique et dans l'ordre économique* (Thèse de doctorat, Paris, 1908), esp. pp. 60-82; Edith Thomas, *Les Femmes de 1848* (Paris, 1948) and *Pauline Roland*, esp. pp. 108-115; A. Ranvier, "Une Féministe de 1848, Jeanne Deroin," *La Révolution de 1848* 4 (1907); Moses, "The Evolution of Feminist Thought in France," pp. 149-73; Marie Collins and Sylvie W. Sayre, eds., *Les Femmes en France* (New York, 1974), pp. 126-52.

13. *Le Droit des femmes*, September 20, 1885.

14. The fullest study of this period is by Patrick K. Bidelman, "The Feminist Movement in France: The Formative Years, 1858-1889" (Ph.D. diss., Michigan State University, 1975), revised as *Pariahs Stand Up! The Founding of the Liberal Feminist Movement in France, 1858-1889* (Westport, Conn., 1982); "Maria Deraismes, Léon Richer, and the Founding of the French Feminist Movement, 1866-1878," *TR/TR* 3-4 (1977: 20-73; "The Politics of French Feminism: Léon Richer and the LFDF, 1882-1891," *HR/RH* 3 (1976): 93-120. See also: Suzanne Grinberg, *Historique du mouvement suffragiste depuis 1848* (Paris, 1926); Richard J. Evans, *The Feminists: Women's Emancipation Movements in Europe, America, and Australasia, 1840-1920* (New York, 1977); Li Dzeh-Djen, *La Presse féministe en France de 1869 à 1914*

(Paris, 1934); Moses, "The Evolution of Feminist Thought in France," pp. 254-89.

15. The text of the Marseille resolution is reprinted in Madeleine Guilbert, *Les Femmes et l'organisation syndicale avant 1914: Présentation et commentaires de documents pour une étude du syndicalisme féminin* (Paris, 1966), pp. 156-57.

16. The most thorough examination of the relationship between French socialism and feminism is the work of Charles Sowerwine: *Sisters or Citizens? Women and Socialism in France since 1876* (Cambridge, 1982), a revision of his *Les Femmes et le socialisme* (Paris, 1978); "Le Groupe féministe socialiste, 1899-1902," *Le Mouvement sociale* 90 (1975), 87-120; "The Organization of French Socialist Women, 1880-1914," *HR/RH* 3 (1976): 3-24; "Women and the Origins of the French Socialist Party," *TR/TR* 3-4 (1977): 104-127; and the work of Marilyn J. Boxer, "Socialism Faces Feminism in France, 1879-1913" (Ph.D. diss., University of California–Riverside, 1975), the chief arguments of which are recapitulated in her "Socialism Faces Feminism: The Failure of Synthesis in France, 1879-1914," in *Socialist Women*, ed. Boxer and Quataert, pp. 75-111; "French Socialism, Feminism and the Family," *TR/TR* 3-4 (1977): 128-67. See also Hélène Heinzely, "Le Mouvement socialiste devant les problèmes du féminisme, 1879-1914" (Thèse de doctorat, Paris, 1957).

17. Auclert, *Le Vote des femmes*, pp. 131, 136-37, 165; *Le Radical*, July 9, 1908 and May 2, 1908.

18. English texts of most documents discussed here may be found in Anderson, *Constitutions and Other Select Documents*, pp. 24, 61-66, 175, 215, 270, 342-45, 457, 507, 525-26. For French texts, the best source is J. B. Duvergier et al., eds., *Collection complète des lois, décrets, ordonnances, règlements, avis du Conseil d'Etat* (Paris, 1834 et seq.), 1:63-67; 3:239-55; 5:352-58; 7:233-42; 12:20-30; 15:1-12; 19:59-73; 30:110-14; 48:560-609.

19. Anderson, *Constitutions and Other Select Documents*, pp. 612 (quoted), 614, 625; Duvergier, *Collection complète des lois*, 71:42-53.

20. For such court cases see M. Dalloz and A. Dalloz (continued by others), eds., *Jurisprudence générale: Recueil périodique et critique de jurisprudence, de législation et de doctrine en matière civile, commerciale, criminelle, administrative et de droit public* (Paris, annual). Quotations from 1893, p. 555.

21. Bidelman, "The Feminist Movement in France," pp. 276, 374-78.

22. Claude Nicolet, *Le Radicalisme*, 2nd ed. (Paris, 1961), p. 42.

23. Albert Thibaudet, *Les Idées politiques de la France* (Paris, 1932), p. 124.

24. *La Patrie*, January 3, 1904.

25. Georges Renard, *Le Régime socialiste* (Paris, 1897), p. 109; italics in original.

26. *Le Radical*, July 17, 1907.

27. Ferdinand Buisson, *Le Vote des femmes* (Paris, 1911), pp. 330-31.

28. C. L. de Ferrer, *Pourquoi voteraient-elles?* (Paris, 1910), p. 4; Auclert, *Le Vote des femmes*, p. 34.

29. *La Citoyenne*, February 13, 1881; reprinted in Erna O. Hellerstein, Leslie P. Hume, and Karen M. Offen, eds., *Victorian Women: A Documentary Account of Women's Lives in Nineteenth Century England, France, and the United States* (Stanford, 1981), pp. 445-46.

30. Jules Michelet, *Le Prêtre, la femme, et la famille* [1845] (Paris, 1890), pp. 2, 266; italics in original.

31. Georges Clemenceau, *La "Justice" du sexe fort* (Paris, 1907), pp. 30-31.

32. Léon Richer, *La Femme libre* (Paris, 1877), p. 238.

33. *Le Combat féministe*, July 1914; italics added.

34. *Le Devoir des femmes françaises*, September 1906, p. 283.

35. *Le Radical*, June 30, 1908.

36. Alfred Fouilée, "La Psychologie des sexes et ses fondements physiologiques," *La Revue des deux mondes*, September 15, 1893, pp. 397-429.

37. France, Ministère du travail et de la prévoyance sociale, *Annuaire statistique (1909)* (Paris, 1910), résumé rétrospectif, p. 22 [hereafter cited in the form: *AS (1909)*]. *Le Radical*, March 5, 1907.

38. Joseph Reinach, as quoted by Buisson, *Le Vote des femmes*, p. 324.

39. See S. Margaret Fuller, *Woman in the Nineteenth Century* [1845] (Columbia, S.C., 1980), p. 136; quotations from Frederic Lees, "The Progress of Woman in France," *The Humanitarian*, February 1901, p. 88; Madeleine Pelletier, "French Feminism," *The Freewoman*, April 25, 1912, p. 451.

40. "The History of the Origins of the International Alliance of Women," Carrie Chapman Catt MSS, Box 7/Folder 10, New York Public Library.

41. See for examples: Theodore Zeldin, *France, 1848-1945*, 2 vols. (Oxford, 1973-1977), 1:346; Evans, *The Feminists, passim*; Ross E. Paulson, *Women's Suffrage and Prohibition: A Comparative Study of Equality and Social Control* (Glenview, Ill., 1973), pp. 43-54.

42. J.-C. Toutain, *La Population de la France de 1700 à 1959* (Paris, 1963), Table 18, p. 66.

43. The authors are indebted to Karen Offen of the Center for Research on Women at Stanford University for stressing to them the importance of depopulation in hampering French suffragism, and for sharing with them her "Depopulation, Nationalism, and French Feminism during the Belle Epoque," a paper presented to the Society for French Historical Studies, Bloomington, Indiana, March 1981. See also Joseph P. Spengler, *France Faces Depopulation* (Durham, N.C., 1938).

44. Data drawn from *AS (1909)*. For recent studies of some of these issues, see: Michael R. Marrus, "Social Drinking in the Belle Epoque," *Journal of Social History* 7 (1974): 120-218; John C. Hunter, "The Problem of the French Birth Rate on the Eve of World War I," *FHS* 2 (1962): 490-503; Angus

McLaren, "Abortion in France: Women and the Regulation of Family Size, 1800-1914," *FHS* 10 (1978): 461-85; Elisabeth A. Weston, "Prostitution in Paris in the Later Nineteenth Century: A Study in Politics and Social Ideology" (Ph.D. diss., State University of New York–Buffalo, 1979).

45. Buisson, *Le Vote des femmes*, p. 34. For a good introduction to the range of feminist concerns, see Karen Offen, "Aspects of the Woman Question during the Third Republic," *TR/TR* 3-4 (1977): 1-19, and her bibliographic essay, "The 'Woman Question' as a Social Issue in Nineteenth Century France," ibid., pp. 238-99. Offen is also the author of a helpful longer study, "The 'Woman Question' as a Social Issue in Republican France before 1914," which she has kindly permitted to circulate in *samizdat* form.

46. Dossier Union fraternelle des femmes, Bibliothèque Marguerite Durand [hereafter cited BMD].

47. For French women and the Napoleonic Code, see Zeldin, *France, 1848-1945*, 1:343-63; Albistur and Armogathe, *Histoire du féminisme français*, 1:359-64.

48. Jeanne Schmahl to [name illegible], January 30, 1895, Lettres Jeanne Schmahl, BMD.

49. See Guilbert, *Les Femmes et l'organisation syndicale*, p. 18.

50. For the development of female education in France, see the special issue of *Penelope, pour l'histoire des femmes* entitled "Education des filles, enseignement des femmes," 2 (1980); the special issue of *HR/RH* edited by Donald N. Baker and Patrick J. Harrigan, entitled "The Making of Frenchmen: Current Directions in the History of Education in France, 1679-1979," 7 (1980); Linda L. Clark, *Schooling the Daughters of Marianne: Textbooks and the Socialization of Girls in Modern French Primary Schools* (Albany, 1983); Antoine Prost, *Histoire de l'enseignement en France, 1800-1967* (Paris, 1968); Joseph N. Moody, *French Education since Napoleon* (Syracuse, 1978). Many of the most important documents are reproduced in P. Chevalier and B. Grosperrin, *L'Enseignement français de la révolution à nos jours*, 2 vols. (Paris, 1971).

51. *La Revue féministe* 1 (1895): 180.

52. Auclert, *Le Vote des femmes*, p. 109; and her *Les Femmes au gouvernail* (Paris, 1923), p. 107.

Chapter Two

1. *L'Entente*, May 1906; unidentified clipping entitled "Le Congrès féministe," Dossier Oddo-Deflou, BMD; *L'Abeille*, January 20, 1901.

2. For the resolutions of the congress, see *Voeux adoptés par le congrès féministe international, tenu à Paris en 1896 pendant les journées 8 au 12 avril* (Paris, n.d.); for the socialist-feminist controversies, Sowerwine, *Sisters or*

Citizens?, pp. 72-73; for the public controversy, Wyona H. Wilkins, "The Paris International Feminist Congress of 1896 and Its French Antecedents," *North Dakota Quarterly* 43 (1975): 5-28.

3. *L'Abeille*, January 20, 1901.

4. For the development of Catholic feminism from this congress, see Steven C. Hause and Anne R. Kenney, "The Development of the Catholic Women's Suffrage Movement in France, 1896-1922," *Catholic Historical Review* 67 (1981): 11-30. See the articles on the congress in Maugeret's *Le Féminisme chrétien* during 1900, especially her "Rapport sur la situation légale de la femme envisagée au point de vue chrétien," May 1900, pp. 139-44 (quoted); Abbé Paul Naudet, *Pour la femme: Etudes féministes* (Paris, 1903), pp. 46-47.

5. Avril de Sainte-Croix, unidentified clipping, Dossier Avril de Sainte-Croix, BMD; *Le Féminisme chrétien*, February 1904, p. 43.

6. Unidentified article by Jane Misme, Dossier Sarah Monod, BMD.

7. Dossier Congrès des oeuvres et institutions féminines, BMD.

8. See the coverage of the congress in *La Fronde* and the stenographic record of the assembly: Marie Pégard, ed., *Deuxième Congrès international des oeuvres et institutions féminines . . . tenu en juin 1900 au Palais des congrès . . .*, 4 vols. (Paris, 1902), esp. vol. 1, for legislative reports.

9. Marguerite Durand, ed., *Congrès international de la condition et des droits des femmes: Tenu à Paris du 5 au 8 septembre 1900: Procès-verbaux. . . .* (Paris, 1901); Dossier Congrès international de la condition et des droits des femmes, BMD, which contains Durand's scrapbook on the meeting; Dossier LFDF, BMD, which contains some correspondence. *La Fronde* gave encyclopedic coverage to the congress. Marie Bonnevial produced a thorough summary in *Le Mouvement socialiste*, October 15, 1900, pp. 503-08, and November 1, 1900, pp. 539-48. The motions adopted are reprinted in Comtesse Pierre Lecointre, *État de la question féministe en France en 1907* (Paris, 1907), pp. 20-24.

10. Emile Faguet, *Le Féminisme* (Paris, 1910), p. 167, quoting the Abbé Bolo. See also Naudet, *Pour la femme*, p. 46.

11. Durand, *Congrès international de la condition et des droits des femmes*, pp. 290-91. See the analysis of the issue in Sowerwine, *Sisters of Citizens?*, pp. 76-79; Boxer, "Feminism Faces Socialism," pp. 95-96.

12. See René Viviani, "Souvenirs anciens," in *Cinquante ans de féminisme, 1870-1920* (Paris, 1921), pp. 5-7; Jean Jolly, ed., *Dictionnaire des parlementaires français: Notices biographiques sur les ministres, députés, et sénateurs français de 1889 à 1940*, 8 vols. (Paris, 1960-1977), 8:3202-3204 [hereafter, *DPF*]; Maria Vérone's sketch of Viviani in *L'Oeuvre*, September 18, 1925; La Française, December 7, 1935; Dossier René Viviani, BMD.

13. Durand, *Congrès international de la condition et des droits des femmes*, pp. 195-205; *La Fronde*, September 10, 1900; René Viviani, "La Femme,"

La Grande Revue, February 1, 1901; *La Lanterne*, September 7, 1900; *La Femme*, April 15, 1901, pp. 57-62.

14. The BMD contains Durand's papers and voluminous materials on her life. Several French theses have been written from them, also available at the BMD. There is also an American dissertation: Sue H. Goliber, "The Life and Times of Marguerite Durand: A Study in French Feminism" (Ph.D. diss., Kent State University, 1975). See also her obituary in *La Française*, January 25, 1936.

15. Quoted by Micheline Morey in her speech to the LFDF, March 28, 1936; MSS in Dossier Marguerite Durand, BMD. See also *Le Figaro*, April 7, 1896.

16. For *La Fronde*, see the sources at the BMD and: Li, *La Presse féministe*, pp. 86-104; Evelyne Sullerot, *La Presse féminine* (Paris, 1963), pp. 38-44; Goliber, "The Life and Times of Marguerite Durand," pp. 13-49; Guilbert, *Les Femmes et l'organisation syndicale*, pp 229, 287-89. The encyclopedic *Histoire générale de la presse française* (Paris, 1972) by Claude Bellanger, Jacques Godechot, Pierre Guiral, and Fernand Terrou manages only one brief mention of *La Fronde* and a footnote in 2,000 pages of text: 3:366. For *La Fronde*'s role in the Dreyfus affair, see Joseph Reinach, *Histoire de l'affaire Dreyfus*, 7 vols. (Paris, 1903-1911), with numerous references of Durand and Séverine, e.g., 3:194-95.

17. For the development of *La Fronde*'s policy on women's suffrage, see the first issue (December 9, 1897), Auclert's article (December 13, 1897), and essays on May 27 and July 3, 1901. See also the Auclert-Durand correspondence at the BMD.

18. For Durand's relations with Catholic women, see Goliber, "The Life and Times of Marguerite Durand," pp. 29-31; Naudet, *Pour la femme*, p. 45.

19. Madeleine Pelletier's diary, August 29, 1914, Dossier Pelletier, BMD. See also *La Fronde*, March 28, 1901; Guilbert, *Les Femmes et l'organisation syndicale*, pp. 295, 401; Li, *La Presse féministe*, pp. 138-39.

20. The delicate question of Durand's sexual life cannot be ignored. She was a beautiful woman, with striking blonde hair, a voluptuous figure, an expensive and stylish wardrobe, well-trained diction, and an unabashedly seductive manner—all of which earned her the label of "the dazzler" (*l'éblouissante*). Durand was discreet and did not flaunt her belief in free love, but neither did she seek to hide it. With a little deviltry, she remarked on more than one occasion, "feminism owes much to my blonde hair." (Quoted by Morey in her memorial speech, MSS in Dossier Durand, BMD.) While at *Le Figaro*, she was the lover of a senior editor, Antonin Périvier, an affair publicly acknowledged when she bore his illegitimate son, Jacques Périvier. Thereafter, the evidence is insufficient. Durand's lovers almost certainly

included René Viviani, quite possibly included Joseph Caillaux, and, it was bruited at the time (certainly with less plausibility), Kaiser Wilhelm II of Germany. It appears likely, although unproven, that her lover(s) were the secret financiers of *La Fronde*. Durand, after all, was an illegitimate child unrecognized by her father and without any inheritance, the divorced wife of a destitute and failed politician, and a person whose only known source of income was from journalism. Somehow she lived as one of the richer women of the feminist movement, personally financing *La Fronde* (which lost a good deal of money) and many other feminist projects.

Harlor, Durand's close associate and successor at the BMD, admitted Durand's long affair with Viviani. Shortly before her death, however, Durand destroyed the love letters and other evidence of her intimate life, including a large correspondence with both Viviani and Caillaux. Caillaux, whose own sexual life figures prominently in prewar French history, wrote letters "deliciously full of heart and affection" according to Harlor. According to the present director of the BMD, Madame Léautey, Durand was also "linked with" (*liée*) other prominent politicians. Rumors about the Kaiser existed because Durand frequently visited Berlin, and Wilhelm escorted her to the theater; she, in turn, wrote flattering articles about him and Germany in both *La Fronde* and *Les Nouvelles*. For more discussion of this aspect of Durand's life, see Goliber, "The Life and Times of Marguerite Durand," pp. 33-34, 47-49; Goliber suggests that Durand considered sexual freedom "was an indication of true liberation" (pp. 48-49). Only the evidence of Harlor's testimony survives in the Dossier Durand, BMD.

For the adverse effect of Durand's behavior on her relations with other feminists, see the correspondence in the Bouglé Collection at the Bibliothèque historique de la Ville de Paris [hereafter, BHVP]. Auclert, for example, wrote to Arria Ly after the feminist electoral campaigns of 1910, proud that she could "muster more votes than Mme. Marguerite Durand seconded by the press and a regiment of lovers" (April 27, 1910). Madeleine Pelletier referred to her as a "demimondaine" feminist (Pelletier to Arria Ly, October 6, 1911). See also the comments of Caroline Kauffmann (Kauffmann to Arria Ly, May 17, 1912).

21. For Bogelot's role in the international council before France joined, see the materials on the London congress of 1899 in the Charlotte Perkins Gilman MSS, Box 1/Folder 6, Schlesinger Library. For the Conférence de Versailles and the origins of the CNFF, see: International Council of Women, *Histories of the Affiliated Councils, 1888-1938* (Brussels, 1938), p. 121; *La Française*, June 3, 1922; Dossiers Sarah Monod and Julie Siegfried, BMD; *La Femme*, during the 1890s.

22. *Le Féminisme chrétien*, August 1900, pp. 225-28.

23. Avril de Sainte-Croix, *Le Féminisme* (Paris, 1907), pp. 173-75.

24. For Auclert's relationship with the CNFF, see *Minerva*, October 19, 1930; Oddo-Deflou to Auclert, December 25, 1901, CP 4248, BHVP. For Kauffmann and the CNFF, see Sowerwine, *Les Femmes et le socialisme*, p. 127. See also *Le Journal des femmes*, May 1901.

25. For the foundation of the CNFF, see International Council of Women, *Histories of the Affiliated Councils*, pp. 121-22; Lecointre, *Etat de la question féministe en France*, pp. 17-18 (reprinting CNFF resolutions); *Journal officiel de la république française*, [hereafter, *JO*], Chambre des députés, documents, October 23, 1901; statutes of the CNFF and brochure, "CNFF," in the Dossier CNFF, BMD; Marie de La Hire, "Le Féminisme en France et les sociétés féministes," *La Revue des lettres*, August 1907, pp. 3-22; *La Femme*, March 15, 1901, pp. 42-43.

26. Zeldin, *France, 1848-1945*, 1:346; italics added.

27. Madeleine Pelletier to Arria Ly, October 19, 1911, Bouglé Collection, BHVP.

28. Estimates of size are based on the publications of each group, the dossiers on organizations at the BMD and the BHVP, and police reports in the Archives du Préfecture de Police [hereafter, APP]. For examples: the highest reported attendance at any meeting of Action sociale in the first years was approximately two hundred for a lecture by Ferdinand Brunetière in 1903 (*Le Féminisme chrétien*, January 1904); reports of the meetings of Solidarité, including the names of participants, were published in the *Journal des femmes* each month, and forty-nine different names were given during the year; the police agent within Suffrage des femmes reported a highest attendance of nearly one hundred (agent's reports, Dossier Vote des femmes, B^A 1651, APP).

29. Sainte-Croix, *Le Féminisme*, p. 178. For feminist concern with the situation in the provinces, see the column "En Province" (title varies) in the *Journal des femmes*, and "Le Mouvement féministe" in *La Française*. See also: Steven C. Hause, "The Failure of Feminism in Provincial France, 1890-1920," *PWSFH* 8 (1982): 423-36.

30. Charles Dawbarn, "The French Woman and the Vote," *Fortnightly Review*, August 1911.

31. Jean Maitron, for example, has studied the social character of 115 women convicted for their rolé during the Commune. He found the overwhelming majority (83 percent) to be from the working class. See the discussion of this in Louise A. Tilly, "Women's Collective Action and Feminism in France, 1870-1914," in *Class Conflict and Collective Action*, ed. Louise A. Tilly and Charles Tilly (Beverly Hills, Calif., 1981), p. 219.

32. This argument is discussed in Chapter Four; for further development, see Steven C. Hause and Anne R. Kenney, "The Limits of Suffragist Be-

havior: Legalism and Militancy in France, 1876-1922," *AHR* 86 (1981): 781-806.

33. Zeldin, *France, 1848-1945*, 1:345.

34. Bidelman compiled a roster of the LFDF at the time of its reestablishment in 1882-1883; of 194 initial members, 96 were men: "The Feminist Movement in France," pp. 276-77 and Appendix H, pp. 374-78. See also Dawbarn's 1911 assertion that "one of the most significant facts about the movement is that men are more bent upon it than women," in his "The Feminist Movement in France," p. 329; and Sainte-Croix's 1910 remark that men are "sometimes more feminist than we are" in an unidentified article in the Dossier Avril de Sainte-Croix, BMD. Auclert noted the difference in signatures on petitions in a letter to Arria Ly, November 3, 1909, Bouglé Collection, BHVP.

35. Société pour l'amélioration du sort de la femme, *Bulletin*, May-August 1900, pp. 95-96; *Le Journal des femmes*, 1902, *passim*; police reports on Suffrage des femmes, Dossier Vote des femmes, B^A 1651, APP.

36. The most explicit rejection of men in the feminist leadership was by Etudes, whose statutes invited male members but denied them office; see the Dossier Oddo-Deflou, BMD. See also Séverine's discussion of a similar policy in the UFSF, in an unidentified article in the Dossier Congrès national de l'UFSF (Lyon, 1914), BMD; and the statutes of the CNFF for their restrictions. For a harsh judgment of this problem, see J. F. McMillan, "The Character of the French Feminist Movement, 1870-1914," in *Actes du colloque franco-britannique tenu à Bordeaux du 27 au 30 septembre 1976: Sociétés et groupes sociaux en Aquitaine et en Angleterre*, ed. Fédération historique du sud-ouest (Bordeaux, 1979), pp. 260-61; Théodore Joran, *Le Suffrage des femmes* (Paris, 1913), p. 72. For interesting feminist reflections on male supporters, see the letters of Pelletier to Arria Ly, esp. August 22 and October 19, 1911, Bouglé Collection, BHVP.

37. Membership lists for the LFDF and an attendance list for the 1889 congress are reproduced by Bidelman, "The Feminist Movement in France," Appendices H, I, J, pp. 374-86. Data for Solidarité are compiled from the reports of meetings in *Le Journal des femmes* and police reports in the APP. Data for *La Française*'s circle are from MacMillan, "The Character of the French Feminist Movement," p. 261. Identifications of leaders are based on the dossiers at the BMD and the BHVP, plus obituaries. Maitron's study found that the overwhelming majority of the women of the Commune were married. Quotation from Léon Abensour, *Histoire générale du féminisme: Des origines à nos jours* (Paris, 1921), p. 280.

38. Auclert, *Les Femmes au gouvernail*, pp. 2-3; *L'Entente*, December, 1905.

39. There is much biographical material on Auclert in her books and in the dossiers at the BMD, BHVP, and APP; her papers survive at the BHVP.

For contemporary sketches of her, see: *Minerva*, October 19, 1930; *Le Féminisme intégral*, April 1913; *La Française*, April 18, 1914; *Les Nouvelles*, April 10, 1914; *La Voix des femmes*, May 18, 1930; *La Lumière*, February 16, 1935. For longer examinations, see: Bidelman, *Pariahs Stand Up!* pp. 106-54; Edith Taïeb's preface to Auclert, *La Citoyenne, 1848-1914* (Paris, 1982), pp. 7-53.

40. For biographies of Vincent, see: *Le National*, July 1900; Amélioration, *Bulletin*, September-October 1903, pp. 373-74; UFSF, *Bulletin annuel-1911*, pp. 15-16; *La Française*, February 28, 1914; *L'Aurore*, March 1, 1914; *Le Jour*, March 3, 1914; *La Femme de demain*, March 1914; *Le Droit des femmes*, March 15, 1914, p. 53; Dossiers Eliska Vincent, BMD and BHVP.

41. For the early years of Solidarité, see Sowerwine, *Sisters or Citizens?*, pp. 68-75; *La Française*, February 20, 1937; Dossier Maria Martin, BMD; Dossier Natalie Lemel, Bouglé Collection, BHVP. For Kauffmann and Solidarité, see: the regular column "Le Vote des femmes" in *Le Journal des femmes; Le Gaulois*, May 19, 1906; Pelletier's reminiscences in *La Fronde*, December 29, 1926; *L'Entente*, May 1906; Dossier Caroline Kauffmann, BMD; Kauffmann-Arria Ly correspondence, Bouglé Collection, BHVP; Sowerwine, *Sisters or Citizens?*, pp. 112-16.

42. There are several sources, some quite moving, for Pelletier's biography. Her dossier at the BMD contains a brief diary and a poignant fragment of an autobiography which she dictated while incarcerated in an asylum in 1939. Her correspondence with Arria Ly, at the BHVP, is very candid, discussing such matters as her asexuality. Her voluminous writings include scientific publications, a remarkable range of feminist and socialist works, and an autobiographical novel (*La Femme vierge*, 1933). For further information on Pelletier, see *Le Droit des femmes*, November 29, 1923; Sowerwine, *Sisters or Citizens?*, pp. 110-28; Boxer, Socialism Faces Feminism," pp. 98-105; Claude Maignien's preface to the volume of Pelletier's reprinted writings, *L'Education féministe des filles et autres textes* (Paris, 1978), pp. 7-55.

43. It was Freemasonry that first drew Pelletier into politics. Masonry had been indirectly open to women since Maria Deraismes joined a lodge in 1882. Masons, however, shared the republican prejudice against the admission of women to political life. Hence, the lodge that had initiated Deraismes was closed and a policy of excluding women from the order maintained. In 1893, Deraismes and Senator Georges Martin founded Droit humain, the first of a series of "mixed lodges" which admitted women. Pelletier joined in the battle to open all of masonry to women.

The best source for the history of women in masonry is Georges Martin's monthly (later, quarterly) *Bulletin mensuel de la maçonnerie mixte*, founded in 1895; see for example, the sketches of Martin in March-April 1919 and of Deraismes in April-June 1921. Much of the argument about the admission of women, including Pelletier's role, can be found in the regular masonic publication, *L'Acacia*; see, for example, Pelletier's articles in May 1905 and June 1906. In addition, the question spawned numerous articles and pamphlets; see: Charles Malato, *L'Admission de la femme dans la franc-maçonnerie* (Paris, n.d.); Dr. Lobit, *De l'admission de la femme dans la franc-maçonnerie* (Paris, n.d.). For a history of the question, see: Elaine Brault, *La Franc-maçonnerie et l'émancipation des femmes* (Paris, 1954). For further discussion of Pelletier's role, Sowerwine, *Sisters or Citizens?*, p. 112. For the founding membership of mixed masonry, see Gerard Serbanesco, *Histoire de la Franc-maçonnerie universelle*, 4 vols. (Paris, 1969), 4:542-45; *Le Devoir des femmes françaises*, May 1911, p. 926; the authors are indebted to Patrick K. Bidelman for sharing these sources on membership with them.

44. Pelletier's account of becoming secretary-general of Solidarité is given in *La Fronde*, August 17, 1926.

45. See Pelletier's foremost feminist work, *La Femme en lutte pour ses droits* (Paris, 1908), esp. pp. 41-44; see also her *La Question du vote des femmes* (Paris, 1909).

46. Madeleine Pelletier, *Le Droit à l'avortement: Pour l'abrogation de l'article 317* (Paris, 1913), p. 15; this pamphlet is a chapter from Pelletier's *L'Emancipation sexuelle de la femme* (Paris, 1911).

47. This interpretation of Pelletier was first developed by Anne R. Kenney in her paper "A Militant Feminist in France: Dr. Madeleine Pelletier, Her Ideas and Actions" (Read at the Fourth Berkshire Conference on the History of Women, Mount Holyoke College, August 1978). Madeleine Pelletier, "Les Suffragettes anglaises se virilisent," *La Suffragiste*, October 1912. For the development of these ideas, see other writings by Pelletier: *L'Amour et maternité* (Paris, n.d.); *La Désagrégation de la famille* (Paris, n.d.); *La Droit au travail pour la femme* (Paris, n.d.); *L'Emancipation sexuelle de la femme*; *Philosophie sociale: Les Opinions, les partis, les classes* (Paris, 1912). Most of these titles are available at the BMD; excerpts from several are included in *L'Education féministe des filles*.

48. Pelletier, *La Femme en lutte pour ses droits*, p. 39; Pelletier, "Le Féminisme et ses militants," *Les Documents du progrès*, July 1909, p. 23; masthead quotation of *La Lutte féministe; La Suffragiste*, January 1912.

49. For Maria Martin, see *Le Journal des femmes*, especially the memorial issue of January 1911; *La Française*, February 20, 1937; *Bulletin mensuel de la maçonnerie mixte*, January 1911; *L'Action féminine*, January 1911; Dossier Maria Martin, BMD; Dossier Maria Martin and Martin-Arria Ly Correspondence, Bouglé Collection, BHVP. For her suffragism, see *Le Journal des femmes*, especially March 1900 and August-September 1901.

50. For Maria Pognon, see: LFDF, *Cinquante ans de féminisme*, pp. 75-76; anonymous manuscript biography in the Dossier Maria Pognon, BMD; *Minerva*, August 16, 1925; Dossier Maria Pognon, Bouglé Collection, BHVP.

51. For Bonnevial, see: LFDF, *Cinquante ans de féminisme*, pp. 78-81; *Le Droit des femmes*, February 1919, pp 21-26; *La Française*, December 14, 1918; Dossiers Bonnevial, BMD and BHVP. For her socialism, see Sowerwine, *Sisters or Citizens?*, pp. 72-76. For her syndicalism and a bibliography of her columns in *La Fronde*, see Guilbert, *Les Femmes et l'organisation syndicale*, pp. 151-52, 165, 177-78, 196, 287-95.

52. The best source for Vérone is the memorial issue of *Le Droit des femmes*, June 1938, esp. pp. 83-86. See also: her columns in *La Fronde*, particularly February-March 1901, and *L'Oeuvre*; *La Française*, June 4, 1938; *Minerva*, June 5, 1938; *Le Temps*, May 25, 1938; Dossiers Vérone, BMD and BHVP.

53. Statutes of Amélioration, Dossier Amélioration, BMD; *Le Radical*, June 19, 1900; Amélioration, *Bulletin*, November-December 1899, p. 28; January-April 1900, p. 36; unidentified biography of Feresse-Deraismes, Dossier Feresse-Deraismes, BMD; *Bulletin mensuel de la maçonnerie mixte*, January 1910, pp. 165-67.

54. For Schmahl, see: *La Française*, January 24, 1909; UFSF, *Bulletin 1914-1916*, p. 78; *Minerva*, October 26, 1930; *L'Entente*, January 1906; *Le Temps*, March 16, 1913; *L'Eclair*, November 17, 1896. For d'Uzès, see her *Souvenirs* (Paris, 1939), and: Jean Puget, *La Duchesse d'Uzès*, 2nd ed. (Uzès, 1972); Duchesse d'Uzès, "Comment j'ai connu le général Boulanger," *Revue des deux mondes*, February 15, 1939; *Le Journal*, February 4, 1933; *Le Temps*, February 11, 1933; Jane Misme, "Madame la Duchesse d'Uzès," *Revue bleue*, August 17, 1897, pp. 178-81; Dossier Duchesse d'Uzès, BMD. For Adam, see *La Nouvelle Revue*, which she founded and edited; her *Idées anti-proudhoniennes sur l'amour, la femme, et le mariage* (Paris, 1858); her *Mes souvenirs*, 7 vols. (Paris, 1902-1910), esp. vol. 7; and Winifred Stephens, *Madame Adam (Juliette Lamber), La Grande Française: From Louis-Philippe until 1917*, 2nd ed. (New York, 1917), quoted, p. 244. For Misme, see her articles in *La Française* and *Minerva*; Dossier Jane Misme, Bouglé Collection, BHVP; *Les Nouvelles*, January 25, 1914; Jane Misme to *Le Journal*, published there on March 22, 1914 (quoted). The Misme collection, given to the city of Paris and subsequently divided, survives in part at the Trocadero Library; it contains no manuscripts.

55. Madeleine Pelletier to Arria Ly, October 6, 1911, Bouglé Collection, BHVP.

56. There are few biographical sources for Oddo-Deflou beyond her dossier at the BMD. See her *Le Sexualisme: Critique de la préponderance et de la mentalité du sexe fort* (Paris, 1906) and discussion of it in *Le Radical*, March 11, 1906, and *Les Annales de l'Ariège*, April 15, 1906. For her contacts with many diverse groups, see their journals; e.g., *Le Féminisme chrétien*, November 1901. For her conservatism in conflict with militants, see *La Française*,

November 10, 1907. For Etudes, see the folder, Groupe français d'études féministes, in the Dossier Groupements femmes (divers), BMD; a brochure, *Groupe français d'études féministes* (Paris, n.d.) in the Dossier Oddo-Deflou, BMD; *La Femme*, June 15-July 15, 1901, October 1904; Lecointre, *Etat de la question féministe en France*, p. 19; *La Française*, February 10, 1907; *Bulletin mensuel de la maçonnerie mixte*, February 1903.

57. For Marbel, see: *Le Féminisme intégral*, October 1913, May-June 1914; Dossier Marbel, Bouglé Collection, BHVP. For the UFF, see the Dossier UFF, BMD, which includes the statutes of the group and a brief history; the group's *Petit almanach féministe illustré*, 1907, p. 33 quoted; Dossier UFF, Bouglé Collection, BHVP, which includes a note by Marbel dated March 5, 1926, explaining her policy. For Martial: *Le Féminisme intégral*, January 1914; *La Française*, May 18, 1929; *L'Heure de la femme*, March 1929; Dossiers on Martial at both the BMD and the BHVP; her *La Femme intégral* (Paris, 1901).

58. Héra Mirtel, "Féminisme mondial," *Les Documents du progrès*, May 1910, p. 436.

59. For Monod, see: *La Française*, December 12, 1912; *L'Action féminine*, December 1911; Dossiers Monod, BMD and BHVP. For Siegfried: *La Française*, June 3, 1922; *Minerva*, November 16, 1930; *The Woman Citizen*, August 26, 1922; *International Women's Suffrage News*, July 1922; *La Femme*, June 1, 1903; Dossiers Julie Siegfried, BMD and BHVP. For Sainte-Croix; her *Le Féminisme; Minerva*, November 30, 1930; *La Française*, April 8, 1939; Dossiers Avril de Sainte-Croix, BMD and BHVP; and especiallly her multivolume scrapbook at the Musée social.

60. Marie d'Abbadie d'Arrast (1837-1913), the first president of the legislative section, was the wife of a wealthy southern landowner whose interest in penal reform had led her to the Conférence de Versailles. (See *La Femme*, December 1932, January-April 1933; *L'Action féminine*, August 1913; *La Française*, September 6, 1913.) Gabrielle Alphen-Salvador (1856-1920), the first head of the hygiene section, was the daughter of a wealthy Touraine family and the founder of a nursing school. (See: *La Française*, September 8, 1907 and November 22, 1908.) The heads of the labor section, Madame Léon Pégard, and charity section, Madame Weill, were both active in the Conférence de Versailles. Indeed, the only exception to the domination of the CNFF by women of charity was the head of the education section, Pauline Kergomard (1838-1925), who was a working teacher; the daughter of one of Guizot's school inspectors of the 1830s, Kergomard came to prominence through a brilliant career in education. (See: Dossier Kergomard, BMD.)

61. Emile Darnaud, quoted in *La Française*, May 9, 1914. For the situation of women in rural France, see: Eugen Weber, *Peasants into Frenchmen: The*

Modernization of Rural France, 1870-1914 (Stanford, 1976), esp. pp. 171-75; Pierre-Jakez Hélias, *The Horse of Pride: Life in a Breton Village* (New Haven, 1978) [trans. of *Le Cheval d'orgueil* (Paris, 1975)], esp. pp. 136-37.

62. For Laguerre and the Société d'éducation, see: Laguerre, *Qu'est-ce que le féminisme?* (Lyons, 1899); *Lyon républicain*, May 17, 1904; *La Femme affranchie*, August 1904; *Les Annales de l'Ariège*, February 12, 1905; *La Fronde*, March 1905; *L'Entente*, June 1905 and June 1906; Dossier Féminisme–France, 1900-1909, BMD; Antonin Choquency, *L'Emancipation de la femme au commencement du XXe siècle* (Lyons, 1902). For the Margueritte brothers, see their many novels, such as Paul's *Nous, les mères*, 2nd ed. (Paris, 1914); their many political essays, such as Paul and Victor's *L'Elargissement du divorce— exposé des motifs et proposition de loi* (Paris, 1902). For their feminism, see: Abensour, *Histoire générale du féminisme*, p. 276; Auclert, *Les Femmes au gouvernail*, p. 123; *La Patrie*, May 7, 1906; *Le Journal*, May 24, 1906; *Le Radical*, November 23, 1907; *Le Journal des femmes*, August-September 1907 and February 1908; *La Française*, January 11, 1919, *L'Humanité*, January 7, 1923; Dossier Victor Margueritte, Bouglé Collection, BHVP.

63. For Darnaud and his group, see: his columns in *Les Annales de l'Ariège; La Fronde*, March 1905; *Le Journal des femmes*, February 13, 1908; *Le Féministe*, December 9, 1909 and February 26, 1911; *La Française*, May 9 and November 15, 1914.

64. The authors wish to thank Yvette Kirby for access to her "Development and Limits of Catholic Social Action in France: The Case of Lyon, 1871-1905" (Ph.D. diss., Harvard University, 1980), pp. 241-45 for Rochebillard. For a broad discussion of liberal Catholicism and the labor movement, see also Parker T. Moon, *The Labor Problem and the Social Catholic Movement in France: A Study in the History of Social Politics* (New York, 1921). For the best recent study of social Catholicism, see Benjamin F. Martin, *Court Albert de Mun: Paladin of the Third Republic* (Chapel Hill, N.C., 1978), which includes a thorough bibliography. For examples of the Catholic interest in the woman question, see Comte d'Haussonville, *Salaires et misères de femmes* (Paris, 1900); Etienne Lamy, *La Femme de demain* (Paris, 1901); A. D. Sertillanges, *Féminisme et christianisme* (Paris, 1908); Naudet, *Pour la femme*; Comtesse Marie de Villermont, *Le Mouvement féministe*, 2 vols. (Paris, 1904).

65. The authors wish to thank Odille Sarti of Indiana University for sharing information and ideas concerning the Ligue patriotique from her forthcoming Ph.D. dissertation, tentatively entitled "La Ligue patriotique des françaises: A Feminine Response to the Secularization of French Society (1901-1933)."

66. For example, an LPF demonstration at Brest in 1903 drew 30,000 participants. By 1906, the LPF numbered 320,000 members, organized in

365 committees at the *arrondissement* level. For more information, see their bulletin, *Echo de la ligue patriotique des françaises*.

67. Ibid., July 1903, p. 200.

68. For the LPF, see the *Echo* and: Martin, *Count Albert de Mun*, pp. 161, 195; Madeleine Rigollot-Converset, *Louise de Hamayde, 1877-1954: Une Animatrice, une vaillante, une modeste* (Troyes, 1956), p. 14; Abbé Stephen Coubé, *Le Patriotisme de la femme française* (Paris, 1916), pp. 12-13; Dossier Groupements catholique (divers), BMD.

69. Dossier Marie Maugeret, Bouglé Collection, BHVP; *La Croix*, August 19, 1923; *Le Féminisme chrétien*, December 1901, p. 355.

70. *Le Féminisme chrétien*, August 1897, p. 119; Li, *La Presse féministe*, p. 145.

71. For an illustration of Maugeret's conservative-nationalist politics, see *Le Féminisme chrétien*, November 1901, pp. 321-30, urging women to remember their power as a conservative influence: "Remember Panama! Remember Fashoda! Remember the Dreyfus affair! Remember the Congregations!" (p. 330) For a good illustration of her feminism, ibid., May 1900, pp. 139-48.

72. The authors are indebted to Patrick K. Bidelman for sharing his paper on right-wing feminism in France. For Copin-Albancelli, see his *Le Pouvoir occulte* (Paris, 1902) and *La Conjuration juive* (Paris, n.d.).

73. For Action sociale, see: Dossier Action sociale de la femme, BHVP; Folder Action sociale de la femme in Dossier Groupements femmes (divers), BMD; anonymous, *Action sociale de la femme* (Angers, 1935), esp. pp. 3-6; the group's bulletin, also entitled *Action sociale de la femme*, esp. January-February 1919, p. 137; April 1920, pp. 50-55; October 1909, p. 375; *Le Journal des femmes*, January 1902; *Le Féminisme chrétien*, December 1901, p. 383; March 1904, pp. 59-60.

74. Wilkins, "The Paris International Feminist Congress of 1896," p. 25.

75. Renaud quotation from Sowerwine, *Les Femmes et le socialisme*, p. 90; Saumoneau quotation from Boxer, "Socialism Faces Feminism," p. 94. In addition to these works, see *La Femme socialiste*; Saumoneau's pamphlets, especially *Principes et action féministes socialistes* (Paris, n.d.); Dossier Renaud, BMD.

76. *Le Petit sou*, October 19, 1900, as quoted by Sowerwine, "The Organization of French Socialist Women," p. 10. For the foundation and character of the GFS, see Sowerwine, "Le Groupe feministe socialiste, 1899-1902," pp. 87-120; Sowerwine, *Sisters or Citizens?*, pp. 81-104; the statutes of the group, published in *La Femme socialiste*, March 1901; Saumoneau's series of articles under the heading "Féminisme socialiste," ibid., 1901-1902.

77. Guesde as quoted by Leslie Derfler, *Alexandre Millerand, the Socialist Years* (The Hague, 1977), p. 156; Millerand in *La Petite république*, March

15, 1903, quoted ibid., p. 221. In addition to Derfler's account of the Millerand case, see Aaron Noland, *The Founding of the French Socialist Party, 1893-1905* (Cambridge, Mass., 1956), pp. 86-114; Claude Willard, *Les Guesdistes: Le Mouvement socialiste en France, 1893-1905* (Paris, 1965), pp. 422-38; Harvey Goldberg, *The Life of Jean Jaurès* (Madison, 1962), pp. 249-59.

78. *Le Radical*, September 3, 1907.

79. *La Femme socialiste*, September 1, 1913 (quoted). For pro-suffragism in *La Femme socialiste*, see the issue of July 1901. For the events of 1900, see Sowerwine, *Sisters or Citizens?*, pp. 75-79. For Bonnevial's appeal for collaboration, see *Le Mouvement socialiste*, November 1, 1900.

Chapter Three

1. *La Lanterne*, September 11, 1900; Viviani, "La Femme," pp. 344-50.

2. *AS (1909)*, résumé rétrospectif, p. 13.

3. *Le Radical*, March 18, 1901 and July 9, 1901; *La Petite république*, May 27, 1901; Auclert, *Le Vote des femmes*, pp. 40-41. Cf. the feelings of moderate feminists about Viviani's articles: *La Femme*, April 15, 1901, pp. 57-62.

4. *Le Radical*, March 7, 1900 and July 9, 1901; Auclert, *Le Vote des femmes*, p. 178; *JO*, Chambre, débats, July 1, 1901; Gautret's text and note, C 5659/ Dossier 1736, Archives nationales [hereafter, AN]; *La Liberté*, May 29, 1901; Jean Le Couteulx du Molay, *Les Droits politiques de la femme* (Paris, 1913), pp. 279-80; Dossier Hubertine Auclert, Bouglé Collection, BHVP.

5. *JO*, Chambre, Débats, July 1, 1901; *JO*, Chambre, documents, No. 2529 (1901); *DPF*, 6:1798-99; Minutes of the Commission of Universal Suffrage, C 7375, AN.

6. Minutes of the Commission of Universal Suffrage, C 7375, AN.

7. *La Femme socialiste*, August 1901; *La Fronde*, July 7, 1901; *Le Journal des femmes*, August-September 1901; Maria Vérone, *Appel à la justice: Addressé par le CNFF à la Chambre des Députés et la Sénat* (Paris, n.d. [1909]), p. 11.

8. Police reports of Suffrage des femmes meetings, April 26, 1904 and May 14, 1904, Dossier Vote des femmes, B^A 1651, APP; Elizabeth C. Stanton, Susan B. Anthony et al., *The History of Woman Suffrage*, 6 vols. (Rochester, N.Y., 1881-1922), 4:23, 27; Evans, *The Feminists*, pp. 204, 251; Edward T. James, ed., *Notable American Women, 1607-1950. A Biographical Dictionary*, 3 vols. (Cambridge, Mass., 1971), 1:312 (Catt); manuscript, "A History of the International Alliance of Women," Catt MSS, Box 7/Folder 10, New York Public Library.

9. *Le Radical*, July 16, 1902; *La Fronde*, July 1, 1904.

10. See Catt's manuscript on the founding of the IWSA, Catt MSS, Box 7/Folder 10, New York Public Library. For her anti-Catholicism, Evans, *The Feminists*, pp. 204, 251; for a discussion of such attitudes in the context of

American suffragism, see Aileen S. Kraditor, *The Ideas of the Woman Suffrage Movement, 1890-1920* (Garden City, N.Y., 1971), chap. 6.

11. Auclert to Durand, June 17, 1904, Dossier Congrès 1904, BMD; *Le Radical*, July 5, 1904. See also the reports on the congress by German feminists in *Die Frauenbewegung* and the *Zentralblatt des Bundes deutscher Frauenvereine*, esp. for June 1, 1904. Copies of these materials may be found in the papers of American feminists who attended. See the Gilman MSS, Box 1/Folder 7, and the Allen MSS, Box 1/Folder 5, both at the Schlesinger Library.

12. *Le Temps*, October 29 and 30, 1904; *La Femme affranchie*, August 1904; *Le Journal des femmes*, October 1904; *La Fronde*, October 1, 1904 and November 1, 1904; Laguerre-Durand correspondence for 1904, Dossier Marguerite Durand à l'Action, BMD; Laguerre's preface to Nelly Roussel, *Trois conférences* (Paris, 1930), p. 11.

13. Minutes of the meeting of Solidarité, October 18, 1904, Dossier Caroline Kauffmann, Bouglé Collection, BHVP; police reports of October 15 (quoted), 27, and 30, 1904, Dossier Vote des femmes, B^A 1651, APP; *Le Radical*, August 29 and November 5, 1904; *Le Journal des femmes*, October 1904; *La Femme de demain*, March 1914; Caroline Kauffmann to Arria Ly, September 13, 1904 and May 28, 1913, Bouglé Collection, BHVP; handbills in the Dossier Hubertine Auclert, BMD.

14. Jeanne Oddo-Deflou, ed., *Congrès national des droits civils et du suffrage des femmes* (Paris, 1908), p. 11; *Le Journal des femmes*, January 1905; *La Fronde*, August 17, 1926; *L'Entente*, May 1906; Dossiers Caroline Kauffmann, BMD and BHVP.

15. *JO*, Documents, December 3, 1904; Sainte-Croix, *Le Féminisme*, pp. 168-69.

16. *Le Radical*, January 3 and April 15, 1902; *L'Aurore*, June 21, 1904; *L'Abeille*, February 1, 1901; Dossier Vote des femmes, 1900-1908, BMD.

17. *Le Radical*, April 21, 1906; *La Femme*, May 1906; *L'Entente*, May 1906, *Le Journal*, May 24, 1906; *La Femme contemporaine*, March 1907; *Le Petit almanach féministe illustré–1907*, pp. 14-15; Auclert, *Les Femmes au gouvernail*, p. 71; brochure on Amélioration, Dossier Amélioration, BMD.

18. For the rally and parade of 1906, see: *L'Humanité*, May 19, 1906; *L'Eclair*, May 22, 1906; *Le Radical*, June 11, 1906 (quoted) and June 25, 1906; Dossier Vote des femmes, 1900-1908, BMD; Dossier Caroline Kauffmann, Bouglé Collection, BHVP; clippings in the scrapbook "L'Opinion de la presse sur Madame Hubertine Auclert et le féminisme, 1876-1914," Bouglé Collection, BHVP; Dossier Manifestations, B^A 1651, APP.

19. *La Voix des femmes*, January 13, 1927; *La Fronde*, October 17, 1926; *L'Autorité*, June 4, 1906; *Le Radical*, June 11, 1906; Dossiers Caroline Kauffmann, BMD and BHVP.

20. For Pelletier's role in French socialism at this time, see Sowerwine, *Sisters or Citizens?*, pp. 110-28; Boxer, "Socialism Faces Feminism," pp. 100-105.

21. *The Times* (London), December 24, 1906; *La Française*, December 30, 1906; *L'Eclair*, January 4, 1907; *Le Journal des femmes*, January 1907; *L'Humanité*, December 22-24, 1906.

22. *Le Petit almanach féministe–1908*, pp. 22-23; *Le Radical*, June 18, 1907; *La Française*, June 23, 1907; Evans, *The Feminists*, p. 193.

23. See Pelletier's correspondence with Arria Ly, especially letters of August 22, October 6, and October 19, 1911, Bouglé Collection, BHVP.

24. Pelletier to Arria Ly, August 22, 1911, Bouglé Collection, BHVP.

25. The conservative aspects of Maugeret's activities have been developed in Bidelman's paper, "Right-Wing Feminism in France."

26. *Le Féminisme chrétien*, January 1903, pp. 1-2; February 1904, pp. 27-31; April 1904, p. 88; January 1905, pp. 1-2; *Le Journal des femmes*, June 1904, Lecointre, *Etat de la question féministe en France*, p. 15; *Le Devoir des femmes françaises*, January 1906, p. 15.

27. *La Femme contemporaine*, October 1903, pp. 6-15; Abbé Henry Bolo, *La Femme et le clergé* (Paris, 1902); Emile Faguet, "L'Abbé féministe," *Revue bleue*, 4th ser., 17 (1902): 609-612; Jules Lemaître, "Le Féminisme," in his *Opinions à répandre* (Paris, 1901), pp. 158-64; Charles Turgeon, *Le Féminisme français*, 2 vols., 2nd ed. (Paris, 1907), quoted, 2:32; Ferdinand Brunetière, *Action sociale du christianisme* (Besançon, 1904). Brunetière accepted women's suffrage as inevitable and urged Catholic women to prepare for it intelligently (*La Femme contemporaine*, January 1904, pp. 8-11). Sertillanges felt women should be better educated first (*Féminisme et christianisme*, p. 145). Naudet preferred an indirect women's suffrage (*Pour la femme*, p. 206). For Lemaître, see also: *Le Féminisme chrétien*, April 1904, pp. 98-99 (quoted); for Turgeon, ibid., December, 1901, pp. 353-62, and January 1903.

28. For her attitudes, see: *Le Féminisme chrétien*, November 1901, pp. 321-28; June 1902, pp. 185-90; February 1901, pp. 61-62; Dossier Vote des femmes, 1900-1908, BMD; IWSA Program, June 1908, in the Anna Howard Shaw Papers, Dillon Collection, Box 22/Folder 510, Schlesinger Library. On cooperation between Catholic and republican feminists, see: *Le Soleil*, June 25, 1906; *Le Peuple français*, June 16, 1906; *L'Entente*, August 1906; Sainte-Croix, *Le Féminisme*, pp. 173-75.

29. *Le Devoir des femmes françaises*, September 1906, pp. 282-89; April 1906, p. 141; *L'Entente*, April 1906; *La Femme contemporaine*, October 1906, pp. 785-90 (quoted); September 1906, pp. 744-47; Unidentified report (1906) in the Dossier Vote des femmes, 1900-1908, BMD (Vincent quote); *L'Eclair*, May 31, 1906; *La Croix*, June 2, 1906.

30. *Le Devoir des femmes françaises*, September 1906, pp. 282-89.

31. *La Femme*, May 1906, p. 74; *Le Devoir des femmes françaises*, January 1907, pp. 16-18; *Echo de la ligue patriotique des françaises*, May 1909, pp. 2-3.

32. Bidelman, "Right-Wing Feminism in France," pp. 3-5; *Le Devoir des femmes françaises*, August 1906, pp. 233-37, 240-42; September 1906, pp. 277-89; October 1906, pp. 313-14; April 1907, pp. 126-27.

33. The authors acknowledge their indebtedness to Odile Sarti for sharing some of these ideas from her forthcoming dissertation on the LPF, especially her conclusions about the LPF's opposition to women's suffrage.

34. *L'Entente*, August 1906.

35. See Auclert's criticism of Durand in *Le Radical*, April 2, 1907.

36. *L'Entente*, July 1906.

37. *La Femme de demain*, July 1913. For the development of Oddo-Deflou's suffragism, see her articles in *L'Entente*, especially in April 1905, May and July 1906; the program of Etudes and an unidentified interview with her in the Dossier Oddo-Deflou, BMD; *L'Action*, February 23, 1910; *Le Petit almanach féministe illustré-1907*, p. 14; the motions adopted by Etudes, listed in Lecointre, *Etat de la question féministe en France*, p. 19.

38. For the CNFF in the early twentieth century, see the Dossier CNFF, BMD, which contains programs of the general assemblies and brochures published by the council; *L'Action féminine*, the official publication of the council from 1909; Sainte-Croix's scrapbook at the Musée sociale; Lecointre's *Etat de la question féministe en France*, pp. 17-19, reprinting the vows adopted in 1903-1906; and the letter of the executive committee of the CNFF to all members, June 1, 1906, Dossier CNFF, Bouglé Collection, BHVP. For suffragism in the CNFF: Unidentified clipping in the Dossier Congrès international de la condition et des droits des femmes, BMD; Sainte-Croix's report to the 1903 general assembly of the CNFF. The authors are indebted to Karen Offen for calling this document to their attention. Sainte-Croix's summary of the CNFF turn to suffragism and a copy of the 1902 resolution may be found in her article in *The Englishwoman* 2 (1909), p. 372.

39. Alice Zimmern, *Woman Suffrage in Many Lands* (London, 1909), pp. 117-18.

40. See Sainte-Croix to Louis Havet, March 30, 1905, Correspondance de Louis Havet, NAF 24,486, Bibliothèque nationale (manuscrits) [Hereafter, BN]; Sainte-Croix, *Le Féminisme*, p. 181.

41. *Le Journal des femmes*, January 1907.

42. For Auclert and the establishment of the CNFF suffrage section, see: *Le Journal des femmes*, January, February, April, and May 1907; *La Française*, March 17, 1907; *La Femme*, April 1907; *Le Petit almanach féministe illustré-*

1908, pp. 12-13. The text of the suffrage petition (showing Auclert's advanced claims) is given in Vérone, *Appel à la justice*, pp. 13-14.

43. See the *Bulletin mensuel de la maçonnerie mixte* and the order's *Convention des loges mixtes de France et des colonies, tenu ... 1910* (Havre, 1910). A copy of this report and other scarce materials on French masonry are in the French masonic collection at the Hoover Institution, Box 12.

44. The best (albeit limited) sources for the provincial activities of the CNFF are the dossier at the BMD and *L'Action féminine*, e.g., June 1909, p. 18, for reports by Alphen-Salvador and Siegfried. For information on evanescent local groups, see the folders in Dossier Groupements femmes (divers), BMD, e.g., Folder on the Association des femmes du Saône-et-Loire.

45. For Roussel, see the preface by Daniel Armogathe and Maïte Albistur in their edition of her *L'Eternelle sacrifiée* (Paris, 1979), pp. 7-25; a sketch by Marbel in the Dossier Nelly Roussel, BMD; *La Voix des femmes*, January 4, 1923; Odette Laguerre's preface to Roussel's *Trois conférences*, pp. 8-13; *Le Féminisme intégral*, December 1913; Dossier Nelly Roussel, Bouglé Collection, BHVP. For Roussel's ideas and her lecture tours, see her collected speeches and writings: *Quelques discours* (Paris, 1907), *Quelques lances rompues pour nos libertés* (Paris, 1910), *Paroles de combat et d'espoir* (Paris, 1919), *Trois conférences*, *Derniers combats* (Paris, 1932), and *L'Eternelle sacrifiée*. She also wrote regularly for *L'Action*; see, for example, her ideas on women's suffrage there, June 8, 1906. Records of her tours survive in some departmental archives; see, e.g., Dossier Conférences sur l'amélioration de la condition féminine, 4 MP 4670, AD-Seine Maritime (Rouen). For comments on her tours, see: *Les Annales de l'Ariège*, August 7 and September 11, 1904; February 12, February 19, April 16, and June 18, 1905; March 4, 1906; *L'Entente*, July 1905; *Le Journal des femmes*, October 1907; *Le Féministe*, January 5 and March 20, 1908.

46. *Le Féminisme intégral*, June 1913; *Les Travailleuses*, April 1911; Li, *La Presse féministe*, pp. 146-47.

47. For biographical information, see the collection of Arria Ly's papers in the Bouglé Collection, BHVP, and the Dossier Arria Ly, BMD. For a harsh judgment on her, see James F. McMillan, "The Effects of the First World War on the Social Condition of Women in France" (D. Phil. thesis, Oxford, 1977), p. 141. For her ideas, see *La Rénovation féministe*, September-December 1908; *La Suffragiste*, October 1911; *Le Matin*, September 4, 1911; *Le Journal*, March 2, 1913.

48. Hubertine Auclert to Arria Ly, May 6, August 5, and November 3, 1909, Bouglé Collection, BHVP; *Le Féministe*, November 25, 1909; *Le Journal des femmes*, May 1909.

49. DPF, 4:1598-99; *La Française*, June 27, 1909; JO, Chambre, Débats, July 10, 1906; Documents, No. 253; Buisson, *Le Vote des femmes*, pp. 326-27,

330-31; *Le Radical*, December 17, 1906 and November 2, 1907; Grinberg, *Historique du mouvement suffragiste depuis 1848*, pp. 107-109.

50. *Le Matin*, July 7, 1906. For more information on the parliamentary group, see: Sainte-Croix, *Le Féminisme*, p. 176; M. Renaudot, *Le Féminisme et les droits publics de la femme* (Niort, 1902), p. 26; Joseph Barthélemy, *Le Vote des femmes* (Paris, 1920), p. 131; *L'Entente*, July 1906; *Les Annales de l'Ariège*, July 22 and 29, 1906; *L'Action*, January 1, 1907; *Le Journal des femmes*, August-September 1907.

51. The cabinet included Viviani at the newly founded Ministry of Labor, Chéron as undersecretary at the Ministry of War, and Caillaux as minister of finance. The minister of foreign affairs, Stephen Pichon, and the second minister of commerce, Jean Cruppi, were husbands of women active in the CNFF and later the UFSF; the first minister of the Marine, Gaston Thomson, was the father of a suffragist. Both the minister of education, Aristide Briand, and the first minister of commerce (later education), Gaston Doumergue, were somewhat sympathetic and later pronounced themselves feminists.

52. Conseil général du département de la Seine, *Procès-verbaux des déli-bérations*, November 20, 1907, AD XIX¹ 1, AN; Buisson, *Le Vote des femmes,* p. 31; *L'Eclair*, November 23, 1907; *Le Radical*, July 9, 1906 and November 24, 1907; *La Française*, December 1, 1907; *L'Entente*, December 1907; Auclert, *Le Vote des femmes*, p. 182.

53. For the pioneering American campaign, see Flexner, *Century of Strug-gle*, esp. pp. 85-88; for international comparisons, see Evans, *The Feminists*, pp. 47, 61, 89, 111. For the text of the Schmahl Law, see Duvergier, *Collection complète des lois*, 107:348-56 (July 13, 1907). For its passage, see *DPF*, 3:924; 5:1663, 1851-52, 1864-65, and 1917; *JO*, Sénat, Débats, July 13, 1907; Buisson, *Le Vote des femmes*, p. 35; Sainte-Croix, *Le Féminisme*, p. 138; Joran, *Le Féminisme à l'heure actuelle* (Paris, 1907), p. 7; *L'Entente*, April and July 1906; *La Française*, October 21, 1906, February 3 and July 28, 1907; *Le Radical*, June 1 and 6, 1907, July 17, 1907; Dossier Jeanne Schmahl, BMD.

54. See the laws and decrees in either Duvergier, *Collection complète des lois*, or *JO*, Documents, for the following dates: January 23 and April 1, 1898; September 17, 1900; January 2 and July 14, 1901; March 14, 1903; March 14, 1905; August 7, 1906; March 27, 1907; February 19 and November 15, 1908. For an illustration of the feminist understanding of these rights as training for other political rights, see *La Fronde*, November 25, 1901.

55. *Le Radical*, September 17, 1906.

56. David R. Watson, *Georges Clemenceau: A Political Biography* (London, 1974), p. 183.

57. Clemenceau, *La "Justice" du sexe fort*, pp. 19, 28.

58. *Le Journal des femmes*, May 1907. Clemenceau's decision involved the expulsion from France of female croupiers.

59. Clemenceau, *La "Justice" du sexe fort*, pp. 30-33.

60. *La Fronde*, June 23, 1901; *Le Journal des femmes*, July 1901.

61. The best source for the programs and congresses of the Radical Party is *Le Radical*. Quotations are from the party program printed on October 10, 1907. The Nancy Program is also reprinted and discussed in Nicolet, *Le Radicalisme*, pp. 48-53; David Thomson, ed., *France: Empire and Republic, 1850-1940* (New York, 1968), pp. 278-83.

62. Minutes of the Commission of Universal Suffrage, 1906-1910, C 7375, AN. See also the papers of Charles Benoist, volumes 10 and 11, Bibliothèque de l'Institut de France, providing evidence of the commission's priorities. Benoist's interests are also clear in his memoirs, *Souvenirs, 1883-1933*, 3 vols. (Paris, 1932-1934), 3:347-72, and his book on electoral reform, *Pour la réforme électorale* (Paris, 1908). For the ultimate development off his thinking, see his *Les Lois de la politique française* (Paris, 1928). Although Buisson wished to raise women's suffrage, he shared the committee's priorities. See his *La Politique radicale* (Paris, 1908), pp. 135-65; *Le Vote des femmes*, pp. 325-31.

Chapter Four

1. *Le Radical*, May 2, 1908.

2. According to the accounts printed in *Le Matin*. Laloë herself, in this account, only thought of "an amusing article." According to her subsequent testimony, Laloë decided to run while doing research for "an austere article" which led to a reading of the Municipal Elections Law; she claimed that it was she who persuaded Vérone to test the law rather than vice versa. For a detailed narrative of the events of 1908, see Steven C. Hause and Anne R. Kenney, "Women's Suffrage and the Paris Elections of 1908," *Laurels* 51 (1980): 21-32. For the newspaper version, *Le Matin* from April 28 to May 5, 1908, plus a retrospective article on May 19, 1908. For Laloë's version, see her "Les Deux féminismes," *La Nouvelle revue*, May-June 1908. For Vérone's account, see her amusing memoir, "Les Impressions d'une candidate," in the Dossier Jeanne Laloë, BMD. See also Joran, *Le Suffrage des femmes*, pp. 121-22.

3. For accounts of the meeting, see the memoirs by Vérone and Laloë; Hause and Kenney, "Women's Suffrage and the Paris Elections of 1908"; *L'Eclair*, May 4, 1908; *Le Matin*, May 2, 1908; the account of an English participant in *Votes for Women*, May 14, 1908, p. 161; the account of Georges Lhermite, who chaired the meeting, in *Le Droit des femmes*, April 15, 1914, pp. 73-74; Auclert's response in *Le Radical*, May 2, 1908; Dossier Elections municipales générales des 3 et 10 mai 1908, B^A 276, APP.

4. For details on the demonstration, see Hause and Kenney, "Women's Suffrage and the Paris Elections of 1908"; Police report, May 5, 1908, Dossier

Hubertine Auclert, B^A 885, APP; Auclert's account in Oddo-Deflou, ed., *Congrès national des droits civils*, pp. 216-17; notes and clippings in the Dossier Jeanne Laloë, BMD; *L'Action*, May 5, 1908; *L'Eclair*, May 4, 1908; *Le Radical*, May 4, 1908.

5. *L'Eclair*, May 4, 1908.

6. One noteworthy exception was Camille Bélilon, who wrote: "Some will say this is violence. Pardon, these are reprisals. Do not men walk over the will, the opinion, of women? In return, women have literally done that with the votes of men. . . . Honor to these courageous women who are mounting the assault. . . ." (*Journal des femmes*, May 1908.)

7. Bureau presidents at two polls defied the government's instructions and counted a total of 527 votes for Laloë; at two other polls, 463 blank ballots were reported. Thus, Laloë received somewhere between 527 and 990 votes; according to Vérone, there were only three true blank ballots, making Laloë's total 987. See Vérone's memoir in the Dossier Jeanne Laloë, BMD; *Le Matin*, May 3, 1908; *L'Eclair*, May 5, 1908. Compare the variety of votes reported in Barthélemy, *Le Vote des femmes*, p. 127; Auclert, *Le Vote des femmes*, p. 18; Li, *La Presse féministe*, p. 75; and the Parisian press on May 4, 1908.

8. Madeleine Pelletier, "La Tactique féministe," *La Revue socialiste*, April 1908, reprinted in *Le Grief des femmes*, ed. Maite Albistur and Daniel Armogathe, 2 vols. (Paris, 1978), 2:105-107; Pelletier's account in her "Le Féminisme et ses militants," p. 24 (quoted); clippings and notes in the Dossiers Madeleine Pelletier and Vote des femmes, 1900-1908, BMD; *Le Radical*, May 11, 1908; *L'Eclair*, May 11, 1908.

9. *Le Journal des femmes*, May and June 1908. Laloë made one more public appearance connected with her candidacy and turned it into a humorous event; thereafter, she declined to speak. See *Le Matin*'s retrospective article on May 19, 1908 and *Le Journal des femmes*, January 1909. Her published account of her race ended by distinguishing between "two feminisms," deploring the one in which women cut their hair and wore trousers: "Les Deux féminismes," p. 410. The LFDF, on the other hand, publicized her campaign as a symbol of what was possible through legalism, eventually claiming credit for it; *Le Droit des femmes*, December 1919, p. 217; April 1922, p. 88.

10. Police reports, June 3 and 4, 1908, and procès-verbaux, Dossier Hubertine Auclert, B^A 885, APP; *Gazette des tribunaux*, June 6 and July 17, 1908; Auclert, *Les Femmes au gouvernail*, p. 77; Pelletier, "Le Féminisme et ses militants," p. 25; *La Suffragiste*, January 1912.

11. *La Française*, June 28, 1908.

12. Madeleine Pelletier to Arria Ly, August 22, 1911 and October 19, 1911. Bouglé Collection, BHVP. For her continuing endorsement of violence, see: "Le Féminisme et ses militants," p. 24; *Gil Blas*, February 26, 1913.

13. For the origins and organization of the congress of 1908, see the Dossier Congrès national des droits civils et du suffrage des femmes, BMD, which includes Vincent-Durand correspondence, minutes of the organizing committee, and Durand's notes on the congress; e.g., Vincent to Durand, May 18, 1908, on Auclert's adhesion. See also Oddo-Deflou's summary in her preface to the report of the congress and her published evaluation of the assembly: Oddo-Deflou, ed., *Congrès national des droits civils*, p. v; *La Liberté d'opinion*, May-June 1908, pp. 70-79.

14. The best sources for such issues at the congress are Oddo-Deflou's volume containing all of the reports presented, the Dossier on the congress at the BMD, and articles in the daily press. See: *Le Journal des femmes*, June and July 1908; *La Française*, June 28, 1908; *Le Radical*, July 1, 1908; *L'Action*, June 26-July 1, 1908.

15. See the sources discussed in note 13, especially Oddo-Deflou's volume.

16. Auclert's speech is reprinted in Oddo-Deflou, ed., *Congrès national des droits civils*, pp. 216-17; additional information on it may be found in *La Liberté d'opinion*, May-June 1908, pp. 70-79.

17. Both Durand and Oddo-Deflou gave interviews to the press stressing the renunciation of violence as the great accomplishment of the congress. See *La Liberté*, July 1, 1908; unidentified interview with Oddo-Deflou, Dossier Oddo-Deflou, BMD.

18. *Le Radical*, July 1, 1908; *Gil Blas*, February 26, 1913 (quoted).

19. *Le Petit almanach féministe illustré-1906*, p. 11. See also UFSF, *Bulletin annuel-1911*, p. 1.

20. *Le Bonnet rouge*, June 3, 1914.

21. Newspapers estimated the crowd at Hyde Park between 250,000 and 500,000. See Andrew Rosen, *Rise Up Women! The Militant Campaign of the Women's Social and Political Union, 1903-1914* (London, 1974), p. 104. For the campaign of marches, see Millicent Fawcett, *Women's Suffrage: A Short History of a Great Movement* [1912] (London, 1970), p. 76.

22. Richard J. Evans, *The Feminist Movement in Germany, 1894-1933* (London, 1976), p. 89.

23. Both the Ministry of the Interior (Police générale) and the Prefecture of Police kept dossiers on the English suffragettes and their tactics. They kept close watch on suffragettes who visited Paris and they collaborated with the English police in keeping track of Christabel Pankhurst. They found no evidence of her contact with French suffragists. Dossier Vote des femmes, 1908-1928, police générale files, F7 13266, AN; Dossier Vote des femmes, BA 1651, APP. Similarly, the Pankhurst Papers at the International Institute for Social History (Amsterdam) show that Christabel did not seek links to French militants during her stay in Paris.

24. Interview with Oddo-Deflou, Dossier Oddo-Deflou, BMD. See *The Times* of London for interesting reflections on the contrast between the two movements and for the French refusal to collaborate in 1908 (June 3 and 22, 1908). For other illustrations of the French attitude, see *Gil Blas*, June 6, 1913 (quoted); *La Française*, June 28, 1908; *La Liberté*, February 10, 1910; *UFSF Bulletin trimestriel*, July-October 1913, pp. 1-2; *La Femme*, November 1910; *L'Equité*, April 1, 1914; *La Femme de demain*, May 1913; Duchess d'Uzès, *Le Suffrage féminin au point de vue historique* (Meulan, 1914), p. 16; Pelletier, "Les Suffragettes anglaises se virilisent, *La Suffragiste*, October 1912" *La Libre parole*, July 2, 1908; *Gil Blas*, February 26, 1913.

25. Dossier Jane Misme, Bouglé Collection, BHVP; Dossier *La Française*, BMD; *La Française*, October 21, 1906; Li, *La Presse féministe*, pp. 148-150; Grinberg, *Historique du mouvement suffragiste*, pp. 89-90; *Les Nouvelles*, January 25, 1914.

26. *Le Journal*, March 22, 1914; Grinberg, *Historique du mouvement suffragiste*, p. 91; *La Française*, December 30, 1906, January 6, 1907, June 28, 1908 (quoted), and April 4, 1914.

27. For Schmahl and the origins of the UFSF, see *La Française*, January 24, 1909; Misme's biography of Schmahl in the Dossier Jeanne Schmahl, BMD; *Revue de l'UFSF, 1922-1923*, p. 1; Grinberg, *Historique du mouvement suffragiste*, pp. 91-92.

28. *La Française*, January 24, 1909.

29. Ibid., February 7, 1909.

30. Ibid., February 21, 1909.

31. Ibid., February 28, 1909.

32. For Auclert and the founding of the UFSF, see: ibid., March 14 and 28, April 18, and November 14, 1909; *Minerva*, October 19, 1930; Dossiers Auclert, BMD and BHVP.

33. For an example of Catholic interest in the UFSF under Schmahl and d'Uzès, see *La Femme contemporaine*, October 1911; *La Française*, June 19, 1910 (quoted). See also the appeal to "women of the elite" in *La Femme*, June-July 1909. For the officers of the UFSF: *La Française*, March 14 and February 21, 1909; Dossier UFSF, BMD.

34. Statutes of the UFSF, February 13, 1909, Dossier UFSF, BMD. There is a long excerpt from these statutes in André Leclère, *Le Vote des femmes en France* (Paris, 1929), pp. 85-88.

35. The most important contributor of this category was Mme. Elie Halévy, wife of the distinguished historian. See the police générale summary report on the UFSF, April 14, 1915, Dossier Rapports et notes concernant l'activité des divers groupements féministes, 1913 à 1928, F⁷ 13266, AN; papers of the UFSF's Paris group, January 26, 1913, Dossier UFSF, BMD; *La Française*,

April 25 and May 23, 1909; Dossier Jeanne Schmahl, BMD; Buisson, *Le Vote des femmes*, pp. 294-95.

36. This argument is developed at greater length in Hause and Kenney "The Limits of Suffragist Behavior." See also Tilly, "Women's Collective Action and Feminism in France, 1870-1914," pp. 207-231.

37. Could it be unimportant in the development of Siegfried's thought that his mother was a president of the CNFF and he grew up in a home filled with feminine and feminist meetings? For his experience with French feminism, see his *lettre-préface* to Louli Sanua [Milhaud-Sanua], *Figures féminines, 1900-1939* (Paris, 1949), pp. 15-16.

38. *La Femme*, November 1910, p. 164.

39. *Le Radical*, January 3, 1902; *Le Journal des femmes*, May 1910.

40. Marguerite Clément, *Conférence sur le suffrage des femmes* (Paris, 1912), p. 3.

41. See Constance Rover, *Women's Suffrage and Party Politics in Britain, 1866-1914* (London, 1967), pp. 12-17; Rosen, *Rise Up Women*, pp. 7-9, 14-15, 62, 69; William L. O'Neill, *Everyone Was Brave: The Rise and Fall of Feminism in America* (Chicago, 1969), pp. 146-68; Eleanor Flexner, *Century of Struggle: The Women's Rights Movement in the United States* (Cambridge, Mass., 1966), pp. 179, 216-19; David Morgan, *Suffragists and Democrats: The Politics of Woman Suffrage in America* (East Lansing, Mich., 1972), p. 24; Evans, *The Feminist Movement in Germany*, pp. 1-3, 42; Richard Stites, *The Women's Liberation Movement in Russia: Feminism, Nihilism, and Bolshevism, 1869-1930* (Princeton, 1978), pp. 213-18, 227-28; Anne F. Scott and Andrew M. Scott, "The Suffragists: A Collective Sketch," in their *One Half the People: The Fight for Woman Suffrage* (Philadelphia, 1975), pp. 164-65; Robert E. Riegel, *American Feminists* (Lawrence, Kans., 1963), pp. 113-36.

42. See Rosen, *Rise Up Woman*, chap. 2 and 3. Also see David Morgan, *Suffragists and Liberals: The Politics of Woman Suffrage in England* (Oxford, 1975), p. 159: "Mrs. Pankhurst brought from her more recent working class association the more desperate, defiant flavour of lower class activism and added her own sense of drama and immediacy." E. Sylvia Pankhurst, *The Suffragette Movement: An Intimate Account of Persons and Ideas* [1931] (Virago ed., London, 1977), pp. 116-70, esp. p. 168, plus the introduction by her son, Richard; Fawcett, *Women's Suffrage*, p. 62; Jill Liddington and Jill Norris, *One Hand Tied Behind Us: The Rise of the Women's Suffrage Movement* (London, 1978).

43. Paulson, *Women's Suffrage and Prohibition*, p. 156; Flexner, *Century of Struggle*, pp. 249-59; Scott and Scott, *One Half the People*, pp. 29-31. Also see the history of the Woman's Party's militancy: Doris Stevens, *Jailed for Freedom* [1920] (New York, 1976).

44. See Evans, *The Feminist Movement in Germany*, pp. 87-92; Jean H. Quataert, *Reluctant Feminists in German Social Democracy, 1885-1917* (Princeton, 1979), pp. 3, 93, 231. For a statement of the Marxist position, see Werner Thönnessen, *The Emancipation of Women: The Rise and Fall of the Women's Movement in German Social Democracy, 1863-1933* (London, 1973), esp. pp. 39-71. Kollantai as quoted by Stites, *The Women's Liberation Movement in Russia*, p. 228; see also pp. 191, 203, 210, 213, 217-18, 222; for Bolshevik arguments against collaboration, see S. Serditova, *Bolsheviki v borbe za zhenskie proletarskie massy (1903-Febral 1917 g.)* (Moscow, 1959), pp. 51-55. For feminist-socialist relations in Italy, see Franca P. Bortolotti, *Socialismo e questione feminile in Italia, 1892-1922* (Milan, 1974), esp. pp. 36-57.

45. For such comparisons, see Auclert, *Le Vote des femmes, passim*; Rosen, *Rise Up Women*, p. 9; Flexner, *Century of Struggle*, pp. 222.

46. Sainte-Croix, *Le Féminisme*, p. 175. See also Zeldin, *France, 1848-1945*, 1:348.

47. Scott and Scott, *One Half the People*, p. 165. Brief biographies of the American suffrage prisoners are in Stevens, *Jailed for Freedom*, Appendix IV, pp. 354-71. A similar pattern existed in New Zealand, for example, where the leader of WCTU suffragism, Kate Sheppard, was the wife of a Christchurch councillor, and the executive committee of the Women's Franchise League included several wives of politicians; see Patricia Grimshaw, *Women's Suffrage in New Zealand* (Auckland, 1972), pp. 36, 50.

48. Georges Wormser, *La République de Clemenceau* (Paris, 1961), p. 206 (quoted). For a detailed introduction to this repression, see Jacques Julliard, *Clemenceau, briseur des grèves: L'Affaire de Draveil Villeneuve-Saint-Georges* (Paris, 1965); Felix Napo, *La Révolte des vignerons* (Toulouse, 1971). For a focus on the involvement of women in such events, see Tilly, "Women's Collective Action and Feminism in France, 1870-1914."

49. *La Française*, December 20, 1908; April 25, 1909; January 23, 1910; June 10, 1922; February 13, 1937; *Le Féminisme intégral*, May 1913; *Le Journal de femmes*, May 1909; *Le Féministe*, April 1 and 15, 1909; Société féministe du Havre, *Le Suffrage municipal des femmes* (Havre, 1913); Dossiers Pauline Rebour, Camille Bélilon, and Julie Siegfried, BMD; Dossier Pauline Rebour, Bouglé Collection, BHVP.

50. Data from Peter V. Meyers, "From Conflict to Cooperation: Men and Women Teachers in the Belle Epoque," *HR/RH* 7 (1980): Pelletier, see *L'Action féministe*, February-March 1910.

51. For women and French education, see Chapter One, note 50. For teachers, see the helpful dissertation by Persis C. Hunt, "Revolutionary Syndicalism and Feminism among Teachers in France, 1900-1921" (Ph.D. diss., Tufts University, 1975), and her "Teachers and Workers: Problems of Feminist Organization in the Early Third Republic," *TR/TR* 3-4 (1977): 168-

204; Francis M. Feeley, "A Study of French Primary School Teachers (1880-1919), and the Conditions and Events Which Led a Group of Them into the Revolutionary 'Syndicaliste' Movement" (Ph.D. diss., University of Wisconsin, 1976). For contemporary suffragist perspectives on the role of teachers, see Jane Misme, *Pour le suffrage des femmes: Le Féminisme et la politique* (Paris, n.d.), p. 9. Albistur and Armogathe reprint some contemporary materials on the syndicalism of teachers in *Le Grief des femmes*, 2:130-34.

52. For the foundation of the FFU, see *L'Action féministe*; Folder L'Action féminine, Dossier Groupements femmes (divers), BMD; *Le Féministe*, November 20, 1910; *La Française*, June 20, 1909 and December 19, 1909; *L'Action féminine*, August, 1910 (quoted); Madeleine Pelletier, "Les Institutrices et le mouvement féministe," *Les Documents du progrès*, May 1910; *L'Entente*, May 1905. For the suffrage question and the FFU, see the debate in *L'Action féministe* from November 1909 through February-March 1910; *L'Action féminine*, August 1910; *Le Féminisme intégral*, October 1913; *La Française*, June 20, 1909 (quoted) and December 26, 1909; Guilbert, *Les Femmes et l'organisation syndicale*, pp. 333-34, 374-78, 387.

53. For feminist skepticism, see *La Française*, April 18, 1909; *Le Radical*, February 9, 1909. For Buisson's biography, see *DPF*, 2:805-807; *Le Journal*, April 8, 1914; Dossier Députés favorables au vote des femmes, BMD. For his role in the committee: *Le Radical*, March 3, 1909; minutes of the Commission of Universal Suffrage, July 12, 1906 and January 22, 1908, C 7375, AN.

54. *JO*, Documents, July 16, 1909, No. 2716; Marguerite Martin, *Les Droits de la femme* (Paris, 1912), p. 115; *La Française*, March 14 and May 6, 1909; Maria Vérone, "Rapport de la section du suffrage du CNFF," Dossier CNFF, BMD; Vérone, "Le Suffrage des femmes," *L'Action féminine*, July 1909, pp. 35-47 (the authors wish to thank Karen Offen for providing them this copy of Vérone's report); Buisson, *Le Vote des femmes*, esp. pp. 42ff. and 292 (quoted). For an example of suffragist pleasure with Buisson, see Grinberg, *Historique du mouvement suffragiste*, pp. 109-110: "When the hour of feminist victory comes, women, in their joy, must remember with recognition the name of Ferdinand Buisson, for his spirit so perfectly and profoundly permeated with the great republican ideals." Durand wrote to Buisson in similar language: "It seems to me impossible to expose with more talent, method, and clarity a thesis so alien to so many of your colleagues." (Durand to Buisson, April 1, 1910, Bouglé Collection, BHVP.)

55. For differing versions of the parliamentary crisis, see: Watson, *Clemenceau*, pp. 206-214; Geoffrey Bruun, *Clemenceau* [1943] (Reprint ed.: Hamden, Conn., 1968), pp. 101-103; Phillippe Erlanger, *Clemenceau* (Paris, 1968), pp. 393-97; Gaston Monnerville, *Clemenceau* (Paris, 1968), pp. 340-50; Wormser, *La République de Clemenceau*, pp. 213-15; Charles W. Porter, *The Career*

of Théophile Delcassé [1936] (Reprint ed.: Westport, Conn., 1975), pp. 272-84; Georges Suarez, *Briand: Sa vie, son oeuvre, avec son journal et de nombreux documents inédits*, 6 vols. (Paris, 1938-1952), 2:219-24.

56. *La Française*, October 17, 1909.

57. Police report on a meeting of Suffrage des femmes, October 11, 1910, Dossier Vote des femmes, B^A 1651, APP.

58. *JO*, Chambre des députés, débats, October 28, 1909; Suarez, *Briand*, 2:252-53.

59. *JO*, Chambre des députés, débats, October 29, 1909; *DPF*, 8:2990-92; *Le Féministe*, November 25, 1909; *La Française*, November 7, 1909.

60. *La Française*, November 14, 1909; *L'Autorité*, November 1, 1909; Dossier Sénateurs favorables au vote des femmes, BMD.

Chapter Five

1. This estimate is based on the membership of the UFSF. Three thousand active suffragists (i.e., excluding nominal suffragists through membership in the CNFF) outside of the UFSF seems an outer limit for 1914, considering Catholic suffragists, socialist suffragists, and republican suffragists from the smaller societies.

2. Jean Finot, *Problems of the Sexes* (London, 1909), p. 249; *L'Action*, February 23, 1910 (Oddo-Deflou quote); M.-L. Bérot-Berger, *La Femme dans le progrès social* (Paris, 1910), p. 13; *Le Féministe*, April 14, 1910 (Réal quote). For other examples of this attitude, see *Le Journal des femmes*, January 1910; Roussel, *Derniers combats*, pp. 18-22.

3. See *DPF*, 2:799-801; *Minerva*, August 30, 1931; *La Française*, February 20, 1910, May 22, 1910 (quoted), and August 7, 1910; *Jus suffraggi* (French ed.), May-June 1920; Thérèse Pottecher, "Le Mouvement féministe en France," pp. 597-98; Sainte-Croix, "Les Françaises et le droit du suffrage," *La Grande Revue*, January 1911, p. 372; Dossiers Cécile Brunschwicg and UFSF, BMD; Dossier Brunschwicg, Bouglé Collection, BHVP.

4. Misme's sketch of Schmahl, Dossier Jeanne Schmahl, BMD.

5. Jeanne Schmahl, "Progress of the Women's Rights Movement in France," *The Forum*, September 1896, p. 86.

6. *La Française*, December 18, 1910. See also Misme's sketch of d'Uzès in the Dossier Duchesse d'Uzès, BMD; Grinberg (a close associate of Brunschwicg's), *Historique du mouvement suffragiste*, pp. 91-92; Joran (sympathetic to Schmahl and critical of Misme), *Le Suffrage des femmes*, pp. 119-120.

7. See Brunschwicg's speech on republicanism to the congress of Brussels in 1912, Dossier Congrès féministe international—Bruxelles, 1912, BMD. On Vincent's ouster (which deeply hurt her, and which was evidently a rejection of her past militancy), see *Le Droit des femmes*, March 15, 1914. For de Witt-

Schlumberger: Abensour, *Histoire générale du féminisme*, p. 280 (quoted); de Witt-Schlumberger's speech, "How to Reach the Society Woman," in the program of the Budapest meeting of the IWSA (1913), p. 19, copy in the Gilman MSS, Box 1/Folder 8, Schlesinger Library; *Minerva*, December 14, 1930; anonymous pamphlet, "Mme de Witt-Schlumberger," Dossier de Witt-Schlumberger, BMD; Dossier de Witt-Schlumberger, Bouglé Collection, BHVP. For her social feminism, see Raoul Froger-Doudement, ed., *Que veulent donc ces féministes?* (Paris, 1926) pp. 57-58; Marguerite de Witt-Schlumberger, *Une femme aux femmes* (Paris, 1909); *Le Féministe*, April 8, 1909; *La Française*, June 5, 1910 and June 23, 1912; *La Femme*, March 1, 1902.

8. See the motion voted at the 1913 congress: "The UFSF is obstinately resolved to restrict itself to the law and legality." UFSF, *Bulletin trimestriel*, July-October 1913, pp. 1-2; Clément, *Conférence sur le suffrage des femmes*, pp. 3, 16.

9. *Le Mouvement féminin*, July 15, 1913.

10. *UFSF, Bulletin annuel-1911*, pp. 4-13.

11. Ibid. See also UFSF, *Bulletin trimestriel*, July-October 1913, p. 30. For Méo's sharp remarks on the prejudice of *instituteurs*, see Meyers, "From Conflict to Cooperation," p. 499 and n. 26.

12. *La Française* published Djénane's list on June 4, 1911; other papers were given in following weeks. For Djénane and her efforts, see also the issues of January 11, 1913, May 22, 1910, and June 26, 1910; UFSF, *Bulletin annuel-1911*, p. 13; *Bulletin de 1912*, pp. 51-52; and *Bulletin trimestriel*, July-October 1913, p. 7.

13. Brunschwicg's report to the UFSF, March 3, 1912, printed in the *Bulletin* of the Ligue d'électeurs, April 1912, pp. 33-34 (quoted); reiterated in her report of May 12, 1913, *Bulletin trimestriel de l'UFSF*, April 1913, p. 1. The provincial groups of the UFSF can be followed in *La Française* and the union's *Bulletin*. The most comprehensive survey is published in UFSF, *Bulletin trimestriel*, July-October 1913, pp. 6-25 and January-March 1914, pp. 4-10. *La Française*, May 9, 1914, gives a summary of growth to that date. For the group at Nice, see *Le Féministe*, 1910-1911. For the strength of the group at Lyons and the 1914 congress, see Dossier Congrès UFSF (Lyons, 1914), BMD. For the demonstration at Brest, see *La Femme socialiste*, April 15, 1913. For the Girondin group, Clément, *Conférence sur le suffrage des femmes*.

14. Little evidence on these groups survives. There are several references to the LFDF program in *Le Droit des femmes*; e.g., May 1914, p. 99. For the CNFF, *L'Action féminine*, e.g., December 1913, p. 580. For Etudes, *Le Féminisme intégral*, July-August 1913. Among the small independent groups were a Groupe féministe de la Somme (Mlle. Poidevin, Amiens), a Société féministe de Saône-et-Loire (Mme. Renaud, Chalon-sur-Saône), an Associ-

ation féminine du Mans (Mme. Pivette), a Ligue des droits de la femme (Lille), Emancipation féminine (Bordeaux), Solidarité féminine de La Rochelle, a Groupe féministe de Bayonne-Biarritz (Mme. Elosu), and a Groupe féministe de l'Hérault (Léa Bérard). See: UFSF, *Bulletin trimestriel*, January-March 1914, p. 10; *L'Equité*, July 15, 1913; *La Vague*, May 9, 1918; *L'Action féminine*, November-December 1915, p. 110; Dossier UFF, BMD. For the federation, see: *La Française*, June 18, August 27, and November 19, 1911; March 3, June 9, September 8, and November 11, 1912; January 4, May 17, and July 12, 1913; March 14 and April 4, 1914; *Les Travailleuses*, December 1911; *La Suffragiste*, June 1912.

15. *Echo de la ligue patriotique des françaises*, February 1914, p. 1.

16. For the UFSF campaign, see the Dossier UFSF, BMD, especially the program of the general assembly of March 1912; *La Française*, March 10, 1912; Dossier Vote des femmes, 1914, BMD. For the campaign at Le Havre, see Société féministe du Havre, *Le Suffrage municipal des femmes; La Française*, October 13, 1912. For the campaign at Amiens, see Buisson, *Le Vote des femmes*, p. 31; Ligue d'électeurs, *Bulletin trimestriel*, April 1911, p. 10; *Le Féminisme intégral*, June 1913; *Le Journal des femmes*, October 1910. Good examples of the cursory debates may be seen in Conseil général du Rhône, *Rapports ... et procès-verbaux des déliberations du conseil: Deuxième session ordinaire de 1912* (Lyons, 1912), p. 1499; Conseil général du département de la Seine-Inférieure, *Rapports et procès-verbaux: Deuxième session ordinaire de 1912* (Rouen, 1912), pp. 455-62.

17. See Goliber, "The Life and Times of Marguerite Durand," pp. 79-89, for Durand's career at *L'Action* and *Les Nouvelles*. Durand's race is exhaustively documented in the Dossier Marguerite Durand, candidate aux élections législatives de 1910, BMD. See also the dossier of her correspondence, especially with Auclert. For examples of her trial balloons, see *Le Matin*, February 14, 1910; *La Liberté*, February 10, 1910; and the report of an interview with her in Dawbarn, "The French Woman and the Vote," pp. 328-29.

18. *La Française*, February 20, 1910 (UFSF quote), April 10, 1910, and April 17, 1910; *La Petite république*, February 16, 1910 (Oddo-Deflou quote); *La Dépêche de Toulouse*, April 10, 1910; *L'Action*, April 21 and May 16, 1910; *Le Journal des femmes*, May and June 1910; Etudes letter to all parliamentary candidates, April 13, 1910, in the Dossier Oddo-Deflou, BMD.

19. *La Française*, January 23 and February 20, 1910; handbill and program for the "great meeting," Dossier Vote des femmes, 1910-1913, BMD; LFDF, *Cinquante ans de féminisme*, p. 22; *La Féministe*, March 17, 1910; *Le Droit des femmes*, April 15, 1914; *L'Action féminine*, February 1910; *Le Journal des femmes*, March, April, and May 1910; Maria Vérone, Chrystal MacMillan, and Marie Stritt, *Woman Suffrage in Practice* (London, 1913), p. 124.

20. The feminist list was published in the grand press on April 5th-6th; see, for examples, *La République française*, April 5, 1910; *Le Soleil*, April 6, 1910. For the legal and financial records of Durand's campaign, see the Dossier Marguerite Durand, candidate aux élections législatives de 1910, BMD. For the collapse of the suffragist races, see *Les Journal des femmes*, May 1910; for the police, see Dossier Elections générales législatives du 24 avril et du 8 mai 1910, B^A 238, APP. *Les Documents du progrès*, July 1910.

21. Copies of the program may be found in the Dossier Marguerite Durand, candidate aux élections législatives de 1910, BMD, and in many daily newspapers for April 15-16, 1910. See also the discussion in Goliber, "The Life and Times of Marguerite Durand," pp. 90-91.

22. For the court ruling see *La Française*, May 15, 1910. For Durand's stormy meeting see the press accounts of April 15-17, 1910, e.g., *Le Figaro* and *L'Humanité* on the 17th; *Le Journal des femmes*, May 1910.

23. *L'Eclair*, April 15, 1910.

24. *Le Temps*, February 12, 1910. For more on Auclert's campaign, see: police report of April 19, 1910, Dossier Hubertine Auclert, B^A 885, APP; *Le Journal des femmes*, May 1910; Auclert, *Les Femmes au gouvernail*, pp. 72-74.

25. For Pelletier's early campaign as a feminist, see *Le Matin*, March 31, 1910; *Le Féministe*, March 3, 1910; Dossier Madeleine Pelletier, BMD. For her campaign as a socialist, see her own accounts: "Les Candidatures féminines," *La Suffragiste*, June 1910; "Ma Candidature à la députation," *Les Documents du progrès*, July 1910 (quoted). A manuscript copy, by Hélène Brion, of one of her speeches survives in the Dossier Pelletier, BMD. For a hostile report, see *Le Soleil*, February 11, 1910; for more sympathetic versions see the clippings in her dossier and the coverage by *Le Journal des femmes*, May 1910. For an analysis of her campaign in the socialist context, see Sowerwine, *Sisters or Citizens?*, pp. 123-24.

26. For Kauffmann's bitter reflections on socialism, Durand, and the 1910 elections, see her letter to Arria Ly, May 17, 1912, Bouglé Collection, BHVP. For her public version of events, see her "Comment je fus candidate," *La Suffragiste*, June 1910. For differing accounts of her campaign, see: *L'Eclair*, April 21, 1910; *Le Journal des femmes*, May 1910.

27. Conflicting reports produced the following counts: Durand, 34/410/ 430/500; Pelletier, 340/349; Auclert, 250/470/500; Kauffmann, 150/200. See *L'Eclair*, April 25, 1910; Durand's "Impressions d'une candidate," in the Dossier Marguerite Durand, candidate aux élections législatives de 1910, BMD; *L'Intransigeant*, April 28, 1910.

28. *Le Féminisme intégral*, June 1913; *La Dépêche de Toulouse*, April 21 and 24, 1910; *Le Journal des femmes*, April and May 1910.

29. Sowerwine, *Sisters or Citizens?*, pp. 124-26; *L'Humanité*, April 27, 1910;

Le Droit des femmes, April-July 1910 and March 1913; *Le Journal des femmes*, May 1910.

30. Quoted in *La Liberté*, February 10, 1910. For other examples of suffragist confidence, see: Pelletier, "La Féminisme et ses militants," p. 19; *Les Travailleuses*, November 1911; UFSF, *Bulletin annuel-1911*, pp. 2-3; Léon Abensour, *Le Probleme féministe* (Paris, 1927), p. 132.

31. Carrie Chapman Catt, "Is Woman Suffrage Progressing?" presidential address to the IWSA, Stockholm, June 13, 1911; text in Catt MSS, Box 1/ Folder 21, Dillon Collection, Schlesinger Library.

32. Abensour, *Histoire générale du féminisme*, p. 276; Sainte-Croix, *Le Féminisme*, pp. 140, 162-63; *L'Aurore*, June 22, 1914. For examples of feminist novels, see: Marcelle Tinayre, *La Rebelle* (Paris, n.d.); Paul and Victor Margueritte, *Femmes nouvelles* (Paris, 1899); Jules Boix, *L'Eve nouvelle* (Paris, 1896); Marcel Prévost, *Les Demi-vierges* (Paris, 1894).

33. Finot, *Problems of the Sexes*, p. 258.

34. *Le Figaro*, April 7, 1896, and *Le Temps*, April 7, 1896, as quoted by Wilkins, "The Paris International Feminist Congress of 1896," p. 17. *L'Autorité*, May 14 and December 22, 1910, May 14, June 4, and September 11, 1913. See also the discussion of press support in the police report of February 8, 1914, Dossier Vote des femmes, B^A 1651, APP; notes in the Dossier Congrès national des droits civils et du suffrage des femmes, BMD; UFSF, *Bulletin trimestriel*, April 1913, p. 10.

35. The league combined the Union française anti-alcoolique and the Société française de tempérance. For its cooperation with suffragists, see: *Le Journal des femmes*, February 1907, March 1907, and May 1907; *La Française*, January 20, 1907; *La Femme*, January 1907; UFSF, *Bulletin de 1912*, p. 6; UFSF, *Bulletin trimestriel*, April 1913, p. 10; UFSF, *Le Suffrage des femmes en France*, 3rd ed. (Paris, 1912), p. 1; UFSF handbills and programs, Dossiers UFSF and Congrès national de l'UFSF, Lyon 1914, BMD; Avril de Sainte-Croix, ed., *Dixième congrès international des femmes* (Paris, 1914), pp. 321-34, 576; Cécile Brunschwicg to Joseph Reinach, April 12, 1911, NAF 24913, BN; Mlle. Levray, *L'Alcoolisme et le vote des femmes* (Paris, n.d.). For international examples of such feminist alliances, see: Alan P. Grimes, *The Puritan Ethic and Woman Suffrage* (New York, 1967) Paulson, *Women's Suffrage and Prohibition*; Grimshaw, *Women's Suffrage in New Zealand*, esp. pp. 21-35; Evans, *The Feminists*, pp. 60-61; Catherine Cleverdon, *The Woman Suffrage Movement in Canada* (Toronto, 1950), p. 11; Flexner, *Century of Struggle*, pp. 181-185; Kraditor, *The Ideas of the Woman Suffrage Movement*, p. 46. For Reinach, see Steve R. Marquardt, "Joseph Reinach (1856-1921): A Political Biography" (Ph.D. diss., University of Minnesota, 1978), pp. 401-415, 452, although he does not develop the link with suffragism.

36. "The 'Rights of Man' which we claim are not those of the masculine being, but of all human beings, since it seems to us that all of humanity is

composed of equal halves, equivalent from all points of view." *Les Droits de l'homme*, January 8, 1911. For the collaboration, see other issues of that review and: *Le Journal des femmes*, May 1907; *L'Action féminine*, June 1, 1909; *Le Féministe*, March 10 and 17, 1910; *La Française*, July 14, 1907; April 30, and December 10, 1911; January 31 and May 2, 1914; UFSF, *Bulletin annuel-1911*, p. 12; UFSF, *Bulletin trimestriel*, January-March 1914, p. 12; Ligue d'électeurs, *Bulletin trimestriel*, April 1911, p. 2; *Le Droit des femmes*, February 15 and May 15, 1914, June 1938; *Le Journal*, April 8, 1914; *Les Cahiers des droits de l'homme*, March 20, 1920; Sainte-Croix, *Le Féminisme*, p. 198; LFDF, *Cinquante ans de féminisme*, p. 22; Dossier Marie Bonnevial, BMD.

37. See the league's *Bulletin trimestriel*, esp. April 1911 for the statutes and program; the *Bulletin* of the UFSF for their collaboration; Dossiers UFSF and Ligue d'électeurs, BMD; *La Française*, April 23, 1911; February 25, 1912; March 10, 1912; February 22, 1913; *Le Radical*, March 24, 1914; Jean du Breuil de Saint-Germain, *La Misère sociale de la femme et le suffrage* (Suresnes, 1911); Barthélemy, *Le Vote des femmes*, pp. 128-29.

38. *La Française*, December 12, 1909.

39. Madeleine Pelletier, "Le Féminisme et les partis politiques en France," *La Suffragiste*, February 1912; Misme, *Pour le suffrage des femmes*, p. 33; *Les Documents du progrès*, February 1910.

40. For Buisson's priorities, see: UFSF, *Bulletin de 1912*, p. 4; *L'Action*, January 23, 1910; Auclert, *Les Femmes au gouvernail*, p. 165. For a different perspective on the proportional representation debates, see David E. Sumler, "Domestic Influences on the Nationalist Revival in France, 1909-1914," *FHS* 6 (1970):517-37.

41. *JO*, Chambre des députés, débats, November 11, 1913; *La Suffragiste*, January 1914; *La Femme de demain*, November 1913; Auclert, *Les Femmes au gouvernail*, pp. 164-68.

42. Minutes, Commission of universal suffrage, 1902-1906 and 1906-1910, C 7375, AN. The papers of Charles Benoist leave no doubt that women's suffrage was an unimportant proposition to him and the committee in comparison to *RP*. See his notes in MS 4534 and MS 4535, Bibliothèque de l'Institut de France.

43. The politics of the proportional representation debate may be followed in detail in Georges Bonnefous and Edouard Bonnefous, *Histoire politique de la IIIᵉ République*, 7 vols. (Paris, 1956-1967), vol. 1.

44. Zeldin, *France, 1848-1945*, 1:719.

45. For the Senate and depopulation, see the discussions in the *JO*, Sénat, débats, January 30 and February 7, 1913, March 5, 1914; for Senator Piot and the strength of natalists in the upper house, see Spengler, *France Faces Depopulation*, pp. 126-27.

46. The historic commitment to women's suffrage may be followed in detail in Sowerwine, *Sisters or Citizens?* and Boxer, "Socialism Faces Fem-

inism." In addition, see *L'Humanité*'s coverage of the party congresses, e.g., September 4, 1906, for Pelletier's speech at Limoges. See also Pelletier's reflections in "Ma Candidature à la députation," and a summary of her role in *Le Petit almanach féministe illustré-1908*, pp. 22-23. For the examples cited, see: *La Française*, November 7, 1909 (Jaurès's speech to the FFU); *JO*, Chambre des députés, débats, June 15, 1910 (Thomas's speech on the Buisson Report); Marcel Sembat, "L'Accession des femmes aux fonctions publique," *Les Documents du progrès*, January 1909; *Revue socialiste*, August 1906 (special issue on women's suffrage); *L'Humanité*, January 19, 1912 (Bracke).

47. Pelletier, "Ma Candidature à la députation," pp. 11-12. See also Auclert's essay, "Le Socialisme n'aurait pas pour résultat l'affranchissement de la femme," in *Les Femmes au gouvernail*, pp. 359-64.

48. See the Albert Thomas papers at the AN, series 94 AP. For avoiding women's suffrage in considering the socialist congresses, 94 AP 333 and 94 AP 405 (Dossiers 9 and 10); for avoiding it in his electoral programs and political interests, 94 AP 475 and 94 AP 476 (elections), 94 AP 332 (politics, 1910-1914).

49. *La Française*, March 17 and December 9, 1912; *L'Humanité*, December 9, 1912. For Jaurès's attitudes about women, see Goldberg, *The Life of Jean Jaurès*, e.g., pp. 375-76. *JO*, Chambre des députés, débats, November 11, 1913 (scrutin no 892).

50. Manuscript text of Pelletier's campaign speech, April 23, 1910, Dossier Madeleine Pelletier, BMD; Pelletier, "Les Candidatures féminines," p. 11.

51. Pelletier, "Le Féminisme et les partis politiques en France" and "Ma Candidature à la députation." On this problem of the conservative socialist attitude toward women and the family, see Guilbert, *Les Femmes et l'organisation syndicale*, pp. 407-408; McMillan, "The Effects of the First World War on the Social Condition of Women in France," p. 102.

52. Madeleine Pelletier to Arria Ly, October 19, 1911, Bouglé Collection, BHVP.

53. For examples of the doubts of bourgeois suffragists, see: *Le Féministe*, May 5, 1908; *La Française*, December 12, 1909 and May 15, 1910.

54. The party, Sowerwine has concluded, "was a male organization devoted to an essentially male preoccupation." See the conclusion to his *Les Femmes et le socialisme*, pp. 233-41. A synthesis of feminism and socialism was "an illusion" in Boxer's conclusion, "Socialism Faces Feminism," p. 107. See also Evans, *The Feminists*, p. 173, on socialist "indifference to women's rights."

55. For a discussion of this attitude, see Charles Thiébaux, *Le Féminisme et les socialistes depuis Saint-Simon jusqu'à nos jours* (Paris, 1906), pp. 123-25; for the "brief delay," see Boxer, "Socialism Faces Feminism," pp. 100-102; Marx, from the "Estranged Labor" manuscript, as translated in Robert C. Tucker, ed., *The Marx-Engels Reader*, 2nd ed. (New York, 1978), p. 80; see

Sowerwine's conclusions on Guesde and feminism, *Sisters or Citizens?*, p. 186; Cf. Auclert's criticism of this socialist theory, *Les Femmes au gouvernail*, p. 359. For the far left, see *Les Documents du progrès*, August 1911; and the debate in Sebastien Faure's *Le Libertaire*, e.g., April 6, 1901, February 13, March 5, 19, 26, and April 23, 1904; July 26, 1908; March 28, 1914; April 4, 1914.

56. Quotations from Suzon (Suzanne Lacore), *L'Equité*, June 15, 1913; excerpts from this article and several others in *L'Equité*'s debate on the relations betwen feminism and socialism are reprinted in Albistur and Armogathe, eds., *Le Grief des femmes*, 2:111-21.

57. For the complexities of working-class anti-feminism, see the discussion of the Couriau affair in Sowerwine, *Sisters or Citizens?*, pp. 135-36, and his longer study, "Workers and Women in France before 1914: the Debate Over the Couriau Affair," *JMH*, 55 (1983): 411-41; for the CGT, see Pellat-Finet's discussion of its relations with feminism in *La Voix du peuple* (the organ of the CGT), e.g., February 9, April 6 and 13, 1914; for Pelletier's conclusions, see her "La Classe ouvrière et le féminisme," *La Suffragiste*, July 1912; see also Pelletier's scathing words on working-class attitudes in her correspondence with Arria Ly, especially letters of August 22 and October 19, 1911, Bouglé Collection, BHVP.

58. Pelletier to Brion, December 27, 1912, Dossier Madeleine Pelletier, BMD (quoted); see also letters of January 7 and 9, 1913. For the foundation of the GdFS, see the detailed account in Sowerwine, *Sisters or Citizens?*, pp. 129-32. See also: *L'Equité*, February 15 and April 15, 1913; *La Française*, May 16, 1914; UFSF, *Bulletin trimestriel*, January-March 1914, p. 3; Dossier La Campagne féministe, F⁷ 13266 (police générale), AN; Dossier Marianne Rauze, BMD; Folder GdFS, Dossier Groupements femmes (divers), BMD; Dossiers Maria Vérone, BMD and BHVP; *La Femme socialiste*, February through April 1913.

59. See Sowerwine, *Sisters or Citizens?*, pp. 132-34 and *Les Femmes et le socialisme*, p. 156 (Saumoneau quotation). See also *La Femme socialiste*, September 1913 through January 1914, especially Saumoneau's article on October 1, 1913; Dossier Louise Saumoneau, Bouglé Collection, BHVP; *L'Equité*, June through November 1913, especially Suzon's articles of June 15, and October 15, 1913, and the responses of August 15 and September 15, 1913. Many of these articles are excerpted in Albistur and Armogathe, eds., *Le Grief des femmes*, 2:115-21. For more on Lacore, see *DPF*, 6:2082-83.

60. Report of Brunschwicg's speech, Dossier Congrès féministe internationale, Bruxelles, 1912, BMD.

61. *La Femme contemporaine*, July 1910, pp. 38-39; *Le Devoir des femmes françaises*, July-August 1910, pp. 577-84; *Le Soleil*, June 2, 1910; Pottecher, "Le Mouvement féministe en France," p. 595; *La Française*, June 12, 1910.

62. *L'Action sociale de la femme*, November 1909, pp. 434-35; July 1910, pp. 323-27; April 1920, pp. 50-55. See the frequent rubrics, "Autour du féminisme" and "Action féminine" in *La Femme contemporaine*; *La Femme catholique contemporaine*, November 1913, pp. 307-311; *Echo de la ligue patriotique des françaises*, February 1914 (quoted).

Chapter Six

1. *Le Droit des femmes*, January 1914; *Le Journal*, December 28, 1913; *L'Humanité*, December 31, 1913; Maria Vérone to Mme. Louis Havet, January 7, 1914, NAF 24508, BN; Dossier Maria Vérone, BMD.

2. Vérone gave a detailed account of the registration campaign in *Le Droit des femmes*, February 15, 1914. See also: *L'Intransigeant*, February 6, 1914; *L'Excelsior*, February 27, 1914; *La Femme de demain*, February 1914; *L'Humanité*, March 8, 1914; police reports, February 2, 1914; Dossier Vote des femmes, B^A 1651, APP; Dossiers Maria Vérone and Vote des femmes, 1914, BMD.

3. *Le Journal*, February 22, 1914.

4. The LFDF court cases may be followed in: *Le Droit des femmes*, February through May 1914; *Le Temps*, February 21, 1914; *L'Autorité*, April 8, 1914; *L'Action*, February 18, 1914; Dossiers Maria Vérone and Votes des femmes, 1914, BMD.

5. *Le Droit des femmes*, January 15 and February 15, 1914; Caroline Kauffmann to Arria Ly, June 12, 1914, Bouglé Collection, BHVP.

6. For Madame Remember, see her articles in *La Suffragiste* and *Le Féminisme intégral*, which includes her most notorious, anti-men articles (e.g., arguing that women should arm themselves against men). For her biography, see *Le Féminisme intégral*, February 1914. See also the many hostile remarks about her in the correspondence of militants in the Bouglé Collection, BHVP: Kauffmann, Pelletier, Camille Bélilon, and Arria Ly all seem to have disliked her a great deal (see, e.g., Pelletier to Arria Ly, November 7, 1913, and Bélilon to Arria Ly, July 10, 1914). For the verdict that Remember was an "unbalanced type," see McMillan, "The Effects of the First World War on the Social Condition of Women in France," p. 141.

7. *La Française*, May 16, 1914 (Misme quote); police report, February 11, 1914, Dossier Rapports et notes concernant l'activité des divers groupements féministes, 1913 à 1928, F7 13266, AN (Ducret quote). For the creation of the LNVF, see the statutes of the group in the Dossier LNVF, MBD: *Le Journal*, February 8, March 17, and April 20, 1914; *Gil Blas*, February 8, 1914; *Le Soleil*, February 8, 1914; *Le Féminisme intégral*, May and June 1914; Camille Bélilon to Arria Ly, March 22, 1914, Bouglé Collection, BHVP; Dossier Vote des femmes, 1914, BMD; *La Femme de demain*, February 1914.

8. For the argument over municipal suffrage versus integral suffrage in 1914 and the conflict between the LNVF and the UFSF, see police reports on LNVF meetings, February 8 and 11, March 17, April 4, and June 30, 1914, Dossier Vote des femmes, B^A 1651, APP, and February 11, 1914, Dossier Rapports et notes concernant l'activité des divers groupements féministes, 1913 à 1928, F7 13266, AN; Camille Bélilon to Arria Ly, March 22, 1914, Bouglé Collection, BHVP: *Le Journal*, March 17, 1914; *La Française*, May 6, 1914; Dossiers UFSF and Vote des femmes, 1914, BMD.

9. For the rivalry between the LFDF and the UFSF in 1914, see *La Française*, May 16, 1914; an interview with Vérone in *Le Rappel*, June 3 and 8, 1914; *Le Droit des femmes*, February 15 and March 15, 1914; undated memorandum of the UFSF central committee (April or May 1914), Dossier UFSF, BMD.

10. Nelly Roussel, "Créons la citoyenne," as delivered March 16, 1914, reprinted in Roussel, *Trois conférences*, pp. 89-115 (quotation, p. 115).

11. Summary of the meeting of Suffrage des femmes, March 13, 1914, Dossier Hubertine Auclert, BMD; *Gil Blas*, March 14, 1914.

12. For the preparations for the demonstration, see *La Française*, March 28, 1914; *Le Radical*, March 27, 1914.

13. *Le Droit des femmes*, April 15, 1914; *La Française*, April 15, 1914 (Misme quotes). For accounts of the demonstration: *Le Petit parisien* (estimating that twenty feminists participated), March 30, 1914; *L'Intransigeant* (stating that most of the crowd was curious men and children), March 30, 1914; *La Libre parole* (claiming that "no, or very few" suffragists were present), March 30, 1914; *L'Action* (reporting a crowd of 200-300, but too few suffragists to make a cortège), March 30, 1914; *Le Radical* (noting that the militants "failed to draw many women"), March 30, 1914.

14. *Le Soleil*, March 30, 1914; *L'Intransigeant*, March 30, 1914; *Le Radical*, March 30, 1914; *L'Action*, March 30, 1914.

15. Estimate given in *Le Droit des femmes*, January 1914, p. 6.

16. UFSF poster for the 1914 elections, Dossier UFSF, BMD. For reiteration of the moderate position on these questions in 1914, see *L'Action féminine*, March 1914; *La Femme de demain*, March 1914; *Le Journal*, March 14, 1914; UFSF, *Bulletin trimestriel*, July-October 1913, p. 2; *La Française*, March 21 and May 16, 1914.

17. *La Française*, March 21, 1914.

18. *JO*, Chambre des députés, débats, February 3, 1914. See also: *La Femme*, February 1914; *L'Action féminine*, March 1914; Ligue des électeurs, *Bulletin*, February 1914; *Le Journal*, March 3, 1914; Dossier Vote des femmes, 1914, BMD.

19. Calculations are based on electoral returns from *Le Temps*, May 1914, and the list of pro-suffrage deputies compiled by the suffrage leagues, Dossier

Vote des femmes, 1914, BMD. See also: *L'Intransigeant*, July 1, 1914; *La Française*, July 5, 1914.

20. For Buisson, see *Le Radical*, April 27, 1914; *DPF*, 2:806 and 7:2556; *La Française*, May 2 and July 5, 1914. For the composition of the commission and the suffragist analysis of it: UFSF, *Bulletin 1914-1916*, pp. 51-52.

21. Valentine Thomson was a member of the UFSF central committee. For her, see *La Vie féminine* (which she edited); *La Française*, June 27, 1914; Gertrude Atherton, *The Living Present* (New York, 1917), pp. 99-118. For Deschanel, see Vérone's article on his presidential election in 1920, *Le Droit des femmes*, March 1920. *Le Journal*, June 23, 1914; *Le Bonnet rouge*, June 3, 1914; Dossier Congrès UFSF—Lyon, 1914, BMD.

22. For Téry, see *Le Matin*, April 28-May 5, May 19, 1908; his open letter to the prefect of the Seine, April 21, 1910, published in *L'Intransigeant*, April 22, 1910; the account of his protest, *Le Soleil*, April 25, 1910; Dossier Marguerite Durand, candidate aux élections législatives de 1910, BMD. For his origination of the poll of 1914; *La Française*, March 14, and May 2, 1914; *Le Féminisme intégral*, April 1914; Dossier Vote des femmes, 1914. BMD. Cf. Li, *La Presse féministe*, p. 208, attributing the poll to Séverine. For the early suffrage record of *Le Journal*, see Paul and Victor Margueritte's article there, May 24, 1906. For suffragist appreciation of the newspaper's role: *Le Journal des femmes*, November 1908. For *Le Journal*'s role in 1914, see almost daily articles there, especially March-May 1914, and the discussions of the paper's activities in *La Française*; the calendars of suffrage activities in *La Française* and *Le Féminisme intégral*; and the Dossier Vote des femmes, 1914, BMD. For a contrasting opinion of *Le Journal*'s suffragism and the conclusion that it was "an enterprising newspaper seeking publicity," see Evans, *The Feminists*, p. 133.

23. *Le Journal*, March 15, 1914 (Roussel quote); *Gil Blas*, May 2, 1914; Dossier Séverine, BMD; *Le Journal* to Amélie Hammer, April 4, 1914, Dossier Vote des femmes, 1914, BMD; LFDF, *Cinquante ans de féminisme*, pp. 26-27; *L'Humanité*, April 26, 1914; *Le Droit des femmes*, April 15, 1914; Misme to *Le Journal*, published there on March 22, 1914; *La Française*, March 14 and 21, April 18, 1914.

24. *Le Journal*, April 25, 1914; *Le Droit des femmes*, May 15, 1914.

25. *Le Journal*, April 27-May 5, 1914; *Gil Blas*, April 27, 1914; *L'Intransigeant*, April 29, 1914.

26. See, for example, the palpable relief that the poll "was not accompanied by reprehensible tumultuous demonstrations," in *Le Petit Parisien*, April 27, 1914.

27. *La Française*, May 2, 1914.

28. The ballots used in the poll were printed with the opinion, "I wish to vote," but had no provision for the opposite opinion; dissenting ballots

required one to change this sentence. For contrast, it is instructive to see the poll conducted by a conservative feminine magazine, *Le Petit écho de la mode*. The magazine had an anti-suffrage editorial policy and published articles on the violence of the English suffragettes. Its readers voted 143,993 to 96,925 against their own enfranchisement. That may have accurately measured the opinion of French women, although conservative readership produced a surprisingly high pro-suffrage total. See *Le Petit Echo* for February and March 1914. For feminist responses, see *Le Droit des femmes*, March 15 and May 15, 1914.

29. See Bernard Lecache, *Séverine* (Paris, 1930), pp. 170-202, esp. pp. 195-96 (quoted). There are materials on her early career in CP 4248, BHVP; on her left-wing activities in B^A 1660, APP; and on her suffragism in the dossier Séverine, BMD. A selection of her articles, edited by Evelyne Le Garrec, has been published under the title *Séverine: Choix de papiers* (Paris, 1982). For her early anti-suffragism, see *Le Figaro*, July 19, 1890; for her interest in women strikers, see her series in *La Bataille syndicaliste*, May 1913. For reaction to her 1914 suffragism: *La Française*, May 16, 1914.

30. Dossiers Amélie Hammer, Vote des femmes, 1914, LFDF, and Congrès UFSF, Lyon, 1914, BMD; *Le Journal*, May 26 and June 10, 1914; *Le Féminisme intégral*, January 1914; *Le Droit des femmes*, May 15, 1914; *La Française*, May 30 and June 6, 1914.

31. *L'Humanité*, May 10, 1914; *Le Droit des femmes*, May 15 and June 15, 1914; *Le Rappel*, June 3 and 8, 1914; *La Française*, June 27 and July 5, 1914; Dossier Vote des femmes, 1914, BMD.

32. *Le Droit des femmes*, March 15, 1914; *Le Journal*, June 24, 1914; summary of the meeting of Suffrage des femmes, March 13, 1914, Dossier Hubertine Auclert, BMD; *Gil Blas*, March 14, 1914; Camille Bélilon to Arria Ly, May 7, 1914, Bouglé Collection, BHVP.

33. *Le Journal*, June 2, 1914; *L'Aurore*, June 3, 1914; *La Française*, June 20, 1914; Dossiers Séverine, Congrés UFSF, Lyon 1914, and Vote des femmes, 1914, BMD.

34. Dossiers Séverine, Manifestation Condorcet, and Vote des femmes, 1914, BMD; *Le Droit des femmes*, June 15, 1914; *Le Journal*, June 24 and July 2, 1914.

35. See Misme's "Les Françaises et les démonstrations de la rue," *La Française*, April 4, 1914, for her general feelings on the subject; an article of July 5, 1914, for her specific misgivings about the Condorcet demonstration.

36. *Le Journal*, July 4, 1914.

37. *La Française*, June 27, 1914; Dossier Manifestation Condorcet, BMD.

38. *La Française*, December 7, 1935; *Le Matin*, July 6, 1914; Dossiers René Viviani and Manifestation Condorcet, BMD; Ministry of the Interior to Prefecture of Police, June 26, 1914, Dossier Manifestations, B^A 1651, APP;

under-secretary of state for beaux-arts to Séverine, July 1, 1914, Dossier Manifestation Condorcet, BMD.

39. *Le Petit Parisien* (July 6, 1914) gave an estimate of 2,000 and the Prefecture of Police report of the demonstration (July 6, 1914), 2,400 (Dossier Manifestations, B^A 1651, APP). Georges Lhermitte claimed 10,000 in *Le Droit des femmes*, April 1922. Most of the daily press, and most feminists, estimated 5,000-6,000; for many such estimates, see the Dossier Manifestation Condorcet, BMD.

40. *La Française*, June 27, 1914 (quoted); for accounts of participants, see *Le Féminisme intégral*, July 1914 and Camille Bélilon to Arria Ly, July 10, 1914, Bouglé Collection, BHVP. For details of the demonstration, see Dossier Manifestation Condorcet, BMD; *Le Journal*, July 6, 1914; *Gil Blas*, July 6, 1914; *Le Bonnet rouge*, July 5, 1914; *L'Autorité*, July 6, 1914. For the LFDF banquet, see *Le Droit des femmes*, May 15 and June 15, 1914; *Le Féminisme intégral*, July 1914; *Le Bonnet rouge*, July 7, 1914; LFDF, *Cinquante ans de féminisme*, p. 22; Dossier Manifestation Condorcet, BMD.

41. Camille Bélilon to Arria Ly, July 10, 1914, Bouglé Collection, BHVP.

Chapter Seven

1. *Le Droit des femmes*, June 15, 1915.

2. The full text of Viviani's appeal is reprinted in Marie d'Espie de la Hire, *La Femme française, son activité pendant la guerre* (Paris, 1917), pp. 7-8. See also the discussion in Abensour, *Histoire générale du féminisme*, p. 306; Yvonne Delatour, "Les Effets de la guerre sur la situation de la française d'après la presse féminine, 1914-1918" (Diplôme d'études supérieures, University of Paris, 1965).

3. Circular letter, de Witt-Schlumberger to all members of the UFSF, August 12, 1914, Dossiers UFSF, BMD and BHVP; handbill with de Witt-Schlumberger's signature, "Appel aux femmes françaises," Dossier de Witt-Schlumberger, BMD (quoted); unidentified obituary of Siegfried, Dossier Julie Siegfried, BMD; Siegfried's speech on the duties of women, *La Française*, January 30, 1915.

4. *La Française*, November 15, 1914.

5. *Le Droit des femmes*, March 15 and June 15, 1915; program of the UFSF, November 14, 1915, Dossier UFSF, Bouglé Collection, BHVP; UFSF, *Bulletin 1914-1916* (quoted).

6. Speech at the Sorbonne, March 7, 1917, quoted in Dossier Julie Siegfried, BMD.

7. *La Fronde*, August 17, 1914 (quoted). For socialist women, see Sowerwine, *Sisters or Citizens?*, pp. 143-46.

8. See the Dossier CNFF, BMD; LFDF, *Cinquante ans de féminisme, passim*; police générale file, La Propagande féminine en faveur de la paix, F⁷ 13266, AN. For Vérone and the Rome congress, see *Le Temps*, May 17, 1914; Dossier Congrès international des femmes (Rome, 1914), BMD. Program of the UFSF congress, May 30-June 1, 1914, Dossier Congrès national de l'UFSF, Lyon 1914, Dossier Congrès national de l'UFSF, Lyon 1914, BMD.

9. For Halbwachs and Duchêne, see Sowerwine, *Sister or Citizens?*, pp. 143-60; for Pelletier, see her *La Guerre, est-elle naturelle?* (Paris, n.d.); her fragmentary World War I diary, especially the entry for August 24, 1914, Dossier Madeleine Pelletier, BMD; Pelletier to Arria Ly, December 21, 1914, Bouglé Collection, BHVP. One of Saumoneau's manifestos is reprinted in Albistur and Armogathe, eds., *Le Grief des femmes*, 2:209. For Brion, see *La Bataille syndicaliste*, July 30, 1914, and the discussion of her pacifism in H. Dubief, "Hélène Brion (1882-1962)," *Le Mouvement social* 44 (1963): 93-97; Annie Kriegel, "Procès de guerre—procès Brion," ibid., pp. 97-99; *La Française*, December 8, 1917 and April 13, 1918.

10. *L'Action féminine*, August 1916.

11. See the discussion in Jane Misme, "La Guerre et le rôle des femmes," *La Revue de Paris* 23 (1916): 206; Léon Abensour, *Les Vaillantes: Héroïnes, martyrs, et remplaçantes* (Paris, 1917), pp. 34-35.

12. Abensour, *Les Vaillantes*, p. 33; Abensour, *Histoire générale du féminisme*, p. 307; Dossier Sainte-Croix, BMD; Folder, Office central de l'activité féminine, in Dossier Groupements femmes (divers), BMD; Dossier Juliette Raspail, BMD; La Hire, *La Femme française*, pp. 171-72.

13. For an introduction to women in the French Red Cross during World War I, see Andrée d'Alix, *Le Rôle patriotique des femmes: La Croix-rouge française* (Paris, 1914); Coubé, *Le Patriotisme de la femme française*; Constance Maud, "What French Women Are Doing," *The Nineteenth Century and After* 83 (1918):1169-71; Mme. Emile Borel, ed., *La Mobilisation féminine en France, 1914-1919* (Paris, 1919), pp. 16-17. For the example of d'Uzès, see her *Souvenirs*, pp. 123-30, and her correspondence with Mme. Raymond Poincaré, in the Poincaré MSS, NAF 16023, BN. For Pelletier, see her war diary in the Dossier Pelletier, BMD. For the leagues: Dossier Elisabeth Fonséque, BMD; *Le Droit des femmes*, March 15, 1915; *L'Action féminine*, July 1916; La Hire, *La Femme française*, p. 177; Maud, "What French Women Are Doing," pp. 1174-75; *La Française*, July 14, 1917; Abensour, *Les Vaillantes*, pp. 100-103.

14. *La Française*, February 13, 1915; *DPF*, 2:800; Dossiers Brunschwicg and de Witt-Schlumberger, BMD; Dossier Brunschwicg, Bouglé Collection, BHVP; *Minerva*, December 14, 1930; Abensour, *Les Vaillantes*, pp. 103-109; Comtesse de Courson, *La Femme française pendant la guerre* (Paris, 1916), pp.

19-31; La Hire, *La Femme française*, pp. 170-75; Maud, "What French Women Are Doing," p. 1180; *International Women's News*, November 1946, p. 22; *L'Action féminine*, September-October 1915.

15. Police reports on UFSF meeting, March 20, 1916, and annual congress, April 22, 1916, Dossier Rapports et notes concernant l'activité des divers groupements féministes, 1913 à 1928, F⁷ 13266, AN; *L'Action féminine*, May 1916; UFSF, *Bulletin 1914-1916*, pp. 4, 22.

16. LFDF, *Cinquante ans de féminisme*, pp. 121-22, UFSF, *Bulletin 1914-1916*, p. 15; *La Française*, April 8, 1916.

17. For the feminist campaign against alcoholism during World War I, see the Julie Siegfried–Joseph Reinach correspondence for 1915-1916, NAF 13566, BN; correspondence, handbills, and brochures in the Dossiers CNFF and UFSF, BMD; clippings in the Dossier Féminisme—France, 1910-1920, BMD; *La Française*, almost weekly during the war, e.g., January 7, 1915; *Le Féminisme intégral*, October 1916; UFSF, *Bulletin 1914-1916*, pp. 15-22; *Le Droit des femmes*, November-December 1916, p. 11; Borel, *La Mobilisation féminine*, p. 85; Marquardt, "Joseph Reinach," p. 408; Atherton, *The Living Present*, pp. 73-98.

18. For examples of extreme chauvinism within the movement, see Remember's *Le Féminisme intégral*, especially for December 1915, April 1916, October 1916, and January 1917. Remember, who also contributed to the *Revue anti-germanique*, was almost pathological in her hatred of Germany: in one article she urged women who traveled always to ascertain that the staff of hotels they visited was entirely French. "In factories, workshops, schools, salons ... all women must without exception pitilessly attack the Germans ..." (*Le Féminisme intégral*, April 1916).

19. The police générale files (F⁷ 13266, AN) contain reports to the Sûreté générale (Ministry of the Interior) on several suffrage groups: see especially the reports of April 23 and 28 (2), 1915. The files of the Prefecture of Police (Bᴬ 1651) contain similar conclusions; see, for example, reports of December 23, 1916, on the UFSF, and May 14, 1917, on Suffrage des femmes.

20. For the congress, see (International Women's Commission for Permanent Peace), *International Congress of Women. The Hague, 28 April-1 May, 1915. Report* (The Hague, 1915); Mary L. Degen, *The History of the Woman's Peace Party* (Baltimore, 1939); Emily Balch, "The International Congress of Women at The Hague," *Home Progress* 5 (1915):111. The French manifesto is reprinted in the report of the congress, pp. 313-15; UFSF, *Bulletin 1914-1916*, pp. 64-66; *La Française*, April 24, 1915; and in *L'Action féminine*, May 1915. The report also prints letters from de Witt-Schlumberger (p. 311) and Siegfried (p. 312). See also: *La Française*, March 27 and April 24, 1915; memorandum by the UFF, April 1915, Dossier UFF, BMD: *Le Droit des*

femmes, June 15, 1915; *L'Action féminine*, May 1915; police report of April 28, 1915, Dossier Rapports et notes concernant l'activité des divers groupements féministes, 1913 à 1928, F⁷ 13266, AN; Marie Chaumont to Camille Bélilon, April 26, 1915, CP 4247, BHVP. For claims of pacifism, see Sainte-Croix to the president of the Dutch national council of women, reprinted in *L'Action féminine*, July-August, 1915; Degen, *The History of the Woman's Peace Party*, p. 79 (quoted).

21. John Williams, *The Other Battleground: The Home Fronts, Britain, France, and Germany, 1914-1918* (Chicago, 1972), p. 291. For similar conclusions, see: Arthur Marwick, *War and Social Change in the Twentieth Century* (London, 1975); Maurice Bardèche, *Histoire des femmes*, 2 vols. (Paris, 1968), 2:357-61. For the contrary conclusion, that the position of women did not greatly change, see McMillan, "The Effects of the First World War on the Social Condition of Women in France."

22. Abensour, *Histoire générale du féminisme*, p. 310.

23. For discussions of the opening of new jobs to women during the war, see McMillan, "The Effects of the First World War on the Social Condition of French Women," chap. 7; Delatour, "Les Effets de la guerre sur la situation de la française," pt. 3. Prewar data drawn from a survey by Senator Gervais, published in *Le Matin*, January 9, 1911, and reprinted in Buisson, *Le Vote des femmes*, pp. 39-40. Conscription and female replacement data from Alain Decaux, *Histoire des françaises*, 2 vols. (Paris, 1972), 2:983; munitions data from Abensour, *Le Problème féministe*, p. 137.

24. Arthur Fontaine, *French Industry during the War* (New Haven, 1926), pp. 43-45, 406.

25. Abensour, *Le Problème féministe*, p. 137. For the development of the thesis that the war chiefly redistributed women within the labor force, see McMillan, "The Effects of the First World War on the Social Condition of Women in France."

26. Data computed from Toutain, *La Population de la France*, Tables 58 and 59, pp. 162-63. See the observations by Thérèse Casewitz in *Jus suffragii*, January 1920. Similar conclusions can be reached by studying the condition of working women during the war. Both the government and private industry exploited women by paying them less than the men they replaced. A CNFF study of 1916 found that women earned about half of the wages of the men drafted; see *Le Féminisme intégral*, July 1916; Abensour, *Les Vaillantes*, pp. 43-45.

27. The Flandin Report surveyed the wartime political roles of women: *JO*, Chambre des députés, documents, October 18, 1918 (no. 5095), esp. pp. 44-45. For the laws mentioned, see Duvergier, *Collection complète des lois*, n.s. 15:310-311 (July 3, 1915); 16:38 (February 2, 1916); 17:120-23 (March 20,

1917); o.s. 70:480 (December 14, 1870). For the law of guardianship, see *La Française*, July 14, 1917; Dossier Amélioration, Bouglé Collection, BHVP; Paul d'Estournelles de Constant, *Les Femmes pendant et après la guerre* (Paris, 1916), pp. 7-8. See André Isoré's legal thesis, *La Guerre et la condition privée de la femme* (Paris, 1919), esp. pp. 481-92.

28. Charles Bouglé, *De la sociologie à l'action sociale: Pacifisme, féminisme, cooperation* (Paris, 1923), p. 109. See also Fernand Crocos, *Les Femmes en guerre* (Paris, 1927), p. 91.

29. Bardèche, *Histoire des femmes*, 2:360-61.

30. For other expressions of this doubt, see Zeldin, *France 1848-1945*, 1:348; McMillan, "The Effects of the First World War on the Social Condition of Women in France," pp. 196-97. For a candid contemporary assertion that the shift of attitudes was temporary, see Abensour, *Histoire générale du féminisme*, pp. 310-11.

31. *The Times* (London), February 3, 1922.

32. See the discussion in Evans, *The Feminists*, pp. 211-28; the argument about British women's suffrage is on p. 222. For a strong argument that "the circumstances of war had inhibited the suffragists nearly as much as their opponents" (in England), see Martin D. Pugh, "Politicians and the Woman's Vote, 1914-1918," *History* 59 (1974): 358-74. For a vigorous rejection of this view, see Arthur Marwick, *Women at War, 1914-1918* (London, 1977), p. 8.

33. This argument was first developed in a different form in Steven C. Hause, "Women Who Rallied to the Tricolor: The Effects of World War I on the French Women's Suffrage Movement," *PWSFH* 6 (1979): 371-81.

34. See the press survey in Delatour, "Les Effets de la guerre sur la situation de la française," pp. 11-12; Dossier Madame Remember, BMD; Madeleine Pelletier, "Le Féminisme et la guerre," *La Suffragiste*, June 1919; Pelletier to Arria Ly, June 6, 1921, Bouglé Collection, BHVP; Dossier Tirage des journaux, F7 12843, AN.

35. Notes générales concernant l'agitation féministe dans les divers dé-partements, 1918-1922, police générale files, F7 13266, AN; UFSF, *Bulletin 1920-1921*, p. 9; unidentified clippings, Dossier Congrès de l'alliance inter-nationale pour le suffrage des femmes, Genève, 1920, BMD.

36. For illustrations of the postwar diffusion of suffragist interests, see the programs of the groups, such as that for the 1921 congress of the UFSF, Dossier UFSF, Bouglé Collection, BHVP. For de Witt-Schlumberger, *L'Il-lustration*, 82 (1924): 435. See also: Dossier Avril de Sainte-Croix, BMD; *Action sociale de la femme*, April 1919, pp. 47-48 (quoted); *Jus suffragii* (French edition), March 1921, pp. 88-89.

37. *L'Humanité*, May 19, 1919. For feminists' comments on the burial of the suffrage question under postwar issues, see: *Jus suffragii* (French edition), July 1919, p. 78; UFSF, *Bulletin 1920-1921*, pp. 46-47; *Le Féminisme intégral*

10 (undated), p. 5. See also the discussion in Delatour, "Les Effets de la guerre sur la situation de la française," pp. 168-69. The foremost feminist recognition of the problem was over the replacement of women in the labor force; see *La Voix des femmes*, May 12, 1921; *Jus suffragii* (French edition), January 1920, pp. 52-53; *Le Droit des femmes*, March 1919.

38. See Pelletier's *Mon Voyage aventureux en Russie communiste* (Paris, 1922); her articles in *La Voix des femmes*, especially in 1921; and her correspondence with Arria Ly, especially a letter of May 13, 1921, Bouglé Collection, BHVP. For others, *La Voix des femmes* is the best source. For communism and feminism, see *L'Ouvrière*, April 1 and June 10, 1922; *La Lutte féministe*, June 25, 1921. For Vérone's attack on Bolshevism, see an unidentified letter to the editor by her in the Dossier Maria Vérone, BMD. For feminism and the Red Scare, see Evans, *The Feminists*, p. 210. For police surveillance, see F[7] 13266, AN, and B[A] 1651 and B[A] 1660, APP.

39. La Vie Féminine, June 1, 1919.

40. Camille Bélilon to Arria Ly, January 4, 1916, Bouglé Collection, BHVP.

41. *La Vie féminine*, February 26, 1916.

42. UFSF, *Bulletin, 1914-1916*, pp. 2, 53; *La Française*, April 27, 1916 (quoted).

43. *JO*, Chambre des députés, documents, April 29, 1915 (no. 847); Barthélemy, *Le Vote des femmes*, p. 131; Leclère, *Le Vote des femmes en France*, p. 137; *L'Echo de Paris*, November 9 and 13, 1916; *Le Droit des femmes*, December 1918; *L'Equité*, March 1916; La Hire, *La Femme française*, pp. 229-30.

44. Roussel in *L'Equité*, March 1916 (quoted). For acceptance: *L'Action féminine*, December 1916, pp. 115-16; police report of February 16, 1916, Dossier Rapports et notes concernant l'activité des divers groupements féministes, F[7] 13266, AN; police report of April 6, 1917, Dossier Vote des femmes, B[A] 1651, AAP; UFSF, *Bulletin 1914-1916*, p. 53. For criticism: La Hire, *La Femme française*, p. 231; *Le Droit des femmes*, May and November-December 1916; Maria Vérone in *L'Oeuvre*, July 4, 1919 (quoted).

45. The Flandin Report, *JO*, Chambre des députés, documents, October 18, 1918 (no. 5095), p. 2; *Le Féminisme intégral*, August 1917.

46. For a survey of international wartime suffrage activities, see Evans, *The Feminists*, pp. 219-28; for Canada, see Cleverdon, *The Woman Suffrage Movement in Canada*, pp. 122-30.

47. See Flexner, *Century of Struggle*, pp. 276-93. For an example of French attention to the role of women in the American presidential elections of 1916, see *Le Journal*, November 6, 1916. For feminist attention to suffrage developments abroad, see *La Française*, 1916-1918, e.g., May 1, 1915; by 1917, such stories were so frequent that Misme grouped them under the heading "Le Suffrage des femmes en marche."

48. Evans, *The Feminists*, pp. 219-20; Stites, *The Women's Liberation Movement in Russia*, pp. 289-96; Great Britain, *The Parliamentary Debates*, House of Commons, 5th ser., 94, June 1917; for French discussion, *Le Féminisme intégral*, August 1917 (quoted).

49. The Flandin Report, *JO*, Chambre des députés, documents, October 18, 1918 (no. 5095); police report on UFSF meetings, April 6, 1917, Dossier Vote des femmes, B^A 1651, APP; *La Française*, January 13 and July 7, 1917; Leclère, *Le Vote des femmes en France*, p. 137; Barthélemy, *Le Vote des femmes*, pp. 131-32.

50. There is a large dossier on Séverine's activities during the war and the 1920s at the Prefecture of Police. Her efforts to resume the suffrage campaign can be found in police reports of April 22, November 2, and December 20, 1916; February 12, July 29, 1917, B^A 1660, APP.

51. *Le Journal*, June 21, 1917 (de Witt-Schlumberger quote); Brunschwicg to the members of the UFSF, February 10, 1917, Dossier UFSF, Bouglé Collection, BHVP; *Le Journal*, April 6, 1917; unidentified clippings, April 1917, Dossier Vote des femmes, campagne 1915-1917, BMD; Dossier Brunschwicg, BMD; *DPF*, 2:799-801; UFSF, *Bulletin 1914-1916*, pp. 51-53 (quoted); circular letter of the Paris group of the UFSF, December 1917, Dossier UFSF, BMD; *La Française*, January 13 and February 24, May 26, June 9, and July 7, 1917; programs of UFF meetings, 1917-1918, Dossier UFF, BMD; *L'Humanité*, May 19, 1919, *L'Heure de la femme*, May 20, 1919; unidentified clipping in the Dossier Julie Siegfried, BMD (quoted).

52. *Le Figaro*, June 21, 1917; *Le Journal*, April 6 and June 21, 1917; *L'Humanité*, June 21, 1917, *L'Excelsior*, June 21, 1917; *Le Droit des femmes*, December 1918; LFDF, *Cinquante ans de féminisme* p. 27; unidentified clippings and letters to Flandin, Dossier Vote des femmes, campagne 1915-1917, BMD; police report on Suffrage des femmes meeting, May 14, 1917, Dossier Vote des femmes, B^A 1651, APP; *Le Féminisme intégral*, August 1917.

53. For Action des femmes: their statutes in Folder Action des femmes, in Dossier Groupements femmes (divers), BMD; Prefecture of Police memorandum, June 4, 1917, and numerous police reports during 1916-1917, police générale files, F^7 13266, AN; *Principes et programme de l'Action des femmes* (Paris, 1917), in Dossier L'Action des femmes, Bouglé Collection, BHVP. For the Comité d'action suffragiste: Prefecture of Police memoranda, January 2, February 3 and 4, 1918, police générale files, F^7 13266, AN; Dossier Jeanne Mélin, Bouglé Collection, BHVP; police report, December 26, 1917, Dossier Vote des femmes, B^A 1651, APP; *La Française*, January 5, 1918.

54. *Principes et programme de l'Action des femmes*, p. 6 (quoted); Dossier L'Action des femmes, Bouglé Collection, BHVP; *La Française*, March 16 and March 30 (quoted), 1918.

Chapter Eight

1. Undated [1918] letter, de Witt-Schlumberger to the UFSF, Dossier UFSF, Bouglé Collection, BHVP (quoted); LFDF manifesto, January 22, 1919, Dossier LFDF, Bouglé Collection, BHVP; *Le Droit des femmes*, February 1919; *L'Oeuvre*, December 16, 1918.

2. See *Le Droit des femmes*, 1919-1920, e.g., discussion of the federation in November 1920. For the charter, see the Dossier LFDF, BMD.

3. For the provincial efforts, see the UFSF *Bulletin 1918-1919* and *Bulletin 1920-1921* plus the reports to the Sûreté générale in Dossier Notes concernant l'agitation féministe dans les divers départements, 1918-1928, F7 13266, AN. For attempts to hold large public meetings in Paris, see the Dossier Rapports et notes concernant l'activité des divers groupements féministes, 1913 à 1928, ibid. *La Française*, December 7, 1918; posters and leaflets in Dossier Amélioration, BMD; *L'Heure de la femme*, April 20, 1919. Notes on the foundation of the Comité, October 27, 1919, Dossier Comité de propagande féministe, BMD; Dossier Louise Brunet, BMD; handbills and programs, Dossier Comité de propagande féministe, Bouglé Collection, BHVP; police memorandum, January 16, 1921, Dossier Rapports et notes concernant l'activité des divers groupements féministes, 1913 à 1928, F7 13266, AN.

4. For Saumoneau, see Sowerwine, *Sisters or Citizens?*, pp. 160-65. In *La Voix des femmes*, see esp. March 3, 1921; in *La Vague*, January 2 and February 6, 1919; in *La Lutte féministe*, February 20, April 3, May 9, and October 1, 1919; June 25, 1921.

5. Annie Christitch, " 'Yes, We Approve,' " *The Catholic Citizen*, July 15, 1919, pp. 51-52. The Fawcett Library (London) holds the papers of the Catholic Woman Suffrage Society; MS carton 135 contains minutes, a diary, and newsclippings for this period. See also the discussion of French Catholics in *L'Action sociale de la femme*, December 1919, pp. 153-54; May 1920, p. 71.

6. Simone de Beauvoir, *The Second Sex* [1952] (New York, 1974), p. 138.

7. Christitch, " 'Yes, We Approve,' " p. 52.

8. See the New York *Times*, December 21, 1919; John T. Ellis, *The Life of Cardinal Gibbons, Archbishop of Baltimore, 1834-1921*, 2 vols. (Milwaukee, 1952), 2:539-43; "Sono avventurati," an allocution "on the mission of woman in society," October 21, 1919. Quotations are from the English text, published in *The Catholic Mind*, December 22, 1919, pp. 453-57. See also the longer text, with introductory remarks, in the *Actes de Benoît XV*, pp. 68-72; the authors wish to thank Karen Offen for providing them with a copy of this text.

9. See *La Française*, May 11, 1918; *Le Gaulois*, May 24, 1906; *Echo de la ligue patriotique des françaises*, May 1925, p. 3. These arguments may be traced in the postwar *Echo* and *Petit écho* of the LPF, especially in the column

"Les Idées de Marthe," written by the league's advisor. The authors wish to thank Odile Sarti for calling this material to their attention.

10. *Jeanne Chenu, 1861-1939. Action sociale de la femme et le livre français* (Paris, n.d.), p. 43; *L'Action sociale de la femme* (Angers, 1935), pp. 5-6; Dossier Action sociale de la femme, BHVP; *L'Action sociale de la femme*, May 1918, pp. 65-69; June 1919, p. 81; September-October 1919, p. 117; December 1919, p. 155; March 1920, pp. 33-35, 153-56 (Mme. Flornoy quote; italics in the original); July-August 1920, p. 158 (Moustier quote); *La Croix*, May 19, 1919; A. Feraud, *La Femme devant les urnes* (Paris, 1918); *DPF*, 7:2534-35; *JO*, Chambre des députés, débats, May 20, 1919.

11. Dossier Levert-Chotard, BMD; Folder, Action sociale de la femme, in Dossier Groupements femmes (divers), BMD; Dossier Duchesse de la Rochefoucauld, Bouglé Collection, BHVP; Dossier Levert-Chotard, Bouglé Collection, BHVP; *Minerva*, March 18, 1934; *L'Action sociale de la femme*, January 1921, pp. 1-2; *Chenu*, p. 43. The prospectus of the UNVF is discussed in Frances I. Clark, *The Position of Women in Contemporary France* (London, 1937), pp. 227-28; a copy of the statutes exists in the Dossier UNVF, BMD.

12. *L'Action sociale de la femme*, September-October 1921, pp. 175-78.

13. See "Note sur les règles en vigeur en matière de réunions publiques ou privées," police générale files, F⁷ 12847, AN. For a full discussion of civil liberties during the war, see Pierre Renouvin, *The Forms of War Government in France* (New Haven, 1927), pp. 27-52. "Liste de principaux groupements féministes, October 1918" and Dossier Rapports et notes concernant l'activité des divers groupements féministes, 1913 à 1928 (quotation from Director of the Sûreté générale to the Prefect of the Loire, March 8, 1918), F⁷ 13266, AN.

14. See *L'Humanité*, March 11, 1919, for the application of these rules to the GdFS. In general, see the police files in F⁷ 13266, AN. *L'Oeuvre*, March 29, 1919 (quoted).

15. *JO*, Chambre des députés, débats, January 9, 1918 (Siegfried quotation); *La Renaissance*, January 19, 1918, and clippings in the Dossier Vote des femmes, 1918, BMD. For Clemenceau, see: *La Française*, February 22, 1919; *Les Travailleuses*, March 1919; *Jus suffragii* (French edition), April 1919, pp. 54-56; *La Lutte féministe*, March 20, 1919; *L'Oeuvre*, February 17, 1919. For Maurras, *L'Action française*, May 21, 1919.

16. *JO*, Chambre des députés, débats, January 24, October 18, and November 12, 1918; January 22 and 30, 1919; ibid., documents, 1918, nos. 4228 and 5095; 1919, nos. 199, 4102, and 5611. Drafts of bills and amendments, Charles Benoist MSS, XI/Dossier 1 (réforme électorale), MS 4535, Bibliothèque de l'Institut de France. Grinberg, *Historique du mouvement suffragiste*, pp. 113-14; Leclère, *Le Vote des femmes en France*, p. 139; Barthélemy, *Le Vote des femmes*, p. 132; Bonnefous, *Histoire politique de la Troisième Répu-*

blique, 3:11-22; *La Française*, October 26, 1918; February 1, 1919; *Les Cahiers des droits de l'homme*, March 20, 1920, p. 6; Dossier Vote des femmes, 1919, BMD.

17. See the essay by Léon Abensour in the Buisson file, Dossier Députés favorables au vote des femmes, BMD; *JO*, Chambre des députés, débats, March 14, 1919 et seq., esp. the debates of March 19 and April 4; Bonnefous, *Histoire politique de la Troisième République*, 3:11-12.

18. *JO*, Chambre des députés, débats, May 8, 1919; *L'Humanité*, May 9, 1919. The debates are also recapitulated in Leclère, *Le Vote des femmes en France*, pp. 147-51; Grinberg, *Historique du mouvement suffragiste*, pp. 121-37.

19. *JO*, Chambre des députés, débats, May 15, 1919; *DPF*, 1:446-47 and 6:2207. See also the sympathetic account of Lefebvre du Prey's speech ("a great loftiness of views, a great force of convictions, and an irrefutable argument") in *La Croix*, May 17, 1919.

20. *JO*, Chambre des députés, débats, May 15, 1919; *DPF*, 2:759-61, and 6:2119-20; Spengler, *France Faces Depopulation*, pp. 125-27; *L'Humanité*, May 16, 1919.

21. *JO*, Chambre des députés, débats, May 20, 1919. Some accounts of the vote (e.g., Grinberg, *Historique du mouvement suffragiste*, p. 137) report different figures, usually 344-97; that was the figure originally reported by the presiding officer, but that was later corrected (*JO*, pp. 2358 and 2366). For recognition of the importance of the speeches by Viviani and Briand, see *La Française*, May 24, 1919; *L'Oeuvre*, September 18, 1925.

22. *La République française*, May 21, 1919.

23. For the Senate's noting of the cabinet's attitude, see the report by Alexandre Bérard, *JO*, Sénat, documents, October 3, 1919, no. 564.

24. See the elaborate computations by Georges Lhermitte in *Le Droit des femmes*, August 1919, pp. 137-39.

25. *L'Action française*, May 21, 1919; *Le Temps*, May 23, 1919.

26. *JO*, Chambre des députés, débats, May 20, 1919.

27. *L'Oeuvre*, May 21, 1919.

28. *Action sociale de la femme*, August 1920, pp. 155-56; clippings in the Dossier Levert-Chotard, BMD; Clark, *The Position of Women in Contemporary France*, p. 22.

29. Lenin's *Women and Society*, as excerpted in the International Publishers edition: *The Woman Question: Selections from the Writings of Karl Marx, Frederick Engels, V. I. Lenin, Joseph Stalin* (New York, 1951), pp. 62-63; *L'Ouvrière*, April 1, 1922.

30. *La Française*, May 31, 1919 (quoted) and November 29, 1919. See also the reports on provincial attitudes in the file Notes générales concernant

l'agitation féministe dans les divers départements, 1918-1922, F⁷ 13266, AN; *L'Heure de la femme*, May and December 1919, November 1922.

31. Roussel, *Derniers combats*, p. 177 (quoted). See also *La Lutte féministe*, April 3, 1919; *Les Cahiers des droits de l'homme*, March 20, 1920, p. 13; clippings in the Dossiers Vote des femmes, 1919, 1920, and 1921, BMD. For consideration of familial suffrage, see *Le Droit des femmes*, May 1920, p. 330; Fonséque's report of December 20, 1920, Dossier Amélioration, Bouglé Collection, BHVP; *Jus suffragii* (English edition), September 1920, p. 190, and March 1921, pp. 88-89; *La Française*, January 22 and February 19, 1921.

32. Louis Martin, "La Femme française et le droit de vote," *La Revue mondiale*, September 15, 1918, pp. 353-69; Louis Martin to Maria Vérone, *L'Oeuvre*, February 14, 1919; *Revue de l'UFSF, 1922-1923*, p. 8; police report on the 1922 UFSF congress at Clermont-Ferrand, Notes générales concernant l'agitation féministe dans les divers départements, 1918-1928, F⁷ 13266, AN; *La Dépêche de Toulouse*, November 17, 1922; Gaston Grémy, ed., *A propos du vote des femmes: La Femme éligible mais non électrice: Opinions et interviews* (Paris, n.d.).

33. See the law in Duvergier, *Collection complète des lois*, n.s., 20:720-21; *La Voix des femmes*, June 23 and July 7, 1921.

34. For Brunet's many efforts, see the Dossiers Louis Brunet, Comité de propagande féministe, and Féminisme–France, 1920-1929, BMD; Dossier Comité de propagande féministe, Bouglé Collection, BHVP. For Vérone's chain letter, see the circular headed "Appel aux françaises" in the Dossier Vote des femmes, 1919, BMD; *Le Droit des femmes*, February 1920.

35. In addition to the newspapers involved, see *Le Droit des femmes*, November 1919, p. 195; December 1919, pp. 213-20; *La Lutte féministe*, December 26, 1919; *La Française*, November 1, 8, 15, and 29, 1919; LFDF, *Cinquante ans de féminisme*, p. 31. Among Vérone's columns in *L'Oeuvre*, see especially those published on October 28, November 10 and 27, 1919.

36. Grinberg, *Historique du mouvement suffragiste*, p. 95; *L'Oeuvre*, November 27, 1919; *Le Droit des femmes*, December 1919, pp. 219-20; November 1922, pp. 221-22; *La Française*, November 29, 1919, October 28, 1922; *Le Journal*, esp. November 7, 1922; Dossiers Comité de propagande féministe and Vote des femmes, 1922, BMD.

37. La Mazière's recollections in *Jus suffragii* (English edition), January 1920, p. 53; *La Française*, October 25, November 1, 8, 15, and 29, 1919; UFSF, *Bulletin 1918-1919*, pp. 76-79; *Le Droit des femmes*, November 1919, pp. 193-95; December 1919, pp. 213-17; *L'Oeuvre*, December 1, 1919.

38. *La Lutte féministe*, April 3 and 24, May 9, October 1 (quoted), and December 26, 1919.

39. La Mazière claimed (*Jus suffragii*, January 1920, p. 53) 390 votes; the LFDF reported (*Le Droit des femmes*, December 1919, p. 217) that same total,

plus 71 for Rauze; Grinberg recorded (*Historique du mouvement suffragiste*, p. 95) 600 for La Mazière; Brion said (*La Lutte féministe*, December 26, 1919) 360 for La Mazière and 503 for Rauze.

40. Invitation to the Deraismes demonstration, June 10, 1919, Dossier Amélioration, BMD; leaflet advertising the demonstration, July 6, 1919, Dossier Vote des femmes, 1919, BMD; *L'Oeuvre*, July 6, 1919; *Le Droit des femmes*, July 1919, pp. 125-27; *L'Heure de la femme*, July 20, 1919. Lhermitte estimated 5,000 diners at the Trocadéro and 3,000 at one of the CNFF's meetings. However, he considered attendance at the banquet to be half the size of the Condorcet demonstration, which he inflated by 100 percent; *Le Droit des femmes*, April 1922, pp. 85-86. For illustrations of such large meetings, see also: *Le Droit des femmes*, December 1919, p. 217; February 1921, pp. 497 and 521-22; *L'Oeuvre*, March 5 and 27, 1921; correspondence, 1921-1922, Dossier UFSF, BMD; program of the LFDF banquet, Dossier LFDF, BMD.

41. Poincaré published his speech as a pamphlet, *Pour le suffrage des femmes* (Paris, 1922), quotation from pp. 4-5. See also *La Française*, January 21, 1922; *Jus suffragii* (English edition), January 1922, pp. 56-57; *La Droit des femmes*, November 1921, p. 713; December 1921, pp. 739-42; *L'Oeuvre*, November 25, December 2 and 4, 1921; clippings in the Dossier LFDF, BMD.

42. For a detailed examination of senatorial conservatism, see Jean-Pierre Marichy's massive *La Deuxième chambre dans la vie politique française depuis 1875* (Paris, 1969), esp. pp. 529-69, and, for women's suffrage, pp. 618-22.

43. *JO*, Sénat, débats, June 20, August 2, and November 22, 1918; January 15 and June 5, 1919; ibid., documents, 1918, nos. 252, 344; 1919, nos. 229, 251.

44. Ibid., documents, October 3, 1919, no. 564. *L'Oeuvre*, May 28 and 30, June 11 and 12, 1919; *La Française*, May 31 and June 7, 1919; *Jus suffragii* (French edition), April 1919, pp. 54-56; August 1919, p. 87; *Le Droit des femmes*, March 1919, p. 49; April 1919, p. 59; July 1919, pp. 117-21; UFSF, *Bulletin 1918-1919*, pp. 1-2, 70-72; *L'Heure de la femme*, May 20, 1919.

45. *L'Oeuvre*, July 25, 1919; *La Française*, October 11, 18, and 25, November 15, 1919 (Raspail quote); *Le Droit des femmes*, November 1919, pp. 197-98; *Jus suffragii* (French edition), October 1919, pp. 2-3; UFSF, *Bulletin 1918-1919*, p. 75; *JO*, Chambre des députés, débats, October 7, 1919 (Bracke quote); ibid., Documents, no. 6970.

46. Bérard did not organize his report in this numbered form—that idea was a feminist condensation. Several varying versions of the "14 points" exist, beginning with one in *La Française*, December 20, 1919. Cf. the lists published in *Le Droit des femmes*, December 1919, pp. 220-21, and Leclère, *Le Vote des femmes en France*, pp. 156-61. The list given above is drawn directly from the report, but follows the general contours of the feminist condensations.

JO, Sénat, documents, October 3, 1919, no. 564. For other examples of the feminist response to the Bérard Report, see *L'Oeuvre*, December 22, 1919; Grinberg, *Historique du mouvement suffragiste*, pp. 148-49.

47. *JO*, Chambre des députés, débats, January 22 and April 26, 1920; June 21, 1921; ibid., documents, 1920, nos. 205 (Guesde Bill), 787; 1921, no. 2830; ibid., Sénat, débats, June 21, 1921. *Le Droit des femmes*, February 1920, p. 75; May 1920, p. 329; June 1920, p. 350; May 1921, p. 577; July 1921, pp. 625, 629-35; February 1922, pp. 33, 36; March 1922, p. 62; July 1922, pp. 156-58. *La Française*, February 14, May 15, and September 9, 1920; January 22 and July 16, 1921; March 4 and 18, February 4, April 8, May 27, June 3, and July 1, 1922. *Jus suffragii*, February 1920, p. 75; January 1921, p. 59; July 1921, p. 152; August 1922, pp. 163-65. *L'Oeuvre*, June 17, 1921; February 23 and June 29, 1922. UFSF, *Bulletin 1920-1921*, pp. 46-47; *La Voix des femmes*, August 10, 1922; *Les Cahiers des droits de l'homme*, special suffrage issue, March 20, 1920; Leclère, *Le Vote des femmes en France*, pp. 163-64; *DPF*, 2:477-78.

48. For the Senate debates, see: *JO*, Sénat, débats, November 7, 14, 16, and 21, 1922. For feminist discussion of the debates, see *La Française*, November 18 and 25, December 2, 1922; *Jus suffragii* (French edition), January 1923, pp. 58-61; *La Voix des femmes*, November 18, 1922; Alice La Mazière, *Le Vote des femmes et le sénat* (Paris, 1923). For the roles of Viviani and Poincaré, see *L'Humanité*, November 21 and 22, 1922; *La République française*, November 7 and 8, 1922; *La Française*, November 25, 1922; *La Croix*, November 8 and 22, 1922; *Le Petit Parisien*, November 22, 1922. A decade later, Brunschwicg defended Poincaré from the feminist criticism that he had failed them: *La Française*, October 20, 1934.

49. See, for example, Zeldin, *France 1848-1945*, 1:360.

50. La Mazière, *Le Vote des femmes et la sénat*, p. 14 (quoted); *Jus suffragii* (French edition), December 1922; *La Fronde*, May 20, 1926 (quoted).

51. *La Française*, November 9, 1918; *L'Oeuvre*, May 28, 1919; *Le Radical*, November 8, 16, 17, and 19, 1922.

52. For a fuller breakdown of these data, see Steven C. Hause, "The Rejection of Women's Suffrage by the French Senate in November 1922: A Statistical Analysis," *TR/TR* 3-4 (1977): 205-237.

53. For suffragist expectations from political leaders see: notes and clippings in the Dossier UFSF, BMD; UFSF, *Bulletin 1920-1921*, p. 4; *Le Droit des femmes*, March 1920, p. 287; *La Française*, February 4, 1922; *Revue de l'UFSF, 1922-1923*, pp. 1-2. For the cabinet's decision not to endorse women's suffrage, see: *L'Oeuvre*, November 11, 1922; *La République française*, November 21, 1922; *L'Humanité*, November 21, 1922; *Le Radical*, November 8, 1922; *La Française*, November 11, 1922; *Le Petit Parisien*, November 22, 1922.

54. For feminist recognition of, and reaction to, this fact, see *La Française*, November 25, 1922; *L'Oeuvre*, November 8, 1922.

Chapter Nine

1. *La République française*, November 22, 1922; *La Croix*, November 23, 1922; *La Française*, November 25, 1922.

2. Vérone quotations: *L'Oeuvre*, May 21, 1919; *Le Droit des femmes*, April 1919, p. 60; December 1922, pp. 249-50; and July 1928, as quoted by Leclère, *Le Vote des femmes en France*, p. 79. UFSF to all senators, July 26, 1919, reprinted in UFSF, *Bulletin 1918-1919*, pp. 72-73.

3. See the recollections of Suzanne Dudit of her interviews with Vérone, in *Minerva*, June 5, 1938; Dossiers Vérone, BMD and BHVP. Clark, *The Position of Women in Contemporary France*, p. 224. See Weiss's *Mémoires d'une européene*, 6 vols., Edition définitive (Paris, 1968-1982), vol. 3, *Combats pour les femmes, 1934-1939* (1980). The authors are indebted to Sabine Jessner for sharing with them her paper on Weiss, "A Question of Method—*La Femme nouvelle*," read at the Berkshire Conference on the History of Women, Mount Holyoke College, August 1978.

4. In addition to the *JO*, see Marichy, *La Deuxième chambre dans la vie politique française*, pp. 620-22; the appropriate volumes of Bonnefous, *Histoire politique de la Troisième République*, e.g., 3:416. For the women in Blum's cabinet, see *DPF*, 1:140-41; 2:799-801; 6:2028-83.

5. Charles de Gaulle, *The Complete War Memoirs* [1955-1960] (1 vol. ed.: New York, 1964), p. 481 (quoted). For his reasoning, see the speculations in Zeldin, *France 1848-1945*, 1:360. For the role of women: Andrée Lehmann, *Le Rôle de la femme française au milieu du XXe siècle*, 3rd ed. (Paris, 1965), pp. 8-9.

6. Lehmann, *Le Rôle de la femme française*, pp. 10-20.

7. Ibid., p. 17; Peter Campbell, *French Electoral Systems and Elections since 1789* (London, 1958), pp. 102-103; Zeldin, *France 1848-1945*, 1:360.

8. Brunschwicg, in *L'Humanité*, May 19, 1919.

9. See, for example, Bérard's speech to the Senate on November 16, 1922, in the *JO*.

10. Ward M. Morton, *Woman Suffrage in Mexico* (Gainesville, Fla., 1962), p. 9.

11. *La Française*, May 9, 1914.

12. See Michelet's *Le Prêtre, la femme, et la famille* for republican hostility to the confessional; Theodore Zeldin, "The Conflict of Moralities: Confession, Sin, and Pleasure in the Nineteenth Century," in *Conflicts in French Society: Anti-clericalism, Education, and Morals in the Nineteenth Century* (London, 1970), pp. 13-50, for an analysis of the rivalry.

13. Alexis de Tocqueville, *Democracy in America* [1835] (Schocken ed.: New York, 1961), 2:237. The quotation appears at the beginning of the Third Book, Chapter Nine, "Education of Young Women in the United States."

14. Ibid., 1:355. The quotation appears at the beginning of the section entitled "Religion considered as a political institution . . ." in Chapter Seventeen of the First Book. For other discussions of the relationship between Protestantism and suffragism, see Evans, *The Feminists*, p. 30; Grimes, *The Puritan Ethic and Woman Suffrage*; Kraditor, *The Ideas of the Woman Suffrage Movement*, chap. 4.

15. For the clearest demonstration of the importance of the WCTU, see Grimshaw, *Women's Suffrage in New Zealand*, esp. pp. 21-35. For other cases, see Cleverdon, *The Woman Suffrage Movement in Canada*; D. Scott, "Woman Suffrage: The Movement in Australia," *Journal of the Royal Australian Historical Society* 53 (1967):299-320; N. MacKenzie, "Vida Goldstein, the Australian Suffragette," *Australian Journal of Politics and History* 6 (1960):194-95; Flexner, *Century of Struggle*, pp. 184-85.

16. Elisabeth A. Weston, "Prostitution in Paris in the Later Nineteenth Century." See in particular chap. 4, where Weston argues that "the decline of the abolitionist movement may have been in part responsible for the growth of a woman's rights movement in France from 1885 on."

17. For several comparisons of this sort, see Evans, *The Feminists*, and Paulson, *Women's Suffrage and Prohibition*. For other specific illustrations, see Fawcett, *Women's Suffrage*, p. 13; Rosen, *Rise Up Women!*, pp. 61-62; Rover, *Women's Suffrage and Party Politics in Britain*, pp. 8-9; Flexner, *Century of Struggle*, pp. 78-104; Ellen C. DuBois, *Feminism and Suffrage: The Emergence of an Independent Women's Movement in America, 1848-1869* (Ithaca, N.Y., 1978), chap. 6.

18. Barbara C. Pope, "Angels in the Devil's Workshop: Leisured and Charitable Women In Nineteenth Century England and France," in *Becoming Visible*, ed. Bridenthal and Koonz, pp. 296-324. For a study of Catholic women's charities in France, see Bonnie G. Smith, *Ladies of the Leisure Class: The Bourgeoisie of Northern France in the Nineteenth Century* (Princeton, 1981), pp. 123-61.

19. Cleverdon, *The Woman Suffrage Movement in Canada*, pp. 5, 14, 214-64. Newfoundland, not united with Canada until 1949, gave women the vote in 1925.

20. The Twelve Tables may be found in Naphtali Lewis and Meyer Reinhold, eds., *Roman Civilization*, 2 vols. (New York, 1951), 1:102-109.

21. Twenty-four of the twenty-eight governments between the Gautret Bill of 1901 and the Senate vote of 1922 were led by lawyers; nearly half of all deputies from the Radical and Radical-Socialist Party in 1906 were lawyers.

See Yves-Henri Gaudemet, *Les Juristes et la vie politique de la Troisième République* (Paris, 1970), pp. 43-48 and annexes.

22. Jeanne Chauvin, "Des Professions accessibles aux femmes en droit romain et en droit français: Evolution historique de la position économique de la femme en société" (Thèse de droit, Paris, 1892).

23. *La Fronde*, November 7, 1901; Auclert, *Le Vote des femmes*, p. 15; UFSF, *Bulletin 1918-1919*, pp. 23-28.

24. The list of the most industrialized departments would add the Vosges and the Ardennes to Table 18, replacing Seine-Inférieure and Pas-de-Calais.

25. *La Vie heureuse*, November 15, 1912 (quoted); *La Française*, July 16, 1921; *Jus suffragii*, July 1921, p. 152; UFSF, *Bulletin 1920-1921*, p. 46; Léon Abensour, essay in Dossier Députés favorable au vote des femmes, BMD; Abensour, *Le Problème féministe*, p. 133.

26. Hubertine Auclert to Arria Ly, August 5, 1909, Bouglé Collection, BMD.

27. Caroline Kauffmann to Arria Ly, November 8, 1909, ibid.

28. *Le Soleil*, April 24, 1910.

29. Levy et al., eds., *Women in Revolutionary Paris*, p. 92; Tilly, "Women's Collective Action and Feminism in France," p. 231. For feminist discussion of this perceived indifference, see Grinberg, *Historique du mouvement suffragiste*, pp. 130-31; Abensour, *Le Problème féministe, pp. 133-34*; Abensour, *Histoire générale du féminisme*, p. 281; *La Française*, November 15, 1908; Amélioration, *Bulletin trimestriel*, September 1900-February 1901, pp. 145-46; *L'Oeuvre*, June 29, 1922.

30. Pottecher, "Le Mouvement féministe en France," p. 593 (quoted): Sainte-Croix, *Le Féminisme*, p. 137.

31. See Mirtel's harsh words on this subject in *Les Documents du progrès*, May 1910, pp. 435-37.

32. Durand in *Les Nouvelles*, January 25, 1914; Ligue d'électeurs, *Bulletin trimestriel*, April 1911, p. 17; *The Times* (London), June 22, 1908; Vérone in *L'Oeuvre*, June 29, 1922 (quoted).

33. Li, *La Presse féministe*, pp. 138-39, 150-52; receipt book for *Le Combat féministe*, Fonds Arria Ly, Bouglé Collection, BHVP; Héra Mirel to Arria Ly, February 3, 1907 and August 29, 1907 (?), ibid.; *La Fronde*, September and October 1903; Goliber, "The Life and Times of Marguerite Durand," p. 45; *La Française*, June 12, 1910 and September 17, 1911; *La Voix des femmes*, January 17 and May 26, 1921; Louise Bodin to Nelly Roussel, March 11, 1920, Bouglé Collection, BHVP.

34. Oron J. Hale, *The Great Illusion, 1900-1914* (New York, 1971), p. 196.

35. Guilbert, *Les Femmes et l'organisation syndicale*, p. 29.

36. Hubertine Auclert to Arria Ly, March 30, 1908, Bouglé Collection, BHVP; cf. Caroline Kaufmann to Arria Ly, November 22, 1905, ibid., in

which Kauffmann praises her for staying in the south and laboring "in feminist isolation."

37. Statutes of the UFSF (1909), Dossier UFSF, BMD; reprinted extensively in Leclère, *Le Vote des femmes en France*, pp. 85-90.

38. These arbitrary examples drawn from recent American research are chosen to illustrate cases where there was very little feminist development yet significant discontent. See: Laura L. Frader, "Grapes of Wrath: Vineyard Workers, Labor Unions, and Strike Activity in the Aude, 1860-1913," in *Class Conflict and Collective Action*, ed. Tilly and Tilly, pp. 185-206; Judy A. Reardon, "Belgian and French Workers in Nineteenth Century Roubaix," ibid., pp. 167-84; Ronald Aminzade, "The Transformation of Social Solidarities in Nineteenth Century Toulouse," in *Consciousness and Class Experience in Nineteenth Century Europe*, ed. John M. Merriman (New York, 1980), pp. 85-105; John M. Merriman, "Incident at the Statue of the Virgin Mary: The Conflict of Old and New in Nineteenth Century Limoges," ibid., pp. 128-48.

39. Martin, in *Le Journal des femmes*, March 1909; Brunschwicg in *La Vie ouvrière*, February 5, 1914, pp. 147-49 (quoted).

40. Marie Guillot, in *Le Féminisme intégral*, March 5, 1914, pp. 276-82; see Guilbert, *Les Femmes et l'organisation syndicale*, pp. 424-25, for further discussion of this confrontation.

41. Mme. Roques quoted by Tilly, "Women's Collective Action and Feminism in France, 1870-1914," p. 228. See *L'Humanité*, March 26, 1907; *La Guerre sociale*, January 30, 1907; *La Voix du peuple*, January 27, 1907.

42. Sainte-Croix, *Le Féminisme*, p. 174; Maugeret, in *Le Féminisme chrétien*, May 1900, p. 137.

43. *La Fronde*, September 1, 1903.

44. Pelletier, *La Femme en lutte pour ses droits*, p. 59.

45. Vow presented to the International Congress of Women, June 1913, text in Dossier Amélioration, BMD.

46. See, for example, *L'Ouvrière*, June 3, 1922.

47. See Arria Ly's "Les Soeurs Bélilon," *La Suffragiste*, January 1914, pp. 4-6; for arguments for sexual emancipation and women's control of their bodies, see Marianne Rauze, *Féminisme intégral* (Paris, 1919). See the strong stand against abortion taken by the CNFF in its congresses and public discussion of this (e.g., Buisson, *Le Vote des femmes*, p. 52). Cf. the writings of Madeleine Pelletier, e.g., *L'Avortement n'est pas un crime*.

48. D'Uzès, *Le Suffrage féminin au point de vue historique*, pp. 2-3.

49. *La Française*, October 27, 1907; Camille Bélilon, in *La Femme*, November 15, 1902, pp. 137-39; Pelletier, *La Femme en lutte pour ses droits*, p. 40.

50. Pelletier to Arria Ly, December 5, 1913, Bouglé Collection, BHVP.

51. *The Times* (London), April 9, 1906.

52. For the Couriau affair, see Sowerwine, *Sisters or Citizens?*, pp. 135-36, and his "Workers and Women in France before 1914." For trade union data, Guilbert, *Les Femmes et l'organisation syndicale*, pp. 14, 29. For the CNFF survey: *Le Féminisme intégral*, July 1916. Madeleine Pelletier to Arria Ly, June 6, 1921, Bouglé Collection, BHVP.

53. For other presentations of solidarism, see Matthew H. Elbow, *French Corporative Theory, 1789-1948: A Chapter in the History of Ideas* (New York, 1953), pp. 107-114; John A. Scott, *Republican Ideas and the Liberal Tradition in France, 1870-1914* (New York, 1951), pp. 157-86; Roger Soltau, *French Political Thought in the Nineteenth Century* (New Haven, 1931), pp. 474-81. Goldberg, *Jaurès*, p. 394 (Herr quotation).

54. Amar, report of 9 Brumaire II, in Levy et al., eds., *Women in Revolutionary Paris*, p. 215.

55. Brunschwicg joined the Radical and Radical-Socialist Party in 1924 and was a leading officer at the party's 1946 congress. *DPF*, 2:800-801.

Bibliography

In the interest of brevity, this bibliography does not list all materials cited in the notes. The principal omissions are: Parisian daily newspapers, feminist periodicals, rare pamphlets and brochures, a full listing of the files and dossiers consulted in each manuscript collection, lesser titles on non-French suffragism, works of indirect importance for this subject.

Manuscript and Archival Materials

Archives départmentales
    Rhône. Especially Series 4 M (associations and individuals)
    Seine-inférieure. Especially Series 1 MP and 4 MP (demonstrations and meetings)
Archives nationales
    Especially Series C (Chamber of Deputies), F7 (police), and AP (personal papers, such as Albert Thomas)
Archives du Préfecture de Police
    Series B^A contains many helpful files, particularly those on elections, Auclert, Séverine, and feminism.
Bibliothèque historique de la ville de Paris
    The huge Bouglé Collection is still undergoing sorting and is difficult to use, but it is of tremendous importance. In addition to numerous dossiers on individuals and groups, it contains much important feminist correspondence, especially letters to Arria Ly.
Bibliothèque de l'Institut de France
    The papers of Charles Benoist
Bibliothèque Marguerite Durand
    The most important source for French feminism: an extremely important and well-organized collection, containing hundreds of dossiers on individuals, organizations, congresses, and many topics. Many dossiers contain valuable primary materials as well as letters. Also the best source for rare pamphlets or periodicals cited.
Bibliothèque nationale (Cabinet de manuscrits)
    Series NAF contains some helpful material in the personal papers of Joseph Reinach, Raymond Poincaré, and Louis Havet.

Bibliothèque du Trocadéro
The Misme collection contains some rare pamphlets.
Fawcett Library (London)
The Fawcett papers provide little help for France, but the collection on the Catholic Women's Suffrage Society is helpful on Catholic feminism.
Institut français d'histoire sociale
Fonds Hélène Brion
International Instituut voor Sociale Geschiedenis (Amsterdam)
The Pankhurst materials include little on France, but the Guesde collection is helpful for some socialist women.
Hoover Institution on War, Revolution, and Peace (Stanford)
File on freemasonry in France, Stephane Lauzane papers, Alice Park papers
Musée social (Bibliothèque du Cédias)
Sainte-Croix scrapbooks
New York Public Library (manuscripts)
Carrie Chapman Catt Papers
Schlesinger Library (Cambridge, Mass.)
Helpful information on international suffragism in the Dillon Collection (Carrie Chapman Catt MSS, Anna Howard Shaw MSS), Charlotte Perkins Gilman Papers, Andrews Papers and Allen Papers.

Official and Semi-Official Government Publications

Dalloz, M. and A. et al., eds. *Jurisprudence générale: Recueil périodique et critique de jurisprudence, de législation et de doctrine en matière civile, commerciale, criminelle, administrative et de droit public* (Paris, annual).
Duvergier, J. B. et al., eds. *Collection complète des lois, décrets, ordonnances, réglements, avis du Conseil d'État* (Paris, annual).
France. Conseil générale du Rhône. *Rapports . . . et procès-verbaux des délibérations du conseil* (Lyons, annual).
――――. Conseil général du département de la Seine. *Procès-verbaux des délibérations* (Paris, annual).
――――. Conseil général du département de la Seine-Inférieure. *Rapports et procès-verbaux* (Rouen, annual).
――――. Conseil municipal de Paris. *Procès-verbaux* (Paris, annual).
――――. *Journal officiel de la République française* (Paris, annual).
――――. Ministère du travail [ministry varies]. Statistique générale de la France. *Annuaire statistique* (Paris, annual).
Gazette des tribunaux. Journal de jurisprudence et des débats judicaires (Paris).

Collections of Reprinted Sources

Albistur, Maïte and Daniel Armogathe, eds. *Le Grief des femmes: Anthologie de textes féminstes du second empire à nos jours*. 2 vols. (Paris, 1978).

Anderson, Frank M., ed. *The Constitutions and Other Select Documents Illustrative of the History of France, 1789-1907* (Minneapolis, 1908).

Chevalier, P. and M. Grosperrin. *L'Enseignement français de la révolution à nos jours*. 2 vols. (Paris, 1971).

Collins, Marie and Sylvie W. Sayre, eds. *Les Femmes en France* (New York, 1974).

Hellerstein, Erna O., Leslie P. Hume, and Karen M. Offen, eds. *Victorian Women: A Documentary Account of Women's Lives in Nineteenth Century England, France, and the United States* (Stanford, 1981).

Levy, Darline G., Harriet B. Applewhite, and Mary D. Johnson, eds. *Women in Revolutionary Paris, 1789-1795* (Urbana, Ill., 1979).

Thomson, David, ed. *France: Empire and Republic, 1850-1940* (New York, 1968).

Reference Works

Bluysen, Paul, ed. *Annuaire de la presse française* (Paris, annual).

Jolly, Jean, ed. *Dictionnaire des parlementaires français: Notices biographiques sur les ministres, députés, et sénateurs français de 1889 à 1940*. 8 vols. (Paris, 1960-1977).

Robert, Adolphe, Edgar Bourloton, and Gaston Cougny, eds. *Dictionnaire des parlementaires français. Comprénant tous les membres des assemblées françaises et tous les ministres français depuis le 1ᵉʳ mai 1789 jusqu'au 1ᵉʳ mai 1889. . . .* 5 vols. (Paris, 1891).

Selected Works of French Feminists

[Action sociale], *Action sociale de la femme* (Angers, 1935).

Auclert, Hubertine. *L'Argent de la femme* (Paris, 1905).

──────. *La Citoyenne, 1848-1914*. Edited by Edith Taïeb (Paris, 1982).

──────. *Les Femmes au gouvernail* (Paris, 1923).

──────. *Le Nom de la femme* (Paris, 1905).

──────. *Le Vote des femmes* (Paris, 1908).

Bérot-Berger, M.-L. *La Femme dans le progrès social* (Paris, 1910).

Bogelot, Isabelle. *Trente ans de solidarité, 1877-1906* (Paris, 1908).

Brion, Hélène. *La Voie féministe* (Paris, 1978).

Brunschwicg, Cécile. *Le Congrès de l'alliance internationale pour le suffrage des femmes, Genève, 6-12 juin, 1920* (Paris, 1921).

Brunschwicg, Cécile. "Féminisme, Le Suffrage des femmes en France," *Les Documents du progrès*, 1913, pp. 229-300.

———. *Le Suffrage des femmes en France* (Leiden, 1938).

Chéliga, Marya, ed. *Almanach féministe, 1899* (Paris, 1900).

Clément, Marguerite. *Conférence sur le suffrage des femmes* (Paris, 1912).

Cruppi, Louise. *Comment les anglaises ont conquis le vote* (Paris, 1919).

Deraismes, Maria. *Ce que veulent les femmes: Articles et discours....* Edited by Odile Krakovitch (Paris, 1980).

Durand, Marguerite, ed. *Congrès international de la condition et des droits des femmes ... 1900: Procès-verbaux* (Paris, 1901).

Feraud, A. *La Femme devant les urnes* (Paris, 1918).

Ferrer, Mme. C. L. *Pourquoi voteraient-elles?* (Paris, 1910).

Grinberg, Suzanne. *Historique du mouvement suffragiste depuis 1848* (Paris, 1926).

International Council of Women. *Histories of Affiliated Councils, 1888-1938* (Brussels, 1938).

International Women's Commission for Permanent Peace, *International Congress of Women. The Hague, 28 April-1 May, 1915. Report* (The Hague, 1915).

Laguerre, Odette. *Qu'est-ce que le féminisme?* (Lyons, 1899).

Lalöe, Jeanne. "Les Deux féminismes," *La Nouvelle revue*, May-June 1908.

La Mazière, Alice. "The Gallant French Senate," *The Woman's Journal*, January 1, 1923.

———. *Le Vote des femmes et le sénat* (Paris, 1923).

Lehmann, Andrée. *Le Role de la femme française au milieu du XXᵉ siècle*. 3rd ed. (Paris, 1965).

LFDF, *Cinquante ans de féminisme, 1870-1920* (Paris, 1921).

Ligue patriotique des françaises. *Compte rendu du congrès de la LPDF à Loirient, le 8 juillet 1909* (Ploermel, n.d.).

———. *Congrès de la Ligue patriotique des françaises, tenu ... Octobre 1907 à Pau et à Lourdes* (Paris, 1908).

Martial, Lydie. *Action du féminisme rationnel. Union de pensée féminine....* (Paris, 1905).

———. *La Femme intégral* (Paris, 1901).

Martin, Marguerite. *Les Droits de la femme* (Paris, 1912).

Minck, Paule. *Communarde et féministe (1839-1901) ... textes*. Edited by Alain Dalotel (Paris, 1981).

Mirtel, Héra. "Féminisme mondial." *Les Documents du progrès*, May 1910.

———. "Nous n'aurons pas encore législatrices en France," *Les Documents du progrès*, July 1910.

Misme, Jane. *Les Dernières obstacles au vote des femmes* (Paris, n.d.).

———. "La Guerre et la rôle des femmes," *Revue de Paris* 23 (1916).

————. "Madame la Duchesse d'Uzès," *Revue bleue*, August 17, 1897.

————. *Pour le suffrage des femmes: Le Féminisme et la politique* (Paris, n.d. [c. 1910]).

Oddo-Deflou, Jeanne, ed. *Congrès national des droits civils et du suffrage des femmes. Tenu . . . les 26-28 juin 1908. Compte rendu. . . .* (Paris, 1908).

————. "Le Congrès national des droits civils et du suffrage des femmes tenu . . . 1908." *Liberté d'opinion* 2 (1908).

————. *Le Sexualisme: Critique de la préponderance et de la mentalité du sexe fort* (Paris, 1906).

Ordre maçonnique mixte universal. *Convention des loges mixtes de France et des colonies, tenu . . . 1910* (Havre, 1910).

Pégard, Marie, ed. *Deuxième congrès international des oeuvres et institutions féminins . . . 1900.* 4 vols. (Paris, 1902).

Pelletier, Madeleine. *Admission des femmes dans la franc-maçonnerie* (Paris, n.d.).

————. *L'Amour et la maternité* (Paris, n.d.).

————. *La Déseagrégation de la famille* (Paris, n.d.).

————. *La Droit au travail pour la femme* (Paris, n.d.).

————. *L'Education féministe des filles et autres textes.* Edited by Claude Maignien (Paris, 1978).

————. *L'Emancipation sexuelle de la femme* (Paris, 1911).

————. "Le Féminisme et ses militants," *Les Documents du progrès*, July 1909.

————. "Le Féminisme à la Chambre des députés," *Les Documents du progrès*, 1911.

————. *La Femme en lutte pour ses droits* (Paris, 1908).

————. *Le Féminisme et la famille* (Paris, 1908).

————. "French Feminism," *The Freewoman*, April 25, 1912.

————. *La Guerre est-elle naturelle?* (Paris, n.d.).

————. "Les Institutrices et le mouvement féministe," *Les Documents du progrès*, May 1910.

————. *Mon voyage aventureux en Russie communiste* (Paris, 1922).

————. "Ma Candidature à la députation," *Les Documents du progrès*, July 1910.

————. *Philosophie sociale: Les Opinions, les partis, les classes* (Paris, 1912).

————. *La Prétendue infériorité psycho-physiologique des femmes* (Paris, 1904).

————. *La Question du vote des femmes* (Paris, 1909).

————. "Les Suffragistes anglaises se virilisent," *La Suffragiste*, October 1912.

————. "La Tactique féministe," *La Revue socialiste*, April 1908.

Rauze, Marianne. *Féminisme intégral* (Vincennes, n.d.).

Rebour, Pauline. *Pourquoi les françaises doivent et veulent voter* (Paris, 1923).

Remember, Madame. *Le Féminisme intégral* (Paris, 1919).

Richer, Léon. *La Femme libre* (Paris, 1877).

Roussel, Nelly. *Derniers combats: Recueil d'articles et de discours* (Paris, 1932).

———. *L'Eternelle sacrifiée*. Edited by Daniel Armogathe and Maïte Albistur (Paris, 1979).

———. *Paroles de combat et d'espoir* (Paris, 1919).

———. *Quelques discours* (Paris, 1907).

———. *Quelques lances rompues pour nos libertés* (Paris, 1910).

———. *Trois conférences* (Paris, 1930).

Sainte-Croix, Avril de, ed. *Dixième congrès international des femmes: Oeuvres et institutions féminines, droits des femmes . . . tenu à Paris le 2 juin 1913. Compte rendu. . . .* (Paris, 1914).

———. *Le Féminisme* (Paris, 1907).

———. "Les Françaises et le droit du suffrage," *The Englishwoman* 2 (1909).

———. *Une morale pour les deux sexes* (Paris, 1900).

Saumoneau, Louis. *Principes et action féministes socialistes* (Paris, n.d.).

Schmahl, Jeanne. *Le Préjugé de sexe* (Paris, 1895).

———. "Progress of the Women's Rights Movement in France," *The Forum*, September 1896.

———. *La Question de la femme* (Paris, 1894).

———. "Women's Suffrage in France," *Englishwoman's Review*, 1902.

Séverine. *Choix de papiers*, Edited by Evelyne Le Garrec (Paris, 1982).

Siegfried, Mme. Jules. *La Guerre et le rôle de la femme* (Paris, 1915).

Société féministe du Havre. *Le Suffrage municipal des femmes* (Havre, 1913).

Union française pour le suffrage des femmes. *Le Suffrage des femmes en France*. 3rd ed. (Paris, 1912).

———. *L'Union française et l'alliance internationale pour le suffrage des femmes* (Paris, 1910).

Uzès, Duchess d'. *Souvenirs* (Paris, 1939).

———. *Le Suffrage féminin au point de vue historique* (Meulan, 1914).

Vérone, Maria. *Appel à la justice: Addressé par le CNFF à la Chambre des Députés et la Sénat* (Paris, n.d. [1909]).

———. *La Femme devant la loi, autour du monde* (Paris, n.d.).

———. *La Femme et la loi* (Paris, 1920).

———. *Maria Vérone parle du féminisme* (Paris, n.d.).

———. *Pourquoi les femmes veulent voter* (Paris, 1919).

———. *Résultats du suffrage des femmes* (Paris, 1914).

———. *La Situation juridique des enfants naturels* (Paris, 1924).

———, and Georges Lhermitte. *La Séparation et ses conséquences* (Paris, 1906).

————, Chrystal MacMillan, and Marie Stritt. *Woman Suffrage in Practice* (London, 1913).

Villermont, Marie, Comtesse de. *Le Mouvement féministe: Ses Causes, son avenir, solution chrétien* (Paris, 1904).

Vincent, Madame. *Electorat et éligibilité des femmes aux conseils des prud'hommes* (Autun, 1907).

————. *La Répression de la traité des blanches et la préservation de la jeune fille. Rapport* (Paris, 1905).

————. *Rapport à la VIᵉ Conference of the International Woman Suffrage Alliance, à Stockholm, 1911* (Paris, 1911).

Voeux adoptés par le congrès féministe international, tenu à Paris en 1896 . . . (Paris, n.d.).

Weiss, Louise. *Mémoires d'une européene.* 6 vols. Edition définitive (Paris, 1968-1982).

Witt-Schlumberger, Marguerite de. *Situation internationale du suffrage des femmes en mars 1918* (Paris, 1918).

————. *Une femme aux femmes* (Paris, 1909).

Contemporary Books and Articles

Abensour, Léon. *La Femme et le féminisme avant la révolution* (Paris, 1923).

————. *Le Féminisme sous le regne de Louis-Philippe* (Paris, 1918).

————. *Histoire générale du féminisme: Des origines à nos jours* (Paris, 1921).

————. *Le Problème féministe: Un Cas d'aspiration collective vers l'égalité* (Paris, 1927).

————. *Les Vaillantes: Héroïnes, martyrs, et remplaçantes* (Paris, 1917).

Acker, Paul. *Oeuvres sociales des femmes* (Paris, 1908).

Balch, Emily. "The International Congress of Women at The Hague," *Home Progress* 5 (1915): 111.

Barthélemy, Joseph. *Le Vote des femmes* (Paris, 1920).

Benoist, Charles. *Les Lois de la politique française* (Paris, 1928).

————. *Pour la réforme électorale* (Paris, 1908).

————. *Souvenirs, 1883-1933.* 3 vols. (Paris, 1932-1934).

Blum, Léon. *Du Mariage* (Paris, 1907).

Bolo, Abbé Henry. *La Femme et la clergé* (Paris, 1902).

Borel, Mme. Emile. *La Mobilisation féminine en France, 1914-1919* (Paris, 1919).

Bouglé, Charles. *De la sociologie à l'action sociale: Pacifisme, féminisme, cooperation* (Paris, 1923).

Bourgeois, Léon. *Les Applications sociales de la solidarité* (Paris, 1904).

————. *La Solidarité* (Paris, 1897).

Broda, Rodolphe. "Le Mouvement en faveur du vote des femmes," *Les Documents du progrès*, July 1909.

——. "Le Vote des femmes," *Les Documents du progrès*, July 1909.

Breuil de Saint-Germain, Jean du. *La Misère sociale de la femme et le suffrage* (Suresnes, 1911).

Brunetière, Ferdinand. *Action sociale du christianisme* (Besançon, 1904).

Buisson, Ferdinand. *La Politique radicale* (Paris, 1908).

——. *Souvenirs, 1866-1916. Conférence faite . . . le 10 janvier 1916* (Paris, 1916).

——. "Suffrage des femmes et le Ligue des droits de l'homme," *Les Cahiers des droits de l'homme*, March 20, 1920.

——. *Le Vote des femmes* (Paris, 1911).

——. "Le Vote des femmes," *Les Documents du progrès*, 1913.

Choquency, Antonin. *L'Emancipation de la femme au commencement du XXᵉ siècle* (Lyons, 1902).

Christitch, Annie. " 'Yes, We Approve,' " *The Catholic Citizen*, July 15, 1919.

Clemenceau, Georges. *La "Justice" du sexe fort* (Paris, 1907).

Coubé, Abbé Stephen. *Le Patriotisme de la femme française* (Paris, 1916).

Courson, Comtesse de. *La Femme française pendant la guerre* (Paris, 1916).

Crouzet-Benaben, Jeanne. "Une Assemblée des femmes en 1913. Le Congrès international de Paris (2-7 juin)," *La Grande revue*, July 10, 1913.

Dawbarn, Charles. "The French Woman and the Vote," *Fortnightly Review*, August 1911.

Dolléans, Edouard. *La Police des moeurs* (Paris, 1903).

Estournelles de Constant, Paul d'. *Les Femmes pendant et après la guerre* (Paris, 1916).

Faguet, Emile. "L'Abbé féministe," *Revue bleue*, 4th ser., 17 (1902).

——. *Le Féminisme* (Paris, 1910).

Fawcett, Millicent. *Women's Suffrage: A Short History of a Great Movement* [1912] (London, 1970).

Finot, Jean. *La Charte de la femme* (Paris, 1910).

——. *Problems of the Sexes* (London, 1909).

Flach, Jacques, "La Souvéraineté du peuple et le suffrage politique de la femme," *Revue bleue*, 1910.

Fouilée, Alfred. *La Démocratie politique et sociale en France* (Paris, 1910).

——. *La Propriété sociale* (Paris, 1909).

Froger-Doudemont, Raoul, ed. *Que veulent donc ces féministes? Opinions et arguments émis depuis cinq cents ans. . . .* (Paris, 1926).

Grémy, Gaston, ed. *A propos du vote des femmes: La Femme éligible mais non électrice: Opinions et interviews* (Paris, n.d.).

Haussonville, Comte d'. *Salaires et misères des femmes* (Paris, 1900).

Isoré, André. *La Guerre et la condition privée de la femme* (Paris, 1919).

Joran, Théodore. *Au Coeur du féminisme* (Paris, 1908).

————. *Autour du féminisme* (Paris, 1906).

————. *Le Féminisme à l'heure actuelle* (Paris, 1907).

————. *Les Féministes avant le féminisme* (Paris, 1910).

————. *Le Mensonge du féminisme* (Paris, 1905).

————. *Le Suffrage des femmes* (Paris, 1913).

————. *La Trouée féministe* (Paris, 1909).

Joseph-Renaud, J. *Le Catéchisme féministe: Résumé de la doctrine sous forme de résponses aux objections* (Paris, 1910).

La Hire, Marie d'Espie de. "Le Féminisme en France et les sociétés féministes," *La Revue des lettres*, August 1907.

————. *La Femme française, son activité pendant la guerre* (Paris, 1917).

Lamy, Etienne. *La Femme de demain* (Paris, 1901).

Lecointre, Comtesse Pierre. *Etat de la question féministe en France en 1907* (Paris, 1907).

Lees, Frederic. "The Progress of Woman in France," *The Humanitarian*, February 1901.

Lemaître, Jules. *Opinions à répandre* (Paris, 1901).

Levray, Mlle. *L'Alcoolisme et le vote des femmes* (Paris, n.d.).

Lobit, Dr. *De l'admission de la femme dans la franc-maçonnerie* (Paris, n.d.).

Malato, Charles. *L'Admission de la femme dans la franc-maçonnerie* (Paris, n.d.).

Maret, Henry. *Pensées et opinions* (Paris, 1903).

Margueritte, Paul and Victor. *L'Enlargissement du divorce—exposé des motifs et proposition de loi* (Paris, 1902).

————. *Mariage et divorce* (Paris, 1900).

Martin, Louis. "La Femme française et le droit de vote," *La Revue mondiale*, September 15, 1918.

Maud, Constance. "What French Women Are Doing," *The Nineteenth Century and After* 83 (1918): 1169-71.

Michelet, Jules. *Le Prêtre, la femme, et la famille* [1845] (Paris, 1890).

Naudet, Abbé Paul. *Pour la femme: Etudes féministes* (Paris, 1903).

Neera, Anna Zuccari. *Les Idées d'une femme sur le féminisme* (Paris, 1908).

Novicow, Jacques. *L'Affranchissement de la femme* (Paris, 1903).

Poincaré, Raymond. *Pour le suffrage des femmes* (Paris, 1922).

Poirson, S. *Mon féminisme* (Paris, 1905).

Pottecher, Thérese "Le Mouvement féministe en France," *La Grande Revue*, January-February 1911.

Reinach, Joseph. *Contre l'alcoolisme* (Paris, 1911).

————. "La Guerre et la lutte contre l'alcoolisme." *Revue bleue* 53 (1915): 432-45.

Renaudot, M. *Le Féminisme et le droits publics de la femme* (Niort, 1902).

Sembat, Marcel. "L'Acession des femmes aux fonctions publiques." *Les Documents du progrès*, January 1909.

Sertillanges, A. D. *Féminisme et christianisme* (Paris, 1908).

Templiez, Ida. "Les Féministes françaises et le mouvement anti-parlementaire," *Les Documents du progrès*, August 1911.

Turgeon, Charles. *Le Féminisme français*. 2 vols. 2nd ed. (Paris, 1907).

Villermont, Comtesse Marie de. *Le Mouvement féministe. Ses causes, son avenir, solution chrétien*. 2 vols. (Paris, 1904).

Viviani, René. "La Femme." *La Grande Revue*, February 1, 1901.

Zimmern, Alice. *Women's Suffrage in Many Lands* (London, 1909).

Secondary Studies

Abray, Jane. "Feminism and the French Revolution," *AHR* 80 (1975): 43-62.

Adler, Laure. *L'Aube du féminisme: Les Premières journalistes, 1830-1850* (Paris, 1979).

Albistur, Maïte and Daniel Armogathe. *Histoire du féminisme français*. 2 vols. (Paris, 1977).

Bachrach, Susan D. "The Feminization of the French Postal Service, 1750-1914." Ph.D. diss., University of Wisconsin, 1981.

Bardèche, Maurice. *Histoire des femmes*. 2 vols. (Paris, 1968).

Barrows, Susanna. *Distorting Mirrors: Visions of the Crowd in Late Nineteenth Century France* (New Haven, 1981).

Bellanger, Claude, Jacques Godechot, Pierre Guiral, and Fernand Terrou, eds. *Histoire générale de la presse française*. Vol. 3, *De 1871 à 1940* (Paris, 1972).

Bidelman, Patrick K. "The Feminist Movement in France: The Formative Years, 1858-1889." Ph.D. diss., Michigan State University, 1975.

———. "Maria Deraismes, Léon Richer, and the Founding of the French Feminist Movement, 1866-1978," *TR/TR* 3-4 (1977): 20-73.

———. *Pariahs Stand Up! The Founding of the Liberal Feminist Movement in France, 1858-1889* (Westport, Conn., 1982).

———. "The Politics of French Feminism: Léon Richer and the LFDF, 1882-1891," *HR/RH* 3 (1976): 93-120.

Bonnefous, Georges and Edouard. *Histoire politique de la IIIᵉ République*. 7 vols. (Paris, 1956-1967).

Boxer, Marilyn J. "French Socialism, Feminism, and the Family," *TR/TR* 3-4 (1977): 128-67.

———. "Socialism Faces Feminism in France, 1879-1913." Ph.D. diss., University of California-Riverside, 1975.

————. "Socialism Faces Feminism: The Failure of Synthesis in France, 1879-1914." In *Socialist Women*, edited by Boxer and Quataert, pp. 75-111.

————. "When Radical and Socialist Feminism Were Joined: The Extraordinary Failure of Madeleine Pelletier." In Slaughter and Kern, *European Women on the Left*, pp. 51-74.

———— and Jean H. Quataert, eds. *Socialist Women: European Socialist Feminism in the Nineteenth and Early Twentieth Centuries* (New York, 1978).

Brault, Elaine. *La Franc-maçonnerie et l'émancipation des femmes* (Paris, 1954).

Bridenthal, Renate and Claudia Koonz, eds. *Becoming Visible: Women in European History* (Boston, 1977).

Campbell, Peter. *French Electoral Systems and Elections since 1789* (London, 1958).

Clark, Frances I. *The Position of Women in Contemporary France* (London, 1937).

Clark, Linda L. *Schooling the Daughters of Marianne: Textbooks and the Socialization of Girls in Modern French Primary Schools* (Albany, 1983).

Cleverdon, Catherine. *The Woman Suffrage Movement in Canada* (Toronto, 1950).

Decaux, Alain. *Histoire des françaises*. 2 vols. (Paris, 1972).

Degen, Mary L. *The History of the Woman's Peace Party* (Baltimore, 1939).

Delatour, Yvonne. "Les Effets de la guerre sur la situation de la française d'après la presse féminine, 1914-1918." Diplôme d'études supérieures, University of Paris, 1965.

Dubief, H. "Hélène Brion (1882-1962)," *Le Mouvement social* 44 (1963): 93-97.

Duhet, Paul-Marie. *Les Femmes et la révolution, 1789-1794* (Paris, 1971).

Duroselle, Jean-Baptiste. *La France et les français, 1900-1914* (Paris, 1972).

Elbow, Matthew H. *French Corporative Theory, 1789-1948: A Chapter in the History of Ideas* (New York, 1953).

Elwitt, Sanford. "Social Reform and Social Order in Late Nineteenth Century France: The Musée Social and Its Friends," *FHS* 11 (1980): 431-51.

Evans, Richard J. *The Feminist Movement in Germany, 1894-1933* (London, 1976).

————. *The Feminists: Women's Emancipation Movements in Europe, America, and Australasia, 1840-1920* (New York, 1977).

Feeley, Francis M. "A Study of French Primary School Teachers (1880-1919), and the Conditions and Events Which Led a Group of Them into the Revolutionary 'Syndicaliste' Movement." Ph.D. diss., University of Wisconsin, 1976.

Flexner, Eleanor. *Century of Struggle: The Woman's Rights Movement in the United States* (Cambridge, Mass., 1966).

Fontaine, Arthur. *French Industry during the War* (New Haven, 1926).

Frader, Laura L. "La Femme et la famille dans les luttes viticoles de l'Aude, 1903-1913," *Sociologie du sud-est* 21 (1979).

Gaudemet, Yves-Henri. *Les Juristes et la vie politique de la Troisième République* (Paris, 1970).

Goldberg, Harvey. *The Life of Jean Jaurès* (Madison, 1962).

Goliber, Sue H. "The Life and Times of Marguerite Durand: A Study in French Feminism." Ph.D. diss., Kent State University, 1975.

Grimes, Alan P. *The Puritan Ethic and Woman Suffrage* (New York, 1967).

Grimshaw, Patricia. *Woman's Suffrage in New Zealand* (Auckland, 1972).

Guilbert, Madeleine. *Les Femmes et l'organisation syndicale avant 1914: Présentation et commentaire de documents pour une étude du syndicalisme féminin* (Paris, 1966).

Harrison, Brian. *Separate Spheres: The Opposition to Women's Suffrage in Britain* (New York, 1978).

Hause, Steven C. "The Failure of Feminism in Provincial France, 1890-1920." *PWSFH* 8 (1982):423-36.

―――. "The Rejection of Women's Suffrage by the French Senate in November 1922: A Statistical Analysis," *TR/TR* 3-4 (1977): 205-237.

―――. "Women Who Rallied to the Tricolor: The Effects of World War I on the French Women's Suffrage Movement," *PWSFH*, 6 (1979): 371-81.

――― and Anne R. Kenney. "The Development of the Catholic Women's Suffrage Movement in France, 1896-1922," *Catholic Historical Review* 67 (1981): 11-30.

―――. "The Limits of Suffragist Behavior: Legalism and Militancy in France, 1876-1922," *AHR* 86 (1981): 781-806.

―――. "Women's Suffrage and the Paris Elections of 1908," *Laurels* 51 (1980): 21-32.

Heinzely, Hélène. "Le Mouvement socialiste devant les problèmes du féminisme, 1879-1914." Thèse de doctorat, Paris, 1957.

Hunt, Persis C. "Revolutionary Syndicalism and Feminism among Teachers in France, 1900-1921." Ph.D. diss., Tufts University, 1975.

―――. "Teachers and Workers: Problems of Feminist Organization in the Early Third Republic," *TR/TR* 3-4 (1977): 168-204.

Hunter, John C. "The Problem of the French Birth Rate on the Eve of World War I," *FHS* 2 (1962): 490-503.

Julliard, Jacques. *Clemenceau, briseur des grèves: L'Affaire de Draveuil Villeneuve-Saint-Georges* (Paris, 1965).

Kirby, Yvette. "Development and Limits of Catholic Social Action in France: The Case of Lyon, 1871-1905." Ph.D. diss., Harvard University, 1980.

Kraditor, Aileen S. *The Ideas of the Woman Suffrage Movement, 1890-1920* (Garden City, N.Y., 1971).

Kriegel, Annie. "Procès de guerre—procès Brion," *Le Mouvement social* 44 (1963): 97-99.

Larkin, Maurice. *Church and State after the Dreyfus Affair: The Separation Issue in France* (London, 1974).

Lacache, Bernard. *Séverine* (Paris, 1930).

Leclère, André. *Le Vote des femmes en France: Les Causes de l'attitude particulière de notre pays* (Paris, 1929).

Li Dzeh-Djen. *La Presse féministe en France de 1869 à 1914* (Paris, 1934).

Liddington, Jill, and Jill Norris. *One Hand Tied Behind Us: The Rise of the Women's Suffrage Movement* (London, 1978).

Loubère, Leo. *Radicalism in Mediterranean France: Its Rise and Decline, 1848-1914* (Albany, 1974).

McLaren, Angus. "Abortion in France: Women and the Regulation of Family Size, 1800-1914," *FHS* 10 (1978): 461-85.

McMillan, James F. "The Character of the French Feminist Movement, 1870-1914." In *Actes du colloque franco-britannique tenu à Bordeaux du 27 au 30 septembre 1976: Sociétés et groupes sociaux en Aquitaine et en Angleterre*, edited by Fédération historique du sud-ouest (Bordeaux, 1979).

————. "The Effects of the First World War on the Social Condition of Women in France." D.Phil. thesis, Oxford, 1977.

————. *Housewife or Harlot: The Place of Women in French Society, 1870-1940* (New York, 1981).

Marichy, Jean-Pierre. *La Deuxième chambre dans la vie politique française depuis 1875* (Paris, 1969).

Marquardt, Steve R. "Joseph Reinach (1856-1921): A Political Biography." Ph.D. diss., University of Minnesota, 1978.

Martin, Benjamin F. *Count Albert de Mun: Paladin of the Third Republic* (Chapel Hill, N.C., 1978).

Marwick, Arthur. *War and Social Change in the Twentieth Century* (London, 1975).

————. *Women at War, 1914-1918* (London, 1977).

Merriman, John M., ed. *Consciousness and Class Experience in Nineteenth Century Europe* (New York, 1980).

Meyers, Peter V. "From Conflict to Cooperation: Men and Women Teachers in the Belle Epoque," *HR/RH* 7 (1980): 493-506.

Monnerville, Gaston. *Clemenceau* (Paris, 1968).

Moody, Joseph N. *French Education since Napoleon* (Syracuse, 1978).

Moon, Parker T. *The Labor Problem and the Social Catholic Movement in France: A Study in the History of Social Politics* (New York, 1921).

Moon, S. Joan. "Feminism and Socialism: The Utopian Synthesis of Flora Tristan." In *Socialist Women*, edited by Boxer and Quataert, pp. 21-50.

―――. "The Saint-Simonian Association of Working Class Women, 1830-1850," *PSWFH* 5 (1977): 274-81.

Morgan, David. *Suffragists and Democrats: The Politics of Woman Suffrage in America* (East Lansing, Mich., 1972).

―――. *Suffragists and Liberals: The Politics of Woman Suffrage in England* (Oxford, 1975).

Morton, Ward M. *Woman Suffrage in Mexico* (Gainesville, Fla., 1962).

Moses, Claire G. "The Evolution of Feminist Thought in France, 1829-1889." Ph.D. diss., George Washington University, 1978.

―――. "Saint-Simonian Men/Saint-Simonian Women: The Transformation of Feminist Thought in 1830s France," *JMH* 54 (1982): 240-67.

Nicolet, Claude. *Le Radicalisme*. 2nd ed. (Paris, 1961).

Offen, Karen. "Aspects of the Woman Question during the Third Republic," *TR/TR* 3-4 (1977): 1-19.

O'Neill, William L. *Everyone Was Brave: The Rise and Fall of Feminism in America* (Chicago, 1969).

Paulson, Ross E. *Women's Suffrage and Prohibition: A Comparative Study of Equality and Social Control* (Glenview, Ill. 1973).

Pope, Barbara C. "Angels in the Devil's Workshop: Leisured and Charitable Women in Nineteenth Century England and France." In *Becoming Visible*, edited by Bridenthal and Koonz, pp. 296-324.

Puget, Jean. *La Duchesse d'Uzès*. 2nd ed. (Uzès, 1972).

Pugh, Martin D. "Politicians and the Women's Vote, 1914-1918," *History* 59 (1974): 358-74.

Quataert, Jean H. *Reluctant Feminists in German Social Democracy, 1885-1917* (Princeton, 1979).

Rabaut, Jean. "1900, tournant du féminisme français," *Bulletin de la Société d'Histoire Moderne* 16 (1983): 5-16.

Rafferty, Frances. "Madame Séverine: Crusading Journalist of the Third Republic," *Contemporary French Civilization* 1 (1977): 185-202.

Ranvier, A. "Une Féministe de 1848, Jeanne Deroin," *La Révolution de 1848* 4 (1907): 11-17.

Renouvin, Pierre. *The Forms of War Government in France* (New Haven, 1927).

Rigollot-Converset, Madeleine. *Louise de la Hamayde, 1877-1954: Une Animatrice, une vaillante, une modeste* (Troyes, 1956).

Robertson, Priscilla. *An Experience of Women: Pattern and Change in Nineteenth-Century Europe* (Philadelphia, 1982).

Ronsin, Francis. *La Grève des ventres: Propagande néo-malthusienne et baisse de la natalité en France (19ᵉ-20ᵉ siècles)* (Paris, 1980).

Rosen, Andrew. *Rise Up Women! The Militant Campaign of the Women's Social and Political Union, 1903-1914* (London, 1974).

Rover, Constance. *Women's Suffrage and Party Politics in Britain, 1866-1914* (London, 1967).

Sanua, Louli. *Figures féminines, 1900-1939* (Paris, 1949).

Scott, Anne F. and Andrew W. *One Half the People: The Fight for Woman Suffrage* (Philadelphia, 1975).

Scott, D. "Woman Suffrage: The Movement in Australia," *Journal of the Royal Australian Historical Society* 53 (1967): 299-320.

Slaughter, Jane and Robert Kern, eds. *European Women on the Left: Socialism, Feminism, and the Problems Faced by Political Women, 1880 to the Present* (Westport, Conn., 1981).

Smith, Bonnie G. *Ladies of the Leisured Class: The Bourgeoisie of Northern France in the Nineteenth Century* (Princeton, 1981).

Soltau, Roger. *French Political Thought in the Nineteenth Century* (New Haven, 1931).

Sowerwine, Charles. *Les Femmes et le socialisme* (Paris, 1978).

———. "Le Groupe féministe socialiste, 1899-1902," *Le Mouvement social* 90 (1975): 87-120.

———. "The Organization of French Socialist Women, 1880-1914," *HR/RH* 3 (1976): 3-24.

———. *Sisters or Citizens? Women and Socialism in France since 1876* (Cambridge, 1982).

———. "Women Against the War: A Feminine Basis for Internationalism and Pacifism?" *PWSFH* 6 (1978): 361-70.

———. "Women and the Origins of the French Socialist Party," *TR/TR* 3-4 (1977): 104-127.

———. "Workers and Women in France before 1914: the Debate over the Couriau Affair." *JMH* 55 (1983): 411-41.

Spengler, Joseph P. *France Faces Depopulation* (Durham, N.C., 1938).

Stephens, Winifred. *Madame Adam (Juliette Lamber), La Grande Française: From Louis-Philippe until 1917*, 2nd ed. (New York, 1917).

Stites, Richard. *The Women's Liberation Movement in Russia: Feminism, Nihilism, and Bolshevism, 1860-1930* (Princeton, 1978).

Suarez, Georges. *Briand: Sa vie, son oeuvre, avec son journal et de nombreaux documents inédits*. 6 vols. (Paris, 1938-1952).

Sullerot, Evelyne, Histoire de la presse féminine en France, des origines à 1848 (Paris, 1966).

——. *La Presse féminine* (Paris, 1963).

Sumler, David E. "Domestic Influences on the Nationalist Revival in France, 1909-1914," *FHS* 6 (1970): 517-37.

Thibaudet, Albert. *Les Idées politiques de la France* (Paris, 1932).

Thibert, Marguerite. *Le Féminisme dans le socialisme français de 1830 à 1850* (Thèse de doctorat, Paris, 1926).

Thiébaux, Charles. *Le Féminisme et les socialists. Depuis Saint-Simon jusqu'à nos jours* (Paris, 1906).

Thomas, Edith. *Les Femmes de 1848* (Paris, 1948).

——. *Pauline Roland: Socialisme et féminisme au XIXe siècle* (Paris, 1956).

Thönessen, Werner. *The Emancipation of Women: The Rise and Fall of the Women's Movement in German Social Democracy, 1863-1933* (London, 1973).

Tilly, Louise A. "Women's Collective Action and Feminism in France, 1870-1914." In *Class Conflict and Collective Action* edited by Louise A. Tilly and Charles Tilly (Beverly Hills, Calif., 1981).

Toulemon, André. *Le Suffrage familial ou suffrage universel intégral: Le Vote des femmes* (Paris, 1933).

Toutain, J.-C. *La Population de la France de 1700 à 1959* (Paris, 1963).

Viollet, Paul. *Histoire des institutions politiques et administratives de la France.* 3 vols. (Paris, 1890-1903).

Watson, David R. *Georges Clemenceau: A Political Biography* (London, 1974).

Weber, Eugen. *Peasants into Frenchmen: The Modernization of Rural France, 1870-1914* (Standford, 1976).

Weston, Elisabeth A. "Prostitution in Paris in the Later Nineteenth Century. A Study in Politics and Social Ideology." Ph.D. diss., State University of New York–Buffalo, 1979.

Wilkins, Wyona H. "The Paris International Feminist Congress of 1896 and Its French Antecedents," *North Dakota Quarterly* 43 (1975): 5-28.

Willard, Claude. *Les Guesdistes: Le Mouvement socialiste en France, 1893-1905* (Paris, 1965).

Williams, John. *The Other Battleground: The Home Fronts, Britain, France, and Germany, 1914-1918* (Chicago, 1972).

Zeldin, Theodore. "The Conflict of Moralities: Confession, Sin, and Pleasure in the Nineteenth Century." In *Conflicts in French Society*, edited by Zeldin, pp. 13-50.

——. *Conflicts in French Society: Anti-clericalism, Education, and Morals in the Nineteenth Century* [St. Antony's Publications, No. 1] (London, 1970).

——. *France 1848-1945.* 2 vols. (Oxford, 1973-1977).

Index

Library of Congress Cataloging in Publication Data

Hause, Steven C., 1942-
  Women's suffrage and social politics in the French Third Republic.

  Bibliography: p.
  Includes index.
  1. Women—Suffrage—France—History. 2. Feminism—France—History. 3. France
—Politics and government—
1870-1940. I. Kenney, Anne R., 1950-   . II. Title.
JN2954.H38   1984   324.6′23′0944   84-42579
ISBN 0-691-05427-4
ISBN 0-691-10167-1 (pbk.)

Steven C. Hause is Associate Professor of History and Anne R. Kenney is Associate Director of the Western Historical Manuscript Collection, both at the University of Missouri at St. Louis.